Integrated Ko

Advanced 2

Integrated Korean

Advanced 2

Eun-Joo Lee   Duk-Soo Park   Jaehoon Yeon

KLEAR Textbooks in Korean Language

This textbook series has been developed by the Korean Language Education and
Research Center (KLEAR) with the support of the Korea Foundation.

Library of Congress Cataloging-in-Publication Data

Integrated Korean : advanced 2 / Eun-Joo Lee... [et al.].
   p. cm. — (KLEAR textbooks in Korean language)
  ISBN 0–8248–2777–5 (pbk. : alk. paper)
   1. Korean language—Textbooks for foreign speakers—English. I. Lee, Eun-Joo.
II. Series.

PL913.I5812 2004
495.7'82421—dc21   00–033782

Camera-ready copy has been provided by the authors.

Photograph and Figure Credits
http://www.ganaani.co.kr—p. 1
http://www.kumsungpub.co.kr/Kumsungpub/webzin/11/matr11_5_2.htm—p. 74a
http://www.kumsungpub.co.kr/Kumsungpub/webzin/11/matr11_5_1.htm—p. 74b
http://www.samul-nori.com—p. 98
http://www.stoo.com/html/stooview/2001/0216/091805556516121611.html—p. 121
http://ynucc.yeungnam.ac.kr/~bwlee/bp.htm—p. 146
http://www.unikorea.go.kr—p. 166
http://www.3asian.com/zboard/data/photo_a/keizu_2.jpg—p. 190
http://www.tangun.co.jp/moviekr/Lists/D0001.htm—p. 217

CONTENTS

제11과 혼인도 맞춤 시대

(Lesson 11: The Age of the "Made-to-Order" Spouse)

Objectives

이 과에서는 21세기 한국의 혼인 풍속에 대한 이야기를 다루었다. 시대가 급변하는 시대이니 만큼 결혼의 풍속 역시 달라졌다. 부끄러움 대신 적극성이, 그리고 중매쟁이 대신 컴퓨터가 만남을 주선하는 현상에 대해서 자세히 알아보자.

This chapter deals with Korean marriages in the 21st century. Naturally, marriage customs are shifting with the rapidly changing times. Let's have a close look at modern matchmaking, in which politeness, instead of shyness, and computers, instead of matchmakers, play an important role.

Pre-reading questions

1. 여러분에게 결혼은 어떤 의미를 갖습니까?

2. 여러분들은 결혼을 목적으로 한 만남을 가져 본 적이 있습니까?

3. 여러분 나라의 전통 결혼 풍습과 최근의 결혼 풍습에 대해 이야기해
   봅시다.

4. 여러분의 이상적(ideal)인 결혼 상대자는 어떤 사람입니까?

Gaining familiarity

1. 중매쟁이, 결혼 상담소, 결혼 정보 회사, 결혼 정보원

2. 미팅, 소개팅

3. 연애 결혼, 중매 결혼, 유전자 맞춤형 결혼

4. 잘하면 술이 석 잔 잘 못하면 뺨이 석 대

이제는 혼인도 맞춤 시대

　대학교 신입생이 되면 가장 먼저 하고 싶었던 일이 몇 가지 있었다. 화장을 해 보고, 술을 마셔 보는 일과 미팅을 해 보는 것이었다. 그 가운데서도 미팅은 모든 신입생들의 특권과도 같은 것이어서 한 학년 내내 미팅 건수를 찾아 이 찻집 저 다방을 전전하기도 했다. 기대가 커서 실망도 많이 겪었지만, 더러 커플로 맺어지는 친구들의 경우를 보면서 언젠가는 나도 이상형의 연인을 만날 수도 있을 것이라는 희망에 하루 서너 번의 만남까지도 기꺼이 감수한 적도 있다.

　가능하면 얼굴이 잘 생긴 사람이 좋겠고 이왕이면[11.1] 좋은 학교에 다니는 머리 좋고 성격도 원만한 파트너가 되기를 바라는 것이 미팅에 임하는 사람들 모두의 바람이었을 것이다. 아무리 세월이 흘러 나이를 먹고 사람을 보는 판단 기준이 달라졌다고 해도 우리 모두가 가지고 있는 이상형의 기준은 쉽게 변하지 않는 것이 사실이다. 재미 삼아 나간 미팅 자리에서도 괜찮은 사람 만나기를 바라는 것이 인지상정이고 보면, 평생을 좌우하는 배우자를 선택하는 일에 있어 자신의 이상형에 대한 기대는 더욱 높아지게 마련이다.[11.2] 그래서인지 우리나라는 예로부터[11.3] 혼인을 위한 준비된 만남이 꾸준히 있어 왔고, 이는 정보화 시대라는 오늘날에도 크게 달라지지 않았다. 이전 세대들이 중매라는 방식의 준비된 만남을 선호했다면 오늘날의 신세대들은 결혼 정보 회사라는 첨단 시스템을 이용하고 있다. 그 방식에 약간의 차이는 있겠지만 이상적인 배우자를 만나고자 하는 열망은 예나 지금이나[11.4] 크게 다르지 않을[11.5] 것이다.

여자는 외모, 남자는 능력

　잘 하면 술이 석 잔일 수도 있고 잘못되면 뺨이 석 대일 수도 있다는 중매는 그동안 우리 나라의 혼인의 역사와 뗄 수 없는 긴밀한 관계를 유지해 왔다. 혼인이 당사자의 의견보다는 집안끼리의 결합으로 인식되어 온 전통 사회에서는 혼인을 성사시키기 위해 신랑, 신부의 집의 중간에서 다리를 놓는 중매쟁이의 구실이 큰 비중을 차지했었다.

　중매는 나중에 중매인들이 결혼 상담소란 것을 개설하면서 본격적인 직업으로 인정받게 되었는데, 그 시기가 1930년 무렵이라고 전해진다.

또한 우리 나라에서 정식 허가를 받은 결혼 상담소는 1959년에 처음 등장하여 아직까지 줄곧 중매 업무만을 담당해 오고 있는 서울결혼정보원이라고 한다. 종로에 위치한 이곳 서울결혼정보원에서 12년째 일하고 있는 김희선 실장은 요즘 젊은이들의 결혼관을 다음과 같이 말한다.

선호하는 배우자의 기준으로 남자는 여자의 외모를 맨 먼저 보고, 여자는 남자의 성실성과 능력을 먼저 본다는 점이 눈에 띈다. 거기에 요즈음엔 자기 배우자는 무조건 예뻐야 하고, 선생이나 약사와 같은 안정된 전문직을 가져야 한다고 말하는 터무니없이 이상만 높은 남자들도 부쩍 늘어나고 있는 추세라고 한다. 또, 요즘 젊은 세대일수록 외모와 가정 환경을 따지는 젊은이들이 눈에 띄게[11.6] 늘고 있다고 한다. 아무리 시대가 바뀌어도 의사, 변호사와 같은 고소득의 전문직을 선호하는 경향이 여전한데, 경제적인 안정을 중요하게 여기는 것은 예나 지금이나 변하지 않는 고전적인 결혼 풍습이기도 하다.

맞선도 컴퓨터로

결혼 정보 회사는 회원으로 가입한 사람들에게 일정액의 회비를 받고 조건에 맞는 배우자 후보를 여러 차례 만나게 하는 혁신적인 시스템으로 21세기형 새로운 개념의 중매로 급부상하고 있다. 컴퓨터를 통해 회원들의 정보 시스템을 구축, 서로 비슷한 조건의 회원들끼리 여러 차례 만남을 갖게 된다. 서로가 서로의 조건을 견주어 본다는 측면에서는[11.7] 전통 중매 방식과 비슷하지만 배우자를 선택할 때 어느 정도 자신의 이상에 맞추어 간다는 점에서는 새로운 개념의 신세대식 만남이라고 할 수 있다.

획일적인 배우자의 조건

결혼 정보 회사들이 이처럼 붐을 일으키게 된 배경은 무엇일까? 무엇보다도[11.8] 혼인에 대한 젊은 세대들의 가치관이 빠르게 변한 것을 근본 원인으로 들 수 있다. 인연이 닿는 사람이 나타나기만을 기다리던 과거 세대와 달리, 합리적인 정보에 근거해서 배우자를 직접 고르겠다는 것이 요즘 젊은이들의 의식이다. 이러한 적극적이고 개방적인 의식이 참신한 아이디어를 선보이는 결혼 정보 회사의 마케팅 전략과 맞아떨어졌기 때문에 큰 효과를 거두고 있는 것이다. 이들의 중매 방식은 가입 회원들에 대한 철저한 확인과 분석을 통해 서로 비슷한 눈높이의 상대를 맺어 주는 것이다. 이를 위해 회원들이 작성해야 하는 설문 조사 항목만도 백여 개에 이른다고 한다. 본인은 말할 것도 없고[11.9] 상대방의 직업, 나이, 학력, 취미, 종교, 출신지, 가정 형편, 월급 같은 상세한 기초 조사를 한 뒤, 여기에 걸맞는 상대를 맞추어 준다. 그러다 보니 신분이나 성격의 차를 뛰어 넘는 평강공주와 온달의 결합은 원천적으로 봉쇄된다고 한다.

또한 조금 딱딱한 분위기에서 상대방의 가족 관계와 취미를 어색하게 물어 보아야 했던 이전의 맞선과는 달리 서로에 대해 어느 정도 파악을 한 뒤에 이루어지는 만남이어서 좀더 화기애애한 분위기에서 만날 수 있다는 점 또한 큰 매력으로 작용하고 있다. 그러나 많은 사람들이 회원에 가입하자마자[11.10] 좋은 사람을 만날 수 있을 것이라고 생각하는데, 이런 환상은 버려야 하며 조건만으로 상대를 판단하지 말고 대화를 통해 서로를 신뢰할 수 있는 마음가짐을 갖는 것이 중요하다고 한다.

유전자 맞춤형 혼인

여러 종류의 결혼 정보 회사 중에는 유전자 정보까지 맞춰 가며 혼인 상대를 찾아 주는 회사도 생겨났다. 디엔에이 분석 업체인 디엔에이 리서치가 결혼 정보 회사 위드와 손잡고, 디엔에이를 분석해 적합한 배우자를 찾아 주는 서비스를 시작했다.

위드에 회원으로 가입한 뒤 머리카락, 침과 같은 분석 자료를 보내면 체질, 성격, 지능, 비만과 같은 파악 가능한 정보를 모아 배우자를 선택할 때 참고 자료로 쓴다고 한다. 건강 기록부를 주고받는 것보다 믿을 수 있다는 게 관계자의 설명이다. 앞으로 과학이 발달할수록 서로 맞춰 가야 할 배우자의 조건도 더 많아지지 않을까 하는 생각이 든다. 결혼 정보 회사 때문에 좀 더 다양한 방법의 만남이 이루어질 수 있다는 것은 좋은 일인 것 같다. 그러나 결혼이 사람을 등급별로 분류하여 기계적으로 짝을 짓는 차가운 시스템으로 변해 가는 것 같아 쓸쓸한 생각도 든다.

이용규 <샘이 깊은 물> 2001년 1월호

New Words

가입하다 to join, become a member (of), participate (in) ▷협회에 가입하다 to join an association

가정 형편 family background, family situation

가치 value, worth, merit. 가치관 sense of values

감수하다 to be ready to suffer ▷비난을 감수하다 to submit to reproach

개방적 frank, candid, open-minded

개설하다 to open (up), establish, set up, found

건강 기록부 record of medical checkups, medical records

건수 number of items (cases); opportunity ▷교통 사고 건수 number of traffic accidents

걸맞다 to be well matched ▷네 옷은 오늘 파티에 걸맞지 않아. Your dress is not suitable for today's party.

견주다 to compare one with another; to compete (with)

결합 joining together, union, combination

결혼관 outlook on marriage. ~관 outlook, view ▷인생관 one's view of life

경향 tendency, trend

고소득 high income

고전적인 classical, classic ▷고전극 classical drama

관계자 persons concerned ▷관계자 외 출입 금지 authorized personnel only

구실 excuse, pretext

근거하다 to be based, founded

급부상하다 to grow rapidly, rise to the surface rapidly

기계적으로 mechanically

기꺼이 gladly, with joy, with pleasure

긴밀하다 to be close ▷긴밀한 협력 close cooperation

꾸준히 steadily, constantly ▷꾸준히 공부하다 to study steadily

눈높이 one's expectations or standards. 눈높다 to aim high

능력 ability, capacity, capability

다방 teahouse, coffee shop

당사자 person [party] concerned, interested party ▷결혼의 당사자 contracting parties in a marriage

대머리 bald head, bald person ▷일찍 대머리가 된 사람 prematurely bald person

등급별 according to rank, grade. 등급 grade, rank. ~별 classified by

등장 appearance, entrance on the stage

마음가짐 one's mental attitude

맞선 meeting [interview] with a view to marriage

맞춤 something made to order, custom-made. 맞춤 옷 made-to-order suit

머리카락 hair

무렵 about, around ▷그 무렵 around that time

미팅 meeting; blind date

바람 one's dearest wish, desire ▷내 집 마련은 우리의 오랜 바람이었다. Owning a home of our own was a dream for years.

배우자 spouse, mate

본격적이다 to be full-scale, genuine, regular, typical ▷본격적인 장마철이 시작되었다. The rainy season has come in earnest.

봉쇄되다 to be blocked, blocked up, sealed up

부쩍 remarkably, greatly

분석 analysis. 분석하다 to analyze

붐 boom ▷붐을 일으키다 to touch off a boom ▷붐을 타다 to ride the crest of the boom

비중 specific gravity, density; importance ▷비중을 차지하다 to take [have] importance

상담소 counselor's office ▷직업 상담소 vocational clinic

상세하다 to be detailed. 상세히 in detail

선호하다 to prefer ▷나는 커피보다 녹차를 선호한다. I prefer green tea to coffee.

설문 questionnaire ▷설문 조사 questionnaire, survey

성격 personality, character ▷성격상의 결점 flaw in one's character

성사 accomplishment, achievement, realization

신뢰 trust, confidence. 신뢰하다 to trust, believe (confide) in

신세대 new generation

씁쓸하다 to be rather bitter ▷씁쓸한 약 bitter medicine

아예 from the very first; never ▷거짓말은 아예 하지 마라. Never tell a lie.

어색하다 to feel awkward, be embarrassed ▷어색한 웃음 forced smile ▷나는 사람들 앞에서 연설하기가 어색했다. It was embarrassing to make a speech in public.

업무 business, duty ▷업무상의 전화 business calls ▷업무용의 차 car for business use ▷업무 보고 business report

업체 company, firm

여전하다 to be as usual; to be as before, as ever ▷우리 할아버지는 기력이 아직도 여전하시다. My grandfather is still going strong, as usual.

열망 ardent wish, burning desire

원만하다 to be harmonious, peaceful ▷원만한 성격 harmonious personality

원천적 original

유전자 gene ▷유전자 조작 gene manipulation

이상 ideal. 이상형 ideal type. 이상적(인) ideal ▷이상적인 남편 ideal husband

인식되다 to be recognised, understood, appreciated

인연 fate, karma; relationship ▷인연이 닿다 to be destined ▷어떤 인연으로 as fate would have it ▷인연을 끊다 to break off relations

인정 recognition, acknowledgment. 인정받다 to be acknowledged, approved, authorized, recognized

인지상정 human nature, humanity ▷불쌍한 사람을 도와 주는 것은 인지상정이다. It is quite natural that one should help a poor person.

일정액 certain amount of money, fixed sum of money

임하다 to deal with, face (meet); to be confronted (by) ▷그는 조용히 죽음에 임했다. He met his death calmly.

전략 strategy, tactics ▷전략을 세우다 to map out a strategy, plan a strategy

전문직 professional occupation

전전하다 to wander (from place to place), roam about

젊은이 youth, young person

정보화 시대 information age ▷정보화 사회 information-oriented society

정식 proper (regular) form ▷정식 결혼 legal marriage ▷정식 교육 regular school education ▷정식으로 in due form, formally

좌우하다 to dominate, influence, affect ▷신문은 여론을 좌우한다. Newspapers influence current thought.

줄곧 all the time, at all hours, constantly ▷줄곧 비가 온다. It rains day in and day out.

중매 matchmaking. 중매쟁이 matchmaker. 중매 결혼 marriage arranged by a go-between

짝 partner, one of a pair, mate

참고 자료 reference materials

참신하다 to be fresh, new

찻집 teahouse

철저하다 to be thorough, complete, exhaustive, all-embracing ▷철저한 연구 thorough study or research ▷철저한 대책 radical [drastic] measure

첨단 advanced, high-end ▷첨단 기술 high-end technology

체질 (physical) constitution ▷체질상의 결함 physical [constitutional] defects ▷나는 감기에 걸리기 쉬운 체질이다. I'm apt to catch cold.

추세 tendency, trend, current ▷일반적 추세 general tendency

출신지 one's hometown, birthplace

측면 side, aspect

침 saliva, spit

터무니없다 to be outrageous, be unreasonable, be groundless ▷터무니없는 거짓말 outrageous lie ▷터무니없는 소문 groundless rumor

특권 privilege (*lit.,* special right)

평강공주와 온달 Princess Pyŏnggang and the commoner Ondal (of the Koguryŏ kingdom; married despite their difference in social status)

합리적(인) rational, reasonable ▷우리 사장님의 경영 방침은 매우 합리적이다. My boss's management policy is very reasonable.

항목 item, head, heading

허가 permission, approval, license ▷허가를 신청하다 to apply for a license ▷허가를 얻다 to obtain permission

혁신적(인) innovative, innovating, progressive

화기애애하다 to be peaceful and harmonious ▷화기애애한 가정 harmonious household

화장 makeup, beauty care ▷화장을 하다 to make up (one's face), apply makeup

환상 fantasy, illusion

회비 membership fee, dues ▷클럽의 회비 club dues ▷회비는 1년에 5만원이에요. The membership fee is 50,000 *won* a year.

획일적 uniform, standardized

Useful Expressions

1. **이왕이면** as long as one is ~; things being what they are; all in all

이왕이면 나하고 같이 가자.

As long as you are going anyway, come along with me.

이왕이면 한국말을 배우겠다.

As long as I am about it (While I'm at it), I might as well take Korean.

2. **~게/기 마련이다** be natural; be expected; be by definition

생명이 있는 것은 죽기/죽게 마련이다.

Life is subject to decay.

약은 쓰기 마련이다.

It is natural for medicine to taste bitter.

3. **예로부터 (= 자고로)** from old times; since time immemorial

예로부터 성공한 사람은 반드시 시간을 중히 여겼다.

There never was a man who achieved success without managing his time carefully.

   자고로 이런 사건은 없었다.
   There is no parallel to this incident in history.

4. **예나 지금이나** as always; as it was in days gone by
   예나 지금이나 다름이 없다.
   It is the same now as it was in days gone by.
   돈에 대한 욕망은 예나 지금이나 마찬가지다.
   The zeal for money is the same today as always.

5. **크게 다르지 않다** be no great difference; be much the same
   결혼 배우자의 기준은 예나 지금이나 크게 다르지 않다.
   People's standards when choosing a partner are much the same as they
   have always been.
   명숙이의 국어 실력은 영어 실력과 크게 다르지 않다.
   The level of Myŏng-suk's Korean is more or less the same as her level
   of English.

6. **눈에 띄게** remarkably; conspicuously
   그 환자의 상태는 눈에 띄게 좋아졌다.
   The condition of the patient is improving rapidly.
   영국의 경제가 요즘 눈에 띄게 좋아지고 있다.
   Recently the U.K. economy has gotten remarkably better.

7. **~는 측면에서는** from the side [angle, viewpoint] of ~
   어떤 측면에서는 그것은 그에게 좋은 일이다.
   Looking at it from one angle, it's good for him.
   다른 측면에서는, 그건 행운이다.
   Looking at it from the other side, it is luck.

8. **무엇보다(도)** more than anything else; above all
   나는 낚시를 무엇보다도 좋아한다.
   I like fishing better than anything else.
   등산은 다른 무엇보다도 재미있다.
   Nothing is more interesting than climbing.

9. **~은/는 말할 것도 없고** not to mention; to say nothing of
   그는 말할 것도 없고 그녀도 모임에 갈 것이다.
   She is going to the party, to say nothing of him.

영어는 말할 것도 없고, 그 사람은 불어와 스페인어도 할 줄 안다.

He can speak French and Spanish, not to mention English.

10. ~자마자 as ~; just as ~; as soon as ~

현수는 성경 책을 읽자마자 졸았다.

Hyŏn-su nodded off as soon as he started to read the Bible.

그가 말을 시작하자마자 큰 폭발이 일어났다.

Just as he began to speak, there was a loud explosion.

Exercises

1. 관련된 단어들끼리 연결하여 문장을 만들어 보세요.

   A: (1) 화장 •   • 만나다

       (2) 배우자 •   • 거두다

       (3) 효과 •   • 맞추어 가다

       (4) 항목 •   • 작성하다

       (5) 이상 •   • 하다

   _____

   _____

   _____

   _____

   B: (6) 가치관 •   • 맺다

       (7) 결합 •   • 봉쇄되다

       (8) 인연 •   • 갖다

       (9) 마음가짐 •   • 바뀌다

   _____

   _____

   _____

   _____

2. 아래의 설명과 맞는 단어나 표현을 보기에서 찾아 쓰세요.

> 보기: 회비, 건강 기록부, 사고 방식, 월급, 맞선

(1) 결혼을 목적으로 중매인이 자리를 마련하는 만남: _____

(2) 회원이 내는 일정액: _____

(3) 매달 직장에서 받는 돈: _____

(4) 생각하고 판단하는 태도나 방식: _____

(5) 개인의 건강에 대한 정보를 기록해 놓은 서류: _____

3. 보기에서 적당한 말을 골라 빈칸을 채우세요.

> 보기: 어느 정도, 더러, 부쩍, 터무니없이, 맨, 내내, 크게

(1) 그 가운데서도 미팅은 모든 신입생들의 특권과도 같은 것이어서 한 학년
    _____미팅 건수를 찾아 이 찻집 저 다방을 전전하기도 했다. 기대
    가 커서 실망도 많이 겪었지만, _____ 커플로 맺어지는 친구들의
    경우를 보면서 언젠가는 나도 이상형의 연인을 만날 수도 있을 것이라는 희
    망에 하루 서너 번의 만남까지도 기꺼이 감수한 적도 있다.

(2) 우리나라는 예로부터 혼인을 위한 "준비된 만남"이 꾸준히 있어 왔고, 이는
    정보화 시대라는 오늘날에도 _____달라지지 않았다.

(3) 선호하는 배우자의 기준으로 남자는 여자의 외모를 _____ 먼저
    보고, 여자는 남자의 성실성과 능력을 먼저 본다는 점이 눈에 띈다.

(4) 거기에 요즈음엔 자기 배우자는 무조건 예뻐야 하고, 선생이나 약사와 같은
    안정된 전문직을 가져야 한다고 말하는 _____ 이상만 높은 남자
    들도 _____ 늘어나고 있는 추세라고 한다. 또, 요즘 젊은 세대일
    수록 외모와 가정 환경을 따지는 젊은이들이 늘고 있다고 한다.

(5) 조금 딱딱한 분위기에서 상대방의 가족 관계와 취미를 어색하게 물어 보아
    야 했던 이전의 맞선과는 달리 서로에 대해 _____ 파악을 한 뒤
    에 이루어지는 만남이어서 좀더 화기애애한 분위기에서 만날 수 있다는 점
    또한 큰 매력으로 작용하고 있다.

4. 밑줄 친 말과 가장 비슷한 단어나 표현을 보기에서 고르세요.

(1) 이왕이면 좋은 학교에 다니는 머리 좋고 성격도 원만한 파트너가 되기를 바라는 것이 미팅에 <u>임하는</u> 사람들 모두의 바람이었을 것이다.
   a. 참석하는　　　　　b. 일하는
   c. 빠지는　　　　　　d. 바라는

(2) 더러 커플로 맺어지는 친구들의 경우를 보면서 언젠가는 나도 이상형의 연인을 만날 수도 있을 것이라는 희망에 하루 서너 번의 만남까지도 기꺼이 <u>감수한</u> 적도 있다.
   a. 이겨낸　　　　　　b. 받아들인
   c. 피한　　　　　　　d. 좋아한

(3) 아무리 시대가 바뀌어도 의사, 변호사와 같은 고소득의 전문직을 선호하는 경향이 <u>여전하다</u>.
   a. 사라진다　　　　　b. 늘어난다
   c. 줄어든다　　　　　d. 바뀌지 않고 남아 있다

(4) 합리적인 정보에 근거해서 배우자를 직접 고르겠다는 적극적이고 개방적인 요즘 젊은이들이 의식이 참신한 아이디어를 <u>선보이는</u> 결혼 정보 회사의 마케팅 전략과 맞아떨어졌기 때문에 큰 효과를 거두고 있는 것이다.
   a. 고르는　　　　　　b. 내놓는
   c. 만드는　　　　　　d. 작성하는

(5) 본인은 말할 것도 없고 상대방의 직업, 나이, 학력, 취미, 종교, 출신지, 가정 형편, 월급과 같은 상세한 기초 조사를 한 뒤, 여기에 <u>걸맞는</u> 상대를 맞추어 준다.
   a. 어울리는　　　　　b. 다른
   c. 보이는　　　　　　d. 찾아 주는

5. 보기와 같이 주어진 말이 들어가는 표현을 만들어보세요.

> 보기: [가정] 가정 환경, 가정 형편, 가정 조사

(1) 중매: _____
(2) 경향: _____

　　(3) 이상: 　　　　　_____

　　(4) 배경: 　　　　　_____

6. 주어진 단어나 표현을 이용하여 문장을 만드세요.

　　(1) ~을/를 해 보다

　　_____

　　(2) ~와/과 달리 ~하다

　　_____

　　(3) 눈에 띄게 ~하다

　　_____

　　(4) ~은/는 말할 것도 없고

　　_____

　　(5) ~의 경우

　　_____

　　(6) ~하자마자

　　_____

　　(7) 무엇보다

　　_____

　　(8) 터무니없이 ~하다

　　_____

　　(9) ~하기 마련이다

　　_____

　　(10) ~측면에서 보면

　　_____

　　(11) ~(으)ㄴ/는 셈이다

　　_____

　　(12) 예로부터

　　_____

7. 본문을 잘 읽은 후 나머지 셋과 관계가 먼 것을 하나 고르세요.

    (1) 혼인   결혼   약혼   회갑

    (2) 회원   회비   회식   가입

    (3) 전문직   고소득   풍속   지위

    (4) 종교   환상   학력   취미

    (5) 직업   중매   맞선   결혼

Comprehension Questions

I. Overall comprehension

1. 결혼할 때에 가장 중요한 것은 무엇일까요?

2. 예전의 결혼 풍속과 최근의 결혼 풍속을 비교해 보고 바뀐 것과 바뀌지 않은 것들에 대해 이야기해 봅시다.

3. 전통 중매 방식과 결혼 정보 회사의 방식과 어떤 점이 다를까요?

4. 여러분의 나라의 결혼 방식과 한국의 결혼 방식은 어떻게 다릅니까?

5. 이 글에서 보편적으로 배우자의 이상형은 어떤 것입니까?

II. Finding details

1. 미팅이란 단어의 뜻은 무엇입니까?

2. "잘 하면 술이 석 잔일 수도 있고 잘못되면 뺨이 석 대일 수도 있다"라는 말의 뜻은 무엇일까요?

3. 서울결혼정보의 김희선 실장이 말한 젊은이들의 결혼관은 어떻습니까?

4. 전통 중매 방식과 신세대식 만남의 차이점은 무엇입니까 ?

_____

5. 결혼 정보 회사들이 호황을 이룬 이유는 무엇입니까?

_____

6. 지은이는 어떠한 마음가짐으로 배우자를 찾아야 한다고 강조했습니까?

_____

7. 결혼 정보 회사들은 어떤 방법으로 회원들을 분류합니까?

_____

8. 지은이는 왜 평강공주와 바보 온달과 같은 만남은 이루어질 수 없다고 했습니까?

_____

9. 결혼 정보 회사를 통한 만남에 대해 지은이는 어떤 견해를 가지고 있습니까?

_____

Related Reading

국제 결혼? 라볶이 같은 거죠!

요즘 피부색이 다른 국제 결혼 커플을 어렵지 않게 만날 수 있다. 국경을 초월한 만남이 많아진 때문이다. 한국인과 결혼해 현재 국내에 살고 있는 외국인은 85개국 출신 2만여 명. 남다른 사연을 가진 이들은 어떤 재미와 어려움이 있을까? 서울에 사는 국제 결혼 커플 두 쌍에게 이야기를 들어 보자.

내 아내는 일본인 – 백원기 씨
"여보, 폐 아파" 어설픈 아내 말에 큰 병원 달려가기도

제 아내의 이름은 미오시 지카코(25세 회사원). 일본 사람입니다. 한국 여자를 두고 왜 일본인하고 결혼했느냐는 질문을 많이 받았습니다. 제 대답은 간단합니다. 지카코는 이 세상에 단 한 명이니까요. 그녀를 처음 만난 것은 5년 전. 우리는 중국 선양에서 유학 중이었습니다. 끙끙거리며 시장 바구니를 들고 가던 그녀를 자전거에 태우면서 사랑이 싹텄죠. 그리고 지난 1월 한국에서 결혼식을 올리기까지 부모님의 반대는 거셌습니다. 외동아들이라서 더욱 그랬죠. 친척들도 제사지낼 때 조상님 뵐 면목이 없다며 한결같이 말렸습니다.

지금은 어떠냐고요? 결혼한 지 1년도 안 됐는데 아내는 시부모 사랑을 독차지하고 있답니다. 어설픈 한국말 때문에 생긴 해프닝이 오히려 온 집안을 웃음꽃을 가득 선사하곤 하지요. 한번은 "배 아파" 대신 "폐 아파"라고 해서, 약국 대신 큰 병원으로 달려간 적도 있다니까요.

문화적인 차이요? 물론 크죠. 그래서 국제 결혼은 어려움도 두 배, 재미도 두 배입니다. 특히 한·일 커플은 양국의 역사 문제 등에 민감하죠. 우린 터놓고 얘기를 나눕니다. 아내는 우익에서 아무리 발버둥쳐도 역사 왜곡 교과서는 일본에서 외면당할 것이라며 핏대를 세웁니다. 오히려 제가 할 말을 잃고 맙니다.

그래도 TV에서 한·일전 축구라도 하면 어림없죠. 서로 자기 나라를 응원합니다. 치킨 내기니까 한치 양보도 없어요. 국제 결혼을 한마디로 표현하라고요? 특별하진 않아요. 세상엔 다양한 방식의 삶이 있죠. 그 중의 하나일 뿐입니다.

한국으로 시집오니 — 미오시 지카코 씨
추석 때 시댁 갔더니 일 너무 많이 시켜 나 싫어하시나 생각도

제 이름은 지카코. 한국인 남편(30세 사업)과 결혼한 지 1년이 안 된 새댁입니다. 지금은 한국말도 조금 늘어 한국 관광 정보를 인터넷으로 일본에 알려 주는 여행사에서 근무하고 있어요. 결혼 생활이요? 정말 하루하루가 핫켄노 렌소쿠(발견의 연속)입니다. 문화가 다르니까 얘깃거리가 마구 샘솟죠. 문화적 차이는 제 생활의 비타민입니다.

물론 힘들 때도 있어요. 지난 추석 때는 부산 시댁에 갔었습니다. 그런데 시부모님께서 너는 이제 손님이 아니라 우리 가족이라고 하셨어요. 너무 기뻤죠. 그리고선 명절 음식 준비가 시작됐는데 하루 종일 일을 했어요. 속으로 "시부모님이 나를 싫어하시나 보다"하고 생각했는데 나중에 그게 한국의 명절 문화임을 알았어요. 시어머니가 며느리와 친해져야 일을 시키는 일본과 달랐습니다.

가끔은 주변 시선이 부담스럽기도 해요. 집 앞 골목을 지날 때면 동네 할머니들이 "일본 색시냐?"며 일제 시대 이야기를 저에게 하세요. 그럼 전 또 시무룩해지죠. 하지만 신나는 일이 더 많아요. 한번은 가게에서 야채 이름을 잊어버려 우물쭈물하고 있는데 주인 아주머니가 "외국 사람이냐?"며 웃더니 콩나물을 한 웅큼 더 얹어 주는 거예요. 한국 사람의 그런 정겨움이 참 좋아요. 국제 결혼이요? 음. . . 매일 매일 계속되는 새로움이죠.

호주에서 온 남편 — 신종숙 씨
내가 부르는 노래 "베리 굿" 박수 치지만, 가사에 담긴 정서는 아는지?

제 남편의 이름은 크리스토퍼 로렌스(36. 주한 영국 문화원 직원). 호주 사람인 그를 처음 만난 건 7년 전. 제가 주한 파푸아 뉴기니 대사관에서 일하고 있을 때였죠. 그는 여행 중인 대학생이었어요. 친구에서 연인으로, 그리고 1년 후 결혼했죠.

좋은 점이요? 무엇보다 서로의 생활을 공유한다는 점이죠. 낮에 회사에서 있었던 일을 함께 얘기하고, 사소한 조언들을 서로 주고받아요. 또 외부 모임은 항상 부부 동반입니다. 초청장 봉투엔 언제나 로렌스 부부 앞이라고 적혀 있어요. 제가 못 가면 남편도 못 가는 것으로 생각할 정도니까요. 이른바 회식 등 남자들만의 세계 때문에 제가 소외당하는 일은 없어요. 또 하나 들자면 가사 분담에 대한 생각이죠. 아내를 도와준다는 게 아니라 너무나 자연스럽게 우리 일로 여깁니다. 물론 아쉬운 점도 있어요. 제가 '봄날은 간다'란 노래를 부르면 남편은 박수를 치며 "베리 굿!"이라고 해요.

하지만 "연분홍 치마~가 봄바람에 휘날리~더라"란 가사에 담긴 알싸한 정서까지 나누긴 힘들죠. 아마도 이게 국제 결혼의 한계가 아닐까 싶어요. 또 호기심 어린 거리의 시선들은 종종 저를 불편하게 해요. 서양 남자와 손잡고 가는 한국 여자가 무척이나 궁금한가 봐요. 그래도 갈수록 국제 커플에 대한 사람들의 인식이 변하고 있음을 느껴요. 7년 전과는 비교할 수 없다니까요. 국제 결혼을 한마디로 표현한다면. . . 글쎄요. 문명의 하모니쯤 될까요?

백년 손님 되어 보니 - 크리스토퍼 로렌스 씨
다른 여자 의자 밀어 주고 한바탕 부부 싸움 문화 차이가 오해 불러

방금 아내가 소개한 크리스입니다. 한국인과의 결혼 생활은 여러모로 인상적입니다. 요즘은 '사위 사랑은 장모'란 말의 의미를 실감합니다. 처가가 있는 부산에 내려가면 장모님은 온갖 생선을 사다가 구워 주시죠. 제가 백년 손님이래요. 서양에선 장모와 사위 관계가 이렇게까지 정겹진 않거든요.

또 아내는 항상 기대보다 더 많이 절 존중해 주죠. 서양의 부부 관계는 꽤 경쟁적입니다. 내 돈과 상대방 돈을 분명하게 가르기도 합니다. 한국에선 모든 게 우리 것이죠. 한국의 부부 관계는 대단히 공동체적입니다. 그래서 인간미가 물씬 풍기죠. 반면 서양의 부부 관계는 합리적이면서도 매정한 느낌이 느껴지는 게 사실입니다.

간혹 문화적 차이로 인한 오해로 부부 싸움도 생기지요. 예를 들어 호주에선 남자들이 여자를 위해 문을 열어 주거나, 앉을 때 의자를 밀어 주는 일은 매우 자연스런 일입니다. 그런데 한국에선 이런 행동이 오해를 빚더군요. 아내는 한국에선 호감이 있는 사람에게만 그렇게 한다고 설명하더라고요. 이런 사소한 다툼은 결국 서로를 이해하는 징검다리 역할을 합니다. 국제 결혼이요? 라볶이같은 것이죠. 서로 다른 재료가 만나서 제3의 맛을 내니까요.

<조선일보>와 영국 교민신문 <코리안 위클리>에서 발췌

국제 결혼 international marriage, 라볶이 spicy Korean dish made up of a mixture of noodles (라면) and rice cake (떡볶이), 국경 border, frontier, 초월하다 to transcend, rise above, 남다르다 to be uncommon, unusual, 사연 story, reason, 폐 lung, 어설프다 to be sloppy, 끙끙거리다 to toil, groan, 싹트다 to begin to develop, 거세다 to be strong, tough, 외동아들 only son, 제사지내다 to hold a memorial service (for the repose of one's ancestors), 면목이 없다 to be shameful, 한결같이 uniformly, 독차지하다 to have all to oneself, 선사하다 to send a gift, 민감하다 to be sensitive, 터놓다 to open one's heart, 우익 right-wing, rightists, 발버둥치다 to struggle, wriggle, 왜곡 perversion, distortion, 외면하다 to turn one's face away, 핏대를 세우다 to get angry, 어림없다 to be far from it, 응원 cheering, 내기 bet, 삶 life, 시댁 husband's parents' family [house], 새댁 newly married woman, 샘솟다 to gush, 색시 bride, 시무룩해지다 to become sulky, get moody, 우물쭈물하다 to hesitate, 콩나물 soybean sprout, 움큼 handful, 정겨움 being kindhearted, 대사관 embassy, 연인 lover, 공유하다 to hold in common, 사소하다 to be trivial, 조언 advice, 부부 동반 gathering for couples, 회식 dining together, 소외 estrangement, 가사 분담 division of labor in the household, 알싸하다 to be irritatingly strong to the taste; to be obscure, 사위 son-in-law, 가르다 to divide, 공동체 communal system, 물씬 strongly, 매정하다 to be cold, heartless, 오해 misunderstanding, 징검다리 stepping stones

Discussion & Composition

1. 본문의 내용에 비추어 볼 때 Related Reading의 만남들은 어떤 만남입니까?

2. Related Reading에 나오는 부부들이 결혼 정보 회사를 통해 만난다고 가정한다면, 그 결혼이 가능했을까요? 가능하지 않다면 왜 그럴까요?

3. 여러분의 나라의 아름다운 결혼 풍속에 대해 이야기해 봅시다. 문제점이 있다면 그것에 대해서도 이야기해 봅시다.

4. 본문 속의 만남과 Related Reading에서의 만남을 참고로 해서 여러분이 생각하는 바람직한 결혼관을 이야기해 봅시다.

Lesson 11   The age of the "made-to-order" spouse

There were a few things I wanted to do right away as a new college student:
wear makeup, drink alcohol, and go on a *mit'ing* (blind date). Of these, *mit'ing* is
like a special privilege granted to first-year students. So for a full semester I
wandered around—first to this teahouse, then that tea shop—looking for dates. I
had high expectations and lots of disappointments. Occasionally, with an eye on
my friends who had formed relationships, I would gladly meet up to three or four
people in one day, thinking that I could also meet my ideal romantic partner.

Everyone who dated may have wanted a partner with (if possible) good looks,
good schooling, a good brain, and a well-rounded personality. It holds true that our
own ideal standard does not change easily, no matter how much time passes by,
how old we become, or how our standards in judging people change. It is human
nature that even on very casual dates we want to meet good people; so our
expectations concerning our ideal mate rise even higher when we go to choose the
partner who will influence the course of our entire life. Perhaps that is why, in
Korea, we have always, since long ago, held prepared meetings for prospective
spouses. This is still largely the case even in today's information society. Past
generations preferred a kind of prepared meeting called *chungmae* 'matchmaking'.
The new generation is using a high-tech system called 'marriage information
companies'. While there are minor differences, the zeal for meeting the ideal
partner is the same today as always.

Women with looks, men with ability

Matchmaking, which at its best can be three cups of wine, and at its worst three
slaps in the face, has maintained its inseparable ties with Korean matrimonial
history. Traditional society perceived marriage more as a union of families than (as
consensus of) the opinions of the persons concerned, and the matchmaker played a
considerable role in the realizing of marriages by acting as a bridge between the
two families.

Later on, matchmakers established matrimonial agencies, and matchmaking came
to be recognized as an actual profession. It is said that this occurred in the 1930s.
Then, in 1959, the first licensed matrimonial agency emerged: the Seoul Marriage
Information Office, which today still runs its matchmaking (-only) business in the
Chongno district. Kim Hŭi-sŏn, who has worked for twelve years as the office's
section chief, had the following to say about contemporary young people's view of
marriage:

(What is noticed is that) Men look first at a woman's appearance as their standard for a desirable mate, and women look at a man's integrity and capability. Nowadays the tendency is toward an increase in men with ridiculously high ideals: his partner has to be attractive in any case and possess a stable, professional job like a teacher or pharmacist. The younger the generation, the more selective he will be about appearance and family background. No matter how times change, women still prefer high-income, professional jobs such as doctors and lawyers. Viewing economic stability as important is, now as before, a classic marriage practice.

The computerized first date

Matrimonial agencies are growing rapidly with a new, 21st-century concept of matchmaking, using a revolutionary system that lets members pay a set fee to meet several candidates matching their specifications. The agencies use computers to create a database of its members, who (use it to) meet other members with matching requisites. This system resembles traditional matchmaking in that both sides size up the qualities of the other. What makes it a new concept, a "new-generation" way of dating, is that people choose their partners in accordance with their own ideal.

Uniform conditions for a partner

What underlies this boom brought about by the matrimonial agencies? The basic reason is that the new generation's values concerning marriage have changed rapidly. Different from previous generations in which one waited for the fated person to simply appear, the new generations are aware that they can choose a partner directly, based on rational information. This positive, candid way of thinking matched perfectly with cutting-edge marketing strategies of matrimonial agencies, thereby yielding big results. The matchmaking method uses thoroughgoing confirmation and analysis of its members to match people of similar aims. The survey questionnaire used for this purpose, which must be filled out by all members, comprises over one hundred items. After making a basic, detailed investigation of the job, age, educational background, interests, religion, birthplace, family background (*lit.*, situation), monthly salary, etc., of the member, and also of other parties whom he or she wants to be matched. From the beginning, (couples with) gaps in social status and personality are blocked.

Another huge appeal of the new system is that unlike the past, when one had to make awkward inquiries about family and interests in an uncomfortable atmosphere, meetings now take place in a somewhat more harmonious atmosphere, since both sides know something about the other person beforehand. Many people think they can meet a good match soon after joining the service, but such a fantasy must be dispelled. It is important not to judge the other person by their conditions, but to have a mutual feeling of trust gained through conversation.

Genetically based marriages

Among a host of matrimonial agencies, some companies look for marriage partners by matching genetic information. DNA Research, a DNA-analyzing industry, joined hands with WITH, a matrimonial agency, and started a service in which DNA is analyzed to find suitable partners.

After becoming a member of WITH, you send (the company) analytical data like hair and saliva. DNA information is used as reference data when you select a partner, making a composite of all available information such as temperament, personality, intelligence, and weight. According to a related person's explanation, this procedure is more reliable than an exchange of health records. I think that as science develops in the future, the number of conditions in matchmaking will increase. It is great that a wider variety of dating methods is being created by the matrimonial agencies, but I am also pessimistic that it may change into an inhumane system of categorizing people into ranks and mechanically matching them into pairs.

Yi Yong-gyu, *Water with a Deep Source*, Jan. 2001

Related reading: International marriage? It's like *rappokki!*

Nowadays it is not difficult to meet international couples with different skin color, because much dating now transcends national borders. There are over 20,000 foreigners from 85 countries living in Korea with a Korean spouse. What are the joys and trials of these people with their unusual stories? Let's hear what two international couples living in Seoul have to say.

My wife is Japanese (Paek Wŏn-gi)

At my wife's sloppy pronunciation, "Honey! My p'ye (lung) hurts!" I once rushed her to a big hospital.

My wife's name is Miyoshi Chikako (25, company employee). She is Japanese. I often get the question, "Why did you put aside Korean women and marry a Japanese woman?" My answer is simple: Because there's only one Chikako in the world. I first met my wife five years ago when we both were foreign students in Shenyang, China. I gave her a ride on my bike when I saw her struggling with the grocery bags she was carrying. Love just blossomed. My parents were strongly opposed to our marrying up to the time of our wedding ceremony last January in Korea, all the more so because I am the only son. My relatives all tried to dissuade me, saying they would not be able to face the ancestors during ancestral rites.

How about now? It has been less than a year since we married, and she is the apple of my parents' eyes. Episodes arising from her sloppy Korean, on the contrary, have served as topics for laughter for the whole family. Once, she said *"P'ye ap'a!"* (my lungs hurt) instead of *"Pae ap'a!"* (my stomach hurts), and we rushed her to a big hospital instead of a drugstore.

Cultural differences? Of course! International marriages are twice the pain and twice the gain. Japanese-Korean couples particularly are sensitive to historical problems between the two countries. We discuss things openly. She becomes livid that no matter how much people stamp their feet at the right-wingers (in Japan), the problem of historical inaccuracies in Japanese textbooks is ignored. I am the one who runs out of words first.

When the Japanese and Korean soccer teams compete on TV, it's a different story altogether. We each root for our own country's team. Neither of us budges an inch because it's a bet of chicken. Size up international marriage in a word? It's no big deal. There are many different lifestyles in the world. It's just one of them.

A bride in Korea (Miyoshi Chikako)
At my in-laws' home for Ch'usŏk, they made me work so hard I even thought they didn't like me.

My name is Chikako. I am a new bride. I married my Korean husband (30, businessman) less than a year ago. My Korean has improved somewhat, and I am working at a travel agency that sends (informs) information about Korean tourism to Japan by the Internet. International marriage? It's really *hakken no rensoku*—continual discovery. Our cultures are different, so we always have heaps of things to talk about. Cultural differences really nourish our relationship.

Of course there are difficult times. Last Ch'usŏk we went to visit my husband's family in Pusan. When my father- and mother-in-law said "You're not a guest anymore, you're a member of the family," I was so happy. Then the preparations for the holiday feast began, and I worked all day long. I thought to myself, "My parents-in-law must hate me. . . . " Later I found out that's just Korean holiday culture. It is different from Japan, where the mother-in-law makes you work only AFTER she and you have become close.

Sometimes I get tired of the attention I attract. Whenever I turn the corner in front of our house, old ladies in the neighborhood say, "Are you a Japanese girl?" and start talking about the Japanese colonial period. I get so sullen. But there are many more exciting things. Once I forgot the name of a vegetable at a store and was speaking hesitantly, and the lady laughed, asking me, "Are you a foreigner?" and she added an extra handful of bean sprouts. I really like this friendliness in Koreans. International marriage? Well, it's something new every single day!

My husband from Australia (Sin Chong-suk)
He claps "Very good!" when I sing, but does he understand the sentiment the song contains?

My husband's name is Christopher Laurence (36, employee of the British Culture Office in Korea). I first met him, an Australian, seven years ago, when I was working at Papua New Guinea's embassy in Korea. He was a college student on vacation. We went from being friends to being lovers, then we married one year thereafter.

Good points? More than anything, we share our daily life. We talk about our work at the office during the day, and give and take bits of advice from each other. We always go to outside meetings as a couple. Invitations that come to us always have "To Mr. and Mrs. Laurence" written on the envelope. They figure that if I can't go, then neither can my husband. There is no such thing as my being excluded by male-only affairs, such as a so-called company dinner. Another thing is the way we think about the sharing of household duties. Rather than "helping out the wife," he regards housework as naturally both our job. There are also bad (*lit.,* regretful) points. When I sing the song 'Spring is Ending', my husband claps and says, "Very good!"

But it's hard to share with him the obscure sentiment found in the lyrics "My pink skirt fluttered in the spring wind. . . ." Perhaps this is one of the limitations to international marriages. Also, every now and then, curious stares on the street make me uncomfortable. A Korean woman walking hand-in-hand with a Westerner can be pretty anxiety-producing. But I feel that people's perception of international couples is changing. It doesn't compare with seven years ago. International marriage in a word? Well, how about 'harmony of civilizations'?

Being a hundred-year visitor (Christopher Laurence)

Misunderstandings arise from cultural differences—a marital dispute when I pulled out a chair for another woman.

My wife just introduced me. I'm Christopher. Married life with a Korean is impressive in many ways. I've come to really understand the meaning of (the expression) 'It is the mother (rather than the father) who loves the son-in-law.' When we go to Pusan, where my wife's parents live, my mother-in-law buys and cooks all kinds of fish for us. They call me the 'hundred-year guest'. Relationships between mothers and sons-in-law in the West are not so tender.

Also, my wife shows me more respect than I expect her to. Western couples are fairly combative. Money is divided into "yours" and "mine." In Korea, everything is "ours." Marriage in Korea is very group-oriented. So our humanity really comes out. By contrast, Western marriages are very rational, but they can seem heartless, too.

We have marital fights stemming from misunderstandings caused by cultural differences. For example, in Australia, it is customary for a man to open the door for a woman, or to pull out her chair for her when she is being seated. But this causes misunderstandings in Korea. My wife explained that in Korea men only do those things for women they are attracted to. These minor spats end up serving as stepping stones leading to mutual understanding. International marriage? It's like *rappokki*: two different ingredients combine to make a new (*lit.,* third) taste.

Excerpted from *Chosŏn ilbo* and *Korean Weekly,* a British newspaper for expatriates

제12과　보신탕 문화를 둘러싼 논쟁들

(Lesson 12: The Controversy Surrounding Canine Meat Culture)

Objectives

이 장에서는 한국의 전통 음식 중 하나인 보신탕에 대해서 알아보고 종종 사회적 이슈가 되고 있는 보신탕 문화가 어떤 관점에서 생각되어야 하는지 토의해 봅시다.

In this chapter you will be able to learn more about traditional Korean *posint'ang* (dog-meat soup), and about the social issues that surround this controversial food.

Pre-reading questions

1. 개고기/보신탕/영양탕 등에 대하여 들어 본 적이 있습니까?

2. 모든 한국 사람들이 개고기를 먹습니까?

3. 다른 나라의 특별한 음식 문화 중에서 재미있거나 이해하기 어려운 것이 있나요?

4. 남들은 먹지만 본인은 먹을 수 없는 음식이 있습니까?

5. 사람이 먹어서는 안 된다고 생각하는 음식이 있다면 무엇입니까?

Gaining familiarity

1. 국제축구연맹 (FIFA)

2. 한국의 음식: 밥, 국, 반찬, 탕, 김치, 국수, 떡, 찜, 부침개, 회

3. 언론 매체: 신문, 텔레비전, 라디오, 인터넷, 잡지

4. 문화, 풍습, 전통, 인습

보신탕 문화를 둘러싼 논쟁들[12.1]

최근 국제축구연맹(FIFA)이 인터넷 홈페이지 뉴스 난에 한국의 보신탕 문화를 비판하는 기사를 실었다.[12.2] 그리고 세계 주요 언론과의 인터뷰를 통해 한국의 개고기 문화를 강력 비판함으로써 한국의 보신탕 문화가 월드컵을 앞두고 '뜨거운 감자'로 대두됐다.[12.3]

BBC 방송을 비롯한 유럽 언론들은 "한국은 즉각 개를 학대하고 먹는 행위를 중단해야 한다"고 촉구한 제프 블래터 국제축구연맹(FIFA) 회장의 말을 대대적으로[12.4] 보도하면서 개를 먹는 한국 사회의 '후진성'을 집중 부각시켰다.

이에 앞서 지난 7월 16일, 영국과 멕시코의 동물 보호 단체는 런던과 멕시코시티의 한국 대사관 앞에서 '개고기 포식 및 개 도살 행위에 항의하는 가두 시위'를 벌여 개를 식용하는 한국의 보신탕 문화를 강력 성토했다.

이들은 유인물을 통해 개고기 문화가 시정되지 않을 경우, 한국 상품 불매 운동을 벌이는 한편 월드컵 공식 스폰서들에게 압력을 넣어[12.5] 대회 후원을 못하도록 하겠다고 경고하기도[12.6] 했다.

이들 시위는 ITV, 채널4TV 등 영국의 TV방송과 아스테카 TV와 라디오 등 멕시코 현지 언론을 통해 생생하게 보도됐으며, 일부 TV는 한국의 개 도살 장면을 폭로하는 특집 프로그램을 긴급 편성해 한국에 대한 부정적인 이미지를 확산시켰다.

개고기를 둘러싼 인터넷상의 논쟁도 뜨겁기는 마찬가지. 전 세계적으로 한국의 개고기 문화에 반대 운동을 펼치고 있는 사이트는 줄잡아[12.7] 50여 곳이나 된다. 대부분의 해외 사이트들은 동물 보호의 차원에서 개 식용을 반대하고 있지만 최근 개고기 식용 자체에 초점을 맞추어[12.8] 반대하는 곳도 점차 늘고 있다.

한국에서 개고기 논쟁을 가장 공격적으로 주도하고 있는 곳은 '개고기 반대 운동 본부.' 해외에까지 널리 알려진 이 사이트는 식용 개 도살 장면 등 끔찍한 사진과 영상 자료 등을 전시해 개고기 반대 여론을 이끌고 있다. 이에 맞서[12.9] "개고기 유통의 합법화"를 주장하는 '개고기 식용화 운동 본부'도 결성돼 인기를 끌고 있다.[12.10]

한국의 보신탕 문화를 공격하는 이들이 내세우는 주된 논거는 그것이 동물 보호에 역행한다는 것. 특히 인간과 가장 친한 개를 식용으로 취급한다는 것은 식인종과 거의 다를 바 없는[12.11] 야만적인 행위라는 것이다.

그러나 이는 문화적 차이를 인정치 않는 서구의 오만이라는 반론도 만만치 않다. 개고기 식용에 찬성하는 이들은 개고기가 식용과 애완견으로 엄연히 구분돼 왔음을 지적하면서, 서양의 잣대로 개고기 문화를 함부로 매도해서는 안 된다고 강조한다.

이들은 또 우리에게 절실한 것은 '문화 사대주의'가 아니라 '문화 상대주의'이며, 개고기 식용을 비난하는 쇠고기 수출국들의 흉계를 꿰뚫어 볼 줄 아는 안목이 필요하다고 주장한다.

기자는 개고기 식용에 대한 찬반 양론을 아래에서 간략히 살펴봤다.

(1) 개는 인간과 가장 가까운 동물이다.

원숭이는 인간의 지능과 가장 가까운 동물로 꼽히고 있고, 유전자 구조로는 돼지가 인간에 가장 가까운 동물로 판명 나 있다. 인간과 친근하기로 따진다면 말도 개나 별반 다를 바 없다.[12.12] 그러나 현재 유럽 대부분의 나라에서 말을 식용으로 삼고 있다.

(2) 개를 가족처럼 애지중지하는 서구인들의 입장에서 볼 때 개를 식용하는 한국인들의 식성은 참으로 이해하기 어렵다.

한국의 식용 문화는 먹는 개고기(구:拘)와 키우는 개(견:犬)를 명확하게 구분하고 있다. 한국인들은 구탕(拘湯)을 먹지 견탕(犬湯)을 먹지는 않는다.

(3) 개를 도살하는 방법이 너무 잔인해서 문명인에 어울리지 않는다.

살아 있는 생선의 몸을 칼로 난도질하여 살점을 떼어먹는 것은 문명인에 어울리는[12.13] 행위인가? 도살의 비극성만 따지자면 굳이 개만 언급할 것이 아니다. 도살당해 죽어 가는 소나 돼지의 모습을 본 적이 있는지 궁금하다.

(4) 보신탕 문화는 결국 동물 학대에 불과하다.

그렇게 동물을 사랑하는 서구인들이 어찌하여 소의 등에 칼을 꽂으며 가지고 노는 투우를 찬미할 수 있는지 이해 못하는 한국인들도 많다.

(5) 개고기를 먹는 것은 동양에서만 볼 수 있는 야만적인 풍습이다.

서구에서도 개를 상식했다는 것이 각종 문헌에 기록되어 있다. 그리고 마지막 개 식육점이 뮌헨에서 1, 2차 세계대전 사이에 문을 닫았다는 기록도 있는 것으로 보아 식용 개나 젖먹이 강아지의 상거래가 유럽에서 그때까지 계속되었음을 알 수 있다.

(6) 한국은 서양인들의 감수성에 충격을 주는 그릇된 식습관을 바꿔야 한다.

왜 우리가 서양인들의 감수성에 맞추어야 하는가? 인구수로만 따져도 세계의 중심은 아시아다. 아시아 사람들 대부분이 개고기를 식용한다. 동양인들의 감수성은 무시되어야 하는가?

(7) 먹을 것이 부족했을 때는 개고기를 먹을 수밖에 없었을 것이나 먹을 것이 지천에 널린 지금은 그 필요성이 없어졌다.

그것은 입을 것이 지천에 널린 지금, 입기 불편하고 가격도 비싼 한복을 입는 한국인의 심성과 크게 다르지 않다. 개고기 식용은 한국의 오랜 전통 문화 가운데 하나다.[12.14]

(8) 개고기가 음지에서 도살·유통되어 위생이 불결하다.

그런 폐해를 막기 위해서라도 개고기 유통의 합법화가 반드시 필요하다.

한편, "개고기를 직접 먹어 봤고 이해하는 희한한 서양인"이라고 자신을 소개한 존 그리핀 서울시립대 평생교육원 강사는 한 일간지에 "보신탕보다 더 심각한 문제는 호랑이나 곰처럼 사라져 가는 야생 동물을 잡아먹는 것"이라고 지적하고, "개는 소나 닭, 돼지처럼 희귀 동물이 아닌 가축이기에 얼마든지 식용으로 키울 수 있다고 믿는다"며 한국의 보신탕 문화를 옹호하는 글을 기고하기도 했다.

<인터넷 한겨레 하니리포터> 2001년 11월 12일, 문성(한별) 기자

New Words

가두 시위 street demonstration ▷그 학생들은 가두 시위를 벌였다. The students held a street demonstration.

가축 domestic animal

간략히 briefly, concisely. 간략 simplicity, brevity. 간략하다 to be simple

감수성 sensibility ▷유진이는 감수성이 예민하다. Yujin has a fine sensibility.

강력(히) strongly

결성하다 to form, organize. 결성되다 to be formed ▷우리는 티벳 탐험대를 결성했다. We organized an expedition into Tibet.

경고 warning. 경고하다 to warn ▷그들은 내 경고를 무시했다. They disregarded my warning. ▷나는 그들에게 위험한 곳에 가지 말라고 경고했다. I gave them warning not to go to dangerous places.

공격적 offensive, aggressive. 공격하다 to attack, assault

그릇되다 to become wrong, go amiss, end in failure ▷그릇된 생각 wrong idea ▷그릇된 판단 misjudgment, miscalculation

기고하다 to write for (a newspaper or a magazine) ▷신문에 기고하다 to write for the paper

기사 article ▷신문 기사 newspaper article

긴급 urgency, emergency. 긴급 명령 emergency order, urgent command. 긴급 회의 emergency conference. 긴급 조치 emergency measures

꿰뚫다 to pierce; to see into (person's heart) ▷꿰뚫어 보다 to see through

끔찍하다 to be appalling, terrible. 끔찍하게 terribly, awfully ▷끔찍한 사고가 일어났다. A terrible accident has happened.

난도질하다 to chop, mince (meat)

논거 grounds (basis) of an argument, data ▷이 교수님의 주장은 논거가 확실하다. Prof. Lee's argument is well grounded.

논쟁 dispute, argument, controversy ▷나는 이 문제로 그와 심하게 논쟁했다. I had a hot argument with him on this matter.

대대적 grand, gigantic, immense, large-scale ▷대대적으로 광고하다 to advertise extensively, place a large advertisement (in a newspaper)

대사관 embassy ▷주미 한국 대사관 the Korean Embassy in Washington, D.C.

도살 slaughter, butchery

동물 보호 단체 animal protection organization

둘러싸다 to surround, enclose ▷기자들이 그 여배우를 둘러쌌다. The reporters surrounded the actress.

마찬가지 sameness, the very same. 마찬가지로 in the same manner ▷이 중고 차는 새 차나 마찬가지다. This used car is as good as new.

매도하다 to denounce, condemn ▷그는 언제나 정부 정책을 매도한다. He always denounces the government's policy.

명예 honor, glory

명확하게 clearly, definitely, precisely ▷이 점을 명확하게 할 필요가 있다. It is necessary to make this point clear.

문명인 civilized person

문헌 documents, written materials, literature

반론 objection, refutation

별반 (not) particularly, especially ▷그의 제안은 너의 제안과 별반 다르지 않았다. His proposal was not any different from yours.

보도하다 to report, inform (people) of, notify (the general public) of ▷신문은 그날그날의 사건을 보도한다. The newspaper informs us of daily events.

부각시키다 to highlight, bring to the fore

부정적인 negative

불결하다 to be dirty, unclean, foul ▷불결한 거리 [장소] filthy street [place]

불매 운동 buyers' [shoppers', consumers'] strike, boycott (movement) against purchasing ▷주부들은 소고기 불매 운동을 벌이기로 합의했다. The housewives agreed to boycott beef.

비극 tragedy

비난하다 to criticize unfavorably, censure, blame, condemn ▷그들은 그를 무능하다고 비난하였다. They criticized him for incompetence.

비판 criticism, comment. 비판하다 to criticize

사대주의 worship of the powerful, toadyism

살점 piece of flesh

~상 on ~; from the viewpoint of ~, in terms of ~ ▷인터넷상 on the Internet ▷교육상 from an educational point of view ▷편의상 for convenience's sake

상거래 business transaction, commercial dealings

상대주의 relativism

상식하다 to eat normally, live on. 상식 staple (daily) food, normal diet ▷아시아 사람들은 대부분이 주로 쌀을 상식한다. Most Asians live chiefly on rice.

생생하게 lively, fresh

서구 the West. 서구 사상 Western ideas. 서구화 Westernization

성토 denounce, censure, debate. 성토하다 to censure, denounce, impeach. 성토 대회 indignation rally

시위 demonstration. 가두 시위 street demonstration

시정되다 to be corrected, be rectified ▷잘못은 즉시 시정되어야 한다. A wrongdoing should be rectified promptly.

식성 taste, culinary preference

식습관 eating habits

식용하다 to use as food, eat. 식용 use as food. 식용화 making something as food

식인종 cannibal, man-eater

싣다 to load, carry; to publish ▷기사를 싣다 to publish an article (in a newspaper)

심각하다 to be serious, grave, acute ▷심각한 인생 문제 serious problem of life

심성 disposition, mentality

안목 good eye (for), appreciative eye, discerning eye, sense of discrimination ▷전문가의 안목 expert's eye ▷안목이 있는 사람 discerning person ▷수잔은 도자기에 대한 안목이 있다. Susan has an eye for pottery.

압력 pressure ▷압력을 가하다 to apply pressure (to) ▷정치적 압력을 가하다 to exercise political influence

앞두고 with (something) ahead ▷우리는 새해를 앞두고 바쁘다. We are busy with the New Year close at hand.

애완견 pet dog

애지중지하다 to love and prize

야만 savagery, savageness ▷야만적인 행위 barbaric behavior ▷야만적인 풍습 savage custom

야생 wild. 야생 동물 wild animal

양론 both arguments, both sides of the argument

어찌하여 why, for what reason ▷오늘은 어찌하여 늦었느냐? Why are you late today?

언론 speech, discussion; the press

엄연히 solemnly, gravely

여론 public opinion

역행하다 to go against

연맹 league, union, federation, confederation, alliance ▷국제 연맹 the League of Nations

영상 자료 visual materials

오만 arrogance, insolence

옹호하다 to protect, safeguard ▷인권을 옹호하다 to defend human rights ▷헌법을 옹호하다 to safeguard the constitution ▷그는 출판의 자유를 옹호하는 일에 몸을 바쳤다. He devoted himself to the protection of the free press.

위생 hygiene, sanitation. 위생 시설 sanitary facilities. 공중 위생 public hygiene

유인물 printed matter

유전자 gene

유통 distribution. 유통하다 to distribute, circulate

음미 tasting, sampling, appreciation, savoring

음지 shady spot, dark place. 양지 sunny spot, bright place

이끌다 to take along with; to guide, lead ▷도박이 그를 파멸로 이끌었다. Gambling led him to ruin. ▷대통령이 나라를 번영의 길로 이끌었다. The president guided the country to prosperity.

인정하다 to admit, recognize, acknowledge, authorize ▷무죄로 인정하다 to presume (a person) to be innocent

일간지 daily newspaper

자체 oneself, itself; one's own body ▷그 생각 자체가 어리석다. The idea itself is absurd.

잔인하다 to be cruel, heartless

잣대 measuring stick; standard

전시하다 to show, exhibit

절실하다 to be earnest, urgent

주도하다 to lead, take the lead in

주되다 to be chief, principal, main ▷주된 산업 chief industry ▷주된 원인 major cause ▷주된 회원 leading members

중단하다 to cease, discontinue, stop

즉각 instantly, at once, immediately

지천 abundance ▷지천으로 in great abundance

집중 concentration, convergence ▷집중 포화 concentrated fire ▷집중 폭격 saturation bombing

차원 (mathematical) dimension ▷제삼차원 the third dimension

찬미하다 to praise, admire ▷신을 찬미하다 to praise god

초점 focus, focal point ▷교수는 그 문제에 초점을 맞추어 강의를 진행했다. The professor delivered a lecture focusing on that issue.

촉구하다 to press, urge, demand, call upon ▷진지한 반성을 촉구하다 to demand someone's serious reflection ▷사임을 촉구하다 to urge someone to resign

취급하다 to treat (in a certain way), handle, deal with

탕 soup; broth

투우 bullfighting, bullfight

특집 special edition. 특집호 special number [issue]

판명 becoming clear. 판명되다 to become clear

편성하다 to draw up, compose, organize ▷프로그램을 편성하다 to put together a program

폐해 evil, abuse, vice, evil practices ▷폐해를 고치다 to correct [remedy] an abuse ▷폐해를 끼치다 to exert an evil influence

포식 predation. 포식하다 to prey upon, catch and eat

폭로하다 to reveal, disclose, expose

학대 cruelty, mistreatment, maltreatment. 학대하다 to be cruel to, mistreat ▷동물을 학대하면 안 된다. We should not be cruel to animals. ▷약자를 학대하다 to oppress the weak

함부로 recklessly, rashly ▷돈을 함부로 쓰다 to spend money recklessly ▷남을 함부로 비판하지 마라. Don't criticize others unreasonably.

합법화 legalization. 합법화하다 to legalize

항의하다 to protest

행위 act, action, behavior, conduct ▷그의 행위는 신사답지 않다. His conduct is unworthy of a gentleman.

현지 the actual spot, the locale ▷현지 사람들 local people ▷현지 시간 local time ▷현지 보고 on-the-spot report

확산시키다 to spread, expand

후원 support. 후원회 support group. 후원자 sponsor

후진성 underdevelopment, backwardness

흉계 evil plot ▷흉계를 꾸미다 to form a wicked design

희귀 동물 rare animal

희한하다 to be rare, curious, scarce, uncommon ▷희한한 물건 rarity ▷희한한 사람 rare person

Useful Expressions

1. **~을/를 둘러싼 논쟁** the controversy [dispute, argument] surrounding ~

   개고기 문제를 둘러싼 인터넷상의 논쟁이 아주 흥미롭다.

   The controversy on the Internet surrounding the dog meat issue is very interesting.

   요즘 교육 문제를 둘러싼 논쟁이 뜨겁게 달아오르고 있다.

   The dispute over the education problem has recently become very heated.

2. **(기사를) 싣다**　publish [carry] (an article)

　　프랑스 신문은 한국의 보신탕 문화를 비판하는 기사를 실었다.

　　A French newspaper carried an article criticizing Korea's dog-eating culture.

　　그는 나이 스물 하나에 신문에 그의 처녀작을 실었다.

　　He published his first work in a newspaper when he was 21.

3. **~이/가 대두하다/대두되다**　gain power; rise; be formed

　　새로운 형태의 민주주의가 대두하고 있었다.

　　A new type of democracy was on the rise.

　　보신탕 문제가 사회적 이슈로 대두되고 있다.

　　The problem of dog eating has arisen as a social issue.

4. **대대적으로**　grandly; immensely; on a large scale

　　현대는 새 자동차를 대대적으로 광고했다.

　　Hyundae placed a large advertisement for a new car.

　　한국 언론들은 그의 결혼을 대대적으로 보도했다.

　　Korean newspapers published his wedding with enormous headlines.

5. **~에게 압력을 넣다**　put pressure on ~; press ~

　　동물 보호 단체들은 월드컵 공식 스폰서들에게 압력을 넣어 대회를 후원하지
　　못하게 했다.

　　Animal protection groups put pressure on the official World Cup sponsors
　　to withdraw their support for the championship.

　　시민 단체는 정부에(게) 압력을 넣어 세금을 내리게 했다.

　　Civilian groups have pressed the government and made it reduce taxes.

6. **~다고/라고 경고하다**　warn [caution] that ~

　　동물 보호 단체는 한국 상품 불매 운동을 벌이겠다고 경고했다.

　　Animal protection groups warned that they would boycott Korean products.

　　그에게 잘못을 되풀이하지 말라고 경고했다.

　　I cautioned him against repeating his errors.

7. **줄잡아**　approximately; roughly

　　한국의 개고기 문화에 반대 운동을 펼치고 있는 사이트는 줄잡아 50여 곳이나 된다.

　　There are about 50 or so Web sites publicizing the movement against
　　Korea's canine-eating culture.

　　초등학교에서 영어를 가르치고 있는 학교는 서울에 줄잡아 100 군데쯤 된다.

　　There are roughly 100 elementary schools in Seoul that teach English.

8. **~에 초점을 맞추다** focus on ~

대부분의 사이트들은 동물 보호의 차원에서 개 식용을 반대하고 있지만, 최근 개고기 식용 자체에 초점을 맞추어 반대하고 있는 사이트도 있다.

Most Web sites have opposed the eating dog meat from the view of animal protection, but recently there are a number of sites which oppose dog eating focusing on the use of dog meat for eating itself.

한국 정부는 경제 성장에 초점을 맞추고 정책을 검토하였다.

The Korean government reviewed its policy focusing on economic growth.

9. **~에 맞서(서)** against ~; in opposition to ~

남성의 권위에 맞서서 싸우는 여성 단체들이 점점 늘어나고 있다.

Women's groups fighting against male authority are expanding gradually.

갈릴레오는 교황청의 천동설에 맞서서 독자적인 지동설을 주장하였다.

Galileo advocated the heliocentric theory of the solar system in opposition to the Vatican's geocentric theory.

10. **인기를 끌고 있다** be winning popularity

코에 장식을 다는 것이 젊은이들 사이에서 인기를 끌고 있다.

It is popular for young people to get their nose pierced.

요즘 전자 상거래가 젊은이들 사이에서 인기를 끌고 있다.

E-commerce is popular among the young these days.

11. **~와/과 거의 다를 바 없다** is hardly different from ~

개를 먹는 것은 식인종과 거의 다를 바 없는 야만적인 행위다.

There is almost no difference between eating dogs and barbaric behavior like cannibalism.

영국의 국민 소득은 독일과 거의 다를 바 없다.

There's almost no difference between the GNP of the U.K. and of Germany.

12. **별반 다름이 없다** be not particularly different

그때 무슨 말을 듣던 나에겐 별반 다름이 없었다. 나는 그 프로젝트에서 손을 떼기로 결정했다.

What I was told at that time didn't make much difference to me. I had already decided to quit the project.

인간도 동물과 별반 다를 바 없다.

Human beings are not particularly different from animals.

13. **~에 어울리다**   match; suit

개를 도살하는 방법이 너무 잔인해서 문명인에 어울리지 않는다.

The method of slaughtering dogs is so cruel that it does not befit a civilized person.

이 실크에 어울리는 물건을 찾아 주세요.

Please find something which matches this silk.

14. **~ 가운데/중의 하나이다**   one of the ~

개고기 식용은 한국의 오랜 전통 문화 가운데 하나다.

Eating dog meat is an age-old part of Korea's traditional culture.

축구는 영국인들이 가장 좋아하는 운동 경기 중의 하나이다.

Soccer is one of the sports that British people like most.

Exercises

1. 아래의 설명과 맞는 단어나 표현을 보기에서 찾아 쓰세요.

> 보기: 가두 시위, 한복, 후원

(1) 위력이나 기세를 떨쳐 보임, 데모: _____

(2) 한국의 전통 의상: _____

(3) 뒤에서 도와 줌. 원조: _____

2. 보기에서 적당한 말을 골라 빈칸을 채우세요.

> 보기: 뜨거운 감자, 오만, 비판, 안목, 잣대

(1) 그러나 이는 문화적 차이를 인정치 않는 서구의 _____(이)라는 반론도 만만치 않다. 개고기 식용에 찬성하는 이들은 개고기가 식용과 애완견으로 엄연히 구분돼 왔음을 지적하면서, 서양의 _____(으)로 개고기 문화를 함부로 매도해서는 안 된다고 강조한다.

(2) 이들은 또 우리에게 절실한 것은 '문화 사대주의'가 아니라 '문화 상대주의'이며, 개고기 식용을 비난하는 쇠고기 수출국들의 흉계를 꿰뚫어 볼 줄 아는 _____이/가 필요하다고 주장한다.

　(3) 최근 국제축구연맹(FIFA)이 인터넷 홈페이지 뉴스 난에 한국의 보신탕
　　　 문화를 ＿＿＿＿＿＿＿＿하는 기사를 실었다.

　(4) 그리고 세계 주요 언론과의 인터뷰를 통해 한국의 개고기 문화를 강력
　　　 비판함으로써 한국의 보신탕 문화가 월드컵을 앞두고 ＿＿＿＿＿＿＿(으)로
　　　 대두됐다.

3. 다음 셋과 관계가 없는 것 하나를 고르세요.

　　 (1) 보신탕　　　　　해물탕　　　　　사철탕　　　　　영양탕
　　 (2) 위생　　　　　　위생 장갑　　　　소독　　　　　　위인전
　　 (3) 관광객　　　　　외국인　　　　　손님　　　　　　승인
　　 (4) 2차 세계대전　　피난민　　　　　독립 기념일　　　구호 물자

4. 밑줄 친 말과 가장 비슷한 단어나 표현을 고르세요.

　　 (1) 원숭이는 인간의 지능과 가장 가까운 동물로 꼽히고 있고, 유전자 구조로는
　　　　 돼지가 인간에 가장 가까운 동물로 판명 나 있다.
　　　　 a. 알려져 있다　　　　　　　　b. 잘못 알려져 있다
　　　　 c. 잘 알려지지 않았다　　　　　d. 판단돼 있다

　　 (2) 이들은 유인물을 통해 개고기 문화가 시정되지 않을 경우, 한국 상품 불매
　　　　 운동을 벌이는 한편 월드컵 공식 스폰서들에게 압력을 넣어 대회 후원을
　　　　 못하도록 하겠다고 경고하기도 했다.
　　　　 a. 반복되지　　b. 고쳐지지　　　c. 조사되지　　　d. 발전되지

　　 (3) 개고기 식용에 찬성하는 이들은 개고기가 식용과 애완견으로 엄연히 구분돼
　　　　 왔음을 지적하면서, 서양의 잣대로 개고기 문화를 함부로 매도해서는 안
　　　　 된다고 강조한다.
　　　　 a. 강조　　　　　b. 비판　　　　c. 무시　　　　　d. 존중

　　 (4) 인간과 친근하기로 따진다면 말도 개나 별반 다를 바 없다. 그러나 현재
　　　　 유럽 대부분의 나라에서 말을 식용으로 삼고 있다.
　　　　 a. 별로　　　　　b. 적게　　　　c. 완전히　　　　d. 무척

5. 보기와 같이 주어진 표현을 이용하여 문장을 만드세요.

> 보기: ~이기 때문에 ~일 것이다
> → 그녀는 선생님이기 때문에 아이들을 잘 가르칠 것이다.

(1) ~에도 불구하고

_____

(2) 왜 ~여야(만)/아야(만) 하는가?

_____

(3) 그렇지만

_____

(4) 특별히

_____

(5) 다름없다

_____

6. 빈도 부사(frequency adverbs)에 대한 용법을 익히고 각 단어를 사용하여 문맥에
   맞게 새로운 문장을 만들어 보세요.

> 보기: 한번도 ~하지 않는다
> → 현수는 몸이 허약하지만 한번도 결석하지 않았다.

(1) 언제나/항상

_____

(2) 보통

_____

(3) 자주

_____

(4) 가끔

_____

(5) 좀처럼 ~지 않는다.

_____

Comprehension Questions

I. Overall comprehension

(1) 지은이는 개고기를 먹는 한국인을 어떻게 생각하고 있습니까?

_____

(2) 다른 나라 사람들은 개고기를 먹는 한국인들의 풍습을 어떻게 생각합니까?

_____

(3) 서로 다른 풍습의 차이를 어떻게 해결해 가야 할까요?

_____

II. Finding details

(1) 한국 사람들은 왜 개고기를 먹습니까?

_____

(2) 누가 인터넷 홈페이지에 한국의 개고기 먹는 풍습을 비판하였습니까?

_____

(3) 서양에는 개고기를 먹은 기록이 있습니까?

_____

(4) 한국인의 개고기를 먹는 풍습을 막는다면 어떤 결과가 예상됩니까?

_____

(5) 보신탕 문화는 동물을 학대시키는 것인가요?

(6) 한국인은 모든 종류의 개를 먹습니까?

_____

Related Reading

왜 개고기는 안 되나

1988년 서울올림픽 때, 한국 정부는 서구의 몇몇 단체들로부터 개고기 소비를 억제하라는 압력을 받아야 했다. 동물 보호주의자인 프랑스의 전 영화배우 브리지트 바르도가 한국에서 유명해지게 된 것도 이때부터이다. 그 뒤 개고기의 거래에 대한 규제들이 만들어졌고, 이 규제들로 인해 개고기의 유통이 음성적으로 됨으로써 위생 관리에 대한 조건들이 더욱 악화되었으며 결국 소비자들이 불이익을 받게 됐다.

지난해 국회 의원 두 명이 이런 규제를 재검토하는 법안을 냈을 때, 한국 정부는 (개고기를 먹는) 이런 관습을 합법화시키는 것이 시기 적절하지 않아 보인다고 말했다. 여기서 정치인들의 말이 그들의 행동으로부터 얼마나 멀어져 있는지 알 수 있다. 정부 사람들 가운데 몇 명이나 개고기를 그들의 음식의 영역에서 제외시켰는지 알려고 하지는 않겠다. 다만 놀라운 점은 개고기 소비를 금지하는 정부의 태도 자체보다 실제로 내세운 이유다. 곧 한국 정부가 개고기 소비를 추방하려 한 것은 동물에 대한 어떤 배려에서가 아니라 국제 무대에서 한국의 이미지를 해칠지 모른다는 이유에서였다.

여기서 나는 한국인의 자존심을 이해할 수 있지만 그래도 약간은 어리둥절할 수밖에 없다. 어떤 정부라도 순전히 국내 정책에 관한 결정을 함에 있어 내부적인 고려 사항들이 아니라 외국으로부터의 압력에 의해 결정하는 일은 실제로 드물기 때문이다. 몇몇 서양 운동 단체가 로비력에 있어서 최고로 통하지만 말이다.

동물류의 소비는 일반적으로 두 가지 문제점을 일으킨다. 첫번째는 그것의 소비 금지의 문제이고, 두번째는 그것을 기르고 소비하기 위해 죽이는 방식에 관련돼 있다. 소비 금지에 관해서 말하자면, 멸종의 위기에 처해 있는 동물들을 빼고는 먹기 위해 죽이는 것을 금지하는 동물과 그렇지 않은 동물을 '구분'하는데 어떤 기준을 따라야 할지를 정하는 것은 솔직히 미묘한 문제이다.

우리는 종종 개가 '인류의 가장 친한' 동물이기 때문에 그것을 먹는 것을 받아들일 수 없다고 말하는 것을 듣게 된다. 그러나 이것은 아주 주관적인 견해일 뿐 아니라, 극히 변하기 쉬운 것이기도 하다. 1세기 전 서부 헐리우드 사람들이라면 누구나 말이 '인류의 가장 친한' 동물이라고 말했을 것이기 때문이다. 그럼에도 말고기는 오늘날 프랑스의 많은 정육점에서 거래되고 있으며, 그렇다고 그 사실이 대중적인 분노를 일으키지도 않는다.

두번째 문제는 동물의 사육 조건과 죽이는 조건에 관한 것이다. 그것은 스페인이나 프랑스 남서부에서 행해지는 투우에 반대해 일어선 사람들이 제기하는 논쟁이기도 하다. 솔직히 나는 개가 어떻게 사육되고 죽임을 당하는지 잘 모른다. 그러나 닭장에서 목만 내밀게 하고 사육하는 닭, 날것으로 먹기 전에 돌에 문대어 분쇄하는 생선, '푸아

그라' 요리를 위해 거위나 오리에게 억지로 많이 먹이는 것보다 더 고통스러운 것은 없을 것 같다. 다른 동물들이 받는 대우에 대해서는 아주 무관심하면서, 사람들이 어째서 개는 다른 동물보다 더 많은 염려를 받을 자격이 있다고 생각하는지 설명하기란 정말 어렵다.

개고기를 먹는 것을 금지하자는 주장은 자기의 문화적 확신에 기초해 다른 나라의 소비 습관에 개입하는 것이다. 인도 사람들이 다른 대륙에 대해 암소 소비를 금하기 위해 압력을 행한 적이 있는가? 문화적인 이유에서 돼지고기 먹기를 거부하는 이슬람 교도들이 다른 나라에 대해 돼지고기를 먹지 말도록 압력을 가하려 한다면 어떻게 받아들여질 것인가? 결국 한국인들이 개고기 먹는 것을 금지시키겠다는 서방인들의 교만 앞에서 우리는 놀랄 수밖에 없다. 누군가 햄버거나 스페어립스를 먹지 못하게 한다면 정작 그들 자신은 이해하지도 못 할 것이다.

채식주의자들처럼 동물 소비를 포기하는 경우를 빼면, 어떤 동물은 소비하고 어떤 동물은 소비를 금하는 것을 가능하게 하는 객관적 논리를 생각해 내기란 불가능하다. 요컨대 개고기 먹는 것을 금하기를 원하는 사람이라면 소고기 먹기를 금해야 좀 더 설득력 있을 것이다.

에릭 비데, 전 유럽연합 파견연구원·사회경제학
http://www.hani.co.kr/section-001031000/2000/001031000200003201914043.html

---

올림픽 the Olympics, 서구 the Western world, 소비 consumption, 억제하다 to restrain, control, 보호주의자 conservationist, protector, 거래 trade, 규제 regulation, restriction, 음성적으로 illicitly, 위생 관리 health control, 악화하다 to worsen, deteriorate, 불이익 disadvantage, 국회 의원 member of the national assembly, 재검토 re-examination, review, 법안 bill, proposal for a new law, 합법화 legalization, 시기 적절하다 to be the appropriate time, timely, 제외시키다 to exclude, make an exception of, 배려 care, concern, 자존심 pride, 어리둥절하다 to become confused, be at a loss, 고려 사항 matters for consideration, ~로 통하다 to be known as ~, 멸종 extinction, 처하다 to be faced with, 미묘하다 to be delicate, subtle, 주관적인 subjective, 대중적인 popular, 분노 anger, rage, 정육점 butcher's shop, 사육 조건 animal rearing conditions, 분쇄하다 to crush, 무관심하다 to be indifferent (to), not care (about), 확신 firm belief, 인도 India, 교만 haughtiness, arrogance, 채식주의자 vegetarian, 설득력 persuasiveness, powers of persuasion

Discussion & Composition

1. 한쪽은 개고기를 옹호하는, 다른 한쪽은 개고기를 반대하는 그룹으로 나누어 서로
   토론을 할 수 있도록 아래에 글을 써보세요.

2. 본문과 Related Reading의 글을 읽어 보고 개고기 식용에 대한 찬반 양론 중에서
동의할 수 있는 것과 동의할 수 없는 것에 대해 토론해 보세요.

3. 먹기 위해 죽이는 것을 금지해야 할 동물과 그렇지 않은 동물을 구분하는 데 어떤
기준이나 객관적 논리가 있을 수 있는지 이야기해 보세요.

Lesson 12 The controversy surrounding canine meat culture

Recently FIFA inserted an article in the news column of its Internet home page criticizing Korea's canine meat culture. Then they strongly criticized that culture through interviews with major global press (agencies), thereby causing that culture to emerge as a "hot potato" in respect to the upcoming World Cup games.

Beginning with the BBC, the European press reported extensively the words of FIFA chairman Sepp Blatter, who called on Korea to "immediately stop the maltreatment and eating of dogs," pointing out in a intense manner the "backwardness" of the canine-eating Korean society.

Previously, on July 16th, animal protection groups in England and Mexico had held street demonstrations in front of the Korean embassies in London and Mexico City to "protest the gluttonous consumption of dog meat and the butchery of dogs," and they strongly denounced the Korean *posint'ang* culture.

These groups used printed matter to give warning that if the canine meat culture was not corrected, they would boycott Korean products and pressure the official World Cup sponsors to withdraw their support from the competition.

These demonstrations were given vivid reportage on ITV and Channel Four TV broadcasts in Britain and in on-the-spot broadcasts on Azteca TV and radio in Mexico. Some stations spread negative images of Korea, quickly putting together special programs with scenes of dogs being slaughtered.

The controversy surrounding the issue is just as heated on Internet sites. No fewer than fifty Internet sites from around the world are spreading a protest movement against Korea's canine-eating culture. Most of the foreign sites oppose the eating of canines out of concern for animal protection, but recently more and more sites are focusing their protest against the eating of canine meat itself.

In Korea, the most aggressive leader in the canine meat debates is the Headquarters for the Movement to Oppose Canine Meat. This site, which has become widely known abroad, has swayed public opinion against canine meat by showing gruesome photographs of the slaughter of canines bred for consumption. On the other side, the Headquarters for the Movement to Make Canine Meat a Food, which advocates the legalization of canine-meat distribution, is [also] gaining in popularity.

The main argument forwarded by those who oppose Korea's *posint'ang* culture is that it goes against animal protection. They say treating "man's best friend" as a food is a barbaric practice only once removed from cannibalism.

But there are not a few who protest this as the "arrogance of Western countries that do not recognize cultural difference." The supporters of canine meat-eating point out that there is a strict distinction between dogs used for eating and those used for pets. They emphasize that canine-meat culture must not be condemned based on Western cultural standards.

They say that what is important (*lit.,* serious) for us is "cultural relativism" rather than "cultural flunkeyism." They assert that we need the vision to see through the evil plot of beef-exporting countries that criticize consumption of canine meat.

I (*lit.,* this reporter) have given a rough outline of the pros and cons of canine-meat eating.

(1) The dog is the animal closest to humans.

The monkey is regarded as the animal closest to humans in intelligence, and it has been ascertained that the pig is closest to humans in terms of genetic structure. If you reckon which animals are dearest to man, there is no difference between the horse and the dog. But most countries in Europe treat horses as a food.

(2) From the point of view of Westerners, who treasure dogs as family members, it is truly difficult to understand the culinary taste of Koreans who eat dogs.

Korean dietary culture clearly distinguishes between canine meat that is eaten (*ku*) and dogs that are raised as pets (*kyŏn*). Koreans eat soup made from *ku*, not from *kyŏn*.

(3) The method used to butcher dogs is cruel and does not suit civilized people.

Is it a civilized act to cut a living fish with a knife and chop it up, or pull off pieces and eat them? Dogs are not the only animals that suffer the tragedy of butchery. I wonder if they have ever seen a cow or pig die from being slaughtered?

(4) *Posint'ang* culture amounts to animal cruelty.

Many Koreans cannot understand how animal-loving Westerners can praise bullfights, where one inserts a knife into a cow's back and plays with it.

(5) Eating dog is a barbaric practice that can be found only in the East.

Documents show that dog was also consumed in Europe. Considering that the last dog-meat shop closed its doors in Munich between the First and Second

World Wars, we know that until that time the selling of dogs and nursling puppies for consumption had continued in Europe.

(6) Koreans must change this mistaken culinary habit that is so offensive to Western sensibility.

Why must we conform to the sensibility of Westerners? Judging by population, Asia is the center of the world. Most Asians eat dog meat. Must we ignore the sensibilities of Asians?

(7) When food was scarce, there was no choice but to eat dog meat; but now that food is plentiful, eating dog meat is unnecessary.

It is not much different from the desire of Koreans to wear uncomfortable, expensive Korean traditional dress, even though clothes are currently plentiful. Dog consumption is a traditional custom in Korea.

(8) Dogs are butchered in unsanitary places. Distributing dog meat is unsanitary.

That is why, in order to avoid injurious effects, the legalization of dog meat distribution is essential.

John Griffin, a lecturer in continuing education at Seoul Municipal College who introduced himself in a daily newspaper as "a rare Westerner who has tried dog meat and understands," pointed out that "A more important problem than *posint'ang* is the capture and consumption of endangered wild animals like the tiger and the bear." He submitted an article in support of Korea's *posint'ang* culture, stating: "Dogs are like chickens and pigs in that they are not endangered animals. I think they can be raised in great numbers for food."

Mun Sŏng, *Internet Hangyŏre Hani reporter,* Nov. 12, 2001

Related Reading: Why is Dog Meat Bad?

In 1988, the year of the Seoul Olympics, the Korean government had to yield to pressure from several European organizations to suppress the consumption of dog meat. It was from this time that Brigitte Bardot, an animal-rights protectionist and former movie actress in France, began to be famous in Korea. Afterwards, regulations concerning the trade of dog meat were created. Due to these regulations, the circulation of dog meat went underground, worsening sanitary conditions. In the end, the consumers were hurt.

Last year, when two assemblymen submitted a bill to re-examine these regulations, the government said it seemed an unseasonable time to legalize the custom (of eating dog meat). This shows how distant the words of the politicians were from their actions. I'm not trying to find out how many among the politicians (actually) had taken dog meat out of their diet. More surprising than the government's attitude in prohibiting dog-meat consumption was its reason for doing so. Its attempt to ban dog-meat consumption did not stem from any concern for animals, but from concern that legalizing [the practice] might harm Korea's image on the international stage.

While I can understand their concern for Korea's self-respect, the situation is also somewhat confused. It is truly rare for any government, in deciding a purely domestic policy, to do so based on pressure from foreign countries rather than on consideration of domestic matters—even if several Western political groups have put forth supreme lobbying efforts.

There are generally two types of problems concerning animal consumption. The first is the problem of forbidding consumption; the second concerns the method of killing animals raised for consumption. Concerning the first problem, except for those species in danger of extinction, it is, frankly, a delicate matter to decide what standards to follow in distinguishing between animals people are forbidden to kill and eat and those they are permitted to kill and eat.

We often hear that we cannot suffer the eating of dogs because they are "man's best friend." This is not only highly subjective, but also extremely capricious. A century ago, people in Hollywood (Old West) called the horse "man's best friend." But these days horsemeat is sold in many French *boucheries*, and this does not incur popular rage.

The second problem concerns the conditions under which the animals are raised and killed. This is the argument raised by people opposed to the bullfight in the south of Spain and France. I do not honestly know how dogs are raised and killed, but nothing could be more painful than chickens raised with only their necks protruding; fish eaten raw after being descaled and smashed with a stone; or geese and ducks force-fed for the purpose of making *foie gras*. It is difficult to explain why, while being utterly unconcerned about how other animals are treated, they deem dogs more worthy of our concern.

The assertion that dog-eating should be disallowed has its roots in cultural convictions and is an intrusion into the consumer practices of another country. Has India ever put pressure on foreign countries to forbid the eating of beef? How would it be regarded if Moslem believers, who do not eat pork for cultural reasons, applied pressure to foreign countries to forbid the eating of pigs? We can only be surprised at the arrogance of Westerners who try to ban Koreans' eating of dog meat. They would never understand if someone tried to keep them from eating hamburgers and spareribs.

Except for cases in which people give up consuming meat, such as vegetarians, it is impossible to imagine an objective logic enabling us to consume certain animals and forbid the consumption of others. In short, people who would forbid eating dog meat would be (more) convincing if they also gave up eating beef.

Eric Bidet, former official researcher at the European Union, Socio-Economics
http://www.hani.co.kr/section-001031000/2000/001031000200003201914043.html

제13과   나의 사춘기

(Lesson 13: My Adolescence)

Objectives

누구나 한번쯤은 사춘기의 경험이 있다. 그 사춘기 때의 추억을 살펴보고 그 추억들이 나중에 어떤 영향을 나에게 주었는지 알아보자.

Everyone experiences adolescence. This chapter looks at one writer's adolescent memories and how they affected his subsequent development.

Pre-reading questions

1. 사춘기 하면 가장 먼저 떠오르는 것은 무엇입니까?

2. 언제 사춘기를 맞이하였습니까? 또 언제 사춘기가 끝이 났는지 기억하고 있습니까?

3. 사춘기 때 사귀었던 친구들과 나누었던 추억들에는 어떤 것이 있습니까?

4. 사춘기 때 가장 하고 싶었던 일은 무엇이었습니까?

5. 첫사랑은 언제 어떻게 누구로부터 시작되었습니까?

6. 사춘기 때 좋아하던 음악이나 소설, 영화나 취미 같은 것이 있었습니까?

Gaining familiarity

1. 6.25: 1950년 6월 25일 시작된 한국 전쟁.
   〔육이오·육이오 동란·육이오 사변·한국 동란·한국 전쟁〕
2. 호: 본명 이외에 쓰는 이름. 허물없이 쓰기 위하여 지은 이름이다. 이광수의 호는 춘원이다.
3. 이광수: 호는 춘원. 계몽주의 문학가. 한국 최초의 근대 장편 소설 '무정'을 매일신보에 연재. '원효 대사', '유정' 등의 작품 남김.
4. 경복궁: 서울에 있는 조선 시대의 궁전.
5. 교외 지도 단속반: 1970-80 년대 학교 밖에서 학생들의 생활을 지도해 주는, 주로 선생님들로 구성된 소규모 단체.
6. 부산: 경상남도 남동부에 있는 광역시. 서울 다음가는 대도시이며 한국 최대의 무역항.
7. 동해 남부선: 부산에서 포항까지 대한민국 남동 해안을 따라 올라가는 철도 노선.
8. 무엇이든 물어 보세요: 시청자의 궁금증을 풀어 주는 한국의 텔레비전 프로그램.

나의 사춘기

누구에게나 자신의 한 시기를 상징하는 몇 장의 그림이 있을 수 있다.[13.1] 실향민인 나의 어머니는 흥남 부두의 참혹했던 기억으로부터 6.25를 회상하신다. 마찬가지로[13.2] 나의 사춘기를 되돌아보면 몇 개의 그림들이 떠오른다. 이광수의 <흙>, 친구, 야구, 영화 <러브스토리>, <알레그로 마 논 트로포>, <데미안>, 동해 남부선, 고호의 <감자 먹는 사람들>, 성.

이광수의 <흙>

이 책을 손에 쥔[13.3] 것은 중학교 1학년 때였는데, 처음으로 '동화'가 아닌 소설에서 문학적 체험을 시작하는 계기가 되었다. 나도 글을 쓰는 사람이 되고자 결심하고, 이광수 선생을 본받아 배운다는 의미에서 일기를 춘원에게 쓰는 편지체로 바꾸어 썼다. 그날그날 있었던 일들, 느낌이 일기장을 가득 채웠다. 춘원에게서 답장은 오지 않고, 붉은 펜으로 쓴 국어 선생님의 주석이 달린 일기장만이 되돌아왔을 뿐이었다. 그때는 왜 그리 부끄러웠는지. 그 후로 일기장의 편지는 국어 선생님으로 수신자가 바뀌었다. 여선생님이었다.

친구

친구는 소년 시절 그 자체의 전부이자 필요 충분한 인간 관계의 핵심이었다. '친구를 위해서' 또는 '친구 때문'이라면 모든 일이 가능할 것 같았다. 특히 '금지된 장난'을 친구들과 함께 남몰래[13.4] 치르는 것은 커다란 즐거움이었다.

영규네 집에 가서 몰래 담배를 피우면서, 우리는 그 엄청난 비밀을 아주 친한 우리 셋만이 공유할 수 있다는 사실에 흥분했다.[13.5] 서울로 전학한 수근이와는 고교 3년 내내 엽서를 주고 받았는데, 어느 가을 녀석이 자기 학교 근처에서 주운 은행잎을 보내 왔다. 나는 그 은행잎을 보면서 온갖 상상력을 더하여 '서울'을 아름다운 도시로 만들었다. 대학 진학 후에 수근이와 나는 경복궁 돌담 밑에 수북이 쌓인 은행잎을 추억과 함께 밟으며 '비목'을 불렀다. 그리고 나서 녀석은 애인이 생겼다고 말했다. 그때부터 서울은 아름답지만은 않았다.

야구

나는 저녁 수업이 끝나면 매일 운동을 했다. 배구부에 들어가 여름 방학 때 합숙을 하기도 하고, 땀을 뻘뻘 흘리며 날이 저물어 공이 보이지 않을 때까지 야구를 하기도 했다. 아령을 하면서 친구들에게 뒤에서 본 내 모습이 정말 역삼각형이 되어 가고 있는지를 수도 없이 묻기도 했다.

그렇게 땀을 흘리고 뛰어도 가슴엔 뭔가 항상 응어리가 남아 있었다. 지금 생각하면 사춘기 열병이었던 것을. 그때는 그게 식욕인지 성욕인지 무엇인지 몰라서 그 응어리를 풀려고[13.6] 틈만 나면 뛰었다. 그리고 엄청나게 먹었다.

영화

좋은 영화 치고 '미성년자 관람 불가' 딱지가 붙지 않은 것은 드물었다. '미성년자'라는 어른들의 기준이 도무지 일방적이고 한심하게 느껴졌던 나로서는 영화를 보기 위해 별수없이 매표소의 아가씨에게 사정하는 도리밖에 없었다.[13.7] 다행히도 당시 부산의 한 극장은 수입이 시원치 않았던지[13.8] 우리 같은 영화광들을 위해 극장 제일 위층 골방을 배려하는 '특혜'를 베풀었다. 나는 그 골방의 단골이었다.

1972년 한 해 동안 부산에서 개봉됐던 외국 영화 중 2편만 빼고 다 보았다. 가끔 '교외 지도 단속반'을 만나기도 했지만, 우리는 화장실 뒷문을 통해 도망가는 길을 알고 있었다. 영화를 보고 나올 때면 항상 영화의 분위기에 동조하게 된다. <러브 스토리>의 제니 같은 여자를 만나 보고도 싶어졌다. 그런데 곤란한 건 그녀가 불치의 병으로 세상을 떠나야 내가 진정한 비극의 주인공이 될 수 있다는 사실이었다.

알레그로 마 논 트로포

베토벤 바이올린 협주곡의 악상을 나타내는 이 단어는 한동안 내가 제목으로 착각한 것이다. 정말 그 협주곡을 들으며 음악의 깊이며 향기를 느낄 수 있었던 것은 그로부터 한참 후의 일이다. 나는 어느 여자 선생님이 좋아한다는 이 음악을 나도 같이 좋아하기 위하여 엄청난 인내

심으로 수도 없이 되풀이해서 들어야 했다. 하지만 마지막 악장까지 듣
는 일은 거의 없었다. 그러면서도 그 이후로 오랫동안 설문지에서 가장
좋아하는 음악을 써 내라고 하면 항상 '알레그로 마 논 트로포'를 썼다.

성

'성'은 그때나 지금이나 우리 사회 청소년들에게 금기시되기는 마찬가
지다. 가끔 비밀스럽게 친구들과 정보 교환을 하기도 하고, '무엇이든 물
어 보세요'를 훔쳐보면서 호기심을 달래기도 했지만, 정말로 '그 누구도'
'성'에 대해 이야기해 주는 사람이 없었다. 그래서 욕정 자체가 죄의식과
연계되면서 나는 갈수록 스스로에게 불결하고 나쁜 아이가 되어 갔다.
앙드레 지드의 <좁은 문>을 읽고는 더 심한 죄책감에 빠졌다.[13.9]

동해 남부선

내 고향 남도 부산에선 여름이면 바닷가의 벌거숭이가 되는 즐거움이
있었다. 하지만 광안리나 해운대보다 나는 친구들과 동해 남부선을 탔
다. 기차를 타고 해안을 따라가면서 한번도 좌석에 앉아 본 적이 없다.
우리는 늘 객차의 문에 매달려 마파람에 얼굴을 비비며 고함을 질러댔
다. 바다에서도 마찬가지였다. 수영 금지 구역을 나타내는 위험선에서 1
미터라도 벗어나야 수영할 맛이 났다.[13.10] 금지된 것은 늘 도전의 대상이
었다.

고호의 <감자 먹는 사람들>

나는 사춘기 시절 혹시라도 명랑하고 쾌활한 소년으로 보이게 될까
봐 조심하였다.[13.11] 그래서 항상 교모를 눌러 쓰고 입술을 군게 다물고
'멜랑콜리한' 분위기를 연출하려고 노력했다. 그건 '나는 남들과는 다르
다'는 첫번째 신호이자, 어떤 영화의 주인공같이 되고 싶은 '나르시시즘'
의 표현이었다.

부산 상공회의소에서 열렸던 미술 전시회에서 나는 고호의 음울한 그
림을 보고, 그 무채색의 그늘에 압도되었다. 그 후로 나는 밝고 화려한
모든 것들을 거부하는 철저한 염세주의자가 되기로 했다. 그러나 그것은
아주 짧은 한때였다.

데미안

이광수의 <흙>을 통해 동화 책 또는 어린 시절과 작별하고 <데미안>을 통해 문학 소년의 출발을 맞이하였다. 그건 혁명이었다. 방황이니, 고통이니, 좌절이니 하는 정말 멋있는 단어들을 만날 수 있었기 때문이다. '데미안과 싱클레어' 때문에 주위의 친구들이 조금씩 가소로워지기 시작했다. 나는 내가 다른 아이들과 상당히 다르거나 특별한 존재라는 생각을 하게 되었다. 내면을 들여다보려고 애썼고 일기장은 더욱 난해한 추상 명사들로 채워지기 시작했다. 평범한 단어가 싫어서 국어 사전을 펴들고 새로운 단어를 탐색하는 밤이 많아졌다.

장용우 <월간 말> 1994년 8월호, 178-179

New Words

가소롭다 to be laughable, ridiculous ▷네가 그를 가르치겠다니 가소롭다. It is
　　ridiculous to imagine you teaching him anything.
개봉되다 to open, releas (a film at the cinema) ▷최근에 개봉된 한국 영화 very
　　recently released Korean film
객차 passenger car, passenger train
거부하다 to reject, refuse ▷딱 잘라 거부하다 to give (somebody) a flat refusal
계기 momentum; beginning ▷계기가 되다 to serve as momentum ▷이것을 계기로
　　with this as a turning point
고통 pain, agony, anguish, suffering. 고통스럽다 to be agonizing, be painful
고함 shout, yell, roar ▷고함을 지르다 to shout, yell
고호 Vincent Van Gogh
골방 back room, small room
공유하다 to share, have in common ▷그들은 재산을 공유하고 있다. They hold
　　property in common.
관람 inspection, viewing. 관람하다 to view, watch. 관람료 admission fee
교모 school cap
금기 taboo ▷금기시되다 to be regarded as taboo
금지 prohibition. 금지하다 to prohibit, ban, forbid
깊이 depth, deepness, profundity ▷바다의 깊이 depth of the sea ▷생각의 깊이
　　profundity of thought

나르시시즘 narcissism

난해하다 to be hard [difficult] to understand, hard to make out ▷난해한 문제
    difficult problem [question]

내면 internal, inside

단골 regular customer

단속 keeping under control, control, supervision ▷단속반 control team, inspection
    team ▷학생을 단속하다 to keep students under control

달래다 to soothe, comfort, calm ▷호기심을 달래다 to satisfy one's curiosity

대상 object, subject ▷이 책은 어린이를 대상으로 쓴 것이다. This book is intended
    for children.

데미안 *Demian* (novel by Hermann Hesse)

도전 challenge

돌담 stone wall

동조하다 to align oneself with, be in tune with, be in sympathy with, agree with
    ▷나는 그의 의견에 동조하지 않는다. I do not sympathize with his opinion.

동화 fairy tale

되돌아보다 to look back, look over one's shoulder ▷과거를 되돌아보다 to think
    back to past days

되풀이하다 to go over again, repeat

드물다 to be rare, uncommon, unusual ▷보기 드문 사건 rare event ▷그가 화를
    내는 것은 드문 일이다. It is unusual for him to get angry.

딱지 sticker, label, tag

떠오르다 to rise, come to mind

마파람 south wind

멜랑콜리하다 to be melancholy

명랑하다 to be bright, cheerful. 명랑하게 merrily, cheerfully

무채색 achromatic color

문학 literature ▷아동 문학 juvenile literature ▷문학 청년 young lover of literature

미성년자 person under age

미술 전시회 art exhibition

방황 wandering, roaming. 방황하다 to wander (about), roam (about) ▷나는 밤새
    산속에서 방황했다. I was roaming over the mountains all night.

배려하다 to consider, give consideration to ▷여러 가지로 배려해 주셔서
    감사합니다. Thank you for your kind consideration.

벌거숭이 naked body

벗어나다 to escape (from), deviate (from)

별수없이 without any better luck, without much choice

본받다 to model (oneself on) ▷본받을 만한 행동 exemplary conduct

부끄럽다 to be shy, embarrassed ▷부끄러워 말을 못하다 to be too shy to talk

부두 quay, wharf

불가 impropriety, disapproval

불치 incurability ▷불치의 병 [불치병] incurable disease

비극 tragedy

비비다 to rub ▷눈을 비비다 to rub one's eye ▷손을 비비다 to rub one's hands

뻘뻘 (sweat) freely, profusely; dripping with sweat ▷땀을 뻘뻘 흘리다 to drip with sweat

사정하다 to beg, entreat, implore, solicit

사춘기 adolescence, (the age of) puberty

상공회의소 chamber of commerce and industry

상상력 power of imagination

상징하다 to symbolize ▷까치는 희소식을 상징한다. The magpie is a symbol of good news.

설문지 survey, questionnaire

성 sex. 성욕 sexual desire. 성 문제 sex problem. 성 지식 knowledge about sex

소설 novel, fiction. 단편 소설 short story. 장편 소설 (full-length) novel

수북이 in heaps, high ▷그릇에 밥을 수북이 담다 to fill a bowl heaping full of rice

시기 time, period

식욕 appetite, hunger

신호 sign, signal

실향민 people who had to move from their hometown because of war [disaster], refugees

쌓이다 to be piled up, be accumulated ▷수북이 쌓이다 to be piled in heaps

아령 dumbbell

악상 theme, motif, melodic subject

악장 movement (of a piece of music), section of a longer musical piece

알레그로 마 논 트로포 *Allegro ma non troppo* (from a concerto by Beethoven)

애쓰다 to take pains (trouble), make an effort, endeavor, strive ▷목적을 이루려고 애쓰다 to endeavor to attain one's aim ▷애쓴 보람이 없었네. I gained nothing for all my trouble.

엄청나다 to be exorbitant, massive, huge. 엄청나게 terribly, absurdly, massively

역삼각형 inverted triangle

연계되다 to be connected, linked (with)

연출하다 to produce (a play) ▷이 연극은 유명한 극작가가 연출했다. This play was produced by a famous playwright.

열병 febrile disease, fever

염세주의자 pessimist

영화 film, movie. 영화광 film fan

욕정 feelings of passion, sexual desire

위험선 danger line, danger signal

은행잎 ginkgo leaf

음울하다 to be gloomy, melancholy ▷음울한 그림 gloomy picture

응어리 stiffness in a muscle; unpleasant feeling, anxiety

인내심 patience, endurance, perseverance

일방적이다 to be one-sided, unilateral ▷일방적인 경기 one-sided game

자체 oneself, itself ▷그 계획 자체는 나쁘지 않다. The plan itself is not bad.

저물다 (the day or year) closes, it grows dark ▷날이 저물도록 till late, till dark
　　　▷날이 저문 후에 after dark

전학하다 to transfer school

존재 existence, being ▷존재 이유 reason for being, raison d'être ▷신의 존재
　　　existence of god

좁은 문 *La Porte étroite,* French novel by André Gide

좌절 breakdown, frustration, setback

죄의식 feeling of guilt (sin)

죄책감 feeling of liability for a crime

주석 notes, commentary

진학 entrance into a school of higher grade

질러대다 to shout (yell, holler) a lot, shout repeatedly ▷진희는 고함을 질러댔다.
　　　Chin-hǔi shouted a lot.

착각하다 to misunderstand, get the wrong end of the stick

참혹하다 to be cruel, brutal, wretched ▷참혹한 짓을 하다 to do a cruel thing,
　　　commit cruelties ▷그것은 정말 눈뜨고 못 볼 참혹한 광경이었다. It was a
　　　really pitiable sight to see.

채우다 to fill up, pack up ▷그녀는 욕조에 물을 채웠다. She filled the bathtub with
　　　water.

철저하다 to be thorough, exhaustive, complete, perfect ▷ 그는 매사에 철저하다. He
　　　is always thorough about anything.

체험 (one's personal) experience

추상 명사 abstract noun

추억 recollection, reminiscence, remembrance, retrospection, reflection

치르다 to experience, go through; to hold (a party or an event) ▷남몰래 치르다 to
　　　experience secretly; to hold (something) secretly

쾌활하다 to be cheerful, gay, cheery, lively ▷쾌활한 성격 cheerful spirit or
　　　personality ▷쾌활한 사람 jolly fellow

탐색 search, hunt. 탐색하다 to search

특혜 special favor, privilege ▷특혜를 주다 to extend a privilege

틈 gap, crack; interval; time ▷틈만 나면 every free moment

편지체 epistolary style, letter style

필요 충분하다 to be necessary and sufficient

한심하다 to be a pity; to be regrettable, lamentable ▷한심한 일 matter of regret ▷나라 일이 자꾸 어지러워지니 한심하다. It is deplorable that the affairs of the nation should get messed up worse and worse.

합숙 (*lit.*, sleeping together) staying together (in a camp for training)

핵심 core, nucleus

혁명 revolution

협주곡 concerto

호기심 curiosity

화려하다 to be splendid, magnificent, gorgeous

회상하다 to recollect, recall ▷그 노인은 젊은 시절을 회상했다. The old man reflected on his younger days.

훔쳐보다 to steal a glance (at), look furtively (at) ▷그는 옆에 앉은 학생의 답안지를 훔쳐보았다. He peeped at the answer sheet of the student sitting next to him.

흙 earth, soil

흥분하다 to be excited ▷흥분하지 말고 내 말을 들어 봐. Don't be excited; listen to me.

Useful Expressions

1. ~(으)ㄹ 수 있다 be able to ~; it is possible that ~

    우리는 불어를 할 수 있는 사람이 필요하다.

    We need a student who is able to speak French.

    누구나 좋아하는 사람이 있을 수 있다.

    It is possible that everybody loves somebody.

2. 마찬가지로 as well as; too; likewise

    그는 야구와 마찬가지로 축구도 좋아한다.

    He likes to play baseball as well as football (soccer).

    영국과 마찬가지로 일본도 운전석이 오른쪽에 있다.

    As in England, Japanese cars have the driver's seat on the right.

3. **~을/를 손에 쥐다** obtain ~, get hold of ~

　　이 책을 손에 쥔 것은 중학교 1학년 때였다.

　　　It was in the first year of middle school that I got hold of this book.

　　김 사장은 거액을 손에 쥐었다.

　　　President Kim obtained big money.

4. **(남)몰래** secretly; in secret; privately

　　나는 몰래 그녀에게 전화 번호를 말했다.

　　　I secretly told her my phone number.

　　그 사람은 남몰래 눈물을 흘렸다.

　　　He shed tears secretly.

5. **~에 흥분하다** be excited by [at] ~

　　그는 흥분 상태에 있다.

　　　His nerves are on edge.

　　사람들은 그 뉴스에 크게 흥분했다.

　　　People were very excited by the news.

6. **응어리를 풀다** relieve anxiety [frustration, pent-up feelings]

　　가슴에 있는 응어리를 풀려고 틈만 나면 뛰었다.

　　　To relieve the feelings of frustration inside me, I ran whenever I had a chance.

　　이산 가족의 한 맺힌 응어리를 풀기 위해서도 하루빨리 통일이 되어야 한다.

　　　To relieve the pent-up grief of the separated families we need to unify the country as soon as possible.

7. **~하는 도리밖에 없다** there is no choice but to ~

　　영화를 보기 위해 별수없이 매표소의 아가씨에게 사정하는 도리밖에 없었다.

　　　The only way to see a film was to beg the woman at the ticket office.

　　대학에 가기 위해서 돈을 버는 도리밖에 없었다.

　　　There is no other way to earn money to pay the university's fees.

8. **시원치 않다** be unsatisfying [unsatisfactory, lacking, wanting]

　　그 사람의 수입은 시원치 않다.

　　　His income is not much.

　　한국 대학생들이 영어 실력이 시원치 않다.

　　　Korean university students' English is not satisfactory.

9. **죄책감에 빠지다** fall into [yield to, be consumed by] a sense of guilt

앙드레 지드의 '좁은 문'을 읽고는 더 심한 죄책감에 빠졌다.

After reading Andre Gide's *La Porte étroite,* I was consumed by an even greater sense of guilt.

영수는 뇌물을 받은 후 심한 죄책감에 빠졌다.

After taking the bribe, Yŏngsu was consumed by strong feelings of guilt.

10. **~(으)ㄹ 맛이 나다** feel like doing ~

수영 금지 구역을 나타내는 위험 선에서 1미터라도 벗어나야 수영할 맛이 났다.

We had to go one meter past the danger line into the prohibited area before we felt like we were really swimming.

드디어 술 마실 맛이 난다.

At last, I feel like drinking.

11. **~게 될까 봐 조심하다** be careful in case ~; be wary of ~

나는 사춘기 시절 혹시라도 명랑하고 쾌활한 소년으로 보이게 될까 봐 조심하였다.

As an adolescent, I was wary of looking like a bright and cheerful young person.

도둑은 주인이 깨게 될까 봐 조심하였다.

The thief was careful in case the landlord got woken up.

Exercises

1. 설명과 맞는 단어를 보기에서 찾아 쓰세요.

> 보기: 동화, 호기심, 회상, 체험

(1) 지난 일을 돌이켜 생각함. 또는 그런 생각: _____

(2) 어린이의 마음을 바탕으로 지은 이야기: _____

(3) 자기가 몸소 겪음. 또는 그런 경우: _____

(4) 새롭고 신기한 것을 좋아하거나 모르는 것을

　알고 싶어 하는 마음: _____

2. 관련된 단어끼리 연결하여 문장을 만들어 보세요.

     (1) 고함(을)   •   • 남다
     (2) 죄책감(에) •   • 피우다
     (3) 응어리(가) •   • 되다
     (4) 담배(를)   •   • 빠지다
     (5) 계기(가)   •   • 지르다

_____

_____

_____

_____

_____

3. 문맥에 맞게 적당한 말을 보기에서 골라 빈칸을 채우시오.

> 보기: 엽서, 비밀, 친구, 특히, 담배

   (1) _____는 소년 시절 그 자체로서 전부이자 필요 충분한 인간
      관계의 핵심이었다.

   (2) '친구를 위해서' 또는 '친구 때문'이라면 모든 일이 가능할 것 같았다.
      _____, '금지된 장난'을 친구들과 함께 남몰래 치르는 것은
      즐거움이었다.

   (3) 영규네 집에 가서 몰래 _____를 피우면서, 우리는 그 엄청난
      _____을/를 아주 친한 우리 셋만이 공유할 수 있다는 사실에
      흥분했다.

   (4) 서울로 전학한 수근이와는 고교 3년 내내 _____을/를
      주고받았는데, 어느 가을 녀석이 자기 학교 근처에서 주운 은행잎을 보내
      왔다.

4. 밑줄 친 말과 가장 비슷한 단어나 표현을 고르세요.

    (1) 나는 저녁 수업이 끝나면 <u>매일</u> 운동을 했다.
        a. 날마다   b. 달마다   c. 가끔   d. 오랜만에

    (2) 배구부에 들어가 여름 방학 때 합숙을 하기도 하고, 땀을 뻘뻘 흘리며 <u>날이</u>
        저물어 공이 보이지 않을 때까지 야구를 하기도 했다.
        a. 해가   b. 달이   c. 시간이   d. 올해가

    (3) 아령을 하면서 친구들에게 뒤에서 본 내 모습이 정말 역삼각형이 되어 가고
        있는지를 수도 없이 <u>묻기도</u> 했다.
        a. 말하기도   b. 확인하기도   c. 뛰어가기도   d. 울어 보기도

    (4) 당시 부산의 한 극장은 수입이 <u>시원치 않았던지</u> 우리 같은 영화광들을 위해
        극장 제일 위층 골방을 배려하는 '특혜'를 베풀었다.
        a. 많았던지   b. 더웠던지   c. 풍부했던지   d. 적었던지

5. 다음 중 나머지 셋과 가장 관계가 없는 단어를 고르세요.

(1) 좌석	의자	극장	신문
(2) 응어리	답답함	자랑스러움	불만족
(3) 거부	거절	승낙	반대
(4) 난해한	쉬운	어려운	곤란한

6. 보기와 같이 주어진 말이 들어가는 단어들을 만들어 보세요.

> 보기: 미술: 미술책, 고대 미술, 미술 작품

    (1) 영화: _____

    (2) 학교: _____

    (3) 비밀: _____

    (4) 운동: _____

7. 주어진 단어나 표현으로 새로운 문장을 만들어 보세요.

> 보기: 실향민
> → 6월25일이 되면 실향민들의 아픔은 더욱 커져 간다.

(1) 필요 충분

_____

(2) 가소롭다

_____

(3) 난해한

_____

Comprehension Questions

I. Overall comprehension

1. 흙, 친구, 야구, 영화, 데미안, 감자 먹는 사람들은 주인공의 어떤 시점에 삶의 변화를 가져다 주었나요?

_____

2. 지은이가 사춘기 시절에 흥미를 가지고 하던 일들은 무엇이었나요?

_____

3. 위에 언급한 사춘기 적 추억을 가져다 준 소재들이 지은이의 인생관을 바꿀 만큼 커다란 변화를 가져다 주었나요?

_____

II. Finding details

1. 지은이가 데미안을 통해 문학적 소년의 출발을 맞이하기 전, 문학적 체험을 시작하는 계기를 가져다 준 소설의 이름은 무엇인가요?

_____

2. 일기장의 검사를 했던 선생님은 어떤 과목을 담당하시는 분인가요?

_____

3. 작가에게 서울이 그렇게 아름다운 도시로 생각될 수 있었던 이유는 무엇인가요?

_____

4. 왜 지은이는 영화의 주인공처럼 비운의 주인공이 될 수 없었나요?

_____

5. 한번도 끝까지 들을 수 없었던 알레그로 마 논 트로포가 지은이의 가장 좋아하는 음악이 될 수 있었던 이유는 무엇인가요?

_____

6. 지은이가 앙드레 지드의 <좁은 문>을 읽고는 더 심한 죄책감에 빠진 이유는 무엇이었을까요?

_____

7. 지은이가 선택했던 나르시시즘의 표현은 어떤 방법이었고 이유는 무엇이었나요?

_____

Related Reading

[나의 20세기] 가야금 인생 50년 . . . 황병기

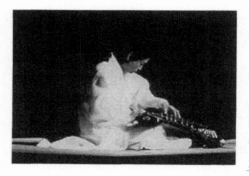

한국전쟁이 일어난 1950년, 나는 경기중학교 2학년 학생으로 부산에 피난했다. 대신동 밭 자리에 급히 세운 천막 피난 학교를 다녔다. 학교에 가는 길에 있는 한 일본식 2층집에 고전 무용 연구소가 있었는데, 나는 이 집에 세 들어 살고 있는 김철옥이라는 노인이 가야금 타는 소리를 듣고 매혹되어 가야금을 배우기로 굳게 결심을 했다.

아버지, 어머니, 누나 등 온 집안 식구가 반대했다. 왜 고리타분한 것을 배우려느냐, 학교 공부에도 시간이 없는데, 더구나 이 전쟁 판에 가야금 배워 신세 망치고 싶으냐는 것이었다. 나는 학교 공부에 아무 지장이 없게끔 할 것이라고 다짐하면서, 아인슈타인 박사 같은 위대한 인물도 바이올린을 배우지 않았느냐고 한사코 우겨댔다.

매일 방과 후 책가방을 든 채 용두산 꼭대기에 피난 와 있던 국립국악원에 가서 가야금을 배우고 귀가하는 것이 일과가 되었다. 53년 서울 환도 후에도 가야금 공부는 계속되었다. 55년 서울대 법대에 무난히 입학함으로써, "학교 공부에 지장이 없게 할 것"이라는 부모님과의 약속이 이행된 셈이어서, 한결 마음 놓고 가야금에 정진할 수 있었다. 법대에 진학하지 못 했다면 가야금을 계속하도록 부모님이 놔 두지 않았을 것이고, 나 스스로도 면목이 없어서 그만두었을 것이다.

그렇게 배운 가야금으로, 대학교 3학년 때는 KBS 주최 전국 국악 콩쿠르에서 최우수상을 받았다. 대학을 졸업하는 59년에 공교롭게도 서울대학교 음악대학에 국악과가 처음 생겨 가야금 강사로 나가게 되었다. 62년부터는 작곡도 시작하였다. 65년 4월에 하와이의 동서문화센터 주최 20세기 음악예술제에 작곡가 겸 연주자로 초청을 받았다. 서양 문물에 밀려 음지에서 사라져 가던 가야금을 내가 붙잡고 배우기 시작한지 14년 만에 바로 서양 사람들 자신이 들어 보겠다고 초청한 것이 꿈만 같았다. 가야금 곡 창

작을 위한 책도, 선배도 전무하여 혼자 힘으로 작곡을 시도한지 겨우 3년. 작품이라고 해 봐야 '숲' '가을' '석류집' 등 곡밖에 없는데, 이 곡을 모두 연주해 달라고 했다.

미국서 돌아온 뒤 나는 명동극장 지배인으로 당시 수입 예정 외화는 모두 보았고, 화학 회사, 다큐멘터리 영화 제작사, 출판사 사장 등 다양한 일을 했다. 그러는 중에도 하루도 가야금을 연습하지 않은 날이 없었다. 직업이 무엇이건, 가야금은 매일 세수하고 이 닦는 일 만큼이나 내 생활의 일부였던 것이다.

그러나 74년에 이화여자대학교에 국악과가 창설되어 전임 교수로 초빙을 받자, 음악을 완전히 그만 둔다던가 음악만을 하든가 결정해야 할 때가 왔다고 생각했다. 불혹을 바라보는 나이였다. 며칠 고심한 끝에 나는 음악을 그만둘 수는 없는 사람이니 앞으로는 모든 잡념을 다 버리고 오직 음악만을 하면서 살아야겠다는 프로 의식을 갖게 됐다. 그 해는 내가 최초로 유럽 순회 공연을 했고 내 작품 중 가장 유명해진 '침향무'를 작곡했으며 첫 작곡집을 출간한 해이기도 하다.

http://bkh.bestmusician.co.kr/hrame1.html

가야금 kayagŭm, Korean musical instrument with 12 strings, 전쟁이 일어나다 war breaks out, 피난하다 to take refuge, 천막 (shelter) tent, 고전 무용 연구소 classical dancing school, 세(를) 들다 to rent a room, 가야금(을) 타다 to play on a kayagŭm, 매혹되다 to be fascinated, 고리타분하다 to be old-fashioned, 신세 one's condition, circumstances, 망치다 to spoil, ruin, destroy, 지장이 없다 to be able to get along, 한사코 persistently, 우기다 to insist, persist, demand one's own way, 방과 후 after school, 귀가 returning home, 일과 daily task, 환도 (Korean government's) returning to Seoul after Korean war, 법대 law school, 이행 performance (of one's duty), 콩쿠르 contest, competition, 공교롭다 to be coincidental, 강사 lecturer, instructor, 동서문화센터 East-West Center, 주최 sponsorship, auspices, 겸 and, as well, 서양 문물 Western civilization,

밀리다 to be pushed, 음지 shady spot, 창작 creation, 전무하다 to be wholly
lacking, 시도하다 to make a trial, 지배인 manager, 수입 import, 예정(의)
pre-arranged, 외화 foreign film, 화학 회사 chemical company, 창설
establishment, 전임 full-time, 초빙 invitation, 불혹 the age of forty, the forties,
고심하다 to work hard, take pains, 잡념 idle thoughts, 순회 a round, a tour,
출간하다 to publish, issue

Discussion & Composition

1. 사춘기 때 본인이 가장 좋아했던 문학 작품이나 음악에 대해서 이야기해 보세요.

2. 사춘기 때 여러분이 했던 '금지된 장난'이 있으면 이야기해 보세요.

3. 지은이가 가야금을 배우게 된 첫번째 동기는 무엇이었나요?

4. 지은이가 부모님의 반대를 극복하기 위해 누구의 예를 들었나요?

5. 자신이 진정으로 하고 싶은 일을 주위의 반대나 그때 당시의 상황 등에 의해
   미루거나 변경한 적이 있으면 자세히 이야기해 보세요.

6. 만약에 난관에 부딪쳤을 때 어떻게 해결해 나가야 할지 이야기해 봅시다.

7. 많은 전통 악기들이 현대의 음악에 밀려 사라져 가고 있습니다. 여러분 나라의
   전통 악기에 대해 생각해 보고, 어떤 특색이 있는지 이야기해 봅시다.

Lesson 13 My Adolescence

Everyone has several pictures (in their mind) that, to them, symbolize a period in their life. My mother, a refugee form the north, recalls the Korean War (6.25) in her memories of cruelty at the Hŭngnam wharf. In the same way, when I recall my adolescence, a number of pictures come to my mind: Yi Kwang-su's *Dirt*, friends, baseball, the movie *Love Story,* Beethoven's *Allegro ma non troppo,* (Hesse's) *Demian,* the Southern East Sea Line, Van Gogh's *The Potato Eaters,* sex.

Yi Kwang-su's *Dirt*

I first got this book as a first-year middle school student. For the first time, it provided my literary experience with novels rather than fairy tales. I had decided to become a writer, and changed (the form of) my diary to a "letter to Yi Kwang-su" with the idea of imitating and learning from him. I filled up my diary with day-to-day events and feelings. No reply came from Yi Kwang-su; only my diary (book) with comments in red pen from my Korean teacher. Why was I so embarrassed, then? After that, I addressed my diary letters to my Korean teacher instead. The teacher was a woman.

Friends

Friends are the totality of adolescence itself, and at the same time the nucleus of necessary and sufficient human relations. It seemed like I could do anything for my friends or because of my friends. I especially took great delight in secretly getting into forbidden mischief with them.

We would go to Yŏng-gyu's house and secretly smoke cigarettes there. We became excited that the grave secret could be known only by ourselves—three close friends. I exchanged postcards with Su-gŭn, who transferred to a school in Seoul, during our three years of high school. One autumn, he sent me a ginkgo leaf he had picked up near his school. Looking at it, I used all of my imaginative power, making Seoul into a beautiful city. After entering college, Su-gŭn and I, together with our memories, stepped through piles of ginkgo leaves beneath the stone walls of Kyŏngbok Palace, and sang *Pimok*. Then he told me he had a lover. From that time, Seoul was no longer just a place of beauty.

Baseball

After classes finished in the evening, I exercised every day. I joined the volleyball club. During summer vacation I participated in training camp, worked up a tremendous sweat, and played baseball in the evening until I could no longer see the ball. While exercising with dumbbells, I would ask my friends if my body, seen from behind, was really becoming triangular.

But despite all the sweating and running, there was always an anxiety in my heart. I think it must have been the fever of adolescence. At that time, I didn't know if it was physical hunger or sexual desire, but I ran every chance I got in order to relieve it. I also ate a lot.

The Movies

As for good movies, nearly all were marked "No minors allowed." The adult standard "minor" was entirely one-sided, and I hated it. If I wanted to see a movie, I had no choice but to beg the young lady at the ticket window. Fortunately, at that time in Pusan there was a theater that, perhaps because it didn't attract many customers, offered movie fans like me the "special favor" of (seats in) a back room on the top floor. I was a regular back-room customer.

In 1972 I saw all of the movies that played in Pusan, except for two. Now and then we ran into an "off-campus guidance patroller," but we knew an escape route through the back door of the bathroom. After it was over, I always felt in tune with the mood of the movie. I wanted to meet a girl like Jenny in *Love Story*. The problem was that I could be a real tragic hero only if she would have to die from an incurable disease.

Allegro ma non troppo

For some time I confused these words, which indicate the tempo (*lit.,* Fr. *accent*) of Beethoven's Violin Concerto, for the title of the piece. Truly, it was a long time after hearing this violin concerto that I understood music's depth and flavor. I had to listen to the piece, which a woman teacher liked and I also wanted to like, many times over, with great patience. But I hardly ever listened up to the final movement. For a long time after that, when asked my favorite music on questionnaires, I would write *Allegro ma non troppo.*

Sex

Then as now, sex was regarded as taboo for young people in our society. In order to satisfy my curiosity, I sometimes exchanged information with my friends in secret and stole glances at the "Go ahead, ask me anything!" program. But in truth, there was no one to tell me anything about it. And so sexual desire itself became connected with feelings of guilt, and, to myself, I became an unclean, bad boy. I became even more guilt-ridden after reading Andre Gide's *Strait Is the Gate*.

The Southern East Sea Line

Back home in Pusan, I enjoyed going naked on the beach in the summer. But instead of going to the Kwangalli or Haeundae (beaches), I would catch the Southern East Sea Line with my friends. We never once took our seats on the train when riding up the eastern coast. We always hung from the entrance door of a passenger coach, exposing our faces to the southward wind, shouting at the top of our lungs. It was the same when we got to the sea. Only when we ventured at least one meter past the danger line indicating the no swimming zone did we feel we were really swimming. We always challenged the forbidden.

Van Gogh's *The Potato Eaters*

During my adolescence, I was careful to avoid looking bright and happy. I always wore my school cap pushed down over my eyes, pursed my lips tightly, and tried to look melancholy. That was the first signal that I was different from others, and an expression of my narcissistic desire to be a movie actor.

At an art exhibition at the Pusan Chamber of Commerce and Industry, I saw some gloomy paintings by Van Gogh. I was overcome by their murky shadows. Afterwards, I decided to become an all-out pessimist, rejecting everything bright and splendid. But that did not last for very long.

Demian

Through Yi Kwang-su's novel *Dirt,* I parted ways with fairy tale books and my childhood years. Through *Demian*, I began my journey as an adolescent literary reader. It was a revolution, because in the book I encountered "confusion," "pain," "frustration," and other delightful words. Because of Demian and Sinclair, my friends began to seem silly to me. I thought I was different from my friends to no small degree, a special existence. I tried hard to look inside myself, and my diary began to be filled with difficult, abstract nouns. I hated everyday words and spent more and more evenings looking for new words in the dictionary.

Chang Yong-u, *Wŏlgan mal*, 1994/8, 178−179

Related Reading: Hwang Byŏng-gi
My twentieth century: Fifty years with the *Kayagŭm*

In 1950, the year the Korean War began, I was a second-year student at Kyŏnggi Middle School. I took refuge in Pusan, where I attended a school for refugees (held in) tents hastily erected among the fields of Taesin Village. There was a classical dance research center in a two-story Japanese-style house I passed on the way to school. I heard an old man, Kim Ch'ŏl-ok, who rented a room there, play the Korean zither. I fell in love with it and firmly resolved to learn the instrument.

My entire family—father, mother, older sister—opposed my plan. They said, "Why do you want to study such an old-fashioned thing? You don't even have enough time to do your schoolwork! And now, with the war on! Do you want to learn the zither and ruin your life?" I persisted to the last breath, promising that I would not let it interfere with my schoolwork, pointing out that great people like Dr. Einstein, too, learned the violin.

Every day after school, carrying my schoolbag, I went to the top of Mt. Yongdu, where the National (Classical) Music Institute had taken refuge. I would study the zither there and then go home. Such was my daily task. My zither studies continued after the South Korean government's return to Seoul (from Pusan) in 1953. In 1955, I got into the Law School of Seoul National University with no problem. Having carried out my promise to my parents that I would "not let it interfere with my schoolwork," I was all the better able to put my mind at ease and devote myself to the zither. If I had failed to enter law school, my parents wouldn't have permitted me to continue playing the zither, and I wouldn't have had the pride to continue.

Having studied the zither in this manner, I won first place at the KBS-sponsored National Classical Music Concours as a university junior. By a lucky coincidence, in 1959, my graduation year, the SNU School of Music opened a National (Classical) Music department, and I went on to become a zither instructor. I started composing for the zither in 1962. In April of 1965, I received an invitation (to participate) as a composer and performer in the "Twentieth-Century Music Arts Festival," sponsored by Hawai'i's East-West Center. It was really incredible to me that Westerners were going to watch me play the zither, an instrument I had taken up fourteen years before, just as Western culture was pushing it into extinction. I had begun experimenting with composition only three years before then, all on my own, entirely without book or teacher to help me. I hadn't written many works: Only 'Forest,' 'Autumn,' and 'Pomegranate House.' They wanted me to play all of them.

After returning from America, I worked as a manager at the Myŏngdong Theater, where I saw all the foreign films that were going to be imported into the country. I worked at many jobs: at a chemical company, at a documentary production center, as chief at a publishing company. But not one day passed that I did not practice the zither. Whatever my job, the zither was as much a part of my life as washing my face and hands and brushing my teeth.

Then in 1974, Ewha Woman's University established its National (Classical) Music Department. When they asked me to be a full-time professor there, I thought, "It's time I decide to either quit music or do music full time." I was getting into my forties. After several days of anguish, I developed a "professional" consciousness, and decided that, as one who could not give up music, I would rid myself of idle thoughts and devote myself to it exclusively. That year I did my first European tour, composed my most famous work, "Agilawood Dance," and published my first collection of compositions.

http://bkh.bestmusician.co.kr/hrame1.html

제14과 교육 문제

(Lesson 14: Problems in Korean Education)

Objectives

이 과에서는 한국 교육의 문제점을 알아보고 그 해결책은 무엇이 있을까
생각해 본다.

In this lesson we will learn about problems in Korean education and
will think about possible solutions.

Pre-reading questions

1. 학원이 무엇인지 아세요? 학원은 어떤 것들을 배우는 곳인지
   알아봅시다.

2. 여러분은 학원에 다녀 본 적이 있나요? 여러분의 경험에 대해 이야기해
   보세요.

3. 개인 교사와 과외 공부를 해 본 적은 있나요? 학교 공부와 비교할 때
   어떤 좋은 점과 나쁜 점이 있습니까?

4. 학원을 다녀 본 적이나 과외 공부를 해 본 적이 있다면, 한꺼번에 여러
   가지를 해 본 적이 있나요?

5. 한국의 초등, 중등학교 학생들의 방과 후 과외 공부 및 학원 가기에
   관한 이야기를 듣고 간단히 의견들을 말해 봅시다.

Gaining familiarity

이 과에 나오는 교육 관련 단어: 명문 대학, 학원, 입시, 유학, 주입식
교육, 비판적 사고, 편입생, 신입생

한국인 교육관 문제 있다

¹미국에 있는 내 한국인 친구 한 명은 최근 서울의 부모로부터[14.1] 이런 전화를 받았다. "돌아오지 말고 미국에서 일자리를 알아 봐. 애들을 한국 학교에 보낼 생각은 아예 하지도 말고."[14.2]

²한국 학생들의 독해력과 수학 실력이 미국보다 높음에도 불구하고[14.3] 한국에선 교육 시스템이 일반의 기대에 크게 못 미치고[14.4] 있다는 인식이 확산되고 있다. 이에 관해 미국의 교육 제도가 몇 가지 중요한 교훈을 줄 수도 있겠지만 궁극적으론 한국인들이 스스로 문제를 해결해야 한다. 미국이 모든 해답을 줄 수는 없기 때문이다.

³한국에서 교육에 대한 일반인들의 기대와 교육 시스템 사이에 간격이 벌어지는 이유는 분명하다. 한국인들은 교육에 너무 많은 것을 기대하고 있다. 대부분의 부모들은 자식이 인생에서 성공하기 위해선 이마에 명문대 도장을 찍어야만 한다고 믿는다. 이들은 마치 군비 경쟁을 하듯[14.5] 교육비 지출 경쟁을 한다. 옆집 아이가 학원을 4곳에 다니면 우리 아이들은 5곳에 다녀야 한다고 생각한다. 그 결과로 수입의 절반 이상이 지출되고 아이들은 전혀 놀 시간이 없어도 말이다.[14.6]

⁴미국인의 눈에는 한국의 부모들은 거의 미치기 직전에 있는 것처럼 보인다.[14.7] 입시 철에 한국의 어머니들이 학교 교문에 서서 자식이 시험을 잘 치기를 비는 모습은 미국에서라면 극단적인 일로 간주될 것이다.

⁵이런 경쟁을 그만두려는 부모들은 비용이 얼마가 들든 자녀들을 해외로 유학 보내려고 한다. 미국 유학의 경우엔 그것이 가족들과의 단절을 의미하고, 어린 자녀들이 섹스, 마약, 총기 등에 노출되는 것을 의미할 수도 있다. 아이들이 잘 적응한 경우엔 한국으로 돌아가려고 하지 않는 문제가 생긴다. 몇 달 전 나는 컬럼비아대 법대의 한국 유학생 6명과 저녁을 할 기회가 있었다. 이들 중 한국으로 돌아가려는 학생은 1명뿐이었다. 우수한 두뇌의 유출은 장차 한국의 장래를 어둡게 할 것이다.[14.8]

⁶한국인들이 모든 비용과 위험을 무릅쓰고[14.9] 자녀들을 미국에 보내려는 이유는 무엇일까? 미국은 몇 가지 교훈을 줄 수 있다.

⁷첫째, 미국에선 암기보다는 비판적 사고를 강조한다. 한국에선 상상이

안 가는 일이겠지만 나는 학창 시절 입시를 위해선 단 하루도 공부해 본 적이 없다. 미국에선 아무리 극성스러운 부모라도 학생들을 주입식 학원에 일주일에 한 번 이상 보내지 않는다.

둘째, 학생들을 능력에 따라[14.10] 가르쳐야 한다. 교사에게 능력이 천차 만별인 학생들을 한 데 모아 가르치는 것은 악몽과 같다. 대부분의 미국 고교는 학생들의 능력에 따라 차등화된 교육을 제공한다. 내가 다니던 고교에선 공부 잘 하는 학생들에게 인근 대학에서 수강하는 것을 허용 하기도 했다. 이런 교육 시스템이 있다면 과외의 필요는 줄 것이다.

셋째, 전문대학에서 4년제 명문 대학으로 편입을 가능하게 하는 등 학생들에게 '2번째 기회'를 주는 프로그램을 만들어야 한다. 미국 교육의 장점 중 하나는 고교 시절 성적이 좋지 않았던 학생도 명문대 학위를 받을 수 있다는 점이다. 내가 다니던 버클리 대학에선 편입생들을 정규 신입생과 똑같이 환영했다.

그러나 미국에서도 당면한 교육 위기에 대한 우려가 크다.[14.11] 보수적 인 조지 부시 대통령이 대통령 선거 기간 중 "어떤 어린이도 뒤쳐지지 않도록 하겠다"며[14.12] 교육 재정 증액을 공약한 것은 미국 교육이 기초적 인 레벨에서 실패했음을 보여 주는 것이다. 미국에선 수백만 명의 학생 들이 제대로 교육받지 못하고 뒤쳐져 있는 실정이다. 미국의 도시와 교 외 지역 학교간의 재정 및 학업 성취도 격차는 갈수록 커지고 있다. 학 교 재정은 지역 주민들의 재산세에 따라 결정되므로 상주 인구가 적은 도시 학교는 교외 지역에 비해 극히 적은 지원을 받는다.

궁극적으로 교육 개혁이 성공하기 위해선 한국인들의 교육관이 바뀌 어야만 한다. 이제 한국의 부모들은 지갑을 내려놓고[14.13] 교육비 지출 경 쟁을 그만두어야 할 것이다. 한국인들이 교육에 대해 보다 균형 잡힌 시 각을 갖지 않는 한 모든 미래의 교육 개혁은 크게 훼손되거나 실패할 수밖에 없다.[14.14] 인생의 성공은 개인의 능력에 달린 것이지 명문 대학 진학에 달린 것이 아니다.[14.15] 한국인들은 얼마나 많은 학생들을 해외로 보낸 뒤에야 이를 깨달을 것인가.

피터 백, www.donga.com, 2000년 5월 30일

New Words

가능하게 하다 to make a matter possible. 가능하다 to be possible, practicable

간격 gap, discrepancy ▷이 두 건물 간의 간격은 15미터이다. There is a 15-meter gap between these two buildings.

간주되다 to be considered. 간주하다 to deem, consider ▷그것은 극단적인 일로 간주된다. It is considered an extreme case.

강조하다 to emphasize ▷선생님은 우리에게 시험에 늦지 않도록 강조하셨다. The teacher emphasized that we should not be late for the exam.

개혁 reform, innovation ▷사회 개혁 social reform

격차 gap, difference

결정되다 to be decided. 결정하다 to decide

경험 experience

공약하다 to pledge, make a public committment ▷공약을 지키다 [어기다] to keep [break] public pledges ▷선거 공약처럼 믿을 수 없는 것은 없다. Election promises always prove to be a gross deception.

과외 extracurricular work, private tutoring ▷과외 공부 out-of-school studies ▷과외 수업 extracurricular lesson

교문 school gate

교외 지역 suburb area

교육 재정 education budget ▷교육 재정의 삭감 reduction of the education budget

교육관 view on education

교훈 lesson, moral. 교훈적인 instructive ▷교훈을 주다 to give a lesson to ▷이 사고는 나에게 좋은 교훈이 되었다. This accident was a good lesson to me.

군비 경쟁 competition at military expense

궁극적으로 ultimately, finally

균형 balance ▷균형 잡힌 to be well balanced ▷균형 잡힌 몸매 well-balanced body

그만두다 to stop, discontinue ▷그는 사업을 그만두었다. He quit his business.

극단적이다 to be extreme ▷그것은 극단적인 예다. That is an extreme case.

극성스럽다 to be frantic, impatient, impetuous ▷극성스러운 우리 엄마 my mom who is too much ▷한국의 부모들은 자녀 교육에 극성스럽다. Korean parents are oversolicitous for their children's education.

기대 expectation ▷그것은 내 기대에 못 미친다. It does not meet my expectation.

기초적인 fundamental, basic ▷기초(적인) 문법 basic grammar

깨닫다 to realize, see, perceive, understand, become aware of ▷나는 상황의 중대성을 깨달았다. I became aware of the seriousness of the situation. ▷내가 실수하였음을 즉시 깨달았다. I saw at once that I had made a mistake.

노출 exposure

능력 ability, capacity, competency

단절 cutting off, separation. 단절하다 to cut off. 단절되다 to be cut off ▷양국간의 국교가 단절되었다. The diplomatic relationship between the two countries was cut off.

당면하다 to face, confront (immediately) ▷당면한 문제 immediate problem [concern, issue]

도장 seal, stamp ▷거기에 도장을 찍었다. I stamped my seal on it.

독해력 reading comprehension ability

두뇌 brain, head ▷두뇌가 명석한 사람 bright person

뒤쳐지다 to fall [lag] behind ▷후반부터 우리 팀은 뒤쳐지기 시작했다. Our team fell behind from the second half (of the game).

들다 to need, cost, require ▷시간이 드는 time-consuming ▷비용이 얼마가 들더라도 at any cost, regardless of expense ▷이 집을 짓는 데 6개월이 들었다. It took six months to build this house.

마약 drug, narcotic ▷마약을 밀매하다 to peddle drugs ▷마약에 중독되다 to become addicted to the use of narcotics

명문대 prestigious university

미치다 to go crazy, be mad

벌어지다 be (wide) open, crack (open), widen, have a margin, differ from ▷두 사람 사이가 벌어졌다. The two people were alienated [estranged] from each other.

보수적이다 to be conservative ▷보수적인 생각 conservative thought [idea]

분명하다 to be clear, obvious, vivid

비용 expenditure, expense ▷그것은 많은 비용이 든다. It costs a lot.

비판적 critical ▷비판적인 사고 critical thought

빌다 to wish, pray ▷행운을 빈다. Good luck.

사고 thinking, thought ▷사고 방식 one's way of thinking

상상 imagination, fancy

상주 인구 permanent residents (in an area)

성공 success, hit, achievement

성적 academic record or achievement ▷그는 학교 성적이 좋다. He has a good academic achievement at school.

성취도 achievement rate

수강하다 to take courses (at a university) ▷나는 이번 학기에 4과목을 수강한다. I'm taking four subjects this semester.

수입 income, earnings, revenue, proceeds

수학 mathematics

시각 viewpoint, perspective, view

실력 real ability, capability

실정 real situation, actual circumstances, real state of affairs ▷실정을 알아보겠다.
I will find out how things stand.

실패하다 to fail, end in failure ▷그는 사업에 실패했다. He failed in the business.

악몽 nightmare, bad dream, hideous dream

암기 learning by heart, memorizing ▷암기는 영어 학습에서 아주 중요하다.
Memorizing is very helpful for the study of English.

암기 memorization

우려 worry, concern, fear. 우려하다 to worry ▷우려할 (만한) 사태 serious situation

우수하다 to be excellent, superior

위기 crisis, critical moment, critical situation

위험 danger, peril. 위험하다 to be dangerous ▷위험을 무릅쓰다 to take a risk
▷위험을 무릅쓰지 않는 사람은 앞으로 나가지 못한다. A man who will not
take a risk will never get ahead.

유출 effluence, outflow, spillage. 유출하다 to flow out ▷두뇌 유출 brain drain
▷금이 해외로 유출됐다. There was an outflow of gold from the country.

유학 studying abroad, studying overseas ▷준호는 미국 유학을 마치고 귀국했다.
Jun-ho returned from study abroad in the States.

의미하다 to mean, signify, imply ▷이는 우수한 두뇌의 유출을 의미한다. This
means a brain drain.

이마 forehead

인근 nearby ▷인근 대학 nearby university

인식 recognition, understanding

일반인 general people, the public

일자리 job, position, employment

입시 entrance exam

입시 철 entrance exam period ▷대학 입시 철 university entrance exam season

장래 the future, the time to come. 장래의 future ▷밝은 장래 bright future
▷장래의 아내 one's future wife ▷장래의 계획을 세우다 to make one's plans
for the future

장점 strong point, merits, advantage ▷장점과 단점 merits and demerits ▷그
계획의 장점은 무엇인가요? What are the merits of the plan? ▷누구나 장점과
단점이 있다. Everybody has strong points and weak points.

장차 in the future, some day ▷장차 어떤 일이 일어날 것인가는 아무도 모른다.
Nobody can tell what will happen in the future.

재산세 property tax

재정 budget, finances

적응하다 to adjust, fit, suit, accord with ▷우리 가족은 한국 생활에 잘 적응해 가고
있다. My family is adjusting well to the Korean lifestyle.

전문대학 technical college

전혀 (not) at all ▷나는 그럴 생각이 전혀 없다. I don't want to do that at all.

정규 신입생 regular freshmen

제공하다 to provide, offer, present

주민 resident, inhabitant, dweller

주입식 cramming method (in teaching) ▷주입식 교육 cramming education

증액 increasing the amount ▷교육 재정 증액 increasing the education budget

지원 support, backup, aid

지출 경쟁 competition in spending

직전 just before

진학 attending a school or a university

찍다 to stamp (a seal) ▷여기에 도장을 찍어라. Stamp your seal here.

차등화 differentiation, gradation ▷차등화된 교육 differentiated [discriminated] education

천차만별 infinite variety ▷천차만별의 사람들 all sorts of people

총기 firearms

최근 the latest date ▷최근에 지은 집 house recently built ▷최근에 그 여자를 만나 보셨어요? Have you seen her lately?

치다 to take, undergo (an exam) ▷내 조카는 올해 수능 시험를 쳤다. My nephew took the Scholastic Aptitude Test.

편입 transfer (from one school [university] to another) ▷편입생 transfer student

학업 성취도 academic achievement rate

학원 private academy, cramming school

학위 university degree. 학위 논문 thesis for a degree ▷학위를 받다 to be granted a degree

학창 school, campus ▷학창 시절 one's schooldays ▷학창 생활 school life

해외 foreign countries, overseas ▷그는 해외 사정에 밝다. He has a thorough knowledge of foreign affairs. ▷나는 여름에 해외로 나갑니다. I am going abroad this coming summer.

허용하다 to allow, permit

확산 spread, dissemination ▷핵 확산 spread of nuclear arms, nuclear proliferation ▷핵 확산 금지 조약 nuclear non-proliferation treaty

확산되다 to be expanded. 확산하다 to expand

훼손되다 to be damaged or ruined. 훼손하다 to damage, ruin ▷국립 공원이 많이 훼손되었다. Many national parks were ruined.

Useful Expressions

1. ~(으)로부터 from ~
   어제 한국에 계신 어머니로부터 전화가 왔다.
   Yesterday there was a phone call from my mother who is in Korea.
   순희로부터 온 편지가 어디 갔나?
   Where is the letter which came from Sunhŭi?

2. ~(으)ㄹ 생각은 아예 하지도 말아 don't ever think about doing ~
   나를 다시 볼 생각은 아예 하지도 말아라.
   Don't ever think about seeing me again.
   내게 다시는 돈을 꿀 생각을 하지 말아.
   Don't ever think of borrowing money from me again.

3. ~(으)ㅁ에도 불구하고 in spite of ~; despite ~
   그는 그 일을 여러 차례에 걸쳐 시도했음에도 불구하고 실패했다.
   Despite the fact that he tried many times, he failed.
   노력했음에도 불구하고 그 결과가 좋지 않았다.
   The result wasn't good, in spite of the effort.

4. ~에 못 미치다 do not meet [reach] ~
   한국의 학교 교육은 일반 대중의 기대에 못 미치고 있다.
   The school education in Korea doesn't meet the expectations of the public.
   북한의 경제는 남한 경제의 반에도 못 미치고 있다.
   North Korea's economy is not half of South Korea's economy.

5. 마치 ~듯(이) (just) as if ~
   그는 내게 마치 미친 듯 덤벼들었다.
   He attacked me as if he were crazy.
   한국어에서는 종종 자음 리을을 마치 모음 취급하듯 한다.
   In Korean, frequently the consonant 'riŭl' is treated as if it is a vowel.

6. ~(어/아)도 말이다 you know; although it is the case that ~
   학원을 다섯 곳에나 보낸대 . . . 아이들이 전혀 놀 시간이 없어도 말이야.
   They said that they are sending kids to five cramming schools . . .
   though their kids do not have time to play, you know.
   자꾸 만나자고 하더라 . . . 시간이 없다는데도 말이다.
   He kept asking me to meet (him) . . . though I said that I didn't have
   time, you know.

7. **거의 ~기 직전에 있는 것처럼 보이다** look as if it is just about to ~
   그는 거의 쓰러지기 직전에 있는 것처럼 보였다.
   > It seemed that he was just about to fall down.

   미국인의 눈에는 이런 한국 부모들은 미치기 직전에 있는 것처럼 보인다.
   > To American eyes, such Korean parents seem on the verge of insanity.

8. **A이/가 B의 장래를 어둡게 [밝게] 하다** A makes B's future dark [bright]
   우수한 두뇌의 유출이 한국의 장래를 어둡게 할 것이다.
   > The outflow of good brains will make Korea's future dark.

   능력 있는 한국의 젊은이들이 한국의 장래를 밝게 한다.
   > Capable young Koreans make Korea's future bright.

9. **~을/를 무릅쓰고** risking ~
   죽음을 무릅쓰고 국경을 넘었다.
   > He crossed the national border, risking his life.

   이와 같은 모든 위험을 무릅쓰고 자녀들을 유학 보내려는 이유는 무엇일까?
   > What are the reasons to send kids overseas, risking all the dangers like this?

10. **~에 따라** according to ~; by ~
    자신의 적성에 따라 전공을 결정한다.
    > People decide their major according to their aptitude.

    법에 따라 결정된 벌금을 내면 된다.
    > You will be all right if you pay the fines decided by law.

11. **~에 대한 우려가 크다** there is great worry [concern] about ~
    한국의 교육 문제에 대한 우려가 크다.
    > There is great concern about Korea's education problems.

    요즘은 테러리즘에 대한 우려가 크다.
    > Nowadays there is great worry about terrorism.

12. **~도록 하다** be sure to do; decide to do
    이번에는 꼭 이기도록 하겠습니다.
    > This time I will try to win for sure.

    컴퓨터 게임을 너무 오래 하지 않도록 해.
    > Don't play computer games too long.

13. **지갑을 내려놓다** stop spending money

한국의 부모들은 이제 그만 지갑을 내려놓고 교육비 지출 경쟁을 그만 두어야
한다.

Korean parents should stop competing for education expenses.

지갑을 내려놓고 과외 수업 경쟁을 그만 두자.

Let's stop spending money for after-school lessons.

14. **~지 않는 한 ~(으)ㄹ 수밖에 없다** there is no choice but to ~ unless ~

계획을 바꾸지 않는 한 실패할 수밖에 없다.

There is no choice but to fail unless we change the plan.

비행기가 30분 안에 오지 않는 한 이번 회의를 취소할 수밖에 없다.

There is no choice but to cancel the meeting unless the airplane comes in
30 minutes.

15. **A에 달린 것이지 B에 달린 것이 아니다** depend on A, not on B

인생의 성공은 개인의 능력에 달린 것이지 명문 대학 진학에 달린 것이 아니다.

Success in life depends not on attending a prestigious university, but
on one's ability.

이 일은 네 마음먹기에 달린 것이지 주변 상황에 달린 것이 아니다.

This one depends on your mind, not on the surrounding situations.

Exercises

1. 관련된 단어들끼리 연결하여 문장을 만드세요.

A:		
(1) 기대에	•	• 많이 들었다.
(2) 인식이	•	• 확산되고 있다.
(3) 문제를	•	• 해결하자.
(4) 간격이	•	• 벌어지고 있다.
(5) 비용이	•	• 못 미친다.
(6) 시험을	•	• 잘 치기를 바란다.

_____

_____

_____

_____
_____
_____

B: (7) 상상이   •   • 찍어라.
    (8) 우려가   •   • 안 간다.
    (9) 능력에   •   • 달린 것이다.
    (10) 지원을   •   • 받았다.
    (11) 도장을   •   • 크다.
    (12) 장래를   •   • 어둡게 한다.

_____
_____
_____
_____
_____
_____

2. 아래의 설명과 맞는 단어나 표현을 보기에서 찾아 쓰세요.

> 보기: 직전, 독해력, 유출, 아예, 명문대, 궁극적으로, 악몽, 암기

(1) 절대로   _____
(2) 글을 읽고 이해하는 능력   _____
(3) 결국   _____
(4) 평판이 좋은 대학교   _____
(5) 바로 전   _____
(6) 밖으로 빠져 나가는 것   _____
(7) 외우기   _____
(8) 나쁜 꿈   _____

3. 보기에서 적당한 말을 골라 빈칸을 채우세요.

> 보기: 아예, 스스로, 전혀, 뿐, 단, 똑같이, 갈수록, 극히

(1) 자신의 문제는 _____ 해결하는 버릇을 기르자.

(2) 점점 날이 _____ 사는 것이 힘든다.

(3) 그 남자와 결혼할 생각은 _____ 하지도 말아라.

(4) 나는 아들 딸 구별 없이 _____ 사랑한다.

(5) 우리 아들은 요즘 _____ 하루도 집에 있는 날이 없다.

(6) 이 일과 그 일은 _____ 관계가 없다.

(7) 이런 테러 사건은 _____ 드문 일이다.

(8) 제시간에 도착한 사람은 나 _____이었다.

4. 밑줄 친 말과 가장 비슷한 단어나 표현을 보기에서 고르세요.

(1) 돌아오지 말고 미국에서 일자리를 <u>알아 봐</u>.
    a. 공부해 봐   b. 알려 봐
    c. 만들어 봐   d. 찾아 봐

(2) 한국의 교육 시스템이 일반의 기대에 크게 못 미치고 있다는 인식이
    <u>확산되고</u> 있다.
    a. 줄어들고   b. 늘어나고
    c. 작아지고   d. 만들어지고

(3) 궁극적으론 한국인들이 스스로 문제를 <u>해결해야</u> 한다.
    a. 답해야   b. 풀어야
    c. 대답해야   d. 해답해야

(4) 일반인들의 기대와 교육 시스템 사이에 간격이 벌어지는 이유는 <u>분명하다</u>.
    a. 불명확하다   b. 정확하다
    c. 분분하다   d. 명확하다

(5) 인생에서 성공하기 위해서는 <u>이마에 명문대 도장을 찍어야 한다</u>.
    a. 명문대에 입학하여야 한다.   b. 명문대를 졸업해야 한다.
    c. 명문대를 졸업한 친구가   d. 명문대를 구경해야 한다.
       있어야 한다.

(6) 미국인의 눈에는 한국의 부모들은 거의 미치기 <u>직전에</u> 있는 것처럼 보인다.
   a. 바로 전에   b. 시작에
   c. 바로 후에   d. 끝에

(7) 어린 자녀들이 섹스 마약 총기 등에 노출되는 것을 <u>의미할</u> 수도 있다.
   a. 문제가 될   b. 뜻할
   c. 상징할   d. 상상할

(8) 한국인들이 모든 비용과 위험<u>을 무릅쓰고</u> 자녀들을 미국에 보내려는 이유는 무엇일까?
   a. 에 무릎꿇고   b. 을 무릎에 두고
   c. 에도 불구하고   d. 이 있지만

(9) 이런 일은 미국에서는 <u>상상이 안 가는</u> 일이다.
   a. 상상할 수도 없는   b. 드문
   c. 상상할 수 있는   d. 혼히 있는

(10) 한국의 부모들은 <u>지갑을 내려놓고</u> 교육비 지출 경쟁을 그만두어야 한다.
   a. 돈 쓰기를 멈추고   b. 지갑을 쓰지 말고
   c. 돈을 꺼내서   d. 지갑을 갖지 말고

6. 보기와 같이 주어진 단어가 들어가는 표현을 3개 이상 써 보세요.

> 보기: [실력] 수학 실력, 외국어 실력, 영어 실력

   (1) 경쟁: _____
   (2) 철: _____
   (3) 유출: _____
   (4) 균형 잡힌: _____
   (5) 개혁: _____

7. 주어진 단어나 표현을 이용하여 문장을 만드세요.

   (1) ~(으)로부터

   _____

(2) ~(으)ㄹ 생각은 아예 하지도 말다

_____

(3) ~(으)ㅁ 에도 불구하고

_____

(4) ~에 못 미치다

_____

(5) 마치 ~듯

_____

(6) ~도 말이다

_____

(7) ~거의 ~기 직전에 있는 것처럼 보이다

_____

(8) ~이/가 ~의 장래를 어둡게/밝게 하다

_____

(9) ~을/를 무릅쓰고

_____

(10) ~에 따라

_____

(11) ~에 대한 우려가 크다

_____

(12) ~도록 하다

_____

(13) 지갑을 내려놓고

_____

(14) ~지 않는 한 ~(으)ㄹ 수 밖에 없다

_____

(15) ~에 달린 것이지 ~에 달린 것이 아니다

_____

Comprehension Questions

I. Overall comprehension

1. 한국의 부모들은 왜 자녀들을 명문대에 보내기 위해서 과다한 경쟁을 합니까?

2. 요즘 한국으로부터의 어린 학생들의 해외 유학이 붐을 이루고 있는데, 그 이유는 무엇입니까?

3. 글쓴이가 말하는 미국의 교육 제도가 주는 세 가지 교훈은 무엇 무엇입니까?

II. Finding details

본문의 글과 내용이 일치하면 □에 ∨ 표를 하세요.

1. 한국의 교육 문제는 심각하다. □
2. 한국 학생들의 수학 실력은 미국보다 낮지 않다. □
3. 한국 교육 시스템은 일반의 기대에 못 미치고 있다. □
4. 미국 교육 시스템이 한국 교육 문제의 모든 해답을 줄 수 있다. □
5. 한국인들은 교육에 너무 많은 것을 기대한다. □
6. 한국 가정에서는 수입의 많은 부분을 자녀 교육비로 지출한다. □
7. 이런 경쟁을 그만두려는 한국 부모들은 자녀들을 해외로 유학을 보낸다. □
8. 해외 유학에 잘 적응한 자녀들은 대부분 한국에 돌아가려 한다. □
9. 한국인들의 교육관이 바뀌어야 교육 개혁이 성공할 수 있다. □
10. 한국인들은 인생의 성공이 개인의 능력에 달린 것이 아니라 명문 대학
    진학에 달렸다고 믿는다. □

Related Reading

서울 강남 일대 어느 족집게 학원 강사의 죽음

96학년도 대학 입시에서 주요 대학 논술 문제를 적중시켜 유명해진 강남 일대 학원 가의 스타 강사 조진만(32) 씨의 갑작스러운 사망이 강남 일대에서 화제가 되고 있다. 그는 17일 새벽 폐렴으로 숨졌다.

조 씨의 사망 소식이 전해지자 이날 밤 수백 명의 학생들이 병원 영안실을 찾았고, 조 씨의 홈페이지에 마련된 사이버 분향소에는 이틀만에 1600여건이나 되는 애도의 글이 올랐다.

조 씨는 연간 억대의 고액 수입을 올리며 최고의 논술 강사로 학생들의 인기를 한 몸에 받았다. 최근에는 한 인터넷 교육 업체의 부사장으로 취임해 사업가로의 변신을 꾀하기도 했다. 그는 학생들에게 특히 인간적으로도 신뢰를 준 것으로 알려졌다. 학생 들은 학업은 물론 신상 문제까지도 조 씨와 상의했다는 것.

학원 강사라면 누구나 부러워할 명성과 고액 수입을 뒤로하고 조 씨가 죽음을 맞이 한 원인은 결국 과로였다. 한 동료 강사는 "학원 강사들에게 학원가는 자기 성취의 장 이면서도 치열한 생존 경쟁의 장이기 때문에 엄청난 스트레스에 시달린다"고 말했다.

그는 "주말이면 식사도 거르면서 12시간씩 강의를 하고 다니는 조 선생이 늘 걱정 이 됐다"며 "직업의 안정성이 보장되지 않는 학원 강사로서 살아남기 위해서는 끊임없 는 자기 개발과 관리가 필요하며 인기가 있을 때 벌어 두지 않으면 안 되는 구조적인 문제점 등이 조 선생을 무리하게 만들었을 것"이라고 말했다.

조 씨는 서울 강남 강동 서초구, 그리고 수도권 평촌 등지의 7개 학원에서 강의를 맡았으며 월수입은 1000만 원대를 훨씬 상회한 것으로 알려졌다. 고소득의 이면에는 고달팠던 '학원 강사의 애환'이 숨겨져 있었다.

<동아일보> 2001년 9월 18일

족집게 (a pair of) tweezers, 논술 문제 essay question, 적중시키다 to predict
correctly, 갑작스러운 sudden, 사망 death, 화제 topic of conversation, issue,
폐렴 pneumonia, 숨지다 to die, 영안실 morgue, 분향소 altar for the dead (*lit.*,
incense burning place), 애도 grief, lamentation, 취임하다 to take office, take
one's post, 변신 change oneself, 꾀하다 to try, attempt, 신뢰 trust, 학업
studying, 신상 문제 personal problems, 명성 fame, reputation, 뒤로하다 to put
something behind, 과로 overwork, overfatigue, 자기 성취 self-achievement, 장

place, 치열한 생존 경쟁 fierce competition of survival, rat-race, ~에 시달리다 to suffer from, 안정성 stability, 보장되다 to be secured, guaranteed, ensured, 자기 개발 self-development, 구조적인 structural, 무리하다 overwork, overstrain, burning the candle at both ends, 고달프다 to be tired, worn out, weary, 애환 joys and sorrows

Discussion & Composition

1. 한국의 사교육비 지출은 정부의 공교육 예산의 30%가 넘는 7조 원으로 추정된다고 합니다. 이런 한국의 과외 교육 문제에 대한 해결책은 무엇이 있을까요? 여러분의 의견을 말해 보세요.

2. 과대 경쟁을 피하려는 부모들은 자녀들을 해외로 조기 유학을 보내고 있고, 조기 유학에는 여러 가지 문제점이 있습니다. 조기 유학의 문제점은 무엇일까요?

3. Related Reading의 '어느 족집게 학원 강사의 죽음'은 한국 교육의 어떤 면을 잘 보여 줍니까?

4. 과연 피터 백 씨가 말하는 미국이 주는 세 가지 교훈이 한국의 교육 문제에 대한 해결책이 될 수 있을까요? 이들 교훈에도 문제가 있다면 무엇입니까? 이에 대한 글을 아래에 써 봅시다.

_____

_____

_____

_____

_____

_____

_____

Lesson 14 Problems in Korean education

Problems in the Korean view of education

One of my Korean friends in the States recently received a phone call from his parents in Seoul: "Don't come back here. Try to find a job in the States. Don't think about sending the children to a school in Korea."

Despite the fact that Korean students have better reading and math skills than American students, the growing perception is that Korea's educational system is unsatisfactory. The American educational system can teach Korea some important lessons in this regard, but in the end, Korea must solve its problems by itself. America cannot provide Korea with all the answers.

There is a clear reason for this gap between the educational system and what the average person wants from it. Koreans expect too much of education. Most parents believe that they must stamp "prestigious university" on their child's forehead if her life is to be successful. They compete in paying educational expenses as though it were an arms race. If the child next door goes to four academies after school, then they think their child must attend five. As a result, half their income is spent (on education), and the children have no time to "be kids" (*lit.*, to play).

To American eyes, such Korean parents seem on the verge of insanity. In America, the sight of Korean mothers standing at the school's entrance praying for their child's test score would be viewed as running to an extreme.

Parents who want to stop the educational wars try to send their children abroad for schooling, no matter what the cost. Studying in America means a break with the family and can also mean their child's exposure to sex, drugs, and guns. A problem arises when children become so well adapted to American life that they do not want to go back to Korea. Several months ago I had the opportunity to have dinner with six Korean students studying at Columbia University's law school. Of them, only one wanted to return to Korea. This sort of brain drain will negatively impact Korea's future.

What is the reason that Koreans risk expense and danger to send their children to America? America can give a few lessons.

First, in the States, critical thought is emphasized over rote memorization. Unimaginable though it may be in Korea, I never studied a single day for my university entrance examination. Even the most frantic parents do not send their child to cram school more than once a week.

Second, one must teach students according to their ability. Teaching students with different levels of ability all at once is an instructor's nightmare. Most U.S. high schools offer "differentiated education" according to each student's ability. At the high school I attended, students who studied well were permitted to attend courses at a local college. This kind of educational system reduces the need for after-school courses.

Third, a program must be created that gives students a "second chance," i.e., allows a student in a technical college to transfer to a four-year prestigious university. One of the strong points of American education is that even students who did not do well in high school can get a degree from a top university. At U.C. Berkeley, where I attended school, transfer students were welcomed the same as regular freshmen.

But in America, too, there is great worry about pressing educational dangers. Conservative President George Bush's public promise during his election campaign to increase the education budget, saying "no child would be allowed to fall behind," shows that American education has failed at a fundamental level. It is a fact that in America, millions of students are unable to receive a good education and are falling behind. The severe disparity in terms of budget and academic achievement between America's inner-city and suburban-area schools continues to increase. A school's budget is determined by the property taxes of area residents. Schools at cities with relatively few permanent residents receive much less support than (schools in) the suburban areas.

Ultimately, Koreans must change their view of education if they are to make an educational revolution succeed. Korean parents must now stop competing with their wallets to pay for educational expenses. Until Koreans gain a more balanced perspective of education, all future educational reforms will be doomed to suffer greatly or fail. Life success depends on an individual's abilities, not on entry into a prestigious university. How many students will Koreans send to foreign countries before they realize this?

Peter Beck, www.donga.com, May 30, 2000

Related reading: The death of a Kangnam academy's "tweezer" instructor

Cho Chin-man (32), star lecturer of the Kangnam district academies, died suddenly in 1996. Famous for his (tweezer-like) successful targeting strategies for essay questions on entrance exams to major universities, Cho's death was the topic of conversation in the Kangnam area. He passed away on the 17th, at dawn, from pneumonia.

The day his death was reported, hundreds of students went to the hospital's mortuary in the evening (to pay their last respects). In just two days, over 1600 messages of condolence were offered at a cyber-altar prepared on his personal Web homepage.

Cho earned a high income of a hundred million *won*, singlehandedly gaining student popularity as the best lecturer for essay questions. He had planned to change to a business career by taking the position of senior vice-president of an Internet educational company. He was known especially for the confidence he imparted to his students on (both) the (professional and the) human level. Students discussed their personal problems with him, as well as educational matters.

Leaving behind a reputation and high earnings that any academy instructor might envy, Cho's ultimate cause of death was over-exhaustion. A colleague said, "For academy lecturers, the academies are sites of self-achievement, but they are also sites of fierce competition for survival. We suffer tremendous stress."

He said that "I always worried about Cho, who taught twelve hours a day on weekends, without eating meals," and that "academy instructors without job security have to tirelessly exercise self-development and control in order to survive, having to make money when they are popular. This kind of structural problem made Cho overdo himself."

Cho took teaching positions at seven academies, such as in Seoul's Sŏch'o, Kangdong, Kangnam wards, and P'yŏngch'on in the metropolitan area. It was revealed that his monthly earnings were well over 10,000,000 *won*. Behind the high income were the "joys and sorrows" of an exhausted academy instructor.

Donga Daily, Sept. 18, 2001

제15과   사물놀이

(Lesson 15: *Samullori,* a Korean Percussion Ensemble)

Objectives

이 장에서는 한국의 대표적 전통 음악 중의 하나인 사물놀이의 유래와
발전 과정에 대해서 알아보고, 사물놀이에 쓰이는 네 가지 악기(꽹과리,
장고, 북, 징)의 기원과 사물놀이가 한국에서뿐만 아니라 세계적으로
인기를 얻게 된 비결에 대해 알아본다.

This chapter examines the origin and development of *samullori,* a
representative genre of Korean traditional music. The origins of four of
its instruments (i.e., *kkwaenggari, changgo, puk,* and *ching*) are
discussed, as well as *samullori*'s domestic and international popularity.

Pre-reading questions

1. 여러분은 현대 음악과 전통 음악 중 어떤 음악을 좋아하나요? 그 이유는 무엇입니까?

2. 여러분은 최근에 콘서트에 가 본 적이 있습니까? 어떤 콘서트였습니까? 누구와 어떻게 가게 됐나요?

3. 국악 연주를 들어 본 적이 있습니까? 여러분의 경험을 이야기해 보세요.

4. 다음의 인터넷 사이트에 가서 여러 가지 국악을 들어 보고 여러분의 느낌을 이야기해 보세요.

   http://www.koreandb.net/KMusic/kmlisten.htm

5. 다음 악기들을 본 적이 있습니까? 악기 이름이 무엇인지 알아봅시다.

Gaining familiarity

1. 국악: 농악, 궁중 음악, 불교 음악, 판소리
2. 악기의 종류: 타악기, 관악기 (목관악기, 금관악기), 현악기
3. 교향악, 피아노 협연, 재즈, 관현악
4. 사물놀이에 쓰이는 악기: 꽹과리, 징, 북, 장고

세계의 음악으로 자리 잡은 '사물놀이'

사물놀이는 우주의 모든 것이 농축되어 있는 음악
교향악단, 피아노 협연, 재즈 그룹과 합동 공연으로 새로운 가능성에 도전

지난 9월 서울 올림픽 공원에서 "세계 사물놀이 대회"가 열렸습니다. 전 세계에서 40여 팀이 참가하여 열띤 경연을 펼친 이 대회야말로 '사물놀이의 세계화'를 잘 보여준 신명나는 한바탕의 축제 마당이었습니다.

쟁과리

평소에 국악은 느리고 슬프고 그래서 재미없는 음악으로만 알고 있었던 사람들이 사물놀이를 들으면 어떤 생각을 할까요? 그런 사람들이 사물놀이에 열광하는 외국인들을 보면 무슨 생각을 할는지 궁금해집니다.[15.1]

장고

'사물'의 뜻

한국의 대표적 타악기인 쟁과리, 장고, 북, 징으로 농악 가락을 연주하는 것을 사물놀이라고 합니다. 그러나 본래 '사물'이라는 용어는 불교 음악에서 나온 말입니다. 바다 속의 물고기를 살려 주기 위해서 두드리는 물고기 모양의 타악기인 목어, 하늘을 날아다니는 새들을 살려 주기 위해서 두드리는 구름을 상징하는 모양으로 된 쇠로 만든 운판, 땅에서 움직여 다니는 네 발 달린 짐승의 영혼을 구제해 주기 위한 짐승 가죽으로 만든 법고, 그리고 마지막으로 인간의 육신과 영혼을 구제해 주기 위하여 두드리는 은은한 소리를 내는 범종이 본디의 사물이었습니다.

북   징

그러면 쟁과리, 장고, 북, 징, 이 네가지 타악기로 연주되는 음악을 '사물놀이'라고 부르게 된 것은 언제부터일까요? 1978년 5월 서울의 공간사랑에서 '김덕수 패 사물놀이'가 농악 리듬을 네 가지 타악기만으로 연주하면서 생겨난 이름입니다. 그때까지만 해도 농악은 야외에서만 연주되었습니다. 그러니까 '사물'은 네 가지 타악기를 가리키고 '놀이'는 그 네 가지 타악기로 농악 가락을 신명나게 연주한다는 의미를 가졌다고 볼 수 있습니다.

김덕수 패 사물놀이의 등장은 1980년대 한국 음악계의 커다란 사건이었습니다. 국내에서의 공연은 물론이고[15.2] 수많은 해외 공연을 통하여 많은 이들에게 충격과 감동을 주면서 한국 음악의 존재를 세계에 알렸던 것이죠. 그 이전의 어떤 공연도 사물놀이만큼[15.3] 폭발적인 인기를 끌지는 못했습니다. 더구나[15.4] 주목할 점은 사물놀이가 청소년 층을 주된 관객으로 끌어들였다는 점입니다.

현대화·서구화를 지향하는 요즘의 청소년들이 좋아할 만한 요소가 사물놀이의 어디에 있는가 하고 의아해 하실 분도 많으리라 생각됩니다. 또한 이런 젊은이들이 전통 음악의 리듬을 그대로 들려 주는 사물놀이의 공연장에서 열광하는 것은 언뜻[15.5] 납득이 가지[15.6] 않는 모습일 것입니다. 더욱이 문화가 다르며, 사고 방식이 다른 나라에서도 찬사를 받고 있다는 사실은 무엇으로 설명해야 할까요.

원초적 리듬, 신명의 놀이

리듬이란 음악의 여러 요소 중에서 가장 원초적이고 강한 호소력을 지니고 있다고들 합니다. 우리의 전통 음악을 보면 많은 장단 속에 변화무쌍한 리듬들을 구사하고 있습니다. 그렇지만 사물놀이가 등장하기 전에는 사람들이 이를 잘 몰랐었던 것이죠. 보물을 바로 옆에 두고도 이를 알아보지 못했던 것입니다. 우리가 몰랐었으니까 남들은 더 말할 나위도 없었을[15.7] 것입니다.

일본인 타악기 반주자 샌바 기요하코는 사물놀이의 공연을 보고 또 합동 연주를 한 후 느낌을 이렇게 말하고 있습니다. "사물놀이와의 만남은 일종의 충격이었습니다. 타악기라면 대체로 북미나 남미, 아프리카 주변이 주류였으므로, 바로 곁에 그렇게 강렬한 것을 지닌 패가 있었을 줄은 몰랐습니다. . . . 사물놀이가 내면적인 것을 깊이 파고 들어간다는 점을 발견할 수 있었습니다."

음색의 대비, 그 절묘한 조화

사물놀이를 구성하고 있는 악기를 살펴보면 각각의 악기가 개성을 갖고 있으면서도 서로 조화를 이루고 있다는 것을 알게 됩니다. 개성과 조화는 물과 기름처럼 서로 안 어울릴 것 같습니다만 사실은 그렇지 않습니다. 개성 있는 사람들이 조화를 이룰 때 멋진 것을 만들어 낼 수 있지요.

꽹과리와 징의 쇠 소리와 장고와 북의 가죽 소리가 대비를 이룹니다. 그러니까 음색에 있어서 서로 매우 다릅니다. 그 음색과 악기의 구조가 다르기 때문에 표현에 있어서도 차이가 있습니다. 어떤 이는 이 네 가지 악기의 특징을 '쇠로 솟구치는 힘, 장고의 세련된 흥, 북의 질박한 맛, 징의 가라앉는 멋'으로 표현하기도 하고, '별, 인간, 달, 해'를 상징하므로 결국 사물놀이는 우주의 모든 것이 농축되어 있는 음악이라고 극찬하기도 합니다.

앞에서도 이야기했지만 사물놀이는 야외에서 연주되던 농악 놀이의 리듬을 다듬어 실내에서 감상하는 음악으로 변모시켜 놓은 것입니다. 이 것이 가능했던 것은 김덕수 패 사물놀이의 뛰어난 기량 때문인데, 그 당시 김덕수 패 사물놀이를 이루고 있었던 김덕수, 이광수, 최종실 등은 대여섯 살에 남사당패에 끼어 들은 애 사당부터 시작한 이들입니다.

애 사당이란 말이 나왔으니까[15.8] 사당패 이야기를 해야겠습니다. 사당패란 조선조 중기 이래로 우리 나라의 농촌과 어촌을 두루 돌아다니며 공연하던 직업적인 유랑 연예인 집단을 말합니다. 사당패는 남사당과 여사당으로 크게 구별되며, 때로는 어린이도 사당패의 일원으로 끼어 들어 공연의 한 몫을 톡톡히 하였는데,[15.9] 이들을 애 사당이라고 불렀습니다.

가장 한국적인 것이 세계적

사물놀이는 이러한 전통 음악의 영역에만 머무르지 않고 새로운 창작 곡으로 국악 관현악단, 교향악단, 그리고 피아노와 협연하기도 했습니다. 그리고, 째즈 그룹과 각 지역의 타악기 연주자들과의 합동 공연을 통해 새로운 가능성에 도전하기도 했는데, 아마도 이것은 사물놀이의 새로운 발걸음이 아닌가 여겨집니다.[15.10]

타악기의 연주로 또한 전통적인 리듬만으로 세계인의 주목을 받은 사물놀이야말로[15.11] '가장 한국적인 것이 세계적이다'라는 말을 실증시켜 준 셈입니다.[15.12]

http://www.changwoncci.or.kr/import/상의지연재/우리음악1.htm

New Words

가능성 possibility, potential
가락 key, pitch, tone
가죽 skin, hide, leather, fur
각각 each, every, all, individually ▷우리는 각각 방이 따로 있다. Each of us has our own room.
감상하다 to appreciate ▷영시는 리듬을 이해하지 못하면 감상할 수 없다. You can't appreciate English poetry unless you understand its rhythm.
강렬하다 to be intense, strong ▷그 광경은 그에게 강렬한 인상을 주었다. The scene made a strong impression on him.
개성 individuality, personality ▷개성이 강한 사람 man of marked individuality
경연 contest, match, competitive performance ▷경연회를 열다 to hold a contest
곁 side, neighborhood, vicinity ▷바로 곁에 nearby, close at hand ▷곁에 두다 to keep a thing close at hand
공연 performance. 공연장 entertainment hall, auditorium
관객 spectator, audience

관현악단 orchestra. 관현악 orchestral music ▷관현악의 반주 orchestral
accompaniment

교향악단 symphony orchestra

구별되다 to be classified (into), be divided (into), be distinguished (from) ▷나무는
상록수와 낙엽수로 구별된다. Trees are divided into evergreens and deciduous
trees.

구사하다 to use freely, make the most of ▷최신 기술을 구사하다 to make full use
of the latest technology ▷영어를 자유롭게 구사하다 to have a good command
of English

구성하다 to compose, constitute ▷사회를 구성하다 to constitute a society

구하다 to relieve, give relief to ▷구제할 수 없는 unrelievable, irremediable

구해주다 to save, rescue, help, give relief to

국악 Korean classical music, Korean folk music (*lit.,* national music). 국악인
Korean classical musician

극찬하다 to speak very highly of (a person); praise (a person) sky-high

기량 ability, talent, capacity

꽹과리 small gong

끌어들이다 to draw (into), bring someone (into) ▷그는 친구를 나쁜 일에
끌어들였다. He enticed his friend to do something wrong.

끼어들다 to intrude (into), break in (on) ▷그는 남의 일에 늘 끼어든다. He always
pokes his nose into other people's business.

남사당 male performers in a troupe of wandering entertainers

납득 understanding

내면적(인) internal, inner ▷내면적 갈등 inner conflict

농악 farmers' music, instrumental music of peasants ▷농악 리듬 rhythm of
farmers' music ▷농악 가락 tone [pitch] of farmers' music

농축되다 to be condensed, concentrated. 농축 concentration

느리다 to be slow, sluggish, slow-going

달리다 to be attached, affixed, appended ▷꼬리표가 달린 트렁크 trunk with a tag
attached

대비 contrast, comparison

대체로 generally, in general, on the whole

대회 large meeting, general meeting

더욱이 besides, moreover, further, furthermore, what's more ▷그는 불어를 쓰지도
못하고 더욱이 읽지도 못한다. He cannot write French, much less read it.
▷더욱이 날씨가 안 좋았다. Besides (i.e., to make things worse), the weather
was bad.

두드리다 to strike, beat, hit

두루 all over, throughout, widely, extensively ▷두루 아는 사실 matter of common knowledge ▷두루 살피다 to look all around

등장 entrance (on the stage), advent, appearance. 등장하다 to show up, appear ▷그녀는 연예계에 혜성처럼 등장했다. She made a comet-like appearance in the world of entertainment.

때로(는) sometimes, occasionally, at times ▷때로 큰 고기가 걸리는 일도 있다. You catch a big fish at times.

레퍼토리 repertoire

마당 yard, court; place, ground; occasion ▷토론의 마당 place for debating ▷이 마당에 on this occasion ▷떠나는 마당에 at this time of one's departure

머무르다 to stay, remain, stop ▷나는 삼촌 댁에 머무르고 있다. I am staying at my uncle's place.

멋 taste, elegance, charm, refinement ▷노래의 멋 flavor of a song ▷멋있는 노래 song full of gusto

모양 look, appearance

목어 wooden fish (used by Buddhist priests)

몫 share, proportion ▷이것이 자네 몫의 전부다. This much has fallen to your lot. ▷각자 자기 몫을 받았다. A share was alloted to each. ▷한몫 주다 to give a share to ▷자기 몫을 요구하다 to claim a share to

반주자 accompanist

발걸음 step, pace, tread ▷무거운 발걸음으로 with a heavy step

범종 bell of a Buddhist temple, temple bell

법고 small stick drum played in front of the statue of Buddha during a Buddhist ritual

변모하다 to change, undergo a change ▷한국인의 사상은 6.25 동란 이후에 여러 면에서 변모했다. The ideas of the Korean have changed in various ways since the Korean War.

변화 무쌍 endless change. 변화무쌍한 ever-changing, kaleidoscopic

보물 treasure

본디 originally, by nature, in itself ▷개는 본디 육식 동물이다. Dogs are carnivorous by nature.

본래 originally, by nature, primarily, from the first ▷그는 본래 매우 부드러운 사람이었다. By nature, he was very gentle.

북 drum

불교 Buddhism. 불교 음악 Buddhist music

사당패 troupe of wandering entertainers

사물 four musical instruments (*lit.,* four things)

사물놀이 a type of traditional Korean percussion music

상징하다 to symbolize ▷이 시의 빨간 장미는 사랑을 상징한다. The red rose in this poem symbolizes love.

서구화 Westernization. 서구화하다 to Westernize

세련되다 to be elegant, polished, refined ▷세련된 문체 elegant writing style

솟구치다 to rise quickly, blaze up

쇠 iron, metal

신명나다 to get enthusiastic (about), be enraptured, enter into the spirit (of things)

신풀이 Korean exorcism

실증하다 to prove, demonstrate. 실증적 positive ▷실증주의자 positivist

악기 musical instrument

애 사당 children in a troupe of wandering entertainers

야외 field, open air ▷아이들은 야외에서 놀기를 좋아한다. Children like to play in the open air.

언뜻 in an instant, in a flash

여기다 to think, consider ▷불쌍히 여기다 feel pity for; have pity on

여사당 female performers in a troupe of wandering entertainers

연주 (musical) performance. 연주하다 to play a musical instrument, perform ▷연주 중에는 들어가면 안 된다. You may not go inside during the performance.

열광하다 to get excited

열띠다 to get excited, become heated ▷열띤 논쟁 heated discussion [argument]

열리다 to be held, take place

열정적이다 to be passionate, ardent, fervent

영역 territory, domain ▷과학의 영역 domain of science

영혼 spirit, soul

외국인 foreigner, alien

요소 element, factor ▷건강은 행복의 중요한 요소다. Health is an essential factor to happiness.

요즘 these days, nowadays ▷요즘엔 물가가 비싸다. Prices are high these days. ▷나는 요즘 그녀와 만나지 못했다. I haven't seen her lately.

용어 terminology, term ▷이것을 의학 용어로 뭐라고 합니까? What is the medical term for this?

우주 universe, cosmos

운판 cloud drum (절에서 부엌에 달아 놓고 식사 시간을 알리는 기구로 청동이나 쇠로 구름 모양으로 만듦)

원초적 basic, original, first

유랑 wandering, roaming. 유랑하다 to wander [roam] about. 유랑 극단 itinerant theatrical troupe. 유랑민 nomadic people, nomads. 유랑자 roamer, vagabond

육신 body, flesh

은은하다 to be dim, vague, indistinct, misty ▷은은한 향기 subtle perfume
▷종소리가 은은하게 들려 왔다. There came the dim sound of a bell to my
ears.

음색 (musical) tone color ▷음색이 좋다. It sounds beautiful. ▷이 바이올린은
음색이 좋다. This violin sounds beautiful.

의아해 하다 to be dubious, suspicious ▷나는 무슨 일인가 하고 의아해 했다. I
wondered what had happened.

이루다 to form, make ▷나는 결혼하여 새 가정을 이루었다. I got married and made
a new home.

인기 popularity ▷인기를 끌다 to obtain popularity

일원 a member (of society)

일종의 a kind of, a sort of ▷이 책은 일종의 안내서이다. This book is a kind of
guidebook. ▷그는 일종의 천재다. He is a genius of a kind.

장고 traditional Korean hourglass-shaped drum

장단 rhythm ▷민지는 장단에 맞추어 춤을 추었다. Minji danced in rhythm to the
music.

전통적 traditional, conventional ▷오랜 전통 time-honored tradition

절묘하다 to be miraculous, exquisite. 절묘한 superb, exquisite, miraculous. 절묘
exquisiteness

점 point, respect, way; standpoint, point of view. 좋은 점 strong point ▷그 점에
있어서 on that point ▷어떤 점에서는 in some respect

정교하다 to be elaborate, exquisite

정화 purification, purgation

조화 harmony, accord, agreement

존재 existence, being, presence ▷나는 그것이 어떻게 존재하게 되었는지 모르겠다. I
don't know how it came into existence.

주되다 to be the head of, take the head of ▷주된 원인 major cause

주류 main current, mainstream

주목하다 to pay attention to. 주목 attention ▷주목(을) 받다 to draw one's attention
▷그 책은 누구에게도 주목을 받지 못했다. Nobody took any notice of the
book.

주변 surroundings, periphery ▷서울과 그 주변에 in Seoul and its vicinity

지니다 to carry, wear, have something along, hold ▷인간은 이성을 지니고 있다.
Man is endowed with reason. ▷그는 아직도 젊음을 지니고 있다. He still
keeps his youthfulness.

지향하다 to intend to do, aim ▷우리가 지향하는 것은 스포츠의 대중화이다. What
we aim at is the popularization of sports.

질박하다 to be simple, plain, simple and honest, homely

짐승 beast, animal ▷짐승 같은 행위 brutal act, brutality ▷그는 짐승만도 못하다. He is worse than a beast.

집단 group. 집단으로 in a group. 집단적으로 as a group ▷집단 토론 group discussion ▷집단 강도 organized burglars ▷집단을 이루다 to form a group

징 large gong

쩨즈 그룹 jazz group

찬사 compliment, laudatory remarks, eulogy

참가하다 to participate in ▷나는 그 프로젝트에 참가했다. I participated in the project.

창작 creation

청중 audience, attendance; hearers, auditors

축제 festival; gala

충격 shock, impact

타악기 percussion instrument

톡톡히 much, quite a lot ▷톡톡히 이득을 남기다 to make a big profit

특징 special or distinctive feature, characteristics. 특징적인 characteristic, distinctive ▷캘리포니아의 특징은 기후와 경치다. The main features of California are the climate and the scenery.

파고 들어가다 to dig into, make a thorough investigation of a matter ▷마음속에 파고 들어가다 eat one's heart out ▷외국시장에 파고들다 to make an inroad into foreign market

패 party, company, group, troupe

펼치다 to spread, extend, expand, unfold ▷자리를 펼치다 to spread a mat

평소(에) (in) ordinary times

폭발적인 explosive

풍미하다 to dominate, predominate ▷그의 예술은 그 세기를 풍미했다. His art was a dominant influence during that century.

한바탕 scene, round ▷한바탕 싸우다 to make a scene (with a person) ▷한바탕 울다 to cry for a spell

합동 joint, united, combined ▷합동 연주회 joint concert ▷합동 공연 joint performance ▷합동 결혼식 group wedding

현대화 modernization, updating. 현대화하다 to modernize, update

협연 co-performance, concerto. 협연하다 to perform in concert (with)

호소력 power of appeal ▷그의 연설은 호소력이 약했다. His speech was of little appeal.

Useful Expressions

1. **~지 궁금하다** I wonder if [whether, how, when, who, what] ~
   민지가 지금 어디 있는지 궁금하다.
   > I wonder where Minji is now.

   무슨 일이 일어났는지 궁금하다.
   > I wonder what happened.

   무슨 일이 일어날지 궁금하다.
   > I wonder what will happen.

2. **~은/는 물론이고** not to mention ~; let alone ~
   영미는 영어는 물론이고 프랑스어도 할 줄 안다.
   > Yŏungmi speaks French, not to mention English.

   그는 학식은 물론이고 경험도 많다.
   > He has experience as well as knowledge.

3. **만큼** not so ~ as; as much as
   금년은 작년만큼 춥지 않다.
   > This year is not so cold as last year.

   기대하지 않았던 만큼 우리는 더욱 기뻤다.
   > We were all the more delighted because we had not expected it.

   나는 그것을 싫증이 날 만큼 먹었다.
   > I have eaten it so much that I am sick of it.

4. **더구나** besides; moreover; in addition
   더구나 비까지 퍼부었다.
   > To make things worse, it was raining hard.

   그는 학식도 없고 더구나 경험도 없다.
   > He has no scholarship, to say nothing of experience.

5. **언뜻** in an instant; in a flash
   그 말이 언뜻 내 귀에 들려 왔다.
   > It came to my ears by chance.

   그의 이름이 언뜻 생각나지 않는다.
   > His name does not occur to me right offhand.

6. **납득이 가다** understand; be convinced of
   그 점은 나도 납득이 잘 간다.
   > I am fully convinced of it.

그의 설명은 납득이 잘 가지 않는다.

Something about his explanation just doesn't sit right with me.

7. **말할 나위도 없다** it goes without saying that ~; it is needless to say that ~

그는 말할 나위 없이 좋은 사람이다.

He is extremely good-natured.

저희 아버지는 말할 나위 없는 신사이십니다.

My father is a gentleman, every inch of him.

8. **~란 말이 나왔으니까** having mentioned ~; speaking of ~

애사당이란 말이 나왔으니까 사당패 얘기를 해야겠습니다.

Having mentioned *aesadang*, we should discuss what it meant by *sadangp'ae.*

텔레비전이란 말이 나왔으니까 하는 얘긴데, 어제 사물놀이 봤니?

Speaking of television, did you watch *samullori* last night?

9. **~에서 한 몫을 톡톡히 하다** play a big role in ~

어린이들이 공연에서 한 몫을 톡톡히 했습니다.

Children played a big role in the performances.

해리 포터 영화에서 애완 동물이 한 몫을 톡톡히 했습니다.

Pets played a big role in the Harry Potter series.

10. **~이/가 아닌가 여겨지다** it is thought that ~ may be

이것이 사물놀이의 새로운 발걸음이 아닌가 여겨집니다.

It is thought that these may be new avenues for *samullori*.

척추 디스크 교체술을 받기에 가장 적합한 사람은 성인이 아닌가 여겨집니다.

It is thought that the best candidates for spinal disc replacement may be adults.

11. **~(이)야말로** the very; indeed; precisely; exactly

나야말로 편지를 했어야 했다.

It is I, not you, who should have written.

이번에야말로 꼭 성공해야 한다.

I must succeed this time or never.

12. **~(으)ㄴ/는 셈이다** amount to; be considered [thought] to be ~

시작이 좋으면 반은 끝난 셈이다.

A good beginning is half the battle.

그 애는 거의 제 여동생인 셈이에요.
She is practically my sister.

Exercises

1. 관련된 단어들끼리 연결하여 문장을 만들어 보세요.

(1) 경연 •   • 구제하다
(2) 영혼 •   • 펼치다
(3) 존재 •   • 알리다
(4) 찬사 •   • 이루다
(5) 조화 •   • 받다
(6) 청중 •   • 사로잡다

_____

_____

_____

_____

_____

_____

2. 아래의 설명과 맞는 단어나 표현을 보기에서 찾아 쓰세요.

보기: 사고 방식, 호소력, 공원, 주류, 개성, 용어, 타악기

(1) 사람들이 들어가 쉬거나 놀 수 있도록 풀밭, 나무,
    꽃 등을 가꾸어 놓은 도시 속의 넓은 장소: _____
(2) 어떤 개념을 나타내는 데 사용하는 말: _____
(3) 다른 사람을 감동시키거나 설득할 만한 힘: _____
(4) 생각하는 방식: _____
(5) 손이나 채로 두드리거나 서로 부딪쳐서 소리를
    내는 악기: _____
(6) 중심이 되고 기본이 되는 줄기: _____
(7) 사람마다 가지고 있는 남과 다른 특성: _____

3. 보기에서 적당한 말을 골라 빈칸을 채우세요.

> 보기: 본래, 대체로, 언뜻, 주요, 어떤, 일종의

(1) 전통과는 거리가 먼 생활을 하는 젊은이들이 전통 음악의 리듬을 그대로
   들려 주는 사물놀이의 공연장에서 열광하는 것은 ＿＿＿＿＿＿ 납득이
   가지 않는 모습일 것입니다.

(2) 사물놀이의 공연을 보고 또 합동 연주를 한 후 느낌을 이렇게 말하고
   있습니다. "사물놀이와의 만남은 ＿＿＿＿＿＿ 충격이었습니다."

(3) 한국의 대표적 타악기인 꽹과리, 장고, 북, 징으로 농악 가락을 연주하는
   것을 사물놀이라고 합니다. 그러나 ＿＿＿＿＿＿ '사물'이라는 용어는
   불교 음악에서 나온 말입니다.

(4) 사물놀이는 그 동안 ＿＿＿＿＿＿ 레퍼토리로 삼아 왔던 영남 농악,
   삼천포 농악 같은 농악 가락뿐만이 아니라 무악의 장단도 개발하여 무대에
   올리는 등 레퍼토리 폭을 넓히고 있습니다.

(5) 국내에서의 공연은 물론이고 수많은 해외 공연을 통하여 많은 이들에게
   충격과 감동을 주면서 한국 음악의 존재를 세계에 알렸던 것이죠. 그 이전의
   ＿＿＿＿＿＿ 공연도 사물놀이만큼 폭발적인 인기를 끌지는 못했습니다.

(6) 타악기라면 ＿＿＿＿＿＿ 북미나 남미, 아프리카 주변이 주류였으므로,
   바로 곁에 그렇게 강렬한 것을 지닌 패가 있었을 줄은 몰랐습니다.

4. 밑줄 친 말과 가장 비슷한 단어나 표현을 보기에서 고르세요.

(1) <u>평소에</u> 국악은 느리고 슬프고 그래서 재미없는 음악으로만 알고 있었던 사
   람들이 사물놀이를 들으면 어떻게 생각할까요?
   a. 평생   b. 보통 때
   c. 일생   d. 비상시

(2) 한국의 대표적 타악기인 꽹과리, 장고, 북, 징으로 농악 가락을 연주하는 것
   을 사물놀이라고 합니다. 그러나 <u>본래</u> '사물'이라는 용어는 불교 음악에서 나
   온 말입니다.
   a. 원래   b. 주로
   c. 본격적으로   d. 주기적으로

(3) 현대화·서구화를 <u>지향하는</u> 요즘의 청소년들이 좋아할 만한 요소가 사물놀
   이의 어디에 있는가 하고 의아해 하실 분들도 많으리라 생각됩니다.
   a. 지양하는   b. 추구하는
   c. 가리키는   d. 부정하는

(4) 어떤 이는 이 네 가지 악기의 <u>특징</u>을 '쇠로 솟구치는 힘, 장고의 세련된 흥, 북의 질박한 맛, 징의 가라앉는 멋'으로 표현하기도 하고, '별, 인간, 달, 해'를 상징하므로 결국 사물놀이는 우주의 모든 것이 농축되어 있는 음악이라고 극찬하기도 합니다.

    a. 특파   b. 특허

    c. 특출   d. 특색

(5) 타악기의 연주로 또한 전통적인 리듬만으로 1980년대를 풍미한 사물놀이야말로 '가장 한국적인 것이 세계적이다'라는 말을 실증시켜 <u>준 셈입니다</u>.

    a. 준 것과 마찬가지입니다   b. 준 것이 아닙니다

    c. 준 것과 차이가 있습니다   d. 준 계산법입니다

5. 보기와 같이 주어진 한자어가 들어가는 단어를 3개 이상 써 보세요.

> 보기: 친 (親, friendly, parents): 친지, 양친, 친척, 친구, 친절

    (1) 사 (四, four): _____

    (2) 물 (物, thing, object): _____

    (3) 화 (化, change, transform): _____

    (4) 자 (者, person): _____

    (5) 내 (內, inside): _____

    (6) 외 (外, outside): _____

6. 보기와 같이 주어진 말이 들어가는 표현을 만들어 보세요.

> 보기: [쇼핑] 쇼핑 객, 쇼핑 백, 쇼핑 차량

    (1) 불교: _____

    (2) 공연: _____

    (3) 문화: _____

    (4) 야외: _____

7. 주어진 단어나 표현을 이용하여 문장을 만드세요.

   (1) 마치 ~처럼

   _____

   (2) 만큼

   _____

   (3) 납득이 가다

   _____

   (4) ~은/는 물론이다

   _____

   (5) ~을/를 말한다

   _____

   (6) ~(이)야말로

   _____

   (7) 한 몫을 톡톡히 하다

   _____

   (8) ~은/는 말할 나위도 없다

   _____

   (9) ~지 궁금하다

   _____

   (10) 경우에 따라서는

   _____

   (11) ~은/는 셈이다

   _____

8. 주어진 단어 중에 나머지 셋과 관계가 먼 단어를 고르세요.

(1)	꽹과리	장고	농악	북
(2)	국악	농악	법고	사물놀이
(3)	남사당	여사당	세계화	사당패
(4)	청중	관중	관객	공연

Comprehension Questions

I. Overall comprehension

1. 지은이는 왜 김덕수 패 사물놀이의 등장을 한국 음악계의 커다란 사건이라고 했습니까?

2. 지은이는 사물놀이가 새로운 창작 곡으로 관현악단, 교향악단, 재즈 그룹과 협연하는 것에 대해 어떻게 생각합니까?

II. Finding details

1. 평소에 일부 한국 사람들은 국악에 대해 어떻게 알고 생각하고 있었습니까?

2. 사물놀이에 사용하는 악기는 무엇입니까?

3. 본디 불교 음악에서 사용되는 사물은 무엇이었습니까?

4. 지은이는 요즘의 청소년들의 특성을 무엇이라고 했습니까?

5. 네 가지 타악기로 연주되는 음악을 사물놀이라고 부르게 된 것은 언제부터입니까?

6. 일본인 타악기 반주자 샌바 기요하코가 사물놀이의 공연을 보고 충격이라고 한 이유는 무엇입니까?

7. 왜 사물놀이는 우주의 모든 것이 농축되어 있는 음악이라고 했습니까?

8. 사당패란 무엇입니까?

9. 애사당이란 무엇입니까?

Related Reading

정명훈-조수미-보첼리 '우정의 무대'

음악계의 '좋은 친구들'이 나란히 한 무대에 올라 우정을 과시한다. 국제적인 명성을 얻고 있는 테너 안드레아 보첼리(42), 소프라노 조수미(37), 지휘자 정명훈(47)이 오는 5월 17일 오후 8시 수원 밤 하늘을 아름다운 선율로 수놓는다. 다음달 15, 17, 18일 수원 야외 음악당에서 열리는 '2000 수원 국제 음악제'의 일환.

정명훈

안드레아 보첼리

이번 콘서트는 이번 음악제의 음악 감독을 맡은 정명훈의 초청을 보첼리가 받아들여 성사됐다. 12세에 시력을 잃은 보첼리는 96년 앨범 '로만차'를 히트시키며 인기 절정에 오른 테너. 94년 '파바로티와 친구들' 공연에 참가하면서 입지를 굳혔다. SBS TV<기분 좋은 밤>의 '결혼할까요' 코너 삽입 곡인 <마이 퓨 론타노>도 보첼리가 부른 노래.

수원 국제 음악제 직전인 5월 11, 13, 15일 도쿄에서 열리는 'NHK 창립 75주년 기념 음악제'도 콘서트 성사에 한몫 했다. 세 사람은 도쿄 공연의 레퍼토리를 수원으로 옮긴다.

흥미로운 것은 세 사람 각각의 친분 관계. 남다른 우정을 쌓아 왔지만 여태까지 한 무대에 선 전례가 없었다. 우선 정명훈과 보첼리는 97년 여름 '파리 세계 가톨릭 청년 대회' 당시 교황 앞에서 함께 공연했으며, 98년 4월엔 정명훈이 이탈리아 로마에서 산타체칠리아 오케스트라를 지휘, 보첼리의 2집 앨범을 녹음한 바 있다.

조수미

조수미와 보첼리의 우정도 각별하다. 상대방의 공연 때 무대를 찾아 축하하는 사이다. 한편 조수미는 지난 94년 예술의 전당서 가진 독창회에서 정명훈과 같이 호흡을 맞춘 적이 있다. 보첼리와 첫 공연을 가지는 조수미는 "세계적인 슈퍼스타 보첼리와 공연하게 돼 기쁘다. 개인적으로 그와 대단히 친하다. 보첼리는 피사, 나는 로마에 살아 종종 식당에도 같이 간다. 맹인이면서도 성격이 밝고 음악에 대한 열정이 뜨겁다"라고 말했다.

수원 콘서트에서 정명훈은 수원 시립 교향악단을 지휘하고, 각각 3~4곡씩 부를 조수미와 보첼리는 베르디 오페라 <리골레토>의 아리아도 이중창으로 부른다. 3만원, 7만원. (0331) 257-4500.

장상용 기자

http://young.hankooki.com/sed_culture/200004/e2000041618424033851278.htm

우정 friendship, 무대 stage, 과시하다 to show off, 국제적 international, 명성 fame, reputation, 테너 tenor, 지휘자 concertmaster, 선율 melody, tune, 수놓다 to embroider, 일환 part, 초청 invitation, 성사 accomplishment, realization, 시력 eyesight, vision, 절정 acme, climax, 입지를 굳히다 to solidify one's footing, 한몫 하다 to play an important role, 레퍼토리 repertory, 친분 friendship, 남다른 to be uncommon, 여태까지 up to now, 가톨릭 Catholic, 교황 the Pope, 전례가 없다 to be unprecedented, 각별하다 to be special, 독창회 solo vocal recital, 호흡을 맞추다 to act in concert with, 종종 often, 맹인 blind person, 열정 passion, 이중창 duet

Discussion & Composition

1. Related Reading의 내용을 잘 읽고 조수미-정명훈-보첼리 공연을 선전하는 짧은 신문 광고를 만들어 보세요.

2. 전통 문화에 대한 다음의 의견을 읽어 보고 여러분은 어떤 의견에 동의하는지 이야기해 보세요. 본문의 내용을 예로 들면서 여러분의 의견은 어떤지 이야기해 보세요.

▶ 전통 문화는 보존을 하는 것이 중요한 것이다. 전통 문화를 변형시키면 그것은 더 이상 전통 문화가 아니다.
▶ 전통 문화는 보존도 중요하지만 새로운 창조를 하는 작업이 더 중요하다.

3. 한국의 전통 음악(예, 판소리, 가야금, 궁중 음악, 농악, 민요) 중 하나를 골라
   인터넷이나 도서관을 이용해 조사해 보고 수업 시간에 5분 정도 발표하세요.

4. 지은이는 가장 한국적인 것이 가장 세계적이라고 했습니다. 한국적이며 세계적인
   것들이 있는 지 조사해 보고, 조사한 것을 정리하여 아래에 글을 써 보세요. 글을
   쏠 때는 다음의 표현을 사용해 보세요.

> ▸ ~(이)야말로
> ▸ 더구나 주목할 점은
> ▸ 대표적
> ▸ 찬사를 받다
> ▸ ~을/를 살펴보다
> ▸ ~을/를 사로잡다
> ▸ ~은/는 셈이다

Lesson 15 *Samullori,* a Korean percussion ensemble

Samullori: Now a world music
Samullori music is a condensing of everything in the universe.
New musical possibilities have been pioneered in co-performances with the
symphony orchestra, piano, and jazz groups.

Last September the World *Samullori* Competition was held at Seoul Olympic Park. The heart-stirring festival, in which some forty ensembles from around the world participated and gave fiery performances, truly showed how *samullori* has become a worldwide art form.

People who thought the national (classical) music was slow, sad, and uninteresting must have been surprised when they heard *samullori* and saw foreigners becoming wild with excitement over it.

The meaning of *samul*

Samullori is the name given to performances of syncopated "farmers' music" using the small hand gong, the hourglass-shaped drum, the barrel drum, and the large gong. But the word *samul* 'the four instruments' originally came from the Buddhist musical tradition. The original 'four instruments' were the wooden temple drum *(mogŏ)*, a fish-shaped percussion instrument struck to save the lives of fish in the water; the cloud drum *(unp'an)*, made of iron, whose shape symbolized a cloud, played to save the lives of birds flying in the sky; the Buddhist drum *(pŏpko)*, made from animal skin, beaten to save the souls of the four-legged beasts moving on the earth; and finally, the faint-sounding Buddhist bell *(pŏmjong)*, sounded to save the flesh and souls of human beings.

So when did music performed with the small hand gong, hourglass-shaped drum, barrel drum, and large gong begin to be called *samullori?* The name came about in May of 1978 at (a venue called) Konggan sarang, where the Kim Tŏk-su *Samullori* Ensemble performed syncopated farmers' music using the four instruments. Until that time, farmers' music had only been performed outdoors. *Samul* refers to the four percussion instruments; and *nori* (lit., play) to the exhilarating performance of farmers' music in which the four instruments are used.

The emergence on the scene of the Kim Tŏk-su *Samullori* Ensemble shook the Korean music world of the 1980s. The ensemble's performances at home and abroad impacted and moved many people, and the existence of Korean music became known to the world. No performance art had ever enjoyed such an explosive popularity. Moreover, what is notable is that the ensemble has attracted young people as its main audience.

I suppose many may wonder: What is there about *samullori* to attract the modernizing, Westernizing young people of today? Why young people go wild at *samullori* performances that bring them the rhythms of traditional music is not immediately obvious. What is more, how can we explain the praise accorded *samullori* in foreign countries with different cultures and ways of thinking?

A performance of primitive rhythms and high spirit

Rhythm is said to be the most primitive and appealing of music's essential elements. Korean traditional music commands endlessly changing rhythms within a multitude of musical meters. But people were not aware of this until *samullori* arrived on the scene. There was a jewel right beside them, but they failed to notice. We ourselves did not know, so how could others?

Semba Kiyohako, a percussion accompanist from Japan, gave his impressions after seeing a *samullori* performance and co-performing with a *samullori* ensemble: "My encounter with *samullori* was a kind of shock. When we think of percussion instruments, we mostly think of North or South America or Africa. I did not know we had such a forceful group of players just next door. . . . I discovered that *samullori* digs deeply into what is inside of us."

Exquisite harmony of contrasting tone colors

One finds that each of the instruments that make up *samullori* has its own personality, yet at the same time, each harmonizes with the others. While such an individuality and harmony may sound like mixing water and oil, this is, in fact, not the case: it is just like individual people harmonizing (their talents) to produce something splendid.

The (shrill) metallic sound of the small and large gongs contrasts with the dull sound of the two skin-covered drums. So the two sides differ greatly in terms of their tonalities. Because of the differences in tonal color and in the instruments' (physical) construction, each possesses a different manner of expression. Some people express the characteristics of the four instruments as "strength blazes from the metal (of the small gong); the refined merriment of the hourglass-shaped drum; the simple and honest flavor of the barrel drum; and the calm grace of the large gong." Some say the instruments symbolize "the stars, humans, the moon, and the sun," highly praising *samullori* as a "condensing" of everything in the universe.

As discussed above, *samullori* was changed, in that the rhythms of (the outdoor spectacle of) farmers' music were embellished and enjoyed indoors. What made this possible was the exceptional talent of the Kim Tŏk-su *Samullori*

Ensemble. The members who made up the ensemble (Kim Tŏk-su, Yi Kwang-su, Ch'oe Chong-sil, etc.) started out as itinerant child performers who had joined a men's troupe of itinerant entertainers.

Having mentioned 'itinerant child performers' *(aesadang),* we should discuss what is meant by 'itinerant entertainers *(sadangp'ae).* The term "itinerant entertainers" dates from the mid-Chosŏn period and refers to professional groups of artists who wandered among Korea's farming and fishing villages performing shows. There were, roughly speaking, male groups and female groups. Sometimes children joined the troupes and played a big role in the performances. Such children were called *aesadang.*

Most local is most global

Samullori has not stayed within the confines of traditional music. New original compositions have been co-performed with the national (classical) orchestra, with symphony orchestras, and with piano. New musical possibilities have been pioneered through co-performances with a jazz group and with other kinds of percussion instruments. It is thought that these may be new avenues for *samullori.*

Samullori, which gained world attention with only percussion playing and traditional rhythms, proves the adage that what is most local is most global.

http://www.changwoncci.or.kr/import/상의지연재/우리음악1.htm

Related Reading: Friends on Stage: Chŏng Myŏng-hun, Cho Su-mi, Bocelli

Three good friends of the music world will display their comradeship side-by-side on stage. World-renowned tenor Andrea Bocelli (42), soprano Cho Su-mi (37), and conductor Chŏng Myŏng-hun (47) will embroider the evening skies of Suwŏn with beautiful melodies on May 17 at 8 P.M., as a part of the Suwŏn International Music Festival 2000 to be held next month (15−17) at the Suwŏn Outdoor Music Hall.

The concert was realized by Bocelli's acceptance of an invitation from the festival's musical conductor, Chŏng Myŏng-hun. The tenor Bocelli, who lost his sight at age 12, reached the height of popularity in 1996 with his hit album *Romanza.* His success had been solidified in 1994 by his participation in *Pavarotti & Friends.* Bocelli sang *Mai Più Così Lontano,* the incidental music for the "Shall I Marry?" segment of SBS TV's "Pleasant Evening."

On May 11, 13, and 15, just prior to the Suwŏn Festival, the three performers will take part in the Music Festival in Commemoration of NHK's 75th Year, to be held in Tokyo. Thus, the Tokyo Festival contributed to the fruition of the Suwŏn event. They will bring the Tokyo repertory to Suwŏn.

Of particular interest is the close friendship shared among the three performers. Although the three are old friends, they have never stood together onstage. To begin with, Chŏng and Bocelli performed together for the Pope at World Youth Day in Paris in 1997; then in 1998, Chŏng conducted the Santa Cecilia Orchestra in Rome and did recordings for Bocelli's second album.

Cho and Bocelli also have a special friendship, attending each other's concerts and congratulating each other. Also, Cho performed (*lit.,* matched breath) with Chŏng at her solo concert held in 1994 at the Seoul Arts Center. Regarding her first concert with Bocelli, Cho said, "I am happy to perform with the world superstar Bocelli. We are close personal friends. He lives in Pisa and I live in Rome. We often go to restaurants together. Although non-sighted, he has a bright personality and a passion for music."

At the Suwŏn Festival, Chŏng will conduct the Suwŏn Symphony Orchestra. Cho and Bocelli will perform three or four songs separately and an aria from *Rigoletto* by Verdi as a duet. Tickets: 30,000/70,000. TEL (0331) 257-4500

Chang Sang-yong, reporter
http://young.hankooki.com/sed_culture/200004/e200004161842403851278.htm

제16과　한국은 '여성 상위'의 사회?

(Lesson 16: Are Women "Superior" in Korean Society?)

Objectives

이 과에서는 한국 사회에서 여성이 차지하는 지위에 대해서 생각해 본다. 한국 사회는 얼핏 보면 남성 중심의 사회 같지만, 자세히 보면 남자를 지 배하는 것이 바로 한국의 여자들이라는 주장이 있다. 한국 사회에서 여성 들이 어떤 역할을 하고 있는지 알아보기로 하자.

This lesson looks at the position of women in Korean society. It is argued that although on the surface Korea appears to be a male-dominated society, in fact it is the women who control the men. Let's find out what kind of role women play in Korean society.

Pre-reading questions

1. 서구 사회와 비교해서 한국 여성들의 지위는 어느 정도 수준이라고 생각하세요?

2. 한국의 가정에서 경제권을 쥐고 있는 사람은 누구일까요?

3. 여러분의 가정에서는 경제권을 쥐고 있는 사람이 누구인가요?

4. 한국에서 모든 집안일을 여자들이 처리하게 된 이유는 무엇이라고 생각합니까?

5. 한국 학부모들, 특히 어머니들의 자식 교육열에 대해서 이야기 해 봅시다.

Gaining familiarity

1. 여성 상위, 여필종부

2. 유교적 이데올로기

3. 장영자 사건

4. 임진왜란, 논개

5. 치맛바람

한국은 '여성 상위'의 사회?

①한국에 살면서 좀처럼 이해할 수 없는 것이 한국 사회에서 여성이 차지하는 지위라는 문제이다. 가끔 텔레비전에 나오는 여자들이 서구 사회에 비해 한국에서는 여성 정치인의 비율이 낮다고 아쉬워하는 모습을 본다. 국회 의원뿐만 아니라 장관이나 차관 등 고위 공무원, 각 기업체 최고 경영자 등 정계와 재계 전체를 통틀어 한국 여성의 사회적 지위는 선진국과 비교할 때 터무니없이[16.1] 낮다. ②똑같은 대학을 나와도 취업이나 승진, 봉급 등에서 여성들은 뚜렷한 이유도 없이 차별을 당하고 평상시에도 남성들보다 열등한 대우를 받는다. 그러니 여성 지도자들이 '여성들의 각성'을 외치며 열변을 토하는[16.2] 것도 무리는 아닌[16.3] 듯하다.

③불평등이 그뿐인가, 수시로 터져 나오는 성희롱 사건이나 여성이기 때문에 받아야 하는 사회적 차별 등을 생각하면 이제 한국도 진정한 남녀 평등 시대를 열어 가야 한다는 주장이 일리 있어[16.4] 보인다.

④한국 사회에서 남녀가 평등하게 대우받지 못하는 것은 분명한 사실이다. 그것도 대부분 여성이 차별을 받는다. 그런데도 나는 여성들이 나약하고 억울하고 불쌍하지 않다. 아니, 오히려 그 반대다. 남성들이 힘이 없고 불쌍해 보인다.

⑤한국에서는 '여성 상위' 사회라고밖에 볼 수 없는 측면이 많다. 그 어떤 나라와 비교해도 사정은 달라지지 않는다. 일본은 물론 미국보다 더 여성의 힘이 센 나라가 바로 한국이다. 이른바 '여필종부'라는 유교적 이데올로기는 사라진 지 오래 되었다. 이것은 결코 역설이 아니다. 궤변은 더 더욱 아니다. 내가 한국은 여성의 힘이 남성을 압도하는 사회라고 생각하는 이유는 다음과 같다.

⑥역사적으로 나라에 위기가 닥쳤을 때 한국 여성들이 보여 준 억척스러운 힘은 남자에게 절대 뒤지지 않는다. 임진왜란 때 평범한 여염집 아낙들이 앞치마에 돌덩이를 실어 날라 일본군을 물리치는 데 앞장섰다는 이야기며, 적장의 허리를 껴안은 채 동반 자살한 논개라는 여인의 이야기를 듣고 나는 적지 않은 감동을 느꼈다.

⑦현대 한국 여성들도 결코 선조들에게 뒤지지 않는다.[16.5] 처음 한국에

왔을 때 나는 한국 사채 업자는 전부 여자인 줄 알았다. 자본주의 사회에서는 자고로[16.6] 돈줄을 움켜쥔 사람이 강자로 군림한다. 따라서 큰손 작은손 가릴 것 없이 사채 시장에 여자가 많다는 것은 그만큼 힘이 세다는 반증이다. 장영자 사건을 필두로[16.7] 굵직한 금융 사고에는 반드시 여자가 개입되어 있는 것도 이러한 나의 생각을 뒷받침해 준다.

⑧ 물론 세계 어느 나라에나 '치맛바람'을 일으키는[16.8] 여자들이 있고, 대형 사고에 여자들이 관계된 경우도 많다. 그러나 대부분 배후에서 조연 역할을 하는 데 그친다. 한국에서처럼 여자가 전면에서 주도권을 행사하며[16.9] 대형 사고를 일으키는 나라는 거의 없다.

⑨ 힘에는 여러 종류가 있다. 간단하게 팔씨름으로 확인할 수 있는 물리적 힘도 있지만, 우리는 지금 그런 물리력보다 경제력이나 정치력 같은 사회적 힘이 더욱 중요한 세상에서 살고 있다. 가정에서도 복잡한 역학 관계는 어김없이 작용한다.

⑩ 한국에서는 '경제권'을 남편이 쥐고 있는 가정이 별로 많지 않은 것 같다. 월급이 온라인으로 입금되어 집에서 통장을 틀어쥐고 있는 아내의 수중으로 고스란히 들어가거나 월급 봉투째 아내에게 가져다 바치고 자신은 용돈을 타서 쓰는 직장인이 태반이다.

⑪ 이따금 그런 친구들에게 "왜 자기가 번 돈을 아내에게 모조리 주고 정작 자신은 돈이 없어서 쩔쩔매느냐?"[16.10]고 물어보면 대답은 한결같다. 자기가 돈을 관리하면 한 달 월급 가지고 보름도 못 버틴다는[16.11] 것이다.

⑫ 결국 그 가정의 주도권을 아내쪽에서 쥐고 있다는 뜻이다. 다들 표면적으로는 여성들이 특유의 꼼꼼하고 치밀한 성격으로 살림을 잘 하기 때문에 돈이 헤프게 없어지지 않는다는 이유를 댄다. 하지만 내막을 들여다보면 여기에도 돈줄을 쥔 자가 힘을 장악하고 관계를 장악하는 자본주의의 생리가 고스란히 관철되고 있다.

⑬ 서구와 비교할 때 한국 여성의 사회적 진출이 미약한 것은 사실이다. 그렇다고 해서 한국을 남성 중심의 사회라고 단정하는 것은 성급한 판단이다. 얼른 보기에는 남자들이 모든 것을 지배하는 것 같지만, 한 꺼풀 벗기고 보면 모든 것을 지배하는 남자를 지배하는 것이 바로 한국의 여자들이다.

⑭ 한국에서는 모든 집안일을 여자들이 처리한다. 밥하고 살림하는 것은 물론 물건을 사고 집을 사고 적금을 붓고[16.12] 심지어 축의금이나 조의금 액수까지 여자들이 알아서 결정한다. 남자들은 아녀자 일에 꼬치꼬치 간섭하는[16.13] 것은 대장부의 도리가 아니라고 생각한다. 음식이 싱겁거나 짜도 아무 소리 않고 그냥 먹는다. 왜 그렇게 사느냐고 물어보면 십중팔구는 '가정의 평화를 지키기 위해서'라고 대답한다.

⑮ 물론 남자든 여자든 통이 크고[16.14] 대범한 것은 좋은 일이다. 그러나 한국 사회에서는 가정에서 이런 기울어진 역학 관계 때문에 많은 문제점이 발생한다. 남자들이 간섭하지 않으니까 여자들은 자기가 하는 일이 다 올바르다고 착각한다.

⑯ 가정 문제에 관한 한 한국 여자들은 남자의 견해에 귀기울이지 않는다.[16.15] 뭐라고 이야기를 하면 으레 "잔소리한다", "시대에 뒤떨어졌다", "구닥다리다"라고 말대꾸나 한다. 그런 소리가 듣기 싫어서 남자들은 아예 간섭을 안 해 버린다. '가정의 평화'를 지키기 위해서다.

⑰ 한 가정의 경제권을 여자가 장악하는 것까지는 이해할 수 있다. 그러나 자녀 교육 문제에 관한 한 한국 남자들이 지금처럼 전권을 아내에게 맡겨 놓아서는 안 된다고 생각한다.

⑱ 남편은 회사 일로 바쁘고 집 바깥에서 보내는 시간이 많다 보니 아내에게 자녀 교육 문제를 전담시킨다. 어머니들의 자식에 대한 애정과 관심은 곧 교육열로 이어진다. 조금 적극적인 어머니들은 다른 아이들이 하지 않는 것을 하나라도 더 가르치려고 안달이다. 그러니까 별 생각 없이 사는 어머니들까지도 최소한 남들 하는 것은 우리 아이도 시켜야 한다는 생각으로 그 뒤를 따른다. 여자들이 인정받기 위해서는 살림을 잘 하는 것도 중요하지만 그보다 자식을 얼마나 출세시키느냐 하는 것이 더 크게 작용한다. 가만 보면 이 부분에서도 유행을 따라가는 것과 똑같은 심리가 작용한다. 옆집 아이가 피아노를 배우면 내 아이에게도 가르쳐야 하고, 옆집 아이가 태권도를 배우면 내 아이에게도 시켜야 한다. 그래 봤자 궁극적인 목표는 단 하나, 자식을 명문 대학에 입학시키는 것이 대한 민국 어머니의 지상 과제다.

⑲ 사정이 이러니 집에서 부모가 자식한테 가정 교육을 하고 싶어도 시

간적 여유가 없다. 한국의 가정 교육은 철저하게 입시 위주인 학교 교육을 보충하는 수준에 머물러 있을 뿐이다.

⑲ 나는 이런 세태의 직접적인 원인이 여자가 잘못하고 있기 때문이라고 생각한다. 어떻게든 자식을 출세시켜야 한다는 그릇된 관념 때문에 여자들의 시야가 그만큼 좁아지는 것이다. 한국 남자들은 '가정의 평화'를 지킨다는 명분으로 귀찮다는 듯이 모든 것을 양보하고 인내해서는 안 된다. 그것은 가장으로서 명백한 직무 유기다. 이대로 가다가는 교육뿐만 아니라 나라 전체가 망한다.

이케하라 마모루 <맞아죽을 각오를 하고 쓴 한국, 한국인 비판>에서 발췌

New Words

가끔 sometimes, every now and then ▷그는 가끔 학교에 지각한다. He is sometimes late for school. ▷나는 가끔 테니스를 친다. I play tennis once in a while.

가장 head of a family [household]

각성 awakening. 각성하다 to awake. 각성시키다 to awaken, disillusion

간단하다 to be simple, brief, short

강자 strong person, the strong ▷강자와 약자 the strong and the weak

개입되다 to intervene (in), be involved (in)

견해 opinion, view ▷나는 그와 같은 견해다. I have the same view as he does.

경제력 economic power

고스란히 wholly, completely, just as it was, with nothing missing ▷그녀는 그의 선물을 고스란히 돌려주었다. She returned her present unopened. ▷나는 음식을 먹지 않고 고스란히 남겼다. I left the food as it was without eating any.

고위 공무원 high-ranking civil servant

관념 idea, notion, thought, conception

관철 accomplishment, realization. 관철하다 to accomplish. 관철되다 to be accomplished, realized

구닥다리 old-fashioned person, old-fashioned stuff

국회 의원 member of the National Assembly. 국회 National Assembly. 의원 member (of the Assembly)

군림하다 to reign, rule

굵직하다 to be thick, significant, big

궁극적인 final, ultimate, eventual

궤변 sophistry, deceptive talk

귀기울이다 to listen to (someone, something) attentively, bend one's ear to (someone, something)

그릇되다 to go wrong [amiss, awry] ▷그릇된 mistaken, wrong, false, incorrect ▷그릇된 생각 false idea, mistaken notion ▷그릇된 행실 misdeed, evildoing, wrong behavior

금융 circulation of money, finance, financing

기업체 enterprise, type of business enterprise

기울어지다 to slant, lean, incline, decline, sink, go down ▷왼쪽으로 기울어지다 to slope to the left ▷숙명론에 기울어지다 to lean towards fatalism

꺼풀 outside layer

꼬치꼬치 inquisitively ▷그는 내게 꼬치꼬치 캐물었다. He questioned me even to the minutest details.

꼼꼼하다 to be a perfectionist, be meticulous

나약하다 to be weak, soft and spiritless, feeble-minded

내막 underlying factor (*lit.,* inner screen [curtain])

단정하다 to decide, conclude

당하다 to suffer, receive, sustain. 부상당하다 to be injured. 도난당하다 to be stolen. 무시당하다 to be despised, be ignored

대범하다 to be big-hearted, broad-minded, of lofty manners

대우 treatment; pay, salary. 대우하다 to treat; to pay. 대우받다 to be treated, receive ▷나는 그에게 부당한 대우를 받았다. I received unfair treatment from him.

대장부 manly man, heroic man

도리 duty, obligation

돈줄 line of credit, source of money ▷돈줄이 떨어지다 to lose one's financial backing ▷돈줄을 움켜쥐다 to control the source of money

돌덩이 piece of stone

동반 자살 joint suicide, suicide pact

뒷받침해 주다 to support, back up

뚜렷하다 to be vivid, clear, distinct

말대꾸 reply, response (in speech or words)

명백하다 to be obvious, evident, clear

명분 one's moral duty [obligation] ▷명분을 세우다 to justify oneself

모조리 all, without exception, thoroughly

물론 of course, naturally ▷물론 그는 그 제안을 거절할 것이다. Naturally, he will refuse the proposal.

물리(적) physical. 물리력 physical strength

물리치다 to defeat, turn down, repulse ▷그 판사는 검은 손의 유혹을 물리쳤다. The judge rejected the temptation of the bribe. ▷우리 군은 열 배가 넘는 적군을 물리쳤다. Our soldiers defeated an enemy force ten times their size.

미약하다 to be feeble, weak, faint

반증 counterevidence, evidence to the contrary

배후 behind the scenes, background ▷그 사건의 배후로 그가 지목되었다. He was suspected of being the brains behind the crime. ▷사실상 그는 배후 세력에 의해 조종당했다. In fact, he was controlled from behind the scenes.

버티다 to endure, tolerate, stand, keep the balance

보충하다 to assist, supplement ▷임산부는 영양을 보충해야만 한다. Pregnant women must have good nutrition. ▷정부는 군의 병력을 보충하기로 결정했다. The government has decided to supplement the strength of the military.

복잡하다 to be complex, complicated ▷복잡한 절차 complicated process ▷이 기계는 구조가 복잡하다. This machine is complicated in structure.

봉급 salary, pay, wages

분명하다 to be clear, evident ▷그 뜻은 아주 분명하다. The meaning is quite clear.

불쌍하다 to be poor, pitiable, pitiful ▷불쌍한 고아 poor orphan ▷그 여자는 그 고아를 불쌍하게 여겼다. She felt sorry for the orphan.

불평등 inequality ▷불평등 조약 unequal treaty

비율 ratio, percentage, proportion

사고 accident, mishap ▷사고가 나서 많은 사람이 사망했다. An accident happened and many lives were lost.

사정 circumstances, situation

사채 시장 private money market

사채 업자 private moneylender, loan shark

살림 housework, domestic chores. 살림하다 to run one's household ▷살림 도구 household goods ▷살림이 어렵다 to make a poor living

생리 physiology

서구 the West (*lit.,* Western Europe) ▷서구 문화 Western culture

선조 ancestor

성급하다 to be hasty, rash

성희롱 sexual harassment

세태 social conditions

수시로 as occasion arises, often, frequently

수중 in the hands (of) ▷수중에 있다 to be in the hands of ▷수중에 넣다 to take possession of

시야 visual field, field of vision, sight, view ▷시야에 들어오다 to come in sight ▷시야가 넓다 [좁다] to have a broad [narrow] view of things

십중팔구 in eight or nine times out of ten, in the majority of cases

아낙(네) woman, wife. 아낙네들 the womenfolk, women

아녀자 children and women; women

아쉬워하다 to be reluctant, loath; to feel the lack of ▷이별을 아쉬워하다 to be reluctant to part

안달이다 to be impatient, overanxious ▷그는 항상 배가 고파서 안달이다. He is always fretting because he's hungry. ▷준호는 시험 결과를 알지 못해 안달이다. Chun-ho was anxious because he didn't know his exam results.

압도하다 to overwhelm, overpower, surpass ▷그 정치인의 연설은 청중을 압도했다. The politician's speech overwhelmed the audience. ▷그는 압도적인 지지로 시장으로 당선되었다. He was elected mayor with overwhelming support.

앞장서다 to be at the head of ▷유행에 앞장서다 to lead fashion ▷그는 앞장서서 교육 개혁을 실행했다. He took the initiative in carrying out educational reforms.

앞치마 apron

애정 affection, love

액수 amount of money

양보하다 to concede, give in, compromise, yield ▷민수는 버스에서 노인에게 자리를 양보하였다. Minsu offered his seat to an old man on the bus.

어김없이 surely, without fail, certainly

억울하다 be feel mistreated [victimized]

억척스럽다 to be steadfast, unyielding, unrelenting ▷미성이는 가족을 부양하기 위해서 억척스럽게 일해야만 했다. Misŏng works steadfastly to maintain her family. ▷모든 사람이 그녀의 지나친 억척스러움에 질렸다. Everyone was fed up with her excessive stubbornness.

여염집 ordinary household

여필종부 wives should be submissive to their husbands

역설 paradox ▷역설적으로 말하면 paradoxically speaking

역학 관계 dynamic relationship

열등하다 to be inferior

열변 passionate eloquence, fervent speech

올바르다 to be straight, upright, straightforward, honest, right

용돈 pocket money, allowance

위기 crisis, emergency ▷위기에 닥치다 to come to a crisis, face a crisis

으레 habitually, regularly, commonly, usually ▷그들은 만나면 으레 싸운다. They quarrel whenever they meet.

이른바 what is called, what we call, so-called ▷이른바 지식인 so-called intellectual ▷그는 이른바 천재다. He is what you might call a genius.

인내하다 to tolerate, endure

인정받다 to receive recognition, be recognized ▷이 교과서는 교육부로부터 인정받았다. This textbook was authorized by the Ministry of Education.

입금 receipt of money, depositing money (into an account)

자본주의 capitalism

작용하다 to operate on, affect, function (as)

장관 minister ▷교육부 장관 minister of Education

장악하다 to hold, seize, grasp ▷정권을 장악하다 to take over the reins of government

재계 financial world

적극적(인) positive, active, constructive

적장 enemy's general, commander of the enemy force

전권 total control, whole [total] power

전담하다 to bear [take] total [whole] responsibility, be fully responsible (for), be solely in charge of (something) ▷사고가 날 때에는 보험 회사가 그 비용을 전담한다. When the accident happened the insurance company took full responsibility for the costs. ▷그 형사는 마약 사범 전담반이다. That detective is in charge of the narcotics squad.

전면 front (side, part), frontage

정계 political world

정작 actually, really, practically ▷그의 대답은 정작 사죄나 다름없다. His reply is, in fact, an apology.

정치력 political power, political influence

정치인 politician, statesman

조연 supporting player, supporting actor

조의금 condolence money

주도권 leadership, initiative

쥐다 to grasp, clasp, grip, clutch

지도자 leader ▷여성 지도자 woman leader

지배하다 to govern, dominate

지상 과제 someone's purpose, someone's ultimate aim, mission

지위 position, status

직무 유기 negligence of one's duty

진정한 true, sincere, earnest ▷진정으로 heartily, from the bottom of one's heart ▷진정으로 걱정하다 to be very anxious

진출 advance, march. 진출하다 to advance, gain ground

차관 vice minister

차별 discrimination ▷인종 차별 racial discrimination

차지하다 to have (a position), have a share (portion); win (a prize) ▷그는 그 웅변대회에서 일등을 차지했다. He won the first prize at the speech contest.

착각하다 to mistake, misunderstand

처리하다 to handle, manage, treat, deal with, take care of

철저하다 to be perfect, be complete ▷그는 철저하게 자신의 신분을 속여 왔다. He completely falsified his identity. ▷철저한 계획은 성공의 지름길이다. Perfect planning is the shortcut to success.

최고 경영자 CEO (chief executive officer)

축의금 wedding gift in cash

출세 rising in the world, making one's way in life ▷그는 가난한 집에서 태어나서 크게 출세했다. Born of a poor family, he made his way in the world.

취업 going to work, commencement of work, employment

측면 side, flank

치맛바람 (*lit.,* skirt's wind) female influence, female power

치밀하다 to be elaborate, fine, nice, delicate, meticulous

태반 mostly, generally, the majority (of) ▷혼자 사는 학생들은 아침밥을 거르는 날이 태반이다. Most students who live on their own skip breakfast. ▷영국은 비 오는 날이 태반이다. It rains most days in Britain.

터무니없다 to be unfounded, unreasonable ▷터무니 없는 말 하지 마라. Don't talk nonsense.

터져 나오다 to get broken, be torn; to explode, burst

통틀어 taking all things together, altogether

특유의 unique, peculiar ▷한국 특유의 미술 Korea's unique arts ▷이 지방 특유의 풍습 customs peculiar to this district

틀어쥐다 to take control, grasp hard

판단 judgment, decision ▷옳은 판단 right judgment ▷네 판단에 맡기겠다. I will leave it to your judgment.

팔씨름 arm wrestling

평등 equality, impartiality. 평등하다 to be equal ▷평등한 권리 equal rights ▷선생님은 학생들에게 기회를 평등하게 주셨다. The teacher gave equal opportunities to the students.

평상시 normal times ▷평상시의 usual, ordinary, normal, common ▷평상시와는 달리 unusually ▷나는 오늘 아침에 평상시보다 일찍 일어났다. This morning I got up earlier than usual.

표면적으로 superficially, outwardly, externally

필두 first on a list; role model ▷그의 이름이 필두에 올라 있다. His name heads the list.

한결같다 to be constant, consistent ▷한결같은 우정 unfailing friendship

헤프게 wastefully, lavishly ▷돈을 헤프게 쓰다 to be too free with one's money

Useful Expressions

1. **터무니없다** be unfounded [unreasonable, for no apparent reason]
    명균이는 터무니없는 가격에 놀라 입을 다물지 못했다.
    Myŏnggyun's jaw dropped at the outrageous price.
    그의 꿈은 터무니없이 무너졌다.
    His dream collapsed for no apparent reason.

2. **열변을 토하다** make an impassioned speech; deliver a fervent speech
    김 선생은 인권 신장을 위해 열변을 토하고 있다.
    Mr. Kim is making an impassioned plea for the extension of human rights.
    그 국회 의원이 열변을 토하자 많은 사람들이 박수를 보냈다.
    When the National Assembly member finished his fiery speech there
    was enthusiastic applause.

3. **~이/가 무리는 아니다** be not unreasonable; be not unnatural
    그렇게 말하는 것이 무리는 아니다.
    It is not unnatural for you to say that.
    그 사람이 돈을 요구하는 것이 무리는 아니다.
    It is not unreasonable for him to demand money.

4. **일리(가) 있다** there is some reason [truth]
    해영이의 말도 일리가 있고 윤주의 말도 일리가 있는 것 같다.
    It seems there is some truth in what both Haeyŏng and Yunju say.
    그 사람의 말에는 일리가 있다.
    There is some point to his words.

5. **~에 뒤지지 않는다** be ahead of others in ~; be second to none in ~
    나는 한국어만큼은 남에게 뒤지지 않을 자신이 있다.
    I'm confident that I'll be ahead of the others at least in Korean.
    그 아주머니는 수다쟁이로 어느 누구에게도 뒤지지 않는다.
    She's second to none when it comes to talking.

6. **자고로** from ancient times; traditionally
    자고로 성공을 하려면 부지런해야 한다.
    They say that one must work hard to be successful.
    자고로 부모님께 효도하는 사람은 복을 받는다.
    From time immemorial, those who look after their parents are fortunate.

7. **필두로** first on the list; as a starting point

그를 필두로 모든 회원이 탈퇴했다.

Starting with him, all the members left the society.

삼일 운동은 유관순 누나를 필두로 시작되었다.

The March First Independence Movement of 1919 began with sister Yu Kwan-sun as the leader.

8. **치맛바람을 일으키다** (exert) women's influence on (something)

한국의 부동산 시장에는 항상 치맛바람을 일으키는 여자들이 있다.

Women are always an influence in the Korean real estate market.

치맛바람을 일으키는 여자들 때문에 한국의 교육이 몸살을 앓고 있다.

The Korean education system is suffering as a result of the influence of women.

9. **주도권을 행사하다** take the leadership [initiative]

이번 회담은 김 장관이 주도권을 행사했다.

Minister Kim took the lead at this conference.

누가 주도권을 행사하느냐 [차지하느냐]에 따라 역학 관계가 달라진다.

The power relationships change depending on who takes the initiative.

10. **쩔쩔매다** become flustered; be at a loss (what to do)

나는 한국어로 이야기 할 때마다 쩔쩔매곤 한다.

I feel flustered every time I speak in Korean.

은서는 무거운 짐을 들고 가느라 쩔쩔맸다.

Ŭnsŏ was carrying such heavy luggage she was at her wit's end..

11. **못 버티다** not hold; not maintain; be unable to keep up

나는 힘이 들어서 더 이상 못 버틸 것 같다.

It was tiring, so I couldn't keep it up any longer.

10,000원으로는 일주일도 못 버틴다.

10,000 ₩ doesn't support me for even a week.

그 기둥은 집의 무게를 못 버티고 쓰러졌다.

The pillar could not support the weight of the house, and it collapsed.

12. **적금을 붓다** deposit installments into a savings account

우리 할머니께서는 한 달에 한번씩 적금을 부으십니다.

My grandmother makes a deposit into her savings account once a month.

매달 적금을 붓기 위해 미현이는 절약하면서 살고 있다.

Mihyŏn is living frugally so that she make a deposit into her savings account every month.

13. **~에 꼬치꼬치 간섭하다** fuss over ~; interfere in ~

집안일에 꼬치꼬치 간섭하는 남자를 여자는 좋아하지 않는다.

Women don't like men who interfere in the housework.

김 교수는 학생들의 사생활에 꼬치꼬치 간섭한다.

Mr. Kim interferes in the private lives of his students.

14. **통이 크다** be of character; be magnanimous

통이 큰 사람들은 작은 일에 마음을 쓰지 않는다.

People of character do not think about small matters.

술을 잘 마신다고 반드시 통이 크고 대범한 사람은 아니다.

A heavy drinker is not necessarily a person of character.

15. **~에 귀기울이지 않다** not pay attention to ~

영수는 선생님 말씀에 전혀 귀기울이지 않는다.

Yŏngsu really doesn't pay any attention to the teacher.

다른 사람의 충고에 귀기울이지 않는 사람은 발전이 없다.

Those who do not listen to the advice of others do not do well.

Exercises

1. 관련 있는 단어들끼리 연결하여 문장을 만들어 보세요.

A: (1) 열변을 •   • 붓다
      (2) 위기에 •   • 닥치다
      (3) 적금을 •   • 토하다
      (4) 시야가 •   • 좁아지다

B: (5) 살림을   •   • 하다
      (6) 전권을   •   • 따라가다
      (7) 심리가   •   • 맡기다
      (8) 유행을   •   • 작용하다

_____

_____

_____

_____

2. 보기에서 적당한 단어를 골라 빈칸을 채우세요.

> 보기: 수중, 입금, 보충, 견해, 앞장, 열변, 여염집, 각성, 측면,
>   적금, 수준, 액수

  (1) 한국에서는 '여성 상위' 사회라고밖에 볼 수 없는 _____이/가
      많다.

  (2) 여성 지도자들이 '여성들의 각성'을 외치며 _____을/를 토한다.

  (3) 임진왜란 때 평범한 _____ 아낙들이 앞치마에 돌덩이를 실어
      날라 일본군을 물리치는데 _____섰다는 이야기가 있다.

  (4) 월급이 온라인으로 _____되어 집에서 통장을 틀어쥐고 있는
      아내의 _____으로 고스란히 들어간다.

  (5) 물건을 사고 집을 사고 _____붓고 축의금이나 조의금의
      _____까지 여자들이 알아서 결정한다.

  (6) 자녀들의 교육 문제에 관한 한 한국 여자들은 남자의 _____에
      귀를 귀기울이지 않는다.

  (7) 한국의 가정 교육은 철저하게 입시 위주인 학교 교육을
      _____하는 _____ 머물러 있을 뿐이다.

3. 보기에서 적당한 단어를 골라 빈 칸을 채우세요.

> 보기: 터무니없이, 좀처럼, 결코, 이따금

(1) 한국은 살면서 ＿＿＿＿＿＿＿이해할 수 없는 것들이 많다.

(2) 여자들의 지위는 ＿＿＿＿＿＿＿ 남자들에게 뒤지지 않는다.

(3) 한국 여성의 사회적 지위는 선진국과 비교해 볼 때 ＿＿＿＿＿＿＿ 낮다.

(4) ＿＿＿＿＿＿＿나는 친구들에게 "왜 자기가 번 돈을 아내에게 모조리 주고 정작 자신은 돈이 없어서 쩔쩔매느냐?"라고 물어 본다.

4. 주어진 단어와 비슷한 뜻을 가진 단어나 문장을 고르세요.

(1) 적금을 <u>붓다</u>.
　　a. 나는 바가지에 물을 부었다
　　b. 그 환자는 자고 일어나면 얼굴이 붓는다
　　c. 아주머니는 한 달에 한번씩 계를 부으십니다

(2) 돈이 없어서 <u>쩔쩔매다</u>.
　　a. 줄을 매다
　　b. 당황해서 어찌할 바를 모르다
　　c. 가방을 매다

(3) 마약을 <u>전담하는</u> 경찰이 있다.
　　a. 돌리다　　　b. 주문하다　　　c. 맡다

(4) 학생들 중에는 아침을 굶는 사람이 <u>태반이다.</u>
　　a. 거의 없다　　b. 조금 많다　　　c. 대부분이다

5. 보기와 같이 주어진 말이 들어가는 단어를 3개 이상 만들어 보세요.

> 보기:　[교육] 가정 교육, 교육 문제, 교육부

(1) 사정: ＿＿＿＿＿＿＿＿＿＿＿＿＿＿＿＿＿＿＿＿＿＿＿

(2) 평등: ＿＿＿＿＿＿＿＿＿＿＿＿＿＿＿＿＿＿＿＿＿＿＿

(3) 차별: ＿＿＿＿＿＿＿＿＿＿＿＿＿＿＿＿＿＿＿＿＿＿＿

(4) 출세: ＿＿＿＿＿＿＿＿＿＿＿＿＿＿＿＿＿＿＿＿＿＿＿

6. 보기와 같이 주어진 단어를 이용하여 다양한 표현을 3개 이상 만드세요.

> 보기: [유행] 유행을 이끌다, 유행에 뒤쳐지다, 유행을 따라가다

(1) 시야: _____

(2) ~을/를 붓다: _____

(3) 용돈: _____

(4) 월급: _____

7. 아래 설명과 맞는 표현을 보기에서 찾아 쓰세요.

> 보기: 확인하다/뒷받침해 주다, 적금을 붓다, 으레, 열변을
> 토하다, 전권을 맡다, 십중팔구, 고스란히, 태반이다,
> 어김없이, 구닥다리

(1) (생각이나 주장을) 증명해 주다 _____

(2) 매달 은행에 돈을 저금하다 _____

(3) 당연히 _____

(4) 생각이나 행동이 구식이고 낡았다 _____

(5) 목소리를 높여 주장하다 _____

(6) 절대적인 권력을 갖고 지휘하다 _____

(7) 틀림없이 _____

(8) 열 중 아홉은, 대부분이 _____

(9) 통째로, 그대로 _____

(10) 대부분이다 _____

Comprehension Questions

I. Overall comprehension

1. 본문은 무엇에 관한 글입니까?

_____

2. 한국은 남성 위주의 사회입니까?

_____

3. 한국 여성들의 표면적인 사회적 지위는 높습니까?

_____

4. 한국 여성들의 가정 경제권의 독점으로 인해 생기는 문제점은 무엇입니까?

_____

II. Finding details

1. 작가는 한국 여성의 지위에 대해 어떤 생각을 가지고 있습니까?

_____

2. 한국 남성들은 왜 아내에게 월급을 고스란히 가져다 줍니까?

_____

3. 작가는 자본주의적 관점에서 볼 때 왜 여자가 강자라고 했습니까?

_____

4. 역사적으로 나라에 위기가 닥쳤을 때 한국 여성들이 보여 준 모습의 예를 두
   가지만 말해 보세요.

_____

5. 가정 문제에 대해서 한국 남자들이 간섭을 하면 여자들은 뭐라고 대꾸합니까?

_____

6. 한국에서 여자들이 인정받기 위해서 중요하게 생각하는 것은 무엇입니까?

_____

7. 한국의 가정 교육이 잘 되지 않는 이유는 무엇인가요?

_____

Related Reading

한국의 ‘펭귄 아빠’들

서울 강남의 한 미국 체인 식당. 시간은 오후 1시쯤. 2층으로 된 넓은 홀이 손님들로 빽빽한데 사방 어디를 둘러봐도 여성뿐이다. 여자 친구와 동행한 남자 대학생 한둘, 엄마 손잡고 온 사내아이 몇 명이 천연 기념물처럼 눈에 띌 뿐, 말 그대로 ‘여인 천하’다.

“남자들은 다 어디 갔느냐”고 묻자 여기 여성 일색인 일행의 대답은 “남자들은 일하지”였다.

“남자들은 일하느라고 바쁘고, 여자들은 돈 쓰며 노느라 바쁘고 . . . 그게 요즘 한국이야.” 중, 고교 동창 모임, 대학 동창 모임, 동네 친구 모임, 자녀들 학교 학부모 모임, 거기에 문화 센터 같은 데서 한두 클래스 수강하고, 헬스클럽에라도 다닐라 치면 “노는 것도 여간 고된 일이 아니다”고 전업 주부들인 일행은 말했다.

“30대엔 아이들 키우느라 정신없지만 40대 들어서 아이들 다 크고 나면 여자들은 그때부터 해방이야. 남자들은 구조 조정이다, 조기 은퇴다 해서 스트레스 잔뜩 받으며 일에 매달리지만, 여자들은 시간이 남아도니 돈 쓸 궁리만 해.”

가정 내 여성의 목소리가 높아진데다 90년대 거품 경제로 소비 문화가 잔뜩 몸에 배면서 주부들의 생활 방식이 바뀌었다는 것이다. 가부장제니, 남존여비니 하는 것도 다 옛말이 되었고 언제부터인가 “남자들이 불쌍한 세상이 되었다”고 그 자리에 모인 주부들은 입을 모았다.

여자는 ‘베짱이’, 남자는 ‘개미’인 것이 일반적인 부부의 모습이라면 ‘개미’보다도 더 고달픈 것은 ‘펭귄’ 아빠들. 자녀들을 외국으로 유학 보내고, 아이들 뒷바라지를 위해 아내도 같이 보낸 후 혼자 남아 돈 버는 아빠가 소위 ‘펭귄 아빠’이다.

펭귄은 종에 따라 한 번에 1-2개의 알을 낳는데 주위가 혹한의 얼음판이다 보니 수컷의 털북숭이 발 위에 암컷이 알을 낳는다. 그리고 나면 수컷은 알이 부화하기까지 수십일 동안 꼼짝도 않고 서서 배의 피부 주름으로 따뜻하게 알을 품는다. 암컷은 그동안 바다로 가서 먹이를 실컷 먹은 후 알이 부화할 때쯤 돌아와 뱃속의 먹이를 반추해 새끼를 먹인다. 반면 쫄쫄 굶은 채 서 있던 수컷은 그제야 먹이를 찾아 바다로 가는데, 너무 기진맥진하면 도중에 쓰러져 죽는 경우도 있다고 한다.

가족들의 외국 생활비를 대느라 조기 유학 가정 아빠들은 스튜디오 같은 단칸방에서 라면으로 식사를 때우는 경우가 다반사라고 하니 자기 희생의 부정이 펭귄에 비교가 되는 것이다.

<한국일보 미주판> 2001년 8월 30일자 권정희 편집위원

체인 식당 franchise restaurant, 빽빽하다 be packed, 사방 in all directions, 동행하다 to go together, 여인 천하 petticoat government, 천연 기념물 national monument, 일색 exclusively, 일행 companions, 동창 모임 old schoolmates' association, 학부모 모임 association of parents of students, 문화 센터 private adult [community] school, 수강하다 to take courses, 여간 ~ 아니다 not easy to ~, 고된 일 tough work, 전업 주부 full-time housewife, 일행 party (of people), 해방 liberation, 구조 조정 structural adjustment, 조기 은퇴 early retirement, 매달리다 to hold on to, 궁리 thinking over, mulling over, 거품 경제 bubble economy, 몸에 배다 to get used to, 가부장제 patriarchy, 남존여비 predominance of men over women (Confucian idea), 옛말 old saying, 베짱이 grasshopper, 개미 ant, 고달프다 to be worn out, 뒷바라지 looking after, caring for, 소위 so-called, 혹한 severe cold, 수컷 male (animal), 털북숭이 hairy person (thing), 암컷 female (animal), 부화하다 to hatch, 꼼짝 않다 to remain motionless, 품다 to brood, incubate (eggs), 실컷 to one's heart's content, 반추하다 to ruminate, chew, 기진맥진하다 to be completely exhausted, 다반사 an everyday experience, 자기 희생 self-sacrifice, 부정 paternal love

Discussion & Composition

1. 본문에서 본 한국 남성들의 문제점은 무엇이라고 생각합니까?

2. 작가가 말한 한국 남성들의 문제점에 대해 그 해결 방안을 이야기해 봅시다.

3. 본문에서 말한 한국 여성의 가정에서의 역할과 여러분의 어머니나 아내의 가정에서의 역할을 비교하여 아래에 글을 써 봅시다.

_____

_____

_____

_____

_____

Lesson 16 Are women "superior" in Korean society?

After living in Korea, I still cannot understand the issue of women's place in Korean society. I often see women on television at a loss over the fact that Korea has a lower ratio of women politicians compared to the West. Not only in the National Assembly, but also in the entirety of Korea's political and economic worlds—high-ranking public officials like cabinet ministers and vice ministers, and top managers in industry—the social position of women is ridiculously low compared to advanced countries. Even if graduated from the same university as men, women are unaccountably discriminated against in employment, advancement, and salary, and are treated as inferior beings. It is no wonder that women leaders belt out fiery speeches calling for a "women's awakening!"

And inequality is not just that. Just think about the all-too-frequent cases of sexual harassment and other forms of social discrimination women must suffer. There is something to be said for the assertion that Korea must open the way for (an age of) true equal rights.

It is clear that in Korean society, men and women are not treated in an equal manner. And in most cases it is the women who are discriminated against. But even so, I am not saying that Korean women are weak, unfairly treated, and deserving of pity. No, quite the opposite: men are the powerless, pitiable ones.

There are many aspects of Korean society that manifest what must be viewed as "female superiority." Korea's situation of "female superiority" cannot be viewed differently no matter what country we compare it with. In fact, in Korea women have more power than (women) in Japan and even America. It has been a long time since the Confucian ideology "wives must be obedient to their husbands" disappeared in Korea. To say so is neither paradox nor sophistry. Let me explain why I think women's power overrides that of men in Korean society.

Historically, whenever the country met with trouble, Korean women have never been less tough than men. During the Imjin (Japanese) invasions, women from ordinary, respectable families took the lead, collecting stones in their aprons and carrying them to (throw in order to) drive off the Japanese soldiers; and then there was Non'gae, the woman who took the enemy general by the waist and plunged with him to their death in a double suicide. These stories moved me considerably when I heard them.

Modern Korean women, too, are no less (strong) than their ancestors. When I first came to Korea, I thought all the private moneylenders were women. Traditionally, in capitalist societies, the person holding the purse (*lit.,* money) strings dominates as leader. No matter whether they are big or small moneylenders, the fact that so many women are in the private money market proves, to the contrary, that women are very powerful. Beginning with the Chang Yŏng-ja incident, women's implication in hefty banking incidents supports my idea.

Of course, women who wield their power are to be found in all countries, and there are many cases of women's involvement in felony fraud. But in most of the cases, the women provide assistance behind the scenes. There is hardly any other country like Korea, in which women take the up-front initiative in perpetrating the felonies.

There are many kinds of power. There is physical power, for example, that can be tested by an arm-wrestling match. But we now live in a world in which social power, like economic and political clout, outweighs physical strength. Surely, complex dynamics are at work in the family, too.

It seems that in Korea there are very few families in which the husband holds the economic power. In a majority of cases, either the salaried man's monthly salary is deposited online and goes entirely into the hands of the wife, who controls the bank passbook; or he hands his pay packet over to his wife and is given some of it for his "allowance."

"Why do you give all of your earnings to your wife, then complain you have no money to spend?" When I ask my friends this question, they always say the same thing. They say if they controlled the money, their monthly salary would not last three weeks.

This means, ultimately, that the leadership in that family is held by the wife. On the surface, men explain the situation by saying women, with their special perfectionism and eye for detail, are better at managing the household, and therefore money does not get wasted. But a look at underlying factors reveals that the situation is shot through with the capitalist notion (*lit.,* physiology) that the person who holds the pursestrings controls the power and the relationship.

It is true that Korean women have not made many social advances compared to the West. But let's not be too hasty in saying that because of this Korea is a male-centered society. At first glance, it seems that men control everything, but a closer look shows that the ones controlling the controllers are the women.

In Korea, women manage all household affairs. Not only do they decide the meals and accounts, but they also buy the (household) goods, buy the house, pay the monthly installments, and even decide the amounts to be given for wedding gifts and condolence money. Men think that it is not a real man's way to fuss over women's affairs. Men just eat their meals, whether too bland or too salty, without comment. When asked why they live that way, nine times out of ten they reply, "in order to keep peace in the family."

Of course, whether male or female, it is a good thing to be magnanimous and big-hearted. But in Korean society many problems arise due to this imbalance in family dynamics. Because men do not interfere, women mistakenly believe that everything they do is correct.

Women do not listen to men's opinions in family matters. If the husband tries to say something, the wife comes back at him with, "Don't preach," "You're behind the times," or "You're old-fashioned." Men hate listening to this, so they just don't interfere—of course, in order to "keep peace at home."

I can understand a woman holding the economic power in a family. But where the children's education is concerned, it is wrong for men to hand over all the power to the wife.

The husband is busy at work and spends a lot of his time outside the home, so he gives his wife total responsibility for the children's education. A mother's love and concern for her children leads to zeal for education. Energetic mothers will be overanxious to have their children learn something that other children haven't learned. Even the otherwise unassuming mother follows other mothers, thinking that her children should do at least what the others are doing. It is important for women to manage their household well so they will be well thought of; but the more important factor at work is how successful they can make their children. It is the same mentality as those who follow the latest trend: If the child next door learns piano, then I must teach my child piano, too. If the child next door learns *t'aekwŏndo*, then I must make my child learn it, too. Ultimately, there is only one goal: the mission of Korean mothers is to have their children enter a prestigious university.

In such a situation, there is no time for parents to teach their children at home. Home education in Korea only remains at the level of supplementing the children's education at school, which is totally geared to university entrance exams.

I think the errors of women are the direct cause of the present situation. The mistaken concept that they must worry about making their children successful has narrowed women's vision. Korean husbands must not view their moral obligation to keep peace in the family as an annoyance and stoically fork over their power. This constitutes neglect of one's duty as head of the family. If this continues, not only education, but the country itself will go to ruin.

From Ikehara Mamoru, *A Critique of Korea That I Wrote at the Risk of My Life*

Related reading: Korea's "penguin daddies"

(I am at) an American franchise restaurant in Seoul's Kangnam district. The time is 1:00 in the afternoon. The wide, two-floor hall is packed with customers. There are only women everywhere I look. One or two male college students with girlfriends, and a few small boys holding Mommy's hand, stand out like national monuments: it is truly a "woman's world."

When I ask, "Where have all the men gone?" an all-female party answers: "The men are at work."

"Men are busy working, women are busy spending money and having a good time . . . that's today's Korea!" Considering they attend middle and high school alumni meetings, university alumni meetings, neighborhood meetings, and parents' meetings at school, then take a few classes at places like the Cultural Center, and then go to the health club, "Having a good time is pretty rough!" according to a group of full-time housewives.

"In their thirties women go crazy raising their children. In their forties, their children are all grown and they are liberated. Men hang on to their jobs, stressed about structural adjustments and early retirement. But women have time on their hands. They just mull over how to spend money."

The lifestyle of the housewife has changed. In addition to having more influence at home, they are now at ease with the consumption culture owing to the bubble economy of the '90s. Words like "patriarchy" and "male dominance" are now things of the past. The women gathered there agreed in saying that, at some point, "the world became a bad place for men."

If the average wife is the grasshopper and the husband the ant, being a "penguin daddy" is even more tiring than being an ant. So-called penguin daddies are dads who send their children abroad to study, then send their wife abroad to mind the children, while remaining home alone to earn money.

Penguins, depending on their breed, lay one or two eggs at a time. Because of the surrounding severe cold and sheets of ice, the female lays the egg(s) on top of the male's hair-covered feet. Then the male stands, without budging, for several weeks until the eggs are hatched, keeping the eggs warm with the skin folds of his belly. In the meantime, the female goes to sea and eats her fill, returning around hatching time to feed the chicks with the food she regurgitates. The male, who has stood so long without eating, can now go to sea to find food, but sometimes he is so utterly exhausted he collapses en route and dies.

Since a father, in order to furnish living expenses for his family staying abroad, normally makes do with a meal of instant noodles in a single room (studio), the comparison of his fatherly self-sacrifice with that of the penguin is an apt one.

Kwŏn, Chŏng-hŭi, *Hanguk ilbo*, American edition, Aug. 30, 2001

제17과 한국의 경제 발전

(Lesson 17: Economic Development in Korea)

Objectives

이 과에서는 지난 40여 년 동안 한국의 경제 발전 과정을 살펴보고,
눈부신 경제 개발을 이루는 과정에서 정부가 한 일은 무엇인가를
알아본다.

In this lesson we will look at Korea's astounding economic development
over the last forty years, and the government's role in the process.

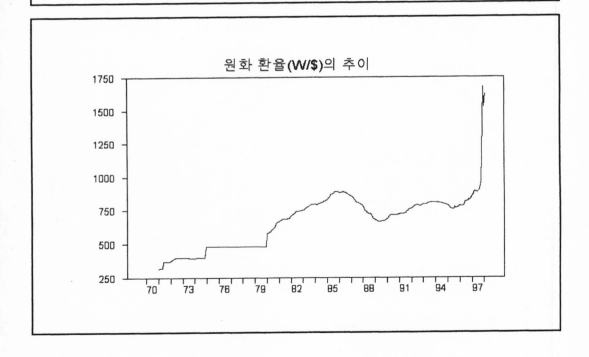

원화 환율(W/$)의 추이

Pre-reading questions

1. 한국의 대기업체 이름 중 아는 이름이 있습니까?

2. 지난 반세기 동안 한국은 어떻게 경제 발전을 이룩할 수 있었을까요?

3. 여러분이 사는 나라의 지난해 GNP 성장률은 얼마였나요?

4. 지난 1960년대부터 최근까지 한국의 연간 평균 GNP 성장률은 어떻게
   변해 왔는지 알아봅시다.

Gaining familiarity

이 과에서 쓰이는 경제 용어:

수입 대체 산업, 국민 총생산, 금융 위기, 외환 위기, 경제 위기, 경제 개발
5개년 계획, 금융 기관의 국영화, 차관, 외채, 수출 장려 정책, 노조 활동,
중화학 공업, 경공업, 오일 쇼크, 경기 침체, 정경 유착, 금융 관리, 단기
상환 외채, 장기 투자, 국제 통화 기금, 불황

한국의 경제 발전

¹ 한반도의 분단 이후 지난 반세기 동안 남한과 북한은 각기 다른 길을 걸어왔다.[17.1] 이 글에서는 분단 이후 남한의 경제 발전을 살펴보고자 한다.

² 남한은 1950년대 후반에는 전후 복구 사업에 치중하였으며[17.2] 별 성과 없는 수입 대체 산업 육성 정책을 펼쳐 나갔다.[17.3] 그 후 1960년대와 1970년대의 놀랄만한 경제적 성취는 남한의 위상을 후진국에서 개발 도상국으로 올려 놓았다.³ 1962년부터 1986년까지 국민 총생산 연 평균 성장률은 8.3%를 기록하고 있다. 그간 국민 총생산의 마이너스 성장을 보인 해는 1979년 오일 쇼크 다음해인 1980년(-5.2%)과 금융 위기를 맞은 1997년(-6%) 두 해뿐이었다.

⁴ 이렇게 눈부신 경제 개발 뒤에는 정부의 주도 면밀한 계획이 있었다.[17.4] 1961년 군사 쿠데타로 정권을 잡은 박정희 정권은 1962년부터 경제 개발 5개년 계획을 펼쳐 나가기 시작했다.⁵ 박정희 정권은 그의 군사 독재 정치로 비난을 받고 있지만 경제 개발에의 공헌은 그 누구도 부인하지 못 하고 있다.[17.5] 정부의 주도적 역할은 다음과 같다. 모든 국내 금융 기관이 국영화되어, 모든 대출업무 및 해외로부터의 차관이 전적으로 정부의 통제 아래 있게 되었고,[17.6] 60년대 이후의 주요 경제 정책은 '수출 장려 정책'이었다.⁶ 국내 수출업자들에게는 무제한의 관세 면제 혜택과 은행으로부터의 자금 융자도 주어졌다. 이와 같은 정부의 계획 경제는 주로 수출 성과가 좋은 대기업이나 재벌 기업에 특혜를 주게 되었다. 결국 이는 삼성, 대우, 현대, 럭키금성(지금의 LG)과 같은 거대한 재벌 기업을 만들어 냈다.

⁷ 이렇게 수출을 장려하는 한편[17.7] 국내 농업을 국제 시장과의 경쟁으로부터 보호하기 위해서 정부는 국내 농산물 가격을 통제하고 농업 시장을 개방하지 않는 정책을 써 왔다. ⁸또한 정부는 기업의 편에 서서[17.8] 노조 활동을 통제해 왔던 것도 사실이다. 정부는 노조 활동을 탄압해 1980년대 초반까지 남한의 노조 활동은 극히 미비했다.

⁹ 제3차 경제 개발 5개년 계획이 시작된 1972년부터 정부는 중화학 공

업의 육성에 박차를 가하기[17.9] 시작했다. 중화학 공업 육성책으로 정유, 석유 화학, 조선, 자동차 산업 등 상당한 중공업 산업 기반을 갖추게 된다. 그러나 방직 산업과 같은 경공업 분야가 침체해 산업간 불균형을 보이기도 한다.

[10] 1979년의 오일 쇼크로 인한 세계 경기 침체와 더불어 박정희 대통령 시해 사건으로 혼란한 정국을 맞았으며, 그 이듬해인 1980년은 사상 최저의 국민 총생산량 마이너스 5.2% 성장률을 보인다.[11] 이와 같은 난국의 해결책으로 전두환 제5공화국은 예전보다 더 많은 외채를 끌어들인다. 1979년의 외채 대 국민 총생산 비율은 33%이었고, 1980년과 1981년에는 각각 45% 및 49%이었다.[12] 다행히도 세계 경제의 회복으로 한국의 경제도 회복되어, 경기는 경기침체 이전의 상태로 돌아 갈 수 있었다. 1988년의 서울의 올림픽 경기의 유치는 국제 사회에서의 한국의 위상을 크게 높이었다. 그 후에도 1997년에 닥친 경제 위기 전까지 지속적인 경제 성장을 해 왔다.

[13] 1997년에 닥친 통화 위기의 원인에는 여러 가지 분석이 있지만 무엇보다도 정경 유착에 따른 비정상적인 국내외 금융 관리에 그 원인이 있다고 본다.[14] 계속해서 늘어난 외채와 단기 상환 조건의 외채의 장기 투자가 결국 외환 위기로 몰고 갔다고[17.10] 보는 견해가 많다. 결국, 국가 경제는 파산 직전에 이르렀으며, 국제 통화 기금 및 세계은행으로부터 거금 미화 302억 불의 구조 융자금을 빌려 그 위기를 모면했다. 그동안 정부와 기업의 노력으로 한국은행은 이를 갚아야 할 2004년 5월보다 훨씬 앞당겨 2001년 8월 23일에 이를 모두 갚았다고 한다.[15] 그러나 현재 남한의 주요 교역국인 미국과 일본의 경제가 불황을 맞고 있기 때문에 남한의 경제는 통화 위기 이전의 경제로 회복하는 데는 보다 많은 시간이 걸릴 것으로 보는 견해가 많다.

박덕수

New Words

각각 each, every, all ▷사람은 각각 생활 방식이 있다. Everyone has his own way of living.

각기 individually, each one ▷사람은 각기 장점과 단점이 있다. Each man has his strengths and weaknesses.

갖추다 to equip, furnish, have ▷그 상점은 갖가지 상품을 고루 갖추고 있다. The store keeps a rich assortment of goods in stock.

갚다 to repay, pay back ▷빚을 빨리 갚아야 한다. You have to repay the debt quickly.

개발 도상국 developing country

개방하다 to open ▷정부는 농산물 시장을 개방해야 하는 부담을 안고 있다. The government has the burden of opening markets for agricultural products.

거금 huge amount of money

거대하다 to be huge, enormous

견해 view, opinion ▷정부는 이와 같은 견해를 나타냈다. The government expressed its opinion like this.

경공업 light industry

경기 침체 economic stagnation, recession

경쟁 competition, rivalry. 경쟁국 competing [rival] country. 경쟁률 competition rate

경제 economy. 경제 개발 economic development. 경제 발전 economic development. 경제 성장 economic growth. 경제 위기 economic crisis. 계획 경제 planned economy ▷경제 개발 5개년 계획 the Five-Year Economic Development Plan

공헌 contribution, service ▷공헌하다 to contribute (to) ▷그는 대외 무역에 크게 공헌했다. He rendered great services to foreign trade. ▷그는 스포츠 발전에 많은 공헌을 했다. He contributed much to the development of sports.

공화국 republic, commonwealth

관세 면제 exemption from tariffs

교역국 trading partner (as a country)

구조 relief, bailout

국내 domestic, internal to a country

국내 농산물 domestic agricultural product

국내외 domestic and international

국민 총생산 Gross National Product (GNP)

국영화 nationalization ▷국영화 되다 (some firm) to become nationalized

국제 사회 international community

국제 시장 international market

국제 통화 기금 International Monetary Fund (IMF)

군사 쿠데타 military coup d'état

군사 독재 정치 military dictatorship

그간 in the meantime, meanwhile ▷그동안 안녕하셨는지요? Have you been well all
these days?

극히 extremely, greatly, excessively

금융 관리 management of finance

금융 기관 financial institution

금융 위기 financial crisis

기록하다 to record, write down

기반 base, basis, foundation, footing ▷가족은 사회의 기반을 이룬다. Families form
the basis of society.

끌어들이다 to pull into, take into, draw in ▷그는 많은 빚을 끌어들였다. He
incurred much debt.

난국 difficult situation, crisis, deadlock ▷1997년 한국 경제는 난국을 맞았다. In
1997, the Korean economy faced a crisis.

노조 활동 labor union activity

놀랄만하다 to be surprising, amazing

농업 agriculture, agricultural industry. 농업 시장 agricultural market

높이다 to raise, lift

눈부시다 to be dazzling, brilliant, striking, remarkable

다행히 luckily, fortunately

닥치다 to fall upon, befall, draw near, come round, approach, be near at hand
▷눈앞에 닥친 위험 impending danger ▷위험이 그녀에게 닥쳐 왔다. Danger
threatened her. ▷파산이 눈앞에 닥쳤다. We were on the verge of bankruptcy.

단기 상환 repayment (of debt) within a short period of time

대 versus, against; to ▷7 대 3 seven to three ▷외채 대 국민 총생산 national debt
to GNP

대기업 big firms, large companies, consortiums

대출 업무 lending business

더불어 together with, in addition to

마이너스 minus, negative ▷마이너스 성장 negative growth

맞다 to meet, go to meet ▷그는 현관에서 손님을 맞았다. He greeted his guests at
the front door. ▷집주인은 그를 따뜻하게 맞았다. He was well received by the
host.

모면하다 to escape, avoid, evade ▷우리는 간신히 위기를 모면했다. We had a
narrow escape.

몰고 가다 to chase, drive, push (into) ▷우리는 돼지들을 우리 속으로 몰고 갔다.
We drove the pigs into the pen.

무제한의 unlimited, unrestricted ▷무제한의 혜택 unlimited benefits

미비하다 to be deficient, defective, imperfect, incomplete, weak ▷미비한 시설 deficient facility

미화 American dollar

박차 spur; acceleration ▷사업에 박차를 가하기 시작했다. She spurred herself into the business.

방직 산업 textile industry

별(로) particularly, in particular, specially ▷별로 좋지 않다. It is not particularly good.

복구 rehabilitation, recovery, restoration ▷복구 사업 restoration task

부인하다 to deny, defy ▷아무리 부인해도 소용이 없었다. There was no use denying.

분단 dividing into sections, division, partition ▷한반도의 분단 partition of the Korean Peninsula ▷분단국 divided country

분석 analysis, research

분야 area, field

불균형 lack of balance, imbalance ▷산업간 불균형 imbalance between industries

불황 recession, business depression ▷세계적인 불황 worldwide recession

비난 criticism, blame, reproach

비율 rate, ratio

비정상적 abnormal

사상 historically (the abbreviated form of 역사상) ▷이런 일은 사상 최초의 일이다. This type of event has no precedent in history.

살펴보다 to look into, examine ▷나는 서류를 잘 살펴보았다. I examined the papers well.

상당하다 to be considerable, fair, good ▷그는 증권에서 상당한 이익을 봤다. He made a considerable sum of money in the stock market.

석유 화학 petroleum chemistry

성과 result, fruit, outcome, performance

성장률 growth rate

성취 achievement, accomplishment, attainment

세계은행 World Bank

수입 대체 산업 import-substitution industry; industries by which imports are substituted by domestic products

수출 export. 수출업자 exporter. 수출 장려 promotion of export

시해 assassination

앞당기다 to do something ahead of its due date ▷만기를 앞당겨 융자금을 갚았다. I paid back the loan before it reached maturity.

역할 role, function

연 평균 annual average

예전 former days

오일 쇼크 the oil shock

올려 놓다 to raise, lift

외채 foreign debt

외환 위기 foreign exchange (currency) crisis

원인 cause, origin, factor ▷분쟁의 원인 cause of dispute ▷이 병의 원인은 아직 밝혀지지 않고 있다. The causes of this illness are not found yet. ▷사고의 원인은 운전자의 부주의였다. The accident was caused by the carelessness of the driver.

위기 crisis, emergency ▷정치적 위기 political crisis ▷금년 말에는 경제 위기가 올 것이다. There will be an economic crisis at the end of this year.

위상 status of (a country or an organization in a bigger community)

유치 lure, enticement ▷관광객을 유치하다 to attract tourists ▷올림픽 경기를 유치하다 to lure the Olympic games

육성 promotion; upbringing ▷육성 정책 promotion policy

융자금 loan ▷구조 융자금 bailout loan

이듬해 the following year ▷그 이듬해 the year following

이르다 to reach, arrive; to result in ▷행복에 이르는 길 road to happiness ▷오늘에 이르기까지 until now ▷결국 그는 그녀와 결혼하기에 이르렀다. He finally ended up marrying her.

이전 before, in former times ▷한 씨 이전에는 누가 주지사였습니까? Who was the governor prior to Mr. Han? ▷그는 이전에는 대학 교수였다. He was formerly a professor at a university.

자금 융자 capital loan

장기 투자 long-term investment

장려 promotion, encouragement ▷수출 장려금 export subsidy

재벌 기업 *chaebol,* (financial) conglomerates

전적으로 totally, overall

전후 복구 사업 recovery (task) after the war

정경 유착 tie between politicians and businessmen

정국 political situation

정권 political power, regime ▷박정희 정권 the Park Chŏng-hŭi regime

정유 oil refinery

정책 policy

조건 condition

조선 shipbuilding

주도 면밀하다 to be meticulous, careful, cautious, scrupulous, circumspect ▷주도 면밀한 계획 meticulous plan

주도적 leading

주로 mainly, principally ▷아버지는 주로 운동을 위해 테니스를 치신다. My father plays tennis mainly for exercise.

중공업 heavy industry

중화학 공업 heavy-chemical industry

지속적이다 to be continual, continuous

직전에 just before

차관 national loan, debt (from overseas) ▷단기 차관 short-term loan

초반 early stage ▷시합의 결과는 초반에 결정되었다. The result of the game was decided in its early stages.

최저 the lowest. 최저가 the lowest price ▷주가는 최저가를 기록했다. Stock prices dropped to an all-time low.

치중하다 to put weight (on), emphasize ▷정부는 중공업 육성에 치중했다. The government emphasized the promotion of heavy-chemical industry.

침체하다 to stagnate, become sluggish (dull) ▷침체된 시장 dull [slack] market

탄압하다 to suppress, oppress, repress, crush

통제 control, regulation, regimentation

통화 currency, medium of circulation ▷통화 위기 monetary crisis ▷통화 관리 currency management

투자 investment. 투자자 investor ▷나는 토지에 많은 돈을 투자하였다. I invested heavily in land.

특혜 privilege, special favor ▷특혜를 받다 [주다] to receive [give] preferential treatment

파산 bankruptcy, insolvency ▷그는 파산 직전에 몰리었다. He was driven to the verge of bankruptcy.

편 side. 우리 편 our side. 상대편 other party, one's opposition ▷편을 짓다 to form a faction

펼치다 to spread, extend, expand, carry out, unfold ▷정부는 수출 장려 정책을 펼쳤다. The government carried out the export promotion policy.

한국은행 the Bank of Korea

해결책 solution

해외 overseas, foreign countries. 해외 여행 overseas travel

혜택 favor, kind indulgence, benevolence ▷혜택을 주다 to bestow a favor on ▷혜택을 입다 [누리다] to receive a favor from

혼란하다 to be confused, disordered, messy, chaotic

회복 recovery, restoration, retrieval, rehabilitation, recuperation. 회복하다 to recover, get back, regain, restore, rehabilitate, retrieve

후반 the second half. 후반전 the second half of the game
후진국 undeveloped country

Useful Expressions

1. **각기 다른 길을 걸어오다/걸어가다** each goes through different ways
   한반도의 분단 이후 남북한은 각기 다른 길을 걸어 왔다.
   > Since the division of the Korean peninsula, North and South Koreas
   > have taken different paths.
   우리는 각기 다른 길을 걸어가고 있었다.
   > We were taking different paths from one another.

2. **~에 치중하다** attach weight [importance] to ~; lay stress on ~
   1950년대 후반에는 전후 복구 사업에 치중하였다.
   > In the second half of the 1950s, we emphasized recovery in the aftermath
   > of the war.
   나는 지금부터 한국어 공부에 더욱 치중해야겠다.
   > From now on, I should focus more on studying Korean.

3. **~을/를 펼쳐 나가다** unfold ~; lay out ~; carry out ~; promote ~
   1960년대부터는 수출 장려 정책을 펼쳐 나갔다.
   > Since the 1960s, an export promotion policy has been carried out.
   지금 한국어 세계화 정책을 펼쳐 나가고 있다.
   > The globalization of the Korean language is now being promoted.

4. **A 뒤에는 B이/가 있다** B is behind A
   경제 개발 뒤에는 정부의 주도 면밀한 계획이 있었다.
   > Behind the economic development, there were meticulous plans by the
   > government.
   훌륭한 사람 뒤에는 훌륭한 어머니가 있다.
   > Behind a great person, there is a great mother.

5. **~은/는 그 누구도 부인하지 못 하다** nobody can deny ~
   박정희 대통령의 경제 개발에의 공헌은 그 누구도 부인하지 못한다.
   > Nobody can deny President Park Chung-hee's contribution to the
   > economic development.
   건강이 무엇보다도 중요한 것은 그 누구도 부인하지 못한다.
   > No one can deny that health is the most important thing.

6. **~의 통제 아래 있다**   be under the control of ~
   3년 동안의 한반도는 미소 양군의 통제 아래 있었다.
   For three years, the Korean Peninsula was under the control of American and Soviet troops.
   아이들은 한동안 부모의 통제 아래 있다.
   Children are under the control of parents for a time.

7. **~는 한편**   while ~
   수출을 장려하는 한편, 국내 농산물은 국제 시장으로부터 보호하였다.
   While promoting exports, they protected domestic agricultural products from the international market.
   나는 대학에 다니는 한편, 집에서 개인 교수도 한다.
   While I attend university, I also do private tutoring at home.

8. **~(의) 편에 서다**   take sides; go over to ~
   한국 전쟁 중에 중공군은 북한의 편에서 유엔군과 싸웠다.
   During the Korean War, taking the side of North Korea, the Chinese Red Army fought against U.N. troops.
   상대편에 서서 그를 지지하는 사람이 많았다.
   There were many people who supported him while siding with the other party.

9. **~에 박차를 가하다**   spur (someone, something) to ~; accelerate or prompt ~
   1970년대에 정부는 중화학 공업의 육성에 박차를 가했다.
   In the 1970s, the government accelerated the promotion of heavy-chemical industry.
   공업화가 농업의 쇠퇴에 박차를 가했다.
   Industrialization aggravated the decline of agriculture.

10. **~(으)로 몰고 가다**   drive, chase [push] into ~
    단기 상환 외채의 장기 투자가 국가 경제를 외환 위기로 몰고 갔다.
    The use of short-term foreign loans in long-term investments drove the national economy into the foreign exchange crisis.
    우리는 소들을 풀밭으로 몰고 갔다.
    We drove the cows out to pasture.

Exercises

1. 관련 있는 단어들끼리 연결하여 문장을 만들어 보세요.

A: (1) 수출 장려   •
         •   역할

       (2) 경제   •
         •   쿠데타

       (3) 개발   •
         •   도상국

       (4) 군사   •
         •   개발

       (5) 주도적   •
         •   정책

_____

_____

_____

_____

_____

B: (6) 관세 면제   •
         •   융자

       (7) 자금   •
         •   혜택

       (8) 노조   •
         •   활동

       (9) 산업간   •
         •   침체

     (10) 경기   •
         •   불균형

_____

_____

_____

_____

C: (11) 장기   •
         •   조건

    (12) 단기 상환   •
         •   유치

    (13) 올림픽 경기   •
         •   투자

    (14) 금융   •
         •   기관

    (15) 위기   •
         •   모면

_____

_____

_____

_____

_____

2. 아래의 설명과 맞는 단어나 표현을 보기에서 찾아 쓰세요.

> 보기: 대출 업무, 단기 상환, 외채, 전후, 후진국, 국영화, 위상

(1) 전쟁이 끝난 뒤: _____

(2) 한 국가의 국제 사회에서의 위치: _____

(3) 못 사는 나라: _____

(4) 산업이나 기업을 국가에서 운영하는 것: _____

(5) 은행에서 돈을 빌려 주는 일: _____

(6) 외국에서 빌려 온 돈: _____

(7) 짧은 기간 안에 돈을 갚는 것: _____

3. 보기에서 적당한 말을 골라 빈칸을 채우세요.

> 보기: 극히, 별, 도, 훨씬, 대

(1) 나는 지금부터 _____ 성과 없는 수학 공부보다는 한국어 공부에
    치중해야겠다.

(2) 1980년대 초반까지 한국의 노조 활동은 _____ 미비했다.

(3) 노동력을 통제해 왔던 것_____ 사실이다.

(4) 축구 시합에서 우리 팀이 호주 팀을 3 _____ 1로 이겼다.

(5) 은행에서 빌린 돈을 만기일보다 _____ 앞당겨 갚았다.

4. 밑줄 친 말과 가장 비슷한 단어나 표현을 보기에서 고르세요.

(1) 분단 이후 남북한은 <u>각기</u> 다른 길을 걸어왔다.
    a. 자기   b. 서로
    c. 매우   d. 무척

(2) 1960년대와 1970년대에는 <u>놀랄만한</u> 경제 성장을 하였다.
　　a. 놀면서　　　　　　　　　b. 적은
　　c. 엄청난　　　　　　　　　d. 기쁠만한

(3) 이런 경제 발전 뒤에는 정부의 <u>주도 면밀한</u> 계획이 있었다.
　　a. 철저한　　　　　　　　　b. 엉성한
　　c. 위험한　　　　　　　　　d. 좋은

(4) 이 사고는 <u>전적으로</u> 네 책임이다.
　　a. 일부　　　　　　　　　　b. 약간은
　　c. 모두　　　　　　　　　　d. 정말로

(5) 수출을 장려하는 <u>한편</u> 국내 농업을 보호했다.
　　a. 반면에　　　　　　　　　b. 한
　　c. 것뿐만 아니라　　　　　　d. 동안

(6) 1980년대 초반까지 노조 활동은 <u>극히 미비했다</u>.
　　a. 하나도 없었다　　　　　　b. 매우 많았다
　　c. 무척 많았다　　　　　　　d. 거의 없었다

(7) 1979년 박정희 대통령 시해 사건으로 정국이 <u>혼란했다</u>.
　　a. 불안했다　　　　　　　　b. 불만스러웠다
　　c. 불행했다　　　　　　　　d. 안정됐다

(8) 그 후에도 1997년 경제 위기 전까지 <u>지속적인</u> 경제 성장을 해 왔다.
　　a. 끝까지　　　　　　　　　b. 계속적인
　　c. 지독하게　　　　　　　　d. 지루하게

(9) 미국과 일본의 경제가 불황을 <u>맞고 있다</u>.
　　a. 겪고 있다　　　　　　　　b. 때리고 있다
　　c. 이기고 있다　　　　　　　d. 매를 맞고 있다

5. 보기와 같이 주어진 단어가 들어가는 표현을 3개 이상 써 보세요.

> 보기: [정부] 한국 정부, 미국 정부, 일본 정부

    (1) 산업: _____

    (2) 경제: _____

    (3) 면제: _____

    (4) 불균형: _____

    (5) 분석: _____

6. 주어진 단어나 표현을 이용하여 문장을 만드세요.

    (1) 각기 다른 길을 걸어오다/걸어가다

    _____

    (2) ~에 치중하다

    _____

    (3) ~을/를 펼쳐 나가다

    _____

    (4) ~뒤에는 ~이/가 있다

    _____

    (5) 그 누구도 부인하지 못 하다

    _____

    (6) ~은/는 ~의 통제 아래 있다

    _____

    (7) ~는 한편

    _____

    (8) ~의 편에 서다

    _____

    (9) ~에 박차를 가하다

    _____

    (10) ~(으)로 몰고 가다

    _____

Comprehension Questions

I. Overall comprehension

1. 본문에서는 무엇이 1960년대부터 한국의 경제 발전을 가능하게 만들었다고 합니까?

_____

2. 지금까지 한국의 국민 총생산이 마이너스 성장을 보인 해는 두 해뿐이라고 했는데, 그 두 해는 언제 언제였으며, 그 두 해에 무슨 일들이 마이너스 성장을 가져 왔습니까?

_____

II. Finding details
본문의 글과 내용이 일치하면 □에 ∨ 표를 하세요.

1. 한국의 경제 성장은 정부의 주도 면밀한 계획이 있었기 때문이다. □
2. 박정희는 1961년 민주적인 선거에 의해 정권을 잡았다. □
3. 박정희 정권의 경제 개발에의 공헌은 컸다. □
4. 박정희 정권부터의 주요 경제 정책은 수출 진흥 정책이었다. □
5. 수출은 장려하면서, 국내 농업을 보호하기도 했다. □
6. 한국 경제는 주로 재벌 위주의 정부의 계획 경제였다. □
7. 1980년대 초반까지 노조 활동은 많았다. □
8. 중공업의 육성이 경공업과의 산업 간의 불균형도 가져왔다. □
9. 1979년부터 1980년대 초반까지 한국의 외채는 상당했다. □
10. 한국은 1997년 금융 위기를 맞아 국제 통화 기금에서 빌린
    거금 302억 불을 만기 이전에 이미 다 갚았다. □

Related Reading

재벌이 문제인가?

　박정희의 제3공화국과 제4공화국 기간 동안에 (1961 – 1979) 정부는 '수출 장려 정책' 및 '중화학 공업 육성책' 등으로 상당한 외채를 일정 재벌 대기업에 치중하여 투자하였다. 이런 재벌을 위주로 한 정부의 계획 경제는 지난 30여 년 동안 놀라울 만한 성과를 보여 왔으며, 전 세계는 이를 격찬해 왔다고 해도 과언이 아니다.

　그런데 1997년에 닥친 금융 위기에 대한 많은 책임을 바로 이 재벌 위주의 경제 구조에 돌리고 있다. 과거에는 이런 재벌 위주의 경제의 성공에 찬사를 보내더니, 이제 바로 이 재벌 구조에 문제가 있다는 말이다. 이와 같은 이유에서 김대중 정부는 금융 구조를 개선함과 동시에 기존 재벌 기업의 구조 조정을 시도하기도 했다.

박덕수

제3공화국 the Third Republic (in Korea), 제4공화국 the Fourth Republic,
상당한 considerable (amount of), 일정 재벌 대기업 certain conglomerate groups,
투자하다 to invest, 을/를 위주로 한 -centered, 계획 경제 planned economy,
성과 achievement, 격찬하다 to praise highly, 고 해도 과언이 아니다 it is not
too much to say that, 책임을 . . . 에 돌리다 to place the responsibility on,
찬사 compliment, praise, 금융 구조 financial structure, 개선 improvement,
기존의 existing, 구조 조정 restructuring, 시도하다 to try, attempt

Discussion & Composition

1. 여러분이 살고 있는 나라의 주요 경제 정책은 무엇인 것 같아요? 토론해 봅시다.

2. Related Reading에서는 한 동안 한국의 경제 발전의 원인은 정부의 재벌을 위주로 한 계획 경제에 있다고 말했다. 그러나 1997년에 닥친 경제 위기의 원인이 또한 재벌의 경제 구조와 국가의 금융 구조에 있다고 지적하고 있다. 다시 말하면, 재벌이 그동안 국가 경제 발전의 원동력으로 칭찬 받아 오다가 1997년 경제 위기 이후에는 경제 위기의 원인으로 지적되고 있는 데, 이를 어떻게 해석해야 할까요?

3. 문제 2에서 제시한 아이러니를 어떻게 설명해야 하는지 연구해서 발표합시다. 주로
   한국 재벌 기업의 생성 과정, 재벌의 구조 및 재벌이 차지하는 한국 경제에서의 위
   치 등에 착안해서 연구해 봅시다. 위의 주제로 여러분이 한 연구 결과를 아래에 써
   보세요.

Lesson 17 Economic development in Korea

For half a century, since the division of the Korean peninsula, North and South Korea have traveled different paths. In this essay, we will look at economic development in South Korea.

In the latter half of the 1950s, South Korea put emphasis on its postwar recovery and carried out an ineffective policy of promoting import-substitution industries. Surprising economic achievements during the 1960s and 1970s raised South Korea's status from "undeveloped country" to that of "developing country." From 1962 to 1986, the average annual growth rate of South Korea's GNP was recorded as 8.3%. Negative growth GNP occurred only in two years: 1980 (-5.2%), the year following the 1979 oil shock; and 1997 (-6%), when the country was hit by a financial crisis.

Behind the brilliant economic development lay careful government planning. After seizing power in a military coup in 1961, the Pak Chŏng-hŭi regime began laying out a Five-Year Plan for economic development. While the regime was criticized for being a military dictatorship, no one can deny its contribution to Korea's economic development. Its leadership role was as follows: all national [domestic] financial institutions were nationalized, and lending institutions and overseas debt were all put under government control. After the 1960s, South Korea's main economic policy was the encouragement of exports. Domestic exporters were given the favor of unlimited exemption from tariffs and (also) capital loans from banks. This planned economy gave special favors to big companies successful in exports and to great financial conglomerates. This (policy) produced the great conglomerates Samsung, Daewoo, Hyundai, and Lucky Goldstar (now LG).

In addition to encouraging exports, the government also controlled agricultural products in order to protect the country's farmers from international competition, and employed a policy that kept Korea's agricultural market closed. Furthermore, the government supported industry and controlled labor power. It also oppressed labor union activities, which were very weak until the early 1980s.

From 1972, when the Third Five-Year Plan was begun, the government began spurring the growth of heavy-chemical industries. Its strategy was to furnish a heavy industrial base of oil refineries, petroleum chemistry, shipbuilding, automobiles, etc. But the light industry fields, like textiles, were sluggish, and an industrial imbalance was created.

After the economic slump owing to the 1979 oil shock, Korea's political situation was thrown into turmoil with the assassination of Pak Chŏng-hŭi. The following year, in 1980, the growth rate of the national GNP was -5.2%, the lowest in the country's history. As a remedy to this difficult situation, the Fifth Republic, under Chŏn Tu-hwan, incurred the most foreign debt ever. In 1979, the ratio between South Korea's foreign debt and its GNP was 33%, and in 1980 and 1981, that ratio was 45% and 49%, respectively. Fortunately, the world economy recovered; and so did Korea's economy, eventually returning to its pre-slump condition. The lure of the 1988 Seoul Olympic Games raised the status of Korea in international society. Afterwards, the country experienced continuous growth until the onset of the economic crisis of 1997.

There have been many analyses as to why the economic crisis of 1997 took place, but the primary cause seems to have been abnormal handling of foreign and domestic finance arising from ties between politicians and businessmen. Many hold the opinion that a continuing rise in foreign debt, and long-term investments based on short-term foreign loans, finally drove Korea to the exchange crisis. In the end, Korea, on the verge of financial bankruptcy, avoided catastrophe by taking out an enormous bailout loan of U.S. $30,200,000,000 from the International Monetary Fund (IMF) and the World Bank. Through the efforts of government and industry, the Bank of Korea repaid the full amount of the debt, originally due in May 2004, at the much earlier date of August 2001. But now, because its biggest trade partners, Japan and the U.S, are experiencing recessions, many people think that it will take much more time before Korea can return to its pre-crisis economy.

Park Duk-Soo

Related reading: Are the conglomerates a problem?

During Pak Chŏng-hŭi's Third and Fourth Republics (1961 – 1979), under the government's "export-encouragement" and "heavy-chemical industry strategy" policies, the government invested lots of foreign loans in a few designated conglomerates. The government's planned economy, centered around the conglomerates, has shown incredible results over the past 30 years. It is no exaggeration to say that the entire world praised it.

But much of the responsibility for the 1997 financial crisis surrounded the economic structure centered around the conglomerates. In the past, there was praise for the achievements of this conglomerate-centered economy, but now there are problems in the conglomerate structure. For such reasons the Kim Tae-jung government, while reforming the financial structure, has attempted to restructure the existing conglomerate industries.

Park Duk-Soo

제18과 남북 통일

(Lesson 18: Unification of North and South Korea)

Objectives

이 과에서는 한반도의 통일을 위하여 우리가 준비해야 할 것은 무엇이 있을까 알아보고 독일 통일이 주는 의미와 교훈을 배우고자 한다.

In this lesson we will consider how to prepare for the reunification of the Korean Peninsula, and what lessons can be learned from Germany's reunification.

Pre-reading questions

1. 한반도는 언제부터 남한 북한으로 나뉘어졌습니까?

2. 왜 이렇게 분단되었는지에 대해 아는 것이 있습니까?

3. 2000년 6월 15일의 남북한 정상 회담에 대해 들어 봤나요?

4. 남북 통일은 언제쯤 될 것으로 생각합니까?

5. 통일을 위해서 먼저 어떤 일들을 해야 할까요?

Gaining familiarity

1. 대한민국, 조선 민주주의 인민 공화국, 남한, 북한, 남조선, 북조선

2. 2000년 시드니 올림픽 개막식 남북한 선수단 공동 입장

3. 평양 학생 예술단

4. 동서독 기본 조약, 베를린 봉쇄 시기, 소련 및 동구 사회주의 붕괴

한반도 통일

1

한반도 통일을 위해 우리가 할 일들

통일을 위해 다음과 같은[18.1] 것들을 준비할 필요가 있겠다. 통일은 단순히 국토가 하나 되는 것만을 의미하지 않는다.[18.2] 정치적으로는 대립되었던 제도를 하나로 만드는 것이고, 경제적으로는 서로 도와 잘 살게 하려는 것이며, 사회적으로는 서로 달라진 민족 문화를 하나로 다시 탄생시키는 것이다. 또한 남북의 주민 모두가 마음속으로 '우리는 한 겨레'라고 느끼게 되는 상태가 바로 통일이다. 즉 통일은 모든 면에서 남북의 주민이 하나가 되고, 서로 이해하며 함께 잘 살기 위한 것이다. 그래서 통일을 하기 위해 남과 북은 서로 노력해야 하는 것이다. 어쨌든 통일이 되면 남한과 북한은 지금까지의 서로 다른 체제 때문에 많은 혼란과 갈등이 일어날 수도 있을 것이다. 따라서 우리는 통일이 되기 전에 준비해야 할 몇 가지 일들이 있다.

첫째, 남북한이 서로를 이해하는 태도가 절실하게 필요하다. 서로를 이해하지 못하는 상황에서 통일이 되면 큰 고통과 혼란이 나타날 것이다. 그래서 우리나라는 북한을 이해하려는 활동을 꾸준히 전개하여 왔다. 얼마 전 평양 학생 예술단이 서울에 와서 공연을 하고, 우리 농구단이 북한을 방문하여 경기를 한 것, 그리고 남한의 가수들이 평양에서 공연을 한 것 등은 바로 그러한 활동인 것이다.[18.3]

둘째, 서로 다른 문화와 언어에서 오는 이질감을 줄여야 한다. 서울에 온 귀순자들은 끝없는 차량 행렬에 놀라고 각종 간판에 어안이 벙벙해졌다고[18.4] 한다. 그들에겐 한자어도 어렵지만 외래어는 더욱 어려웠을 것이다. 반면, 평양을 방문한 남한 사람들은 전투적 용어가 넘쳐나는 정치적 간판에 질리고 낯선 억양과 용어 때문에 말을 알아듣는데 시간이 걸렸다고 한다. 그러므로 서로 다른 문화와 언어의 이질감을 줄이기 위하여 남한과 북한의 잦은 왕래가 필요하다.

셋째, 어려운 북한 경제가 나아져야 한다. 북한 경제의 주름살이 펴져야[18.5] 남한의 경제적 부담이 줄어들 것이다. 북한 경제가 나아지려면 무엇보다 북한 스스로의 개혁과 개방이 이루어지도록 도와 주어야 한다.[18.6] 그리고 우리 스스로도 노력하여 부강한 경제력을 키워야 할 것이다.

넷째, 전쟁을 억제하고 평화를 정착시켜 통일을 이루는 준비를 해 나가야 할 것이다. 통일을 너무 조급하게 생각하지 말고, 하나하나[18.7] 이루어 나가는 준비가 필요하다. 이산 가족의 만남, 남북 정상 회담, 예술, 문화, 체육, 학문 등의 교류를 통하여 평화적 분위기를 만들어 나가야 할 것이다.

노재완, 조선일보 <nk.chosun.com> 2001년 11월 26일

2
독일 통일의 의미와 시사점

독일은 우리 남북한과는 달리 분단 후 지방 정부 관리들의 묵인 하에[18.8] 민간 교류가 진행되어 왔었다 (물론 베를린 봉쇄 시기(1948-1949)에는 일시 중단). 1972년 동서독 기본 조약 체결 후 매년 수백만 명의 상호 방문 교류와 정부 수준의 경제 교류, 합작 투자 및 협력이 이루어졌다. 이것만 보아도[18.9] 서독과 동독은 서로가 노력했고, 그에 따른 결과물이 통일이었다고 볼 수 있는 것이다. 결국 교류를 통해, 동독이 서독의 자유주의적 자본주의 체제에 압도되어 통일이 된 것이다. 어떤 이들은 과거 독일 통일이 소련 및 동구 사회주의의 붕괴로 갑작스럽게 다가왔다고 하지만, 사실 그것은 그렇지 않았다. 위에서 언급했듯이[18.10] 분명 독일 통일은 끊임없는 노력과 이해를 통해서 이룩한 노력의 결실이다.

독일 통일의 근본적 원인을 찾아보면 다음과 같은 것이 있다.

첫째, 동독인들의 서독 경제에 대한 기대일 것이다. 당시 서독은 세계 최고의 경제 대국이었다. 이러한 경제적 여유로움이 동독인들로 하여금 통일을 원하게[18.11] 만든 요인이라 할 수 있겠다.

둘째, 앞서 제시했던 것과 같이[18.12] 동서독간의 대규모적인 인적 물적 교류 협력일 것이다. 이것은 서로를 알게 하는 원동력이 됐고, 실질적으로 서로가 하나가 되는 것이 훨씬 더 유리하다는 인식을 심어 주게 됐던 것이다.

셋째, 서독 정부의 탈이데올로기적 경제 외교일 것이다. 다시 말하면[18.13] 서독은 통일을 염두에 두고 계속해서 인도적 지원을 아끼지 않았다는 점이다.

넷째, 독일 통일은 두 독일 간의 합의로만 이루어진 것은 아니다. 독일의 분단 역시 한반도 분단과 같이 연합군의 분할 통치로 인해 발생된 것이기[18.14] 때문에 이러한 열강들의 동의를 얻어야만 했던 것이다. 당시 서독의 콜 총리는 미국, 소련, 영국, 프랑스 등과 외교적 협상을 통해 독일 통일의 공식적 지지를 얻어냈다. 여기에는 서독의 소련에 대한 파격적 선심 외교, 즉 경제적 지원이 가장 힘이 컸던 것으로 보여진다.

이상에서 알 수 있는 것과 같이[18.15] 한반도의 통일도 갑자기 찾아오지는 않을 것이다. 물론 독일처럼 언젠가는 통일이 되겠지만, 통일의 기회가 온다 해도[8.16] 그것을 잡을 수 있는 여력이 있어야 그런 기회를 잡을 수 있는 것이다.

<조선일보> 통일로 가는 길

New Words

각종 every kind, every variety ▷각종 신문 all kinds of newspapers
간판 signboard
갈등 complication, conflict, discord, trouble
갑작스럽게 suddenly
개방 opening ▷개방 사회 open society
개혁 reform, reformation, innovation ▷많은 사람들이 교육 제도의 개혁을 요구한다.
　　Many request a reform in the educational system.
결과물 resulting product, outcome
결실 fruit, fruition, result
경제 economy. 경제 교류 economic exchange. 경제 대국 major economic power.
　　경제적으로 economically
계속해서 continually, continuously
고통 pain, agony
공식적 official
공연 performance ▷연극 공연 performance of a play

관리 government officials

교류 interchange ▷문화 교류 cultural exchange

국토 national territory or land

귀순자 defector ▷많은 북한을 탈출한 귀순자들이 남한에 들어오고 있다. Many
    defectors who escaped from North Korea are coming into South Korea.

근본적 fundamental

기대 expectation

기회 opportunity

꾸준히 steadily, constantly

끊임없는 endless ▷끊임없는 노력이 그의 성공 비결이었다. Endless effort was the
    secret of his success.

끝없는 endless ▷끝없는 노력의 대가 fruit of endless effort

나아지다 to become better, get better ▷그의 건강이 많이 나아졌다. His health got
    much better.

낯선 unfamiliar, strange, unknown ▷낯선 얼굴 unfamiliar face [person]

넘쳐나다 to overflow ▷기운이 넘쳐나다 to be full of vigor, be in high spirits

놀라다 to be surprised, be alarmed

농구단 basketball team

다가오다 to approach, come near ▷다가오는 새해에는 담배를 끊어야지. I should
    quit smoking in the coming year.

단순히 simply, merely

달라지다 to become different, change ▷그는 몰라보게 달라졌다. He has changed
    beyond recognition.

대규모적인 on a large [grand] scale

대립되다 to be opposed to, be confronted with (each other). 대립하다 to oppose,
    confront ▷남북한은 아직도 군사적으로 대립하고 있다. North and South Korea
    are still confronting each other in a military sense.

동구 사회주의 the socialism of Eastern Europe

동독 East Germany

동서독 기본 조약 the basic treaty between East and West Germany

동의 consent, assent ▷동의를 얻다 to gain someone's consent

면 aspect, face ▷모든 면에서 in every aspect

무엇보다 more than anything else

물론 (as a matter) of course

물적 physical, material. 물적 증거 physical evidence. 물적 자원 material resource

민간 교류 civilian exchange

바로 very, just, true ▷이것이 바로 남북한이 가야 할 길이다. This is the very way
    North and South Korea should go.

방문 교류 visits and exchanges

벌어지다 to happen, occur ▷큰 사고가 벌어졌다. A big accident occurred.

봉쇄 시기 blockade period, closing period

부강하다 to be rich and strong ▷부강한 나라 rich and powerful country

부담 burden, load, charge, responsibility. 부담스럽다 to be burdensome ▷남에게 너무 큰 부담을 주지는 말아라. Do not lay a heavy burden on others.

분단 division, separation ▷한반도의 분단 the division of the Korean Peninsula

분명 clearly, obviously

분위기 atmosphere, ambience ▷나는 그 식당의 조용한 분위기를 좋아한다. I like the quiet atmosphere in that restaurant.

분할 통치 rule by partition, divide and rule ▷1945년부터 약 3년 동안 남북은 각각 미군과 소련군의 분할 통치하에 있었다. After 1945, for about three years, the South and the North were under the divided rule of American and Soviet troops, respectively.

붕괴 collapse, fall, breakdown, crumbling ▷광산의 갱도가 붕괴되었다. The mine roof caved in.

사회적으로 socially

상태 form, condition, state

상호 mutual ▷상호 방문 교류 mutual visits and exchanges

상황 condition, aspect

서독 West Germany

소련 Soviet Union (Union of Soviet Socialist Republics)

시사점 suggestions, lessons ▷이 사건이 우리에게 주는 시사점이 많다. This case gives us many lessons.

실질적으로 practically

아끼다 to be economical, be sparing ▷그는 사업에 돈을 아끼지 않았다. He didn't spare money in his business.

압도되다 to be overwhelmed ▷나는 엄숙한 분위기에 압도되었다. I was overwhelmed by the solemn atmosphere.

어안이 벙벙하다 to be dumbfounded, amazed, struck dumb

어쨌든 anyhow, anyway ▷어쨌든, 시간이 없으니 빨리 갑시다. Anyway, since there is not much time let's go quickly.

억양 intonation

억제하다 to suppress, repress, restrain, constrain ▷가능하면 감정을 억제하라. If possible, suppress your emotions.

여력 remaining power or financial ability ▷여력이 있으면 어려운 이웃을 도와라. If you have spare money, help (your) poor neighbors.

여유로움 surplus, richness; complacency ▷삶의 여유로움 richness of life

연합군 Allied Forces

열강 great powers, superpowers

염두 mind, thought ▷염두에 두다 to keep (something) in mind

예술단 performing arts group, performance group

왕래 journey, traffic, interaction ▷요즘 남북한 간에 잦은 왕래가 있다. Nowadays, there are frequent interactions between North and South Korea.

외교적(인) diplomatic

외래어 loanwords, words of foreign origin

요인 cause, reason

용어 terminology, term

원동력 motive power, driving force

유리하다 to be profitable, advantageous, favorable ▷상황이 우리에게 유리하다. The situation is favorable to us.

이데올로기 ideology

이산 가족 separated families

이질감 sense [feeling] of difference [disparateness]

인도적 humane, humanitarian ▷인도적 지원 humanitarian aid [support]

인식 cognition, recognition, perception, knowledge, impression ▷그녀는 그에게 좋은 인식을 심어 주었다. She made a good impression on him.

인적 (being) human. 인적 자원 human resource ▷인적 물적 교류 협력 personnel and material exchange and cooperation

일시 once, one time

일어나다 to happen, occur, rise

자본주의 capitalism

자유주의적 liberal

잦다 to be frequent, often ▷겨울에는 화재가 잦다. Fires are frequent in wintertime.

전개하다 to unfold, develop, spread out, unroll ▷전개되다 to be unfolded, developed ▷이 사건은 앞으로 어떻게 전개될까? What will be the future developments of this affair?

전쟁 war

전투적 combat, military

절실하게 desperately, urgently

정상 회담 summit meeting

정착시키다 to make (something) settle down, make (something) fixed ▷한국에 민주주의를 정착시킨지 50년이 지났다. It has been over fifty years since democracy was settled down in Korea.

정치적으로 politically

제도 system, institution, organization

제시하다 to present, show ▷나는 사장에게 대안을 제시했다. I presented an
    alternative plan to the president.
조급하게 hastily
주름살 wrinkles (on skin)
준비하다 to prepare
줄이다 to reduce, diminish, lessen, decrease
중단 interruption, stopping, breaking off
즉 in other words
지방 정부 local government
지지 support, upholding, backing ▷우리는 이에 대한 정부의 공식적 지지를
    얻어냈다. We obtained official support from the government.
진행되다 to proceed, progress
질리다 to become disgusted with, get sick of, become fed up with ▷나는 이제
    미역국에 질렸다. I am sick and tired of seaweed soup.
차량 행렬 procession of cars
체결 conclusion (of an agreement or treaty) ▷평화 조약의 체결 conclusion of a
    peace treaty
키우다 to grow, bring up
탄생시키다 to make (something) be born
탈- de-, anti-, withdrawal from ▷탈색 decoloration, 탈당 withdrawal from a
    political party, 탈공산주의 anti-communism
태도 behavior, manner
통일 unification
파격적 exceptional, unprecedented, extraordinary, special, abnormal, irregular,
    ▷파격적 가격 special price ▷파격적 승진 exceptional promotion ▷파격적
    선심 외교 extraordinarily generous diplomacy (the use of patronage for
    political advantage)
평화 peace
하나하나 one by one
한 겨레 one people
한자어 Sino-Korean words, words in Chinese characters
합의 agreement, consent
합작 투자 joint investment
협상 negotiation
혼란 confusion, disorder, disarrangement
활동 activity, motion

Useful Expressions

1. **다음과 같은** (like) the following
   통일을 위해 다음과 같은 것들을 준비를 해야 하겠다.
   For unification we have to make the following preparations.
   다음과 같은 순서로 문제를 해결합시다.
   Let's solve the problem in the following order.

2. **~만을 의미하지 않는다** do not only mean ~; mean more than ~
   통일은 단순히 국토가 하나 되는 것만을 의미하지 않는다.
   Unification does not only mean the national territory becoming
   one.
   결혼은 두 사람이 한 집에서 함께 사는 것만을 의미하지 않는다.
   Marriage means more than two people living together in a house.

3. **~에서 오는** coming [originating] from ~
   서로 다른 문화와 언어에서 오는 이질감을 줄여야 한다.
   The sense of difference which comes from different cultures and
   languages should be reduced.
   사고 방식이 다른 데에서 오는 의견 차이를 줄여야 한다.
   The opinion gap which comes from different ways of thinking should
   be reduced.

4. **어안이 벙벙하다** be amazed; be struck dumb
   대도시에 오니까 어안이 벙벙하다.
   As I come to a big city, I am amazed.
   그 소식을 듣고 그는 잠시 어안이 벙벙했다.
   The news struck him speechless for a while.

5. **~의 주름살이 펴져야 한다** should get better ~
   북한 경제의 주름살이 펴져야 한다.
   North Korea's economy should be getting better.
   우리집 가계의 주름살이 펴져야 하겠다.
   My household budget should be getting better.

6. **~도록 도와 주다** help someone do ~
   나는 철수가 숙제를 빨리 끝내도록 도와 주었다.
   I helped Chŏlsu finish his homework.

북한의 개혁과 개방이 이루어지도록 도와 주어야 한다.

We need to help North Korea achieve reform and openness.

7. **하나하나**   one by one; step-by-step

가구를 하나하나 사 가는 것은 재미있다.

It is fun to buy furniture piece by piece.

통일을 조급하게 생각하지 말고, 하나하나 이루어 나가는 준비가 필요하다.

Not being in a hurry for unification, we need to prepare to achieve things step-by-step.

8. **~의 묵인 하에**   under the auspices of ~; with ~'s connivance

독일에서는 지방 정부 관리들의 묵인 하에 민간 교류가 진행되어 왔었다.

In Germany, civilian exchanges have been going on under the auspices of local government officials.

경찰의 묵인 하에 불법적인 마약 매매가 있어 왔다.

With the silent approval of the police, sales of illegal drugs have been going on.

9. **~만 보아도**   looking at ~ alone

이것만 보았을 때도 독일 통일은 노력의 결과물이었다는 것을 알 수 있다.

Looking at this alone, we can tell that German unification was a result of effort.

이것 하나만 보아도 그가 얼마나 착한지 알 수 있다.

Even looking at this alone, we know how good he is.

10. **위에서 [앞에서] 언급했듯이**   as I mentioned above [before]

위에서 언급했듯이 독일 통일은 끊임없는 노력의 결실이었다.

As I mentioned above, German unification was the fruit of endless effort.

앞에서 언급했듯이 통일은 빨리 올 것 같지 않다.

As I mentioned before, unification won't come soon.

11. **A(으)로 하여금 ~게 하다**   make A do ~

서독의 경제적 여유로움이 동독인들로 하여금 흡수 통일을 원하게 했다.

The economic prosperity of West Germany made East Germans want to have unification by absorption.

우리는 북한의 지도자들로 하여금 시장 경제를 추구하도록 도와야 한다.

We need to help North Korean leaders pursue an open-market economy.

12. **앞서 제시했던 것과 같이** as I showed [presented] earlier

　　앞서 제시했던 것과 같이 동서독 간에는 대규모적인 교류 협력이 있었다.
　　　As I showed earlier, there was large-scale exchange and cooperation
　　　between East and West Germany.
　　앞서 제시했던 것과 같이 남북한도 탈이데올로기적 교류 협력을 추구해야 한다.
　　　As I indicated earlier, North and South Korea should pursue exchange and
　　　cooperation beyond their ideological differences.

13. **다시 말하면** in other words

　　다시 말하면 통일을 염두에 두고 인도적 지원을 아끼지 않았다는 것이다.
　　　In other words, keeping unification in mind, they were preparing
　　　humanitarian aid.
　　다시 말하면 우리도 북한에 인도적 식량 지원을 아끼지 말아야 한다.
　　　In other words, we should generously give humanitarian food aid to North
　　　Korea.

14. **~(으)로 인해 발생된 것** a thing caused by ~; an event that occurred due to

　　북한의 식량난은 지난 몇 년간의 홍수로 인해 발생된 것이라고 한다.
　　　They said that the food crisis in North Korea occurred due to flooding
　　　they had had for the last several years.
　　9월 11일의 뉴욕 WTC 건물의 파괴는 테러리스트로 인해 발생된 것이었다.
　　　The destruction of New York's World Trade Center on September 11 was
　　　caused by terrorists.

15. **이상에서 알 수 있는 것과 같이** as we can learn from the above (discussion)

　　이상에서 알 수 있는 것과 같이 한반도의 통일도 갑자기 찾아오지는 않을
　　것이다.
　　　As we can learn from the above discussion, the unification of the Korean
　　　Peninsula won't come suddenly.
　　이상에서 알 수 있는 것과 같이 통일을 위해서는 이를 준비하는 노력이
　　필요하다.
　　　As we can learn from the above discussion, we need to make an effort to
　　　prepare for it.

16. **~다/라 해도** even if (one says that) ~

　　아무리 통일의 기회가 온다 해도 그것을 잡을 수 있는 여력이 있어야 그런
　　기회를 잡을 수 있는 것이다.
　　　Even if a chance for unification comes, we will be able to grasp the
　　　chance only if we have enough power to hold.

네가 날 죽인다 해도 난 눈 하나 깜짝 안 한다.

Even if you say that you will kill me, I won't be scared at all.

Exercises

1. 관련된 것들끼리 연결하여 문장을 만들어 보세요.

(1) 인식을　　　•　　　• 잡아라.

(2) 활동을　　　•　　　• 전개하였다.

(3) 지원을　　　•　　　• 아끼지 않았다.

(4) 동의를　　　•　　　• 심어 주었다.

(5) 기회를　　　•　　　• 얻었다.

_____

_____

_____

_____

_____

2. 아래의 설명과 맞는 단어나 표현을 보기에서 찾아 쓰세요.

> 보기:　합작 투자, 이산 가족, 인적 물적 교류, 이질감, 외래어

(1) 서로 다르게 느끼는 느낌: _____

(2) (남한과 북한에) 떨어져 사는 가족: _____

(3) 사람과 물건이 오고가는 것: _____

(4) 외국어에서 온 한국어에서 쓰는 단어: _____

(5) 하나 이상의 회사나 개인이 돈을 내서 사업을 함: _____

3. 보기에서 적당한 말을 골라 빈칸을 채우세요.

> 보기: 단순히, 바로, 어쨌든, 끝없는, 하나하나, 갑자기, 훨씬

(1) ＿＿＿＿＿＿＿＿ 그만 싸우고 악수해라.

(2) 남북한의 통일은 ＿＿＿＿＿＿＿＿ 찾아오지 않을 것이다.

(3) 일을 너무 조급하게 서두르지 말고, ＿＿＿＿＿＿＿＿ 풀어 나가자.

(4) 출퇴근 시간에는 ＿＿＿＿＿＿＿＿ 자동차 행렬을 볼 수 있다.

(5) 남북의 주민 모두가 마음속으로 '우리는 한 겨레'라고 느끼게 되는 상태가
＿＿＿＿＿＿＿＿ 통일이다.

(6) 결혼은 ＿＿＿＿＿＿＿＿ 두 사람이 한 집에 사는 것만을 의미하지 않는다.

(7) 이것보다 저것이 ＿＿＿＿＿＿＿＿ 더 좋아 보인다.

4. 밑줄 친 말과 가장 비슷한 단어나 표현을 보기에서 고르세요.

(1) 통일은 단순히 국토가 하나 되는 것만을 <u>의미하지</u> 않는다.
   a. 결정하지   b. 뜻하지
   c. 상징하지   d. 말하지

(2) 즉 통일은 모든 면에서 남북의 주민이 하나가 되고, 서로 이해하며 함께
   살기 위한 것이다.
   a. 다시 말하면   b. 또한
   c. 그리고   d. 첫째

(3) <u>따라서</u> 우리는 통일이 되기 전에 준비해야 할 몇 가지 일들이 있다.
   a. 다음과 같이   b. 따라와서
   c. 그래서   d. 그러므로

(4) 낯선 억양과 용어 때문에 말을 <u>알아듣는데</u> 시간이 걸렸다고 한다.
   a. 아는데   b. 하는데
   c. 이해하는데   d. 설득하는데

(5) 스테이크를 너무 먹었더니 <u>질린다</u>.
    a. 배가 부르다   b. 싫증난다
    c. 졸립다   d. 찔린다

(6) 남한과 북한의 잦은 <u>왕래</u>가 필요하다.
    a. 교통   b. 교류
    c. 왕복   d. 외교

(7) 부모님이 이일을 알았지만 <u>묵인했다</u>.
    a. 인정했다   b. 천천히
    c. 부인했다   d. 급하게

(8) <u>이것만 보아도</u> 그가 얼마나 친절한 사람인지 알 수 있다.
    a. 이것만 봤지만   b. 이것만 보았을 때도
    c. 이것만 봤어도   d. 이것만 보니까

(9) <u>위에서 언급했듯이</u> 독일의 통일은 끊임없는 노력의 결실이다.
    a. 위에서 말했듯이   b. 위에서 봤듯이
    c. 위에서 봤어도   d. 위에서 들었듯이

(10) <u>다시 말하면</u> 통일을 염두에 두고 인도적인 지원을 아끼지 않았다는 점이다.
    a. 다시 쓰자면   b. 즉
    c. 또 다시   d. 또

5. 보기와 같이 주어진 단어가 들어가는 표현을 3개 이상 써 보세요.

보기: [국토] 한국 국토, 미국 국토, 일본 국토

(1) 대립: _____

(2) 체제: _____

(3) 부담: _____

(4) 붕괴: _____

(5) 인식: _____

(6) 지지: _____

6. 주어진 단어나 표현을 이용하여 문장을 만드세요.

    (1) 다음과 같은

      _____

    (2) ~만을 의미하지 않는다

      _____

    (3) ~에서 오는 ~

      _____

    (4) 어안이 벙벙하다

      _____

    (5) ~도록 도와 주다

      _____

    (6) ~하나하나

      _____

    (7) ~과는 달리

      _____

    (8) ~의 묵인 하에

      _____

    (9) ~만 보아도

      _____

    (10) 위에서/앞에서 언급했듯이

      _____

    (11) ~로 하여금 ~게 하다

      _____

    (12) 앞서 제시했던 것과 같이

      _____

    (13) 다시 말하면

      _____

    (14) ~(으)로 인해 발생된 것

      _____

    (15) 이상에서 알 수 있는 것과 같이

      _____

    (16) ~이/가 ~한다 해도

      _____

Comprehension Questions

I. Overall comprehension

1. 본문에 제시된 남북 통일을 위해서 우리가 할 일 4가지를 영어로 요약해 보세요.

_____

_____

2. 분단 후 동서독의 상황이 남북한과 다른 점은 무엇이었습니까?

_____

_____

3. 본문에서 제시하는 독일 통일의 근본적 원인 4 가지를 영어로 요약해 보세요.

_____

_____

II. Finding details
본문의 글과 내용이 일치하면 □에 ∨ 표를 하세요.

1. 통일은 국토가 하나 되는 것만을 의미한다.   □
2. 남북한은 서로 이해하려는 태도가 필요하다.   □
3. 남북한은 다른 문화와 용어에서 오는 이질감을 줄이기 위해 잦은
   왕래가 필요하다.   □
4. 북한이 경제적으로 나아지어야 통일 후 남한의 경제적 부담이 줄어든다. □
5. 통일은 조급하게 생각할 문제이다.   □
6. 동서독은 분단 후 소규모의 교류 협력이 있었다.   □
7. 독일의 통일은 소련 및 동구 사회주의 붕괴로 갑작스럽게 왔다.   □
8. 서독의 경제적 여유로움이 동독인들이 통일을 원하게 만들었다.   □
9. 서독 정부의 탈이데올로기적 경제 외교는 통일에 도움이 되지 않았다. □
10. 독일의 분단도 연합군의 분할 통치로 인해 발생됐다.   □
11. 독일은 통일에 대한 열강들의 동의를 얻어야만 했다.   □
12. 한반도의 통일은 갑자기 찾아 올 것이다.   □

Related Reading

남북한 통일 방안의 차이점

남북한은 서로 다른 통일 방안을 내세우고 있다. 남한은 '민족 공동체 통일 방안'을 제시하고 있다. 남한의 통일 방안은 7천만 민족이 다 함께 행복하게 잘 살기 위하여 남북이 함께 단계적인 노력을 통해 통일을 완성해 나갈 것을 제시하고 있다. 남북은 서로 다른 체제로 나뉘어 50여 년 동안 단절된 생활을 해 왔기 때문에 제도가 다르고, 살아가는 방법과 사물을 보고 느끼는 감정까지도 달라져 있다. 남북이 당장 함께 어우러져 살아가기에는 장애가 많음을 인정하고, 함께 살 수 있는 분위기를 개선하기 위한 노력으로부터 통일에 접근해 가자는 것이다. 남한은 민족 공동체 통일 방안에서 통일을 3단계로 나누어 제시하고 있다.

1단계는 화해 협력의 단계이다. 오랫동안 서로 다른 환경 속에서 생활한 탓에 믿지 못하게 되었던 과거를 이겨내고 남북이 화해하며 신뢰를 회복하는 일이 중요하다. 여러 방면의 교류와 협력을 통해서 민족 전체의 복지와 이익을 향상시키는 단계이다. 정치적 화해, 군사적 신뢰 관계 형성, 경제·사회·문화적 교류와 협력을 통해 민족의 이질감을 극복하는 데 뜻이 있다.

2단계는 남북 연합의 단계이다. 화해 협력의 단계에서 이루어진 서로에 대한 신뢰를 바탕으로 남북 간의 평화 정착을 이루는 과정이다. 남북 연합 단계에서는 정치적 통합을 이루기 위해 남북한이 연합하여 여러 가지 공동 기구들을 창설하게 된다. 이들 공동 기구에서 국가 통합, 즉 정치와 제도의 통합을 위한 동질성 회복의 여러 가지 방법이 논의되고 결정되는 과정이다.

3단계는 통일 국가의 완성이다. 한 민족, 한 국가의 통일 국가를 완성하는 단계이다. 남북 연합의 단계에서 제정한 통일 헌법에 따라 남북한 자유 총선거를 실시하여 통일 국회를 구성하고, 모두가 다 함께 잘 살게 되는 통일 정부를 수립하는 과정이다.

북한이 제시하고 있는 통일 방안은 '고려 연방제 통일 방안'이다. 북한은 '통일 방안'에서 "남한과 북한이 각각 상대방의 사상과 제도를 그대로 두고, 남북이 동등하게 참가하는 통일 정부를 세우자"고 주장하고 있다. 남북한의 현 정부를 지역 정부로 두고, '고려 민주주의 연방 공화국'이라는 연방 정부를 세우자는 것이다.

북한은 연방 정부를 구성하기 전에 남한에서 해결되어야 할 조건을 제시하고 있다. 그 조건은 남한에서 미군을 철수시켜야 하고, 공산주의자들의 자유로운 활동을 보장하고, 공산주의자들도 정치에 참여할 수 있는 정권이 허용되어야 한다는 것이다. 연방 정부는 정치적, 군사적으로 외국과의 동맹 등을 맺지 않는 중립 국가가 되어야 한다고 주장하고 있다.

북한의 '고려 연방제 통일 방안'에는 통일의 중간 과정에 대한 구체적인 설명이 없다. 다만, 통일 국가 수립 절차로서 민족 통일 정치 협상 회의 개최, 통일 방안 협의 결정, 고려 민주 연방 공화국 선포를 제시하고 있다. 통일을 실현함에 있어서는 통일이라는 목표 달성 못지않게 목표를 달성하는 과정과 방법이 중요하다. 그러나 북한은 통일을 달성하는 방법에 있어 민족 전체의 의사가 반영되는 민주적인 총선거 방식이 아닌 소수가 참여하는 '정치 협상'을 통해 달성하려 한다.

우리는 남북의 통일 방안을 잘 살펴보고 비교하여, 민족을 위한 진정한 통일의 방법을 생각해 보아야 하겠다.

조선일보, <nk.chosun.com> 남북한 통일 방안의 차이점은 뭔가요?

통일 방안 unification policy, 민족 공동체 national community, 단계적인 gradual, 완성하다 to complete, accomplish, 사물 objects, things, 감정 feeling, emotion, 당장 immediately, that particular time, 어우러지다 to join together, to be harmonized, 장애 obstacles, hindrance, 개선하다 to improve, 접근하다 to be near, to approach, 화해 협력 reconciliation and cooperation, 탓 fault, 이겨내다 to win, overcome, 신뢰 trust, 회복하다 to recover, 복지 welfare, 이익 benefit, 향상시키다 to make something improve [progress], 극복하다 to overcome, 연합 union, ~을/를 바탕으로 on the basis of ~, 평화 정착 peace settlement, 통합 union, 공동 기구 joint organization, 창설하다 to establish, set up (an organization), 동질성 회복 recovery of homogeneity, 제정하다 to establish, formulate (a law), 헌법 constitution, 총선거 nationwide election, 국회 national assembly, 수립하다 to establish (a government), 사상 ideology, thought, 동등하게 equally, 공산당 Communist Party, 연방 정부 federal government, 철수시키다 to have something withdraw, 보장하다 to guarantee, secure, ensure, 참여하다 to participate, 정권 regime, 동맹 alliance, 중립 국가 neutral nation, 중간 과제 intermediate task, 구체적인 concrete, 절차 step, procedure, 정치 협상 political negotiation, 개최 holding/opening (a meeting), 선포 declaration, 목표 달성 achievement of the aim, 살피다 to investigate, examine, 진정한 real, true

---

Discussion & Composition

1. 남북한의 화해와 신뢰 회복을 위해 우리가 쉽게 할 수 있는 민간 차원의 교류 협력에는 어떤 것들이 있을까요? 한두 가지 씩 말해 보세요.

2. 남북한 언어의 이질성을 보여 주는 예를 찾아봅시다. 인터넷 웹사이트
   <nk.chosun.com>에서 북한 말 배우기를 통해 남한 말과 다른 표현을 다섯 가지씩
   찾아 수업 시간에 발표하세요.

3. 윗글의 주장과는 달리 어떤 사람들은 북한이 경제적으로 나아지면 통일이 더욱
   어려워 질 것이라고 주장하기도 합니다. 여러분은 이에 대해 어떻게 생각하세요?
   이에 관한 여러분의 생각을 아래에 써 보세요.

_____

_____

_____

_____

_____

_____

_____

_____

_____

_____

_____

_____

_____

_____

_____

_____

_____

_____

Lesson 18 Unification of North and South Korea

Unification of the peninsula
1. What we should do for the unification of the peninsula

The following are necessary preparations we must make for Korean unification. Unification does not mean simply unifying a piece of land. Politically, it means unifying (two) conflicting systems. Economically, it means living in prosperity and in cooperation. Socially, it means re-forming a single national culture from two divergent ones. Furthermore, unification also means that all the citizens of the North and South feel in their hearts, "We are one people." In short, unification is North and South becoming one in every aspect, with mutual understanding and for co-prosperity. So North and South Korea must make efforts toward their unification. Nonetheless, if unification comes about, much confusion and struggle may arise because of the North's and South's differing systems. So there are several things we must do before unification.

The first thing that is desperately necessary is for the North and the South to have an understanding attitude in respect to each other. If they do not understand each other, unification may bring great pain and confusion. Accordingly, South Korea has steadily fostered activities aimed at trying to understand North Korea. For example, not long ago, the Pyongyang Student Arts Group came to Seoul to perform, and our basketball team visited North Korea to compete, South Korean singers held a concert in Pyongyang, etc.

Second, feelings of alienation arising from our different cultures and language must be curtailed. It is said that North Korean defectors coming to Seoul are astonished at the sight of long lines of automobiles and dumbstruck at the varieties (*lit.,* at each kind) of advertising signs. Chinese words are difficult for them, and foreign words even more so. It is also said that South Koreans who visited Pyongyang were disgusted at the political signs overflowing with militant terminology and required lots of time to understand (the North Koreans) because of (their) unfamiliar intonation and vocabulary. So, frequent intercommunication between the two Koreas is necessary in order to reduce the feelings of unfamiliarity between the different cultures and languages.

Third, North Korea's burdened economy must improve. Their problems [wrinkles] must be resolved [ironed out] to lessen the economic burden on South Korea. If the North Korean economy is to improve, first of all we must help them to reform themselves and to open up. And we, too, must make efforts to cultivate a strong economy of our own.

Fourth, we must prepare for unification by limiting war and ensuring peace. What is necessary is not to think hastily of unification, but to prepare for each step of the way. We must create a peaceful atmosphere through reunions of separated families, normalization talks between the North and the South, and exchanges in the arts, culture, gymnastics, and scholarship.

No Chae-an, *Chosun Daily,* Nov. 26, 2001

2. German unification: Meanings and lessons

Germany differs from Korea in that after its national division, civilian exchanges were carried out with the consent of regional government officials. (Of course, they were suspended for a time during the Berlin blockade period (1948 – 1949)). After the conclusion of the fundamental treaty between East and West Germany in 1972, every year there were achieved tens of thousands of reciprocal exchange visits, government-level economic exchanges, joint investments, and other examples of cooperation. These examples clearly show that West and East Germany made reciprocal efforts that (ultimately) resulted in unification. Finally, unification resulted when, through their exchanges, East Germany was overwhelmed by West Germany's liberal capitalism. Some people have said that German unification in the past came about suddenly as a result of the collapse of the Soviet Union and Eastern Europe, but that is not the case. As mentioned above, Germany's unification was the fruit of efforts achieved through tireless effort and understanding.

The basic causes of Germany's unification are as follows.

First was the East German people's expectations of the West German economy. At the time, West Germany was the greatest economic power in the world. Its economic surplus, it can be said, was one reason the East Germans longed for unification.

Second, as shown above, there was cooperation in (realizing) large-scale personal and material exchanges between East and West Germany. This became a driving force for (gaining) knowledge about each other, and really instilled (into the people) a consciousness that unification would be more advantageous.

Third was West Germany's anti-ideological economic diplomacy. Again, keeping unification in mind, West Germany was never sparing in its continuous provisions of humanitarian aid.

Fourth, German unification was not realized only by agreement between the two Germanies. Because Germany's division, like that of the Korean peninsula, came about because of partition by the Allied Forces, they also needed the agreement of the Great Powers. The then prime minister, Kohl [Helmut], managed to get formal support for German's unification through diplomatic negotiations with America, the Soviet Union, Great Britain, France, etc. Here, West Germany's extraordinarily generous diplomacy with the Soviet Union—meaning its economic assistance—had the greatest impact.

As can be understood from the above, the unification of the Korean Peninsula will not come suddenly. Of course, like Germany, Korea will be unified someday, but when the opportunity comes, we will be able to grasp it only if we have the reserve strength to do so.

Chosun Daily <nkchosun.com>, The Road to Unification

Related reading: Differences in the unification plans of North and South Korea

The North and the South both propose different plans for unification. The South proposes a "National Community Plan for Unification." The South's unification plan is for the North and South to achieve unification through gradual effort, in order that the 70,000,000 Korean people can live together happily and prosperously. Because the North and South have been divided into different systems and have lived separated for over 50 years, their institutions, way of life, and even the way they look and feel about things, are different. Recognizing that presently there are many obstacles to unifying, the South begins its approach to unification with efforts to improve the atmosphere of North–South coexistence. In its "National Community Plan for Unification," South Korea proposes a unification plan divided into three stages.

The first stage is that of reconciliation and cooperation. Due to having lived for a long time in different environments, it is important to overcome our distrustful past, to reconcile, and to recover faith in one another. This stage is meant to improve the welfare and circumstances of all the people through exchange and cooperation in many areas. It is significant as a way to overcome the sense of disparity felt by the people through political reconciliation, the formation of trustful military ties, economic, social, and cultural exchange, and cooperation.

The second stage is the union of North and South. In this stage, a peace settlement between the two sides will be realized, based on the mutual trust gained from stage one. In this stage, the North and South will come together and establish many joint organizations for the purpose of bringing about political unity.

The process will involve using joint organizations to discuss and make resolutions about different methods for the recovery of homogeneity leading to unity of the state, both politically and institutionally.

The third stage is the completed, unified state: one people, one nation. In this stage, in accordance with the constitution formulated in stage two, we will carry out free nationwide elections in North and South Korea, form a unified national assembly, and establish a unified government so that all may live together in prosperity.

The unification plan proposed by North Korea is the "Koryŏ Federation Unification Plan." In its plan, North Korea maintains that "the North and South will each keep their own respective ideals and institutions as they are, and establish a unified government in which North and South can participate equally." The present governments of the North and South would function as regional governments, on which a federal government called a "Koryŏ Democratic Federated Republic" would be set up.

North Korea proposes conditions for South Korea that must be solved before a federated government can be formed. Those conditions are: to make the American Army withdraw; to guarantee the free activities of Communists; and to allow a regime in which the Communist Party can participate. They assert that the federated government must be a neutral state without political or economic ties to foreign countries.

In the North's "Koryŏ Federation Unification Plan," there is no concrete explanation about any intermediate process for unification. But as a procedure for the establishment of a unified nation, the North proposes holding political negotiations for national unification; negotiation for and agreement on unification plans; and the declaration of a Koryŏ People's Federated Republic. Just as important as accomplishing the goal of unification is the process and methods by which unification is to be achieved. In its plan, the North wishes to achieve unification through "political negotiations" participated in by a few, not by means of democratic general elections reflecting the intentions of the entire people.

We must look carefully at the plans for North-South unification, compare them, and think of a real unification method for the Korean people.

Chosun Daily <nkchosun.com> Homework Classroom, The Road to Unification, "What are the differences between the unification plans of the North and South?"

제19과 한국인의 이름

(Lesson 19: Korean Names)

Objectives

이 과에서는 한국인의 이름을 살펴보고 각 성씨와 이름에 대한 유래나 변천 과정을 알아본다. 한국 이름 문화에 대한 이해를 넓히고 한국어로 된 자기 자신의 이름을 지어 보자.

This chapter looks at the origins and development of Korean personal names and surnames. You will be able to better understand this aspect of Korean culture and try to create your own name in Korean.

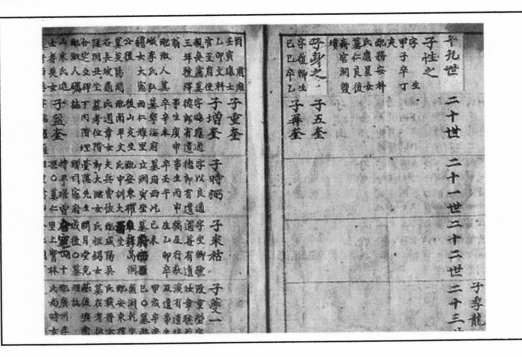

Pre-reading questions

1. 여러분은 자기 이름에 대해서 만족하는 편입니까?

2. 누가 여러분의 이름(first name)을 지었습니까?

3. 여러분의 이름에 특별한 사연이나 의미가 담겨져 있습니까?

4. 본인의 이름을 바꾸게 된다면 무엇으로 바꾸고 싶으며 그 이유는 무엇입니까?

5. 여러분이 자녀들의 이름을 짓게 된다면 어떤 이름을 지어 주고 싶습니까? 그 이유는 무엇입니까?

6. 여러분이 아는 한국인 이름 중에서 좋아하는 한글 이름이 있습니까?

Gaining familiarity

1. 한국에서는 여성이 결혼하여도 자기의 성을 바꾸지 않습니다.

2. 성, 이름, 호, 자, 관명, 아명

3. 일제 시대 ← 조선 시대 ← 고려 시대 ← 삼국 시대 (고구려, 신라, 백제)

4. 양반, 상민, 천민, 농민

5. 삼국사기, 삼국유사

한국인의 이름

1. 이름은 그 사람의 인격과 명예와 책임까지 나타낸다. 그러므로 자기 이름을 지키려고 목숨까지 버린 사람은 수없이 많다.[19.1] 제 이름답게 살아야 한다는 정신은 공자의 '정명(바른 이름) 사상'을 들먹이지 않더라도[19.2] 우리 마음속 깊은 곳에 도사리고 있다.[19.3] 셰익스피어는 "이름은 인간성과 아무 관계가 없으며, 한갓 누구를 가리키는 표시에 지나지 않는다"[19.4] 하고, 노자도 "어떤 이름으로 이름을 삼을 수 있지만 반드시 그 이름이어야 할 까닭은 없다"고 하면서 이름에 담긴 뜻을 대수롭지 않게 말하지만, 많은 사람이 스스로 가장 자랑스럽게 내세우고 싶어 하는 것이 바로 자기 이름이다.

2. 양반 사회에서는 이름을 함부로 부르지 않았고 남들이 보는 앞에서 제 이름을 써 들고 앉아 있는 것을 가장 큰 형벌로 여겼던 때도 있었다고 하니 우리가 이름을 얼마나 소중하게 생각했는지 알 만하다. 어느 사람이나 어떤 물건의 현재와 미래가 그 이름에 달려 있다고 믿기 때문에 이름 짓기란 모든 창작 활동 가운데서 가장 힘을 기울이는 일이라고 해도 지나친 말은 아닐 것이다.[19.5]

우리말 이름과 한자 이름

3. 우리나라의 사람 이름은 예로부터 우리말 이름과 한자 이름, 두 가닥으로 내려왔는데, 요즈음 들어 서양말 이름도 몇몇 눈에 띈다.[19.6] 한자가 들어오기 전에는 우리 겨레가 모두 다 우리말 이름을 썼던 것은 두말할 나위도 없다.[19.7] <삼국사기>나 <삼국유사>에 보이는 "박혁거세, 석탈해, 김알지, 수로, 아사달, 해부루, 거칠부"나 "연개소문, 을지문덕"이나 "을파소, 마리, 부루, 미루, 해루, 맛둥, 누리마로" 따위가 한자 이름처럼 보이지만 모두 우리말 이름이다.

4. 한자가 들어와 임금을 비롯한 양반들이 한자 이름을 쓰기 시작하면서 오랫동안 떳떳하게 써 오던 우리말 이름은 상놈 이름으로 밀려났다. 그뿐만 아니라, 본디 지녔던 밝고 힘차고 아름답던 이름이 상놈에게 걸맞은 천한 뜻 이름으로 떨어지고 말았다. 이렇게 내려오는 동안, 양반 이

름은 중국 이름을 본떠 '성 한 자, 이름 두 자 (성명 세 자)'라는 이름 틀이 굳어졌고, 한자 이름은 양반 자리를 나타내는 이름으로 머릿속에 못 박혔다.[19.8] 한편, 우리말 이름은 천한 사람 이름 자리로 내려앉는데 조선 시대 마지막에 양반 제도가 느슨해지면서 비로소 평민들 사이에서도 한자 이름을 쓰는 사람이 나타나기 시작했다.

어쨌거나, 우리말 이름은 몇 천 년 동안 우리 일상 생활 속에 끈끈하게 이어져 왔다. 소설 <임꺽정>(홍명희 지음)에 나오는 "삽살개미치, 도야지, 쥐불이, 말불이, 매야지, 마당개, 마당쇠" 따위 상놈들 이름뿐만 아니라 양반들 이름으로도 그대로 살아 있었다. 양반들은 어릴 때 부르는 '아명'과 어른이 된 뒤에 쓰는 '관명'과 '자'와 '호' 따위 네 가지 이름을 함께 썼는데, 여기서 아명이 바로 우리말 이름이다. '아명'은 상놈들 이름과 마찬가지로 천한 뜻을 나타낸 이름으로 병 없이 잘 자라라고 '돌'이나 '쇠' 따위로 짓기도 하고 귀신의 시샘에서 벗어나라고 "개, 말, 소, 돼지, 똥" 같은 더러운 이름으로 지었다. 어느 임금의 아명이 "개똥이"였던 것은 널리 알려진 일이다. 또 여자 이름은 양반 상놈 가리지 않고 모두 우리말 이름을 썼는데 다만, '명월, 사임당, 허 난설헌'처럼 기생이나 시인, 화가들은 호나 이름에 한자 이름으로 쓴 것을 더러 볼 수 있다.

일제 시대에 이른바 "민적(호적)"을 만들면서 상놈에게는 없던 성씨를 새로 만들어 주고 우리말 이름을 저들 마음대로 모조리 한자로 고친 것이 빌미가 되어 여자들과 평민들도 모두 한자 이름을 새로 얻게 된다. 하지만 이 한자 이름은 민적에만 올라 있었지 집안과 마을에서는 한결같이 우리말 이름만 썼다. 곧 이어[19.9] 한자 이름은 "창씨 개명(성씨를 새로 만들고 이름을 일본식으로 고침)"으로 잠깐 사라졌다가 광복 뒤에 되살아나는데 이때부터 모든 겨레가 두루 한자 이름을 쓰게 된다. 더욱이[19.10] 우리 호적에도 일제 시대 때의 제도를 그대로 물려받아 반드시 한자 이름만 올리도록 하여 한자 이름을 짓지 않을 수 없게[19.11] 만들었다. 이렇게 해서 우리말 이름은 까마득히 잊혀지고 한자 이름이 오랜 역사와 전통을 지닌 우리 이름 행세를 하게 되었다. 이것이 우리 이름이 걸어온 발자취다.

한편, 나라를 되찾은 뒤 "나를 알고 나를 찾자"는 깨우침과 더불어 겨레의 주체성과 자주성을 되살리자는 생각이 싹트면서 틀에 박힌 생각에서 벗어나려는 바람이 일고, 이 바람에 힘입어 한때 아주 사라지는 듯하던 우리말 이름이 사회 한구석에서 조심스럽게 되살아났다. 처음엔 남의 눈치에 아랑곳하지 않는[19.12] 몇몇 줏대 있는 분들이 나서서 온갖 어려움을 무릅쓰고 우리말 이름의 씨를 뿌리더니 이십, 삼십 년 지난 뒤 가슴 열린 젊은이들 사이에 뿌리를 내려서 1980년대에는 새로 태어나는 어린이들 가운데 열에 서넛을 우리말 이름으로 지었다. 이런 우리말 이름 짓기는 남녘뿐만 아니라 북녘에도 비슷하다고 한다.

소박하고 고운 이름들

우리말 이름은 그동안 얽매여 왔던 한자의 획수, 항렬자, 그리고 "이름 석자"라는 "이름 틀"에서 벗어나 부르기 쉽고 듣기 좋은 우리말로 지은 이름이라 할 수 있다. 이러한 우리말 이름의 만듦새는 다섯 갈래로 나눌 수 있는데, 첫째, 한 낱말로 지은 이름으로 옛말에서 찾아낸 "미루, 새암, 가람, 누리, 미르"와 "아람, 아름, 송이, 노을, 우리, 하늘, 샘" 같은 예쁘고 고운 낱말 이름과 "고은(곱다), 포근(포근하다), 한결(한결같다), 아롱(아롱다롱하다), 바름(바르다), 푸름(푸르다), 빛남(빛나다)" 같은 부드럽고 귀여운 것들이 있다. 둘째, 두 세 가지 낱말을 모아 지은 것으로 "난(나는) + 새, 꽃 + 비, 단 + 비, 늘 + 봄, 외 + 솔, 한 + 길, 새 + 한 + 별" 따위와, 셋째, 두 낱말을 모아 한 글자씩 뽑아서 새로 만든 것으로 "곱슬(곱다 + 슬기롭다), 슬용(슬기 + 용기), 살미(살갑다 + 미덥다)" 따위와, 넷째, 한 두 글귀를 줄여서 만든 "어진이(어진 + 이), 샘지니(샘 + 지닌 + 이), 예소라(예쁜 + 소리 + 내어라)." 다섯째, 글월을 줄이거나 그대로 만든 것도 있다. "박차 오름, 박차고 나온 놈이 샘이나, 강산에 꽃님 아씨, 우람히 너른 바위, 가까스로 얻은 노미" 들이 그 보기이다.

이렇게 힘차게 뻗어나가던 우리말 이름은 1980년대를 고비로 1990년대에 들어와서 주춤거리는 것이 눈에 띄고 몇몇 사람은 다시 한자 이름으로 바꾸는 일도 일어난다. 그 까닭을 알아보면 먼저, 앞에서 본 첫째에서 넷째까지의 방법으로는 새로운 이름을 더 짓기 어렵다는 것을 들

수 있다. <우리말 이름 짓기 책>(한글 이름 짓기 사전)에 많은 보기를
들어 놓았지만 쓸 만한 이름은 이미 동이 나고[19.13] 말았다. 우리말 이름
가운데 같은 이름이 늘어나고 있는 것을 보면 알 수 있다. 다음으로, 이
름 때문에 놀림감이 되는데 어린아이가 참아 내기 어렵다는 것이다. 그
리고 어릴 때 이름으로는 나무랄 데 없으나 어른이 되면 아무래도 가벼
워서 맞지 않는다는 것들이다. 마지막으로 위의 다섯째 방법으로 지은
이름은 너무 길어서 쓰기가 어렵다고 한다.

우리말 이름 짓는 길

그렇다면 여기서 이름 짓는 길을 새로 찾아내야 하고 이를 디딤돌로
삼아 더 멀리 힘차게 펼쳐 나가야 할 것이다. 어디서 어떻게 그 길을 찾
을 것인가? 그 길은 오직 하나 옛날에 잃어버린 진짜 우리 이름의 참모
습을 알아내는 데서 비롯해야 한다. 우리 조상들의 이름에서 우리 이름
의 틀과 본보기를 찾는 것이 바람직하다.[19.14]

동명성왕의 이름 '주몽'은 고구려 말로 '활을 잘 쏘는 사나이'이고 '수
로'는 '우두머리', '박혁거세'는 '밝은 누리를 펼치는 사람'이고 '탈해'는
'알을 토한 사람'이고 '거칠부'는 '용감한 사나이'란 말이고 '알지'는 '알에
서 나온 사람'이란 말이다. 이로 미루어 우리말 이름의 원형을 짐작할
수 있다. 그런데 앞에서 말한 다섯째 방법이 바로 이 이름의 틀과 맞아
떨어진다. 우리는 이미 그 길을 찾아내었고 올바른 길로 가고 있었던 것
이다. 다만, 고정 관념에서 벗어나지 못했기 때문에 그것을 깨닫지 못하
고 있을 뿐이다. 이름이 길다는 것은 흠잡을 일이 아니다. 오히려 같은
이름(동명 이인)에서 벗어나는 오직 하나뿐인 길이라 하겠다. 우리말 이
름 쓰기는 우리 조상들이 힘차고 떳떳하고 자랑스럽게 지어 부르던 우
리 이름을 찾아 새롭게 되살리는 일이다.

요즈음 들어 이른바 "JP, DJ, YS" 따위 지도층에 있다는 사람들 이름
을 로마 글자로 쓰는 일이나 회사나 상표, 가게 이름에 서양말 이름이
지나치게[19.15] 번지는 것은 그 옛날 한문 글자를 받아들이면서 우리말을
벼랑으로 몰아낸 것과 비슷하다.

김정섭, 우리말 바로 쓰기 모임 회장, <샘이 깊은 물> 2001년 2월호에서 편집

New Words

가까스로 barely, just, with difficulty ▷가까스로 5시까지 그 일을 마칠 수 있었다. I barely finished the job by 5 o'clock.

가닥 piece, cut(ting), strip, strand, fork (of a road)

갈래 branch, division, section, fork (of a road)

걸맞다 to be well matched

겨레 race, nation, people, brethren

고구려 Koguryŏ, the northernmost of the Three Kingdoms on the Korean Peninsula from 37 B.C. to A.D. 668

고비 climax, crest, peak, crisis, critical moment ▷한 고비 넘다 to pass the crisis [worst] ▷병이 한 고비 넘다 (of a sick person) to get out of danger, get off the critical list

고정 관념 fixed idea, prejudice, preconception

곱다 to be pretty, beautiful, nice-looking, lovely; to be sweet, pure-minded ▷고운 여자 pretty woman ▷고운 목소리 sweet (nice) voice ▷마음씨가 곱다 to be kindhearted, pure in mind (heart)

공자 Confucius (Chinese philosopher)

관명 one's adult [grown-up] name, official title

광복 restoration of independence in 1945 (from Japanese colonial rule)

구석 corner. 구석방 inner room, back room ▷마음 한구석에 somewhere in the back of one's mind, somewhere at the bottom of one's heart

귀신 ghost; evil spirit

글월 letters, literature; letter, epistle; sentence (= 글)

기울이다 to bend, put (one's mind to); to direct (one's attention to), concentrate (one's mind, energy, powers on) ▷다른 사람 말에 귀를 기울이다 to give ear to (lend an ear to, listen to) what people tell one ▷마음을 기울여 공부하다 to keep one's mind on one's studies, devote oneself to one's studies

까닭 reason, cause ▷까닭 없이 without any reason ▷무슨 까닭으로 for what reason

까마득하다 to be far off (in space or time), distant, remote ▷까마득히 distantly, remotely ▷까마득한 옛날 long, long time ago; remote antiquity ▷새는 벌써 까마득히 멀리 날아갔다. The bird has flown far away in the sky.

깨닫다 to realize, perceive, understand; to become aware of ▷잘못을 깨닫다 to realize one's own mistake

깨우침 awakening, realization

끈끈하게 persistently, tenaciously

나서다 to come out (forth), appear, present oneself ▷무대에 나서다 to appear on the stage, make an entrance ▷정계에 나서다 to embark upon a political career

남녘 south, the south side (= 남쪽); South Korea

낱말 word, vocabulary

내세우다 to set forth, claim, advocate, display (one's learning)

너르다 to be wide, spacious, roomy ▷너른 마당 wide yard

노자 Lao Tzu (the founder of Taoism)

놀림감 object of derision or teasing

누리 the world, this world [archaic] (= 세상) ▷온 누리에 all over the world

눈치 perceptiveness in social situations, tact, intuition, expression, manner ▷눈치를 보다 to read another's face

느슨해지다 to become loosened, relaxed

늘어나다 to lengthen, expand, increase

대수롭다 to be important ▷대수롭지 않게 말하다 to speak lightly of, attach little importance to ▷그게 뭐 대수로운 일이야? Is that an important thing anyway?

더러 occasionally, sometimes

더불어 together with

도사리다 to harbor (feelings, thoughts), lurk (in the mind) ▷그녀에겐 나에 대한 나쁜 감정이 도사리고 있다. She harbors ill-feeling against me.

도야지 pig (= 돼지)

동명 이인 different person of the same name

되살리다 to revive, return to life, rekindle

되살아나다 to revive, return to life

두루 all round, widely, extensively

들먹이다 to mention, refer to, specify by name

디딤돌 stepping-stone, step

떳떳하다 to be fair, honorable ▷빚을 갚지 않는 것은 떳떳하지 못한 일이다. It is not honorable not to pay one's debts.

마음대로 as one wishes, of one's own accord, freely

만듦새 make, workmanship, craftsmanship ▷만듦새가 좋다 (나쁘다) to be of fine (poor) workmanship ▷이 외투는 만듦새가 좋다. The make of this coat is fine.

명예 honor, reputation, prestige

모조리 all, without exception, thoroughly

목숨 life ▷목숨을 잃다 to die; to be killed

몰아내다 to drive out, kick out

무릅쓰다 to risk, brave, face (adversity, danger, etc.) ▷그는 부모의 반대를 무릅쓰고 결혼했다. He got married in spite of his parents' opposition.

물려받다 to inherit (from), take over, obtain by transfer ▷사업을 물려받다 to take over the business ▷재산을 물려받다 to inherit property

미덥다 to be trustworthy, dependable, reliable ▷미더운 사람 reliable [trustworthy] person

민적 register of the population, census register, family register

밀려나다 to be driven out (from) ▷그는 사장 자리에서 밀려났다. He was squeezed out of the president's seat.

바르다 to be straight; to be upright, honest, straightforward ▷바른 길 straight road ▷바른 사람 honest man ▷바른 말을 하다 to tell [speak] the truth, tell what is right

박차다 to kick hard, give a vigorous kick ▷굴러오는 복을 박차다 to toss aside a piece of good luck ▷모든 장애를 박차고 나가다 to go ahead, sweeping aside all obstacles

박히다 (of a nail, etc.) to get stuck, embedded, driven in; to be taken ▷가시가 내 손가락에 박혔어요. A thorn got stuck in my finger.

반드시 certainly, without fail

발자취 tracks, traces, footprints

번지다 (of liquid, etc.) to spread, run ▷잉크가 종이에 번지다 ink spreads on [runs over] the paper ▷독이 온 몸에 번졌다. Poison spread all through the body.

벗어나다 to get out of (difficulties, etc.); to free oneself from ▷가난에서 벗어나다 to overcome poverty ▷위기에서 벗어나다 to circumvent a crisis

벼랑 cliff, precipice

본보기 example, model ▷애국심의 좋은 본보기 fine example of patriotism

북녘 north, the north side (= 북쪽); North Korea

비로소 for the first time (after something happened), not . . . till . . . ▷사람은 건강을 잃고서야 비로소 그것이 얼마나 고마운지를 알게 된다. People do not know the blessing of health till they lose it.

비롯하다 to begin, originate. 비롯하여 beginning with, including ▷이번 행사에는 시장을 비롯해서 20명이 참석했다. There were twenty present, including the mayor, at this event.

빌미 cause of trouble, cause (of an event)

뻗어나가다 to extend, stretch out

사나이 a man, a male

살갑다 to be kind, warmhearted

삼국사기 *The Record of the Three Kingdoms*

삼국유사 *Memorabilia of the Three Kingdoms*

삼다 to make, use . . . as ▷사위로 삼다 to make a person one's son-in-law

삽살개 a kind of shaggy Korean dog

상놈 commoner, ill-bred fellow, vulgar man, man of low birth

상표 trademark, brand

셰익스피어 (William) Shakespeare

소중하다 to be important, valuable, precious ▷소중하게 생각하다 to consider important

쇠 metal

스스로 by oneself, of one's own accord, for oneself

슬기롭다 to be intelligent, sagacious, wise, bright ▷슬기로운 아이 sensible child

시샘 jealousy

싹트다 to sprout, bud, begin to develop

쏘다 to shoot, discharge

아랑곳하다 to be concerned with, take an interest in ▷아랑곳 하지 않다 to not care

아롱다롱하다 to be variegated, mottled

아명 childhood name

아씨 young lady (polite but archaic term of address or reference to an unmarried woman)

양반 the aristocratic class; the nobility of the Chosŏn dynasty

어쨌거나 however, anyway

얽매다 to tie [bind] up tight ▷사람을 얽매다 to tie a person up ▷물건을 얽매다 to bind things fast

여기다 to think of, regard (as), consider

오직 only, merely, solely

오히려 rather, on the contrary

올리다 to put on record, enter (a name) ▷이름을 전화 번호부에 올리다 to put one's name in the telephone directory ▷사건을 역사에 올리다 to record an event in history ▷새 말을 사전에 올리다 to enter a new word in a dictionary

올바르다 to be upright, correct, honest

우람하다 to be grand, magnificent, impressive, imposing

원형 original form, prototype

인격 character, personality

일다 to rise, go up, become active ▷바람이 일 것 같다. The wind seems to be rising. ▷파도가 일고 있다. The sea is running high.

일제 (abridged form of 일본 제국주의) Japanese imperialism ▷일제 시대 period of Japanese occupation (1910−1945)

자 name or style taken at the age of twenty; one's "courtesy name"

자랑스럽다 to be boastful, proud. 자랑스럽게 boastfully, proudly

자주성 independence, sovereignty

잠깐 (for) a moment ▷잠깐 동안 in a minute, for a little while

정신 mind, soul, spirit

제도 system, regime

조상 ancestor, forefather, progenitor

조선 시대 Chosŏn dynasty (1392−1910)

주체성 independence, autonomy

주춤거리다 to hesitate, waver, hold back, shy away ▷주춤거리며 말하다 to say hesitantly, falter ▷살까말까 주춤거리다 to hesitate to buy

줏대 strength of character, moral fiber, conviction ▷줏대 있는 사람 man of principle ▷줏대가 없다 to lack backbone

지나치다 to go beyond, go too far, go to excess ▷지나치게 먹다 to overeat ▷지나치게 일하다 to work too hard

지도층 the ruling class

짐작하다 to guess, conjecture, estimate

창작 creation, production

책임 responsibility, liability, accountability. 책임감 sense of responsibility

천하다 to be lowly, humble ▷천한 사람 humble person

토하다 to throw up, spit

틀 convention, formality, frame, framework ▷틀에 박힌 생각 conventional idea, stereotype

펼치다 to unfold, spread, open

포근하다 to be soft and comfortable

표시 indication, expression, sign

한갓 only, alone ▷한갓 빵만으로는 살지 못한다. We cannot live on bread alone.

한결같이 consistently, invariably

한구석 a corner, a nook, secluded place ▷시골 한구석이 박히다 to be stuck in a secluded village

한편 on the other hand, besides

함부로 recklessly, thoughtlessly

항렬자 generation name, Chinese character used in the names of family members of a particular generation

행세하다 to pose as, assume the air of

형벌 punishment

호 pen name, title

호적 census registration, family register

획수 number of strokes (in a Chinese character)

흠잡다 to find fault with ▷흠잡을 데가 없다 to be faultless

힘차다 to be full of strength, energetic

Useful Expressions

1. **수없이 많다** be countless [innumerable, incalculable]
   하늘에는 수없이 많은 별이 반짝이고 있었다.
   Countless stars were twinkling in the sky.
   미국에 한국 유학생들이 수없이 많다.
   In America, Korean students are innumerable.

2. **~을/를 들먹이지 않더라도** even though you don't refer to [mention] ~
   공자의 말을 들먹이지 않더라도 이것은 사실이다.
   This is true even though we don't mention the teaching of Confucius.
   성경 말씀을 들먹이지 않더라도, 예수의 가르침은 사랑이다.
   You don't have to refer to the Bible; the teaching of Jesus is love.

3. **~에 도사리고 있다** harbor in ~
   부자가 되고 싶은 욕심은 모든 사람의 마음속에 도사리고 있다.
   Everyone harbors in their mind the desire to become rich.
   허영심이 그 여자의 마음속 깊은 곳에 도사리고 있었다.
   Deep in her mind lurks a sense of vanity.

4. **한갓 ~에 지나지 않다** be nothing but; only
   이름은 인간성과 아무 관계가 없으며, 한갓 누구를 가리키는 표시에 지나지
   않는다.
   Names have nothing to do with human nature, and they are nothing more
   than a sign indicating a certain person.
   그 아이가 아무리 힘이 세도, 한갓 어린 아이에 지나지 않는다.
   However strong she is, she is still only a child.

5. **~다고/라고 해도 지나친 말은 아닐 것이다** it's no exaggeration to say that ~
   이름 짓기가 모든 창작 활동 가운데서 가장 힘든 일이라고 해도 지나친 말은
   아닐 것이다.
   It's no exaggeration to say that choosing a name is one of the most
   difficult creative activities.
   독일말이 가장 배우기 어려운 말이라 해도 지나친 말은 아닐 것이다.
   It would be no exaggeration to say that German is the most difficult
   language to learn.

6. **눈에 띄다** catch one's eye; be conspicuous [noticeable]

요즈음 들어 서양말 이름도 몇몇 눈에 띈다.

A few Western names are noticeable these days.

요새는 길거리에 머리를 염색한 학생들이 많이 눈에 띈다.

You can see a lot of students in the street with dyed hair these days.

7. **~은/는 두말할 나위도 없다** it goes without saying that ~; it is needless to say that ~

한자가 들어오기 전에는 우리 겨레가 모두 우리말 이름을 썼던 것은 두말할 나위도 없다.

It goes without saying that before the arrival of Chinese characters we all used native Korean names.

국제화 시대에 외국어를 많이 배워야 할 필요가 있다는 것은 두말할 나위도 없다.

It goes without saying that in the age of globalization we need to learn foreign languages.

8. **~에 못 박히다** be nailed in (one's heart); be stung to the quick; feel a deep rancor [grudge]

한자 이름은 양반 자리를 나타내는 이름으로 머릿속에 못 박혔다.

Chinese-character names were recognised as representing the status of the *yangban*.

영수는 영희의 말에 가슴에 못이 박혔다.

Yŏngsu had his feelings deeply hurt by Yŏnghŭi's remark.

9. **곧 이어** at once; immediately (thereafter); directly

서울로 돌아오자 나는 곧 이어 그의 집으로 달려갔다.

As soon as I returned to Seoul I went straight to see him.

나는 호텔에 도착하자마자 곧 이어 그에게 전화를 걸었다.

I telephoned him as soon as I arrived at the hotel.

10. **더욱이** besides; moreover; in addition (to that); what's more

당신이 모른다면 더욱이 나 같은 사람이야 알 리가 없지요.

If you don't know, still less do I know.

그는 잘 알아듣는데다가 더욱이 한번 배운 것은 잊어버리지 않는다.

He learns easily, and what is more, he remembers what he has learnt.

11. **~지 않을 수 없다**   cannot help (doing) ~; cannot but (do) ~; have to ~

그렇게 강력히 권한다면 내가 사지 않을 수 없겠다.

If you recommend it so strongly (like that), I'll have to buy it.

나는 쓴웃음을 웃지 않을 수 없었다.

I could not help smiling a bitter smile.

나는 대학 입학을 포기하지 않을 수 없었다.

I had to give up going to the university.

12. **~에 아랑곳하지 않다**   be unconcerned about ~; take no notice of ~

남의 눈치에 아랑곳하지 않고 그는 자기가 좋아하는 일에 몰두했다.

He took no notice of others and immersed himself in the work he enjoyed.

다른 사람의 눈총에 아랑곳하지 않고 그들은 큰소리로 노래를 불렀다.

They ignored other people's looks and sang loudly.

13. **동이 나다**   run out; be out; be exhausted; be sold out

쓸만한 이름은 동이 나고 말았다.

The usable names had been exhausted.

휘발유가 동이 났다.

We have run out of gas.

14. **~이/가 바람직하다**   it is desirable [advisable] that ~

자네 혼자 거기 가는 것은 바람직하지 않다.

It is not advisable for you to go there alone.

암에 대한 정기 검진을 받는 것은 바람직하다.

It is desirable that you should have a periodic checkup for cancer.

15. **지나치게**   too much; overly

너는 네 병에 대해서 지나치게 걱정한다.

You worry too much about your illness.

그녀는 그에게 지나치게 관심을 보였다.

She showed excessive concern for him.

Exercises

1. 관련된 단어들끼리 연결하여 문장을 만들어 보세요.

    (1) 참아내기   •   • 없다
    (2) 두 갈래로 •   • 내리다
    (3) 행세를   •   • 어렵다
    (4) 뿌리를   •   • 나누어지다
    (5) 나무랄 데 •   • 하다

_____

_____

_____

_____

_____

2. 아래의 설명과 맞는 단어나 표현을 보기에서 찾아 쓰세요.

> 보기: 형벌, 소중하다, 기울이다, 임금, 유래, 힘차다, 느슨하다

    (1) 범죄에 대한 법률에 있어서의 효과로서
        국가가 범죄자에게 가하는 제재: _____

    (2) 중하다, 귀중하다, 귀하다, 아끼다: _____

    (3) 마음이나 생각을 한 쪽으로 쏠리게 하다: _____

    (4) 군주 국가에서 나라를 다스리는 사람: _____

    (5) 사물의 처음 생겨난 바: _____

    (6) 힘이 있고, 씩씩하다. 기운차다: _____

    (7) 탁 풀려 긴장감이 없다. (끈이나 나사가)
        팽팽하거나 단단하지 않고 헐렁하거나 헐겁다: _____

3. 보기에서 적당한 말을 골라 빈칸을 채우세요.

> 보기: 본보기, 디딤돌, 고정 관념, 참모습, 아무래도

(1) 그렇다면 여기서 이름 짓는 길을 새로 찾아내야 하고 이를 ＿＿＿＿＿＿＿
   로 삼아 더 멀리 힘차게 펼쳐 나가야 할 것이다.

(2) 어디서 어떻게 그 길을 찾을 것인가? 그 길은 오직 하나 옛날에 잃어버린
   진짜 우리 이름의 ＿＿＿＿＿＿＿을 알아내는 데서 비롯해야 한다.

(3) 우리 조상들의 이름에서 이름의 틀과 ＿＿＿＿＿＿＿를 찾는 것이
   바람직하다.

(4) 다만, ＿＿＿＿＿＿＿에서 벗어나지 못했기 때문에 그것을 깨닫지 못하고
   있을 뿐이다.

(5) 어릴 때 이름으로는 나무랄 데 없으나 어른이 되면 ＿＿＿＿＿＿＿
   가벼워서 맞지 않는다는 것들이다.

4. 밑줄 친 말과 가장 비슷한 단어나 표현을 보기에서 고르세요.

(1) 이름 짓는 길을 새로 찾아내야 하고 이를 <u>디딤돌</u>로 삼아 더 멀리 힘차게
   펼쳐 나가야 할 것이다.
   a. 계기   b. 모범   c. 본보기   d. 다리

(2) <u>본디</u> 지녔던 밝고 힘차고 아름답던 이름이 상놈에게 걸맞은 천한 뜻
   이름으로 떨어지고 말았다.
   a. 앞으로   b. 본래   c. 뒤로   d. 자랑스럽게

(3) 우리는 이미 그 길을 찾아내었고 올바른 길로 가고 있었던 것이다. 다만,
   <u>고정 관념</u>에서 벗어나지 못했기 때문에 그것을 깨닫지 못하고 있을 뿐이다.
   a. 늘 가지고 있는 생각   b. 잘못된 생각
   c. 올바른 생각   d. 지루한 생각

(4) 다만, 고정 관념에서 벗어나지 못했기 때문에 그것을 깨닫지 못하고 있을
   뿐이다. 이름이 길다는 것은 <u>흠잡을 일이 아니다</u>.
   a. 잘못된 일이다   b. 바람직한 일이다
   c. 잘못이 아니다   d. 흠 잡을만하다

(5) 요즈음 들어 이른바 "JP, DJ, YS" 따위 지도층에 있다는 사람들 이름을
로마 글자로 쓰는 일이나 회사나 상표, 가게 이름에 서양말 이름이 지나치게
번지는 것은 그 옛날 한문 글자를 받아들이면서 우리말을 <u>벼랑</u>으로 몰아낸
때와 비슷하다.

   a. 해결책   b. 궁지   c. 발전   d. 활성화

5. 다음 단어를 사용하여 문장을 만들어 보세요.

> 보기: 동이 나고 말았다
> → 한글 이름 짓기 사전에 많은 보기를 들어 놓았지만,
>   쓸만한 이름은 이미 동이 나고 말았다.
> → 항아리에 물이 동이 나고 말았다.

(1) ~에 달려있다

_____

(2) ~해 버리다

_____

(3) ~할 수 있었을 텐데

_____

(4) ~하기도 한다

_____

(5) 까다롭다

_____

6. 주어진 단어 중에 나머지 셋과 관계가 먼 단어를 고르세요.

(1) 고구려   임금   백제   조선
(2) 양반   규수   평민   천민
(3) 조상   후손   선조   국민
(4) 백부   고모부   부부   이모부

Comprehension Questions

I. Overall comprehension

1. 옛날에는 노자나 셰익스피어가 언급한 것처럼 이름의 중요성이 부각되지 않았나요?

   _____

2. 이름 짓기가 힘든 이유는 무엇 때문인가요?

   _____

3. 본인의 이름이 자기 자신을 잘 나타낸다고 생각합니까?

   _____

II. Finding details

1. 양반에게 가장 큰 형벌은 무엇이었습니까?

   _____

2. 한글 이름과 한자 이름의 차이점은 무엇인가요?

   _____

3. '창씨 개명'이란 무엇인가요?

   _____

4. 양반들이 천한 이름을 사용한 이유는 무엇인가요?

   _____

5. 성을 갖지 못한 사람들도 성을 가지게 된 계기는 어떤 것이었습니까?

   _____

6. 우리말 이름 짓기가 힘든 이유는 무엇인가요?

   _____

7. 삼국사기나 삼국유사에 나오는 이름들은 한자 이름인가요, 아니면 서양의 성씨가
   유입된 것인가요, 아니면 순수 고유한 우리말 이름인가요?

   _____

8. 임금이나 양반들이 한자 이름을 쓰면서 우리말 이름의 위치는 어떻게 되었습니까?

   _____

9. 어른이 된 뒤에 쓰는 이름은 무엇입니까?

_____

10. 남한과 북한의 우리말 이름 짓기의 현황은 어떻습니까?

_____

Related Reading

성씨 이야기

성씨가 언제부터 생겨났는지는 자세히 알 수 없지만, 초기의 성은 주로 사람들이 살던 지역이나 산, 강에서 따 온 것으로 보인다. 중국의 옛 문헌에도 신농씨(神農氏)의 어머니는 강수(姜水)에 살았다고 하여 성을 강(姜)씨로 정했으며 순(舜) 임금의 어머니는 요허(姚虛)에서 났다 하여 성을 요(姚)씨로 했다고 되어 있다.

왕이 내려준 성씨

우리나라에 성이 나타난 것은 삼국 시대부터였다. <삼국사기>와 <삼국유사>에는 고구려의 시조 주몽이 국호를 따라 자신의 성을 고(高)씨라 했으며, 충신들에게 극(克)씨, 중실(仲室)씨, 소실(小室)씨를 성으로 하사하였다고 한다. 그 밖에도 많은 왕들이 신하에게 성을 하사하였으나 고구려에서 온 성은 지금 거의 없어졌다. 오늘날 고씨들은 거의가 탐라 고씨 계열이고 고주몽의 후손인 고씨들이 일부 강원도 횡성에 살고 있다고 한다.

백제에서는 시조인 온조가 부여에서 났다 하여 부여(扶餘)씨 또는 여(餘)씨라는 성을 썼다. 백제에는 전씨, 마씨, 성주 도씨, 부여 서씨가 있었다. 그 밖에 백, 사, 협, 해, 연, 진, 목, 국처럼 팔족의 족장들에게 왕이 내린 성씨들이 있었다. 신라 시대에는 박(朴), 석(昔), 김(金)의 세 성이 그 기원과 함께 내려오고 있으며 유리왕 때에 육부의 촌장들에게 내렸다는 최(崔), 정(鄭), 손(孫), 배(裵), 설(薛), 이(李) 여섯 개의 성이 오늘날까지 내려오고 있다. <삼국사기>에는 삼국 시대에 성을 쓴 사람보다는 안 쓴 사람들이 많았으며 주로 중국에 왕래한 사신들과 유학자 그리고 장보고처럼 무역을 한 사람들이 성씨를 사용했다고 쓰여 있다.

우리나라에 성씨의 체계가 갖추어진 것은 고려 시대였다. 태조 왕건은 개국 공신과 지방 호족 세력들에게 성씨를 내렸는데 홍유, 배현경, 신숭겸, 복지겸 들의 개국 공신들이 각각 부계 홍(洪)씨, 경주 배(裵)씨, 평산 신(申)씨, 면천 복(卜)씨의 시조가 되었다. 신라 사람인 김신은 태조를 보필하여 권(權)씨 성을 하사받고 안동 권씨의 시조가 되었다. 고려 중기 문종 때인 1055년에는 성을 붙이지 않은 사람은 과거에 급제할 자격을 주지 않는다는 법령을 내린 것으로 보아 이 무렵에 관리나 귀족층들에게는 성을 쓰는 것이 보편화되었음을 알 수 있다.

귀화한 성씨들

조선 초기에 와서 양민들도 성을 쓰는 것이 보편화되었다. 그러나 노비와 천민은 조선 후기까지 성을 가질 수 없었다. 1909년 새로운 민적법이 시행되면서 성을 가지고 있지 않던 이들도 희망에 따라 성을 붙여 쓸 수 있게 되었다. 성이 없던 이들은 이웃이나 대갓집의 성을 따기도 하고 동 서기나 경찰이 마음대로 성을 지어 주기도 하면서 성을 갖게 되었다.

1985년의 인구 및 주택 조사에 따르면 우리나라에는 총 274개의 성이 있고 본관은 3435개가 있는 것으로 나타났다. 가장 많은 성씨는 김(金)씨로 전체 가구 수의 21.7퍼센트를 차지했고 이(李)씨 14.8퍼센트, 박(朴)씨 8.5퍼센트, 최(崔)씨 4.8퍼센트, 정(鄭)씨가 4.4.퍼센트로 그 뒤를 잇고 있으며, 강(姜), 조(趙), 윤(尹), 장(張), 임(林), 한(韓), 신(申), 오(吳), 서(徐), 권(權)씨들이 우리나라 성씨의 일 퍼센트 이상을 차지하고 있다. 인구 백 명 미만의 희귀 성도 40여 개가 있는데 주로 호적 기재 착오로 인한 경우와 고아 출신들의 입적, 외국인의 귀화로 최근 만들어진 성씨였다.

우리나라의 274개 성씨 가운데는 외국에서 들어온 귀화 성씨가 130여 개나 된다. 귀화 성씨 가운데는 중국에서 들어온 것이 가장 많고 고려 시대에는 몽골, 여진, 위구루, 아랍, 베트남, 일본들을 비롯하여 여러 민족들이 우리나라에 귀화하여 성씨를 형성했다. 고려 시대 충렬왕비인 제국공주를 따라와 귀화한 몽골인 후라타이는 연안 이씨의 시조가 되었고, 태조 이성계를 도와 개국에 공을 세웠던 여진인 퉁두란은 이지란이라는 이름을 받고 청해 이씨의 시조가 되었다. 귀화 성씨 가운데는 덕수 장씨, 한양 조씨처럼 백만 명이 넘는 인구를 가진 것도 있고, 섭(葉)씨, 마(麻)씨, 풍(馮)씨, 초(楚)씨 같은 희귀한 성도 많이 있다.

<샘이 깊은물> 2001년 2월호

초기 beginning, 지역 region, 따오다 to pick, cite from, 문헌 records, materials, 신농씨 Divine Husbandman (legendary founder of Chinese agriculture), 순 임금 mythical successor of Emperor Yao, 시조 founder, progenitor, 국호 name of a country, 충신 loyal retainer, 하사 royal gift, 탐라 old name for Cheju Island, 계열 (biological) order, a faction, 후손 descendants, 족장 patriarch, 기원 origin, 촌장 village chief, 사신 envoy, 유학자 Confucian scholar, 무역 trading, 체계 system, 갖추어지다 to be equipped with, 개국 공신 meritorious retainer at the founding of a dynasty, 호족 powerful family, 보필하다 assist, 과거 highest-level state examination to recruit ranking officials during the Chosŏn Dynasty, 급제 passing an examination, 법령 statute, laws, 관리 governmental official, 귀족층 aristocratic class, 보편화되다 universalize, 귀화 naturalization, 양민 law-abiding citizen, 보편화 generalization, 노비 slave, 천민 man of low (humble) birth, the poor, 민적법 law for census registration, 시행 enforcement, 대갓집 powerful family, 동 서기 neighborhood clerk, 가구 household, 본관 one's ancestral home, 희귀성 rare surname, 호적 기재 착오 erroneous census entry, 고아 orphan, 입적 entry in a register, 여진 Jurchen people who founded the Jin Dynasty (in Chinese history), 위구루 Uighur people, 아랍 Arab

Discussion & Composition

1. 자신의 성의 유래를 알면 이야기해 보세요.

2. 한글 이름만 고집하는 것이 좋은지 아니면 외국에서 유래된 성이나 한자 이름을 계속 사용해야 좋은지 이야기해 봅시다.

3. 여러분이 알고 있는 이름들 중에서 그 유래나 어원이 다른 나라에서 유입된 이름들에 대해 이야기해 봅시다.

4. 여러분이 알고 있는 희귀한 성씨에 대해서 이야기해 봅시다.

5. 본문에서 언급된 한글 이름을 적어 보고 가장 마음에 드는 것 하나를 골라 그 이유를 친구들에게 말해 보세요.

Lesson 19 Korean names

A name shows a person's character, reputation, and even her or his responsibilities, so many people have given their life in order to protect their name from dishonor. Even without reference to Confucius' philosophy of proper (or correct) naming, the feeling (*lit.*, spirit) of needing to live up to one's name lurks deep in our hearts. Shakespeare said that names have nothing to do with human nature, they are nothing more than a sign indicating a certain person; and Lao Tzu said that "a man can take a name for himself, but there is no reason that it must be that name." This shows they attached little importance to the meaning a name contains; but for many people, their own name is precisely the thing they proudly wish to put forward.

Names were not used recklessly in *yangban* society. One can see the importance Koreans attached to names in that there were cases when holding up one's written name while seated in public was deemed the greatest punishment. Because we believe a person or object's present and future depends on his or its name, it's no exaggeration to say that choosing a name is one of the most difficult creative activities.

Native Korean names and Chinese-character names

People in Korea have had two types of names since ancient times: native Korean names and Chinese-character names. Recently, our eyes have also met with a few Western names. Until Chinese characters entered Korea, of course, Koreans all used native Korean names. Names like *Pak Hyŏkkŏse, Sŏkt'alhae, Kimaltchi, Suro, Asadal, Haeburu, Kŏch'ilbu; Yŏn'gaesomun, Ŭlchimundŏk; Ŭlp'aso, Mari, Puru, Miru, Haeburu, Mattung,* and *Nurimaro,* appearing in *The Record of the Three Kingdoms* and *Memorabilia of the Three Kingdoms,* appear to be Chinese-character names, but in fact are all native Korean names.

With the arrival of Chinese characters, the *yangban*—beginning with the king—began using Chinese-character names. At the same time, they rejected the native Korean names they had used so honorably until then. Native Korean names were thereafter regarded as proper to people of low social status. What is more, even the bright, powerful, beautiful names they had originally used also dropped in status to "low"-sounding names suitable for the lower classes. As this practice was passed down, the framework for Chinese-based *yangban* names—a one-character surname and two-character personal name (three characters for the entire name)—solidified. Chinese-character names soon became fixed in people's minds as indicating a *yangban*'s (social) position. On the other hand, native Korean names declined in status to indicate a person of low birth. Only when the *yangban* system loosened at the end of the Chosŏn period did commoners begin using Chinese-character names.

At any rate, native Korean names persistently continued to maintain their presence in Korean daily life for several thousand years. In the novel *Imkkŏktchŏng* (written by Hong Myŏng-hŭi) are found not only commoners' names like *Sapsalgaemich'i, Toyaji, Chwiburi, Malburi, Maeyaji, Madang'kkae,* and *Madangsoe,* but also *yangban* names as they existed at the time. Altogether, a *yangban* used four names: a "child's name" used when young; his "official title" used after he reached adulthood; his "pseudonym"; and his "pen-name." Of these, the child's name was his native Korean name. Just like the commoner's name, the child's name indicated humble meanings. Names like "Stone" or "Metal" were used to wish one a good life and good health. Dirty names like "Dog," "Horse," "Cow," "Pig," and "Dung" were used so the person might escape the envy of ghosts. It is widely known that one Korean king had the child's name "Dog Dung." Women, whether aristocrat or commoner, all had native Korean names. Sometimes we can see that *kisaeng*, poets, and painters used Chinese characters for their pen-name or personal name, such as *Myŏngwŏl, Saimdang,* and *Hŏ Nansŏlhŏn.*

During the Japanese colonial period, so-called census registers were created, and commoners were given surnames, something they previously had never possessed. Since the Japanese arbitrarily changed all native Korean names into Chinese-character names, women and commoners received new Chinese-character names, too. But these Chinese-character names were only for use in the census registers. Everyone used native Korean names in the villages and at home. Soon after, Chinese-character names disappeared for a while due to the (colonial) policy of creation of new names (adopting a Japanese name); then their use returned after Liberation. All Koreans used Chinese-character names from then on. Moreover, Koreans kept using the census registers from the Japanese colonial period, and the people were instructed to use only Chinese-character names. In this way, our native Korean names were utterly forgotten, and Chinese-character names assumed the air of those names we used through our long history and tradition. Such is the path native Korean names have traveled.

On the other hand, after recovering our country, there began to blossom, together with an awakening that we should "know ourself and find ourself," the idea that we should revive our autonomy and independence. There arose a trend (*lit.*, energy) seeking to break free from fixed ideas. Owing to this trend, certain quarters of society began to carefully revive the nearly extinct native Korean names. At first, some strong-minded people emerged who, unconcerned with what others thought, braved all kinds of difficulties to reestablish native Korean names. This new trend took root among open-minded youngsters in twenty to thirty years. In the 1980s, thirty or forty percent of all newborns were given a Korean name. This practice took place not only in the South, but also in the North.

Simple and pretty names

Native Korean names broke free from the framework of the member of character strokes, "generation" names and the name frame consisting of three characters, and are easy to pronounce and pleasant to the ear. The methods used to construct these names may be divided into five categories. First, there are single-word names that existed in ancient times such as *Miru* (field), *Saeam* (fountain), *Karam* (river), *Nuri* (world), *Mirŭ* (dragon); names from pretty words like *Aram, Arŭm* (armful); *Song'i* (blossom, cluster); *Noŭl* (twilight) *Uri* (we); *Hanŭl* (heaven); *Saem* (fountain); and "cute," soft-sounding names like *Koŭn* (from *kopta* 'pretty'), *P'ogŭn* (from *p'ogŭnhada* 'mild'), and *Pinnam* (from *pinnada* 'shining'). Second, there are names formed from two or three words, like *Nansae* (*nan* [from *nanŭn* 'flying'] + *sae* 'bird'), *Kkotbi* (*kkot* + *pi* 'flower rain'), *Tanbi* (*tan* + *pi* 'sweet [refreshing] rain'), *Nŭlbom* (*nŭl* + *pom* 'eternal springtime'), *Woesol* (*woe* + *sol* 'lone pine tree'), *Han'gil* (*han* + *kil* 'one path'), and *Saehanbyŏl* (*sae* + *han* + *pyŏl* 'a new star'). Third, there are newly invented names, in which an element is selected from each of two words, like *Kop* + *sŭl* (*kopta* + *sŭlgiropta* 'pretty and wise'), *Sŭl* + *yong* (*sŭlgi* + *yong'gi* 'wisdom and bravery'), and *Salmi* (*salgapta* + *midŏpta* 'warmhearted and trustworthy'), etc. Fourth, one or two phrases may be contracted to create names like *Ŏjini* (*ŏjin* + *i* 'compassionate person'), *Saemjini* (*saem* + *chinin* + *i* 'person holding a fountain [inside of her]'), and *Yesora* (*yeppŭn* + *sori* + *naeŏra* 'make a cute noise'). Fifth, there are sentences, either shortened or used as they are: *Pakch'a orŭm* 'rising up with a kick'; *Pakch'ago naon nomi saemi na* 'to envy a person who rose up with a kick'; *Kangsan e kkonnim assi* 'flower girl in the rivers and mountains'; *Uramhi nŏrŭn pawi* 'majestically wide rocks'; and *Kakkasŭro ŏdŭn nomi* 'a guy we almost missed getting'.

Native Korean names, which were making such headway, reached a peak in the 1980s, then conspicuously slowed down upon entry into the 1990s, when some people began changing to Chinese-character names. This happened for several reasons. First, it was difficult to make new names using the first four methods listed above. Many examples are contained in the *Korean Name-Making Dictionary* and in the *Han'gŭl Name-Making Dictionary*, but people ran out of names worth using. This is evidenced in the growing number of the same native Korean names. Next, children find it difficult becoming an object of ridicule due to their names. And one's childhood name, although perfect as a child's name, comes to sound light and (may be) regarded as unsuitable when he or she becomes an adult. Finally, names created using the sentence (i.e., the fifth) method are too long and too difficult to use.

Ways to make native names
We must find new ways to make our names, then use them as stepping-stones to push and spread them into wider usage. Where and how will we find that path? There is only one way: it begins by examining actual native Korean names we have long forgotten. It would be desirable for us to find our model and framework for naming in the names of our ancestors.

The sage-king Tongmyŏng's name "Chumong" means 'man skillful at archery' in the Koguryŏ language. *Suro* means 'the top', *Pak Hyŏkkŏse* means 'person who unfolds a bright world', *T'arhae* means 'person who coughed up an egg', *Kŏch'ilbu* means 'brave man', and *Alchi* means 'person born from an egg'. Judging from these examples, we may ascertain the archetypes of native Korean names. It is the sentence method above, then, that matches most correctly with the archetypal framework. So we have already found the path, and at one time we were heading in the right direction. But because we could not break free from fixed notions about naming, we did not realize the fact. Having a long name is nothing to be critical of. On the contrary, it is the only way to break free from the practice of duplicated names. Using native Korean names means we are discovering and newly revivifying the names our ancestors once created and used with vigor, honor, and pride.

Contemporary use of roman letters for names of people in leadership positions like JP, DJ, and YS, or the spreading use of Western languages for company names, brand names, and stores, is similar to our adoption long ago of Chinese characters, when we drove our own language over a cliff.

Kim Chŏng-sŏp, Chairman, Group for the Correct Usage of the Korean Language (exerpted from the Feb. 2001 issue of *Saem i kip'ŭn mul*)

Related reading: The story of surnames
We have no way of knowing exactly when our names first came about, but early names were mainly taken from the area or natural features (mountain, river) where people lived. In ancient Chinese documents, it is written that Shennongshi's mother lived in Jiangshui, so her name became Jiang; and Emperor Shun's mother was born in Yaoxu, and given the surname Yao.

Surnames handed down by kings

Korean surnames first appeared during the Three Kingdoms period. *The Record of the Three Kingdoms* and *Memorabilia of the Three Kingdoms* state that the Koguryŏ founder Chumong named himself Ko after his country and gave his loyal retainers the surnames Kŭk, Chungsil, and Sosil as a royal gift. Many other kings gave surnames to their retainers, but names from Koguryŏ have mostly disappeared. Most people named Ko today belong to the T'amna Ko clan. It is said that a number of Kos descended from Chumong live in Hoengsŏng, Kangwŏn province.

Paekje founder Onjo is said to have come from Puyŏ and used the surnames Puyŏ and Yŏ. In Paekje lived the Chŏn, Ma, the Sŏngju To, and the Puyŏ Sŏ clans. Additionally, there were the surnames Onjo bestowed on his eight patriarchs: Paek, Sa, Hyŏp, Hae, Yŏn, Chin, Mok, and Kuk. From the Silla period, three surnames, Pak, Sŏk, and Kim, have been passed down, as well as six surnames that King Yuri gave to his six village chiefs, surnames still in use today: Ch'oe, Chŏng, Son, Pae, Sŏl, and Yi. *The Record of the Three Kingdoms* states that during the Three Kingdoms period, more people lacked surnames than possessed them. Those who used surnames were mostly envoys who journeyed back and forth from China, Confucian scholars, and people engaged in commerce, like Chang Pogo.

Korean surnames were systematized during the Koryŏ period. King T'aejo gave surnames to his meritorious retainers and to powerful local families. The four retainers Hong Yu, Pae Hyŏn-gyŏng, Sin Sung-gyŏm, and Pok Chi-gyŏm each became founder of the Pugye Hong clan, the Kyŏngju Pae clan, P'yŏngsan Sin clan, and the Myŏnch'ŏn Pok clan, respectively. Kim Sin of Silla counseled King T'aejo, and received from the King the surname Kwŏn. He became the founder of the Andong Kwŏn clan. In 1055, in the mid-Koryŏ period, during King Munjong's reign, a statute was established disqualifying people without surnames from the state examinations. This tells us that by that time, surnames had become universalized among the officials and the aristocracy.

Naturalized surnames

By the early Chosŏn period, the use of surnames become universal even among common citizens. Servants and the lowborn, however, could not have surnames until the late Chosŏn period. In 1909, with the enforcement of new census registration laws, people without surnames could, if they desired, have and use surnames. Such people took the surname of their neighbor or master, or neighborhood clerks and police authorities made names arbitrarily for them.

According to a population and housing survey conducted in 1985, there are 274 surnames used in Korea, and 3,435 ancestral homes. The most frequent surname is Kim, accounting for 21.7% of all families, followed by Yi at 14.8%, Pak at 8.5%, Ch'oe at 4.8%, and Chŏng at 4.4%. The surnames Kang, Cho, Yun, Chang, Im, Han, Sin, O, Sŏ, and Kwŏn each occupy over 1% of the total. There are some 40 rare surnames each owned by fewer than 100 persons. Mostly these surnames result from erroneous census entries, entries for the orphaned, or naturalized foreigners.

Of Korea's 274 surnames, 130 are "naturalized" from foreign countries. Among these, Chinese surnames are the most numerous. In the Koryŏ period, many people from Mongolia, Djurchin, Uighur, Arabia, Vietnam, and Japan became naturalized and created surnames. The Mongolian Hurat'ai, who followed Princess Cheguk, consort of King Ch'ungnyŏl, to Korea and became naturalized, became the founder of the Yŏnan Yi clan. The Djurchin T'ungduran, who helped King T'aejo (Yi Sŏng-gye) and performed meritorious deeds at the opening of the new dynasty, received the name Yi Chiran and became the founder of the Ch'ŏnghae Yi clan. Among naturalized surnames, some are used by over 1,000,000 people—like the Tŏksu Chang and the Hanyang Cho clans—and many are very rare, like Sŏp, Ma, P'ung, and Ch'o.

Saemi kip'ŭn mul, Feb. 2001, 114

제20과 춘향전

(Lesson 20: The Story of Ch'unhyang)

Objectives

춘향전은 한국의 대표적인 고전으로 오랫동안 한국인들에게 사랑받아 왔다. 한국의 대표적인 연애 소설이라 할 수 있는 춘향전을 읽어 보고 춘향전에 배어 있는 한국인들의 전통적 사고 방식과 가치관을 알아본다.

The purpose of this chapter is to read *Ch'unhyangjŏn*, a classical work long appreciated by Koreans as their representative traditional love story. From it, we will learn about traditional Korean thought and values.

Pre-reading questions

1. 여러분이 알고 있는 전래 소설이나 동화가 있습니까? 심청전, 흥부와
   놀부 등 알고 있는 전래 소설이나 동화에 대해 이야기해 보세요.

2. 전래 소설이나 동화의 공통점은 무엇이라고 생각합니까?

3. 조선 시대의 과거 제도에 대해 아는 것이 있습니까?

4. '암행 어사'는 어떤 일을 하는 사람인지 아세요?

5. 춘향전은 여러 번 영화화되었습니다. 가장 최근의 영화는 임권택
   감독의 '춘향뎐'입니다. 여러분은 춘향전 영화를 본 적이 있습니까?
   여러분의 경험에 대해 이야기해 보세요. 영화를 본 적이 없으면 다음의
   인터넷 사이트에 가서 영화 평을 읽어 보세요.

   http://movie-reviews.colossus.net/movies/c/chunhyang.html

Gaining familiarity

1. 과거시험, (장원) 급제, (암행) 어사

2. 효자, 효녀, 열녀, 충신

3. 동고 동락, 독수 공방, 천생 연분, 백년 가약

4. 판소리: 춘향전, 심청전

춘향전

1. 조선 숙종 대왕 (1674－1720)때 전라도 남원에 월매라는 기생이 있었는데, 월매는 나이 40이 넘어 성 씨라는 양반과의 사이에서 구슬 같은 딸을 낳았다. 월매는 딸을 춘향이라 부르면서, 보옥 같이 길렀다. 춘향이는 얼굴이 뛰어나게 아름다운데다가 비길 데 없는 효녀였고 어질고 착하고 예절 바르고 글공부에 뛰어나서 남원에서 칭찬하지 않는 사람이 없었다.

2. 이때 충신의 후손인 이한림이라 하는 양반이 임금님의 명을 받아 남원 부사로 내려왔다. 이 사또에게는 이몽룡이라는 16살 되는 아들이 하나 있었다. 이 도령은 과거 시험을 보려고 밤낮 열심히 글공부를 하고 있었다. 어느 따뜻한 봄날 이 도령은 방자를 불러,

이 도령: 이 고을에 경치 좋은 곳이 어디냐?

방자: 글공부하시는 도령님이 좋은 경치를 찾음은 옳지 못합니다.

이 도령: 너 무식하기 짝이 없구나![20.1] 옛날부터 아름다운 강산을 구경하는 것은 글 짓는데 근본이 되는 거야.

방자는 여러 좋은 곳을 말했는데, 이 도령은 광한루로 가자고 했다. 사또의 허락을 받은 뒤, 나귀를 타고 방자를 데리고 광한루에 이르렀다. 이 도령은 광한루에서 한잔 술을 마시고 절경을 보고 있을 때 꾀꼬리는 울고 노랑벌, 흰나비가 향기를 찾아 날아다녔다.

3. 이날은 마침 5월 단오날이라 춘향이는 광한루 근처에서 그네 놀이를 하고 있었다. 그네 줄을 두 손에 갈라 잡고 흰 보선발로 발을 구를 때 버들 같은 고운 몸이 하늘로 치솟았다.

이 도령: 방자야, 저 건너 꽃 속에서 오락가락 희뜩희뜩 얼른얼른하는 게 뭐냐?

방자: 다른 게 아니라,[20.2] 이 고을 기생이던 월매란 사람의 딸
           춘향이란 아이입니다. 제 어미는 기생이나 춘향이는
           글공부도 많이 하여 양반 집 따님과 다름이 없습니다.
이도령: 허허, 기생의 딸이라니 빨리 가서 불러 오너라!

방자는 도령님의 분부로 춘향이한테 가서,

방자: 애 춘향아, 큰일 났다. 사또 자제 도령님이 광한루에
           오셨다가 너 노는 모습을 보고 불러오라는 명령이시다.
춘향: (화를 내며) 너 미쳤구나. 도령님이 어찌 나를 알아서
           부른단 말이냐? 네가 내 말을 종달새처럼 지껄였나
           보구나!

이렇게 말한 뒤에 춘향이는 집으로 돌아가 버렸다.

4. 방자는 도령님의 분부로 춘향이를 데리러 춘향이 집에 찾아가니 모
   녀가 마주 앉아 점심을 먹고 있었다.

춘향: 너 왜 또 오는 거니?
방자: 도령님은 네가 글을 잘 쓴다하여 청하는 것이란다.[20.3]
           잠깐만 다녀 가라 하시더라.

춘향이는 갈 마음이 났으나 어머니의 뜻을 몰라 묵묵히 앉아
있는데,

춘향 모친: 간밤 꿈에 청룡 한 마리가 보이기에 무슨 좋은 일이
           있을까 하였더니, 우연한 일이 아니구나. 듣자하니[20.4] 사또
           자제 도령님의 이름이 꿈 몽자 용 용자라니 내 꿈이
           신통하게 맞춘 것 같구나. 그러나 저러나 양반이
           부르시는데 안 갈 수 있겠니? 잠깐 다녀 오너라.

그제야 춘향이는 못 이기는 체하고 일어나서 광한루로 건너갔다.

이 도령: 네 성은 무엇이며 나이는 몇 살이냐?

춘향: 성은 성 씨고 나이는 열여섯입니다.

이 도령: 허허 그 말 반갑구나. 나와 성이 다르고 나이는 동갑이라
          우리 좋은 연분이니 평생 동고 동락하면 어떻겠냐?

춘향: 충신은 두 임금을 섬기지 않고 열녀는 남편을 바꾸지
          않는 법입니다. 도령님은 귀공자고 저는 천한 몸이에요.
          한번 정을 맡긴 후에 저를 버리시면 저는 평생
          독수 공방하면서 홀로 울어야 합니다. 그러니 그런 분부
          다시는 마십시오.

이 도령: 우리 둘이 인연을 맺을 때는 하늘에 맹세하고 맺을 거다.
          그래서 오늘 밤 너의 집에 찾아가겠다.

5. 춘향이가 돌아간 뒤 이 도령은 춘향이 말소리가 귀에 쟁쟁하고 고운
   태도가 눈에 삼삼하여 해 지기만 기다렸다. 날이 어두워지자 방자가
   비추는 호롱 불을 따라 남 몰래 춘향이 집을 찾아갔다.

방자: 애, 춘향아. 잠들었니? 도령님이 와 계시다.

춘향이는 이 말을 듣고 가슴이 울렁거렸다. 허둥지둥 문을 열고
나와 건넌방에 가서 어머니를 깨워,

춘향: 방자가 도령님 모시고 오셨어요!!

춘향 모친: (뛰어나와) 도령님 문안드리겠습니다.

이 도령: 춘향이 모친인가? 평안한가?[20.5] 자네 딸 춘향이와 백년
          가약을 맺고 싶은데 자네의 마음은 어떠한가?

춘향 모친: 그런 말씀 마시고 노시다가 가시기나 하시지요.[20.6]

이 도령: 대장부가 먹은 마음이니 제발 허락하여 주게.

이 도령의 애원에 춘향이 모친은 마침내 두 사람의 결합을 허락하였
다.

6. 두 사람은 하늘에 맹세한 후, 이날 밤부터 꽃다운 사랑과 온갖 뜨거운 정을 나누었다. 이렇게 한 해가 꿈 같이 지나갔다. 그런데, 어느 날 이 사또는 승진하여 한양(지금 서울)으로 떠나게 되었다. 그래서 이 도령도 춘향이를 두고 떠나야 했다. 이 말을 들은 춘향이는 너무도 기막혀서,

춘향:　　　　(슬프게 울면서) 도령님! 우리가 처음 만나 하늘에 맹세한 백년 가약은 어떻게 된 거예요? 제 몸이 천하다고[20.7] 함부로 버리셔도 되는 건가요? 정말 죽고 싶어요.

이 도령:　　춘향아 울지 마라! 너를 두고 가야 하니 나 어찌 답답하지 않겠니? 지금 너를 두고 떠난다고 너를 잠시인들[20.8] 잊겠느냐? 과거에 급제하거든 너를 꼭 데리러 오마.[20.9]

춘향이는 낭군을 한양으로 떠나보내고 슬픔으로 세월을 보내고 있었다.

7. 그런데 남원에는 변학도라는 고집이 세고 성격이 좋지 않은 양반이 새 부사로 오게 되었다. 변 사또는 이미 춘향이가 예쁘다는 소문을 듣고 춘향이를 불러오게 했다. 사람들이 춘향이는 기생이 아니고 이 몽룡과 백년 가약을 맺었다고 말했지만 듣지 않았다. 이리하여 드디어 변 사또 앞에 춘향이가 나타났는데 한눈에 혹한 변 사또는 춘향이에게 사또 수청을 들게 했다. 춘향이는 거절했고 변 사또는 계속 고집했다.

춘향:　　　　충신은 두 임금을 섬기지 않으며 열녀는 두 남편을 섬기지 않습니다. 분부가 그러하니 사는 것이 죽느니만 못합니다.[20.10]

변 사또:　　(화를 내며) 이년 들어라. 사또의 명을 따르지 않은 죄로 너를 엄벌에 처하겠다.

춘향:　　　유부녀를 겁탈하는 것은 죄가 아니고 무엇인가요?
변 사또:　(벌벌 떨며) 여봐라! 이년을 형틀에 올려 매고 매를 쳐라!

춘향이는 죽도록 매를 맞으면서도 변 사또의 말을 듣지 않았다. 변 사또는 반은 죽고 반은 산 춘향이를 감옥에 가두었다. 춘향이는 이 도령 오기만 기다리면서 옥중에서 슬픔으로 나날을 보냈다.

8. 한편 이 도령은 서울로 올라간 뒤 밤마다 춘향이가 그리워서 잠을 잘 수가 없었다. 과거 시험에 급제하면 춘향이를 만날 수 있다고 믿고 열심히 시험 준비를 했다. 몇 년이 지난 후 이 도령은 과거 시험에서 장원으로 급제하였고 임금님은 이 도령을 불러 전라도 암행 어사로 명하였다. 드디어 이 도령의 평생의 소원이 이루어진 것이다. 부모님께 하직 인사를 하고, 걸인처럼 꾸민 후 부하들과 함께 전라도로 향하였다. 남원 근처에서 농부들한테서 변학도의 학정과 춘향이의 기막힌 처지를 자세히 들었다.

9. 어사는 밤중에 춘향이 집에 들어가서,

어사:　　　그 안에 누구 있느냐?
춘향 모친: 뉘시오?
어사:　　　나네.
춘향 모친: 나라니 뉘신가?
어사:　　　이 서방이네.
춘향 모친: 이 서방이라니?
어사:　　　허허 장모 망령 났군. 나를 몰라? 나를?

춘향 모친은 무척 반가워하며 손을 잡고 들어가서 촛불 앞에 앉혀 놓고 자세히 살펴보니 걸인 중에 상걸인이었다.

춘향 모친:(기가 막혀) 이게 웬 일이요?

어사: 한양으로 올라간 후 부친의 벼슬이 끊어져서 집안이
             망하고 부친은 서당 선생으로 가시고 모친은 친정으로
             가시고 나는 춘향이에게 돈이나 얻어 갈까 하고 내려
             왔네.
춘향 모친: (기가 막혀) 도대체 내 딸 춘향이를 어찌 할 건가?
어사: 장모, 그러나 저러나 춘향이나 좀 보아야겠네.

10. 이리하여 그날 밤 옥에 갇힌 춘향이를 찾아갔다.

춘향 모친: 춘향아, 춘향아, 너의 서방인지 남방인지 걸인이 하나
             내려 왔다. 만나 보아라.
춘향: 이게 웬 말이에요! 서방님이 오시다니.[20.11] 꿈속에서 보던
             임을 생시에 본단 말이에요! 이제 죽어도 한이 없겠어요.
             (임의 형상을 자세히 보더니) 여보 서방님, 내 몸 하나
             죽는 것은 서러운 마음 없지만 서방님은 어쩌다 이
             지경이 되셨나요?
어사: (춘향이가 슬프게 울고 있을 때) 춘향아 서러워 마라.
             사람 목숨은 하늘에 매인 것이니 설마 네가 죽겠느냐?
             하늘이 무너져도 솟아날 구멍이 있는 거다. 내일 다시
             보자구나.[20.12]

어사는 작별하고 춘향이 집으로 돌아왔다.

11. 그 다음날은 변 사또의 생일 잔치가 광한루에서 크게 벌어졌다. 근
처의 여러 고을에서 많은 수령들과 양반들이 모였다. 화려한 음식이
차려졌다. 비단 옷을 입은 기생들이 덩실덩실 춤을 추고 모두가 흥
에 넘쳐 있었다. 그때 어느 걸인이 들어서며,

걸인: 여봐라. 사또에게 여쭈어라. 먼 데 사는 걸인이 좋은
             잔치에 왔으니 술상이나 받고 싶어 한다고 여쭈어라.

이리하여 걸인은 술과 밥을 얻어 먹고 있는데, 양반들은 흥이 나서 글짓기를 시작했다.

걸인:　　　배불리 먹고 그저 가기 미안하니 저도 시 한 수 짓겠습니다.

걸인은 다음과 같은 시를 써 주고 나가 버렸다.

> **금동이의 아름다운 술은 일만 백성의 피요**
> **옥소반의 맛 좋은 안주는 일만 백성의 기름이라**
> **촛불의 눈물이 떨어질 때 백성의 눈물이 떨어지고**
> **노래 소리 높은 곳에 원망 소리 높구나**

12. 잠시 후 "암행 어사 출두요!, 암행 어사 출두요!, 암행 어사 출두요!"

외치는 소리, 강산이 무너지고 천지가 뒤집힌 듯하였다. 이윽고 변 사또는 땅바닥에 무릎을 꿇고 어사 앞에 엎드렸다. 어사는 당장 변 사또의 파직을 명하였다. 그리고 형리에게 명하여 옥에 갇힌 죄수를 모두 데려오도록 하여 한 사람씩 죄를 다시 물은 뒤에 억울한 사람을 풀어 주었다. 그러다가,

어사:　　　저 계집은 무슨 죄냐?
형리:　　　변 사또의 수청을 거절하고 수절하겠다고 관청 뜰에서 사또에게 반항한 춘향입니다.
어사:　　　네가 관청 뜰에서 사또에게 반항하였으니 어찌 살기를 바라느냐? 내 수청도 거절할 거냐?
춘향:　　　높은 절벽의 바위가 바람이 분들 무너지며, 청송, 녹죽 푸른색이 눈이 온 들 변하겠습니까? 어서 죽여 주십시오.
어사:　　　얼굴을 들고 나를 보아라!

춘향이가 고개를 들어 대 위를 살펴보았다. 이것이 꿈이냐, 생시냐! 어젯밤 걸인으로 왔던 낭군이 어사로 앉아 있는 것이 아닌가! 춘향이는 너무도 기쁘고 행복해서 낭군을 끌어 앉고 한없이 울었다.

13. 어사는 전라도를 두루 돌아본 뒤에 춘향이를 데리고 한양으로 올라 갔다. 임금님께서는 춘향이를 이몽룡의 부인으로 승인하였고 이몽룡은 여러 높은 벼슬을 하게 되었다. 이몽룡은 부인 춘향이와 더불어 백 년을 동락하면서 삼남 이녀의 훌륭한 자녀를 두게 되었다.

손호민, 원문에서 축약 및 각색

New Words

가약 marriage vow, pledge of eternal love ▷백년 가약을 맺다 to exchange marriage vows

간밤 last night

갈라 잡다 to hold (two swing ropes) with each hand. 가르다 to divide, split, sever

강산 rivers and mountains, landscape, scenery

거절하다 to refuse, reject, turn down

건너 the other (opposite) side of, over there ▷건너 마을 village on the other side

건넌방 opposite room, room on the opposite side (= 건넛방)

걸인 beggar (= 거지)

겁탈하다 to rape, rob, plunder

결합 union, combination

경치 scenery, scenic beauty, view

계집 female, woman (usually derogatory)

고을 district of a province, county

고집 stubbornness, obstinacy ▷고집이 세다 to be stubborn, obstinate, pigheaded

과거 시험 state examinations in old Korea

관청 government office

광한루 Kwanghan Tower in Namwŏn, setting of the Ch'unhyang story

구슬 gem, bead

귀공자 young noble

그네 swing

그러나 저러나 at any rate, anyhow, anyway, in any case

그립다 to be longed for, be dear ▷그리운 추억 happy memories ▷그리운 사람 person dear to one

그저 without doing anything, without giving any reason ▷그저 가다 to go without doing anything, go without giving any reason

그제야 for the first time, at last, not . . . until, only then

근본 foundation, basis, root, source

글 짓다 to write a composition, compose a piece

글공부 studying (one's books). 글 learning, literature, letters

금동이 golden jar. 동이 small jar. 물동이 water jar

급제하다 to pass (an examination) (= 합격하다)

기(가) 막히다 to be dumbfounded, amazed, stunned

기생 female entertainer [singing and dancing girl] in traditional society of Korea, Korean geisha

꽃답다 to be beautiful, lovely [pretty] as a flower ▷꽃다운 청춘 bloom of one's youth ▷꽃다운 처녀 beautiful young girl

꾀꼬리 Korean nightingale, oriole

꾸미다 to decorate, disguise oneself ▷걸인으로 꾸미다 to disguise as a beggar

꿈 몽자 용 용자 the character 몽 meaning 'dream', and the character 용 meaning 'dragon'

끊어지다 to break (down), be cut, be terminated

끌어안다 to hug, embrace tightly, hold (a person) to one's breast

나귀 donkey (= 당나귀)

나누다 to share (with) ▷정을 나누다 to share love (with)

남방 the south side ▷서방인지 남방인지 either the west side or the south side, your husband or something (남방 is meaningless in this context). 서방인지 남방인지 is a contemptuous expression to refer to the beggar-like husband of Ch'unhyang.

남원 Namwŏn, a city in the southeastern part of North Chŏlla Province

낭군 one's dear husband

넘치다 to overflow, brim over

노랑벌 yellow bee

녹죽 green bamboo

농부 farmer, peasant, peasantry

뉘시오? contraction of 누구시오? Who are you? (= 누구세요?)

다녀 가다 to drop in for a short visit (and then go), call at (a house), stop at (a place), drop [look] in (on a person). 다녀오다 to drop in for a short visit (and then come)

다름(이) 없다 to be same, similar, as good as, no different (from)

단오(날) the fifth day of the fifth lunar month, the May Festival (when women play on swings and men have wrestling matches)

당장 on the spot, then and there, at once, immediately

대 stand, rest ▷대 위 on top of a stand

대장부 manly man, chivalrous man ▷대장부가 먹은 마음 the resolution that a manly man has made (a relative clause form of 대장부가 마음(을) 먹다 a manly man made up his mind [made a resolution, is determined])

덩실덩실 (dancing) lively, joyfully, cheerfully ▷덩실덩실 춤을 추다 to dance a spirited dance

데리다 to take (a person) along with one, be accompanied by, be attended by

도대체 in the world, on earth, at all

도령(님) young gentleman, unmarried boy (as addressed by servants) in old Korea (The contemporary form 도련님 refers to one's husband's younger brother.)

독수 공방하다 to live alone, live apart from one's husband (*lit.*, to keep an empty room alone)

동갑 same age, person of the same age ▷우리는 동갑이다. We are of the same age.

동고 동락하다 to share one's joys and sorrows (with), share the pleasures and pains of life (with)

두다 to keep, have ▷이남 사녀를 두다 to have two sons and four daughters

두루 all around, throughout (= 골고루), far and wide (= 널리) ▷두루 돌아보다 to look all around

뒤집히다 to be turned inside out

들어서다 to step in

떠나보내다 to send one off

뛰어나게 preeminently, outstandingly, by far

뜰 yard, garden, ground

뜻 intent, intention, mind, wish, want

마주 앉다 to sit face-to-face (with each other, with a person, opposite a person)

마침내 at last, finally, in the end

망령 나다 to be in one's dotage. 망령 dotage, senility

망하다 to perish, die out ▷집안이 망하다 family goes down

매를 치다 to whip, cane, flog. 매 rod, whip, 치다 to hit, strike, beat, knock

매이다 to be tied, be bound up with ▷일에 매이다 to be tied down to the job ▷우리 목숨은 하늘에 매여 있다. Our lives are at the mercy of Heaven.

맹세하다 to swear, pledge, make an oath, vow

맺다 to knot, tie, form, make, contract

명 order, command (= 명령). 명하다 to order, command

명령 bidding, order, command

모녀 mother and daughter

모습 features, looks, appearance, shape, figure

모시다 to accompany, escort, attend, serve (a senior person)

모친 one's mother (honorific form of 어머니 (= 어머님))

목숨 life ▷귀한 목숨 one's precious life ▷목숨을 걸고 at the risk of one's life

몰래 secretly, stealthily, furtively ▷남 몰래 (= 남 모르게) by stealth, avoiding others' notice

못 이기는 체하다 to pretend not to be able to do otherwise (*lit.,* one pretends that one cannot win)

무너지다 to collapse, fall down ▷하늘이 무너져도 솟아날 구멍이 있는 거다. There is a way out of every situation, however bad.

무식하다 to be ignorant, illiterate

무척 very, extremely, exceedingly

묵묵히 silently, mutely

문안 asking [inquiry] after the health of another, sending kind regards. 문안드리다 to ask after the health of a senior person, send kind regards to a senior person

미치다 to become insane, go out of one's mind, go crazy

반항하다 to resist, oppose, disobey, rebel against

발을 구르다 to stamp one's feet; to push up (a swing) by pressing the pedal forward with the feet

방자 servant, footman (in old Korea)

배불리 heartily, to one's heart's content. 배불리 먹다 to eat one's fill, eat heartily

백성 the people, common people [obsolete] (= 국민)

버들 willow

벌어지다 to happen, arise, develop, open

벼슬 government post, official rank [obsolete] (= 관직) ▷높은 벼슬을 하다 to obtain a high post in the government

보선 traditional Korean socks usually made of cotton (= 버선). 보선발 feet in Korean socks

보옥 jewel, precious gem (= 보석)

부사 (old term for) mayor, county chief (currently 시장 mayor, 군수 county chief)

부친 one's father (honorific form of 아버지) (= 아버님)

부하 subordinate, follower, man under one's charge

분부 order, command, bidding of a superior. 분부하다 to bid, order, command

불러 오다 to summon, bring (*lit.,* to call someone and come)

비길 데 없다 to be unparalleled, have no comparison. 비기다 to compare. 데 place

비단 옷 silk dress. 비단 silk fabrics, satin

비추다 to flash (the beam) on, shed (light) on

사또 an honorific term for a governor, mayor, county chief, local magistrate (in old Korea)

살펴보다 to look all around, look into, examine, observe

삼남 이녀 three sons and two daughters ▷삼남 이녀의 자녀를 두다 to have three sons and two daughters

삼삼하다 to be unforgettably vivid (= 선하다) ▷눈에 삼삼하다 [선하다] to be vivid to one's eyes

상걸인 the most wretched of beggars

생시 one's lifetime

서당 village schoolhouse in old Korea

서러워 마라 Don't feel sad. ▷서러워하다 to grieve, feel sad, have a heavy heart

서방 Mr. (a familiar title used within the family, especially to one's husband, son-in-law, or younger brother-in-law)

설마 by any means; hardly; on no account; surely (not)

섬기다 to serve, be devoted to (one's master)

성격 character, personality

세월 time and tide, times

소문 rumor, hearsay, news

소원 one's desire, one's wish

솟아나다 to spring out

수 piece, poem ▷시 한 수 짓다 to compose a poem

수령 provincial mandarin, magistrate

수절하다 to remain chaste, remain faithful to one's deceased husband

수차 several times, time and again

수청 bed service ▷수청(을) 들다 to serve (one's master) as a mistress in old Korea, (기생) to give her body from time to time to the local magistrate

숙종 대왕 Sukchong the Great (1674 – 1720), the nineteenth king of the Chosǒn dynasty

술상 drinking table ▷술상을 받다 to get a drinking table

승인하다 to approve, admit, acknowledge

승진하다 to be promoted

신통하게 marvelously, admirably

안주 appetizers (hors d'oeuvres) served with drinks

암행 어사 secret inspector-general, undercover emissary of the king. 암행 travelling in secret. 어사 royal emissary

애원 entreaty, appeal, supplication

어미 mother [vulgar], mother animal

어질다 to be wise, gentle, considerate

어쩌다(가) how, by doing what, by chance (= 어찌 하다가) ▷어쩌다 이 지경이 되셨나요? What has happened to you that you have come to this miserable condition?

어찌 how, in what way, by what means ▷어찌 나를 알아서 부른단 말이냐? How could (he possibly) know me that (he) summons me?

억울하다 to suffer unfairness, feel victimized, be mistreated

얻어 가다 to get something for free

얻어 먹다 to beg ▷친척한테서 얻어 먹다 to live off one's relatives

얼떨결에 on the spur of the moment, in a moment of bewilderment ▷얼떨결에 그렇게 말해 버렸어요. I said so in my bewilderment. ▷얼떨결에 버스를 잘못 탔어요. I took a wrong bus on the spur of the moment.

얼른얼른하다 to glisten (mimetic word)

엄벌 severe [heavy] punishment ▷엄벌에 처하다 to sentence (one) to a heavy punishment

엎드리다 to lie on the ground, prostrate oneself, throw oneself down on the knees

여봐라 hey! (as when a magistrate calls out his men) [archaic] (derived from 여기 보아라)

여쭙다 to tell, say, inform, ask, inquire

연분 preordained tie, bond, fate, relation (= 인연)

열녀 heroine, woman of chaste reputation, exceptionally virtuous woman

예절 바르다 to be well mannered, have good manners. 예절 propriety, etiquette, manners. 바르다 to be correct, straight

오락가락 coming and going, milling (mimetic word)

옥소반 jade tray, small jade dining table

옥에 갇히다 to be imprisoned. 옥 prison, jail

옥중 inside of a jail

온갖 every kind of, all sorts of, all manner of

외치다 to shout out, call out, cry out

우연하다 to be accidental, incidental

울렁거리다 to palpitate, throb, pound, beat

원망 resentment, reproach, grievance, grudge

유부녀 married woman (lit., woman having a husband)

이년 "you bitch (wench)" [vulgar]

이르다 to arrive, reach

이윽고 after a while, before long

인연 karma, fate, tie, bond, relation (= 연분) ▷인연을 맺다 to form a relation

임 lover, sweetheart

임금(님) king, monarch

자네 you, your (familiar speech style)

자녀 children

자세히 minutely, in full, in detail

자제 son, sons, child, children

작별하다 to part, take leave, say good-bye

장모 man's mother-in-law

장원 the highest passing mark in the state examination in old Korea ▷장원(으로)
　　　급제하다 to win the first place in the state examination

쟁쟁하다 to be clear, sonorous, resonant

적응 adaptation. 적응하다 to adapt oneself (to), adjust oneself (to) ▷새 환경에
　　　적응하다 to adapt to new circumstances

전라도 Chŏlla Province (comprises both 전라남도 South Chŏlla Province and
　　　전라북도 North Chŏlla Province; in the Chosŏn dynasty, the south-north
　　　division was not made)

절경 magnificent view, fine scenery

절벽 (sheer) cliff, inaccessible precipice

정을 맡기다 to set one's affections on (a person) (= 정을 주다)

종달새 lark, skylark

죄 sin, crime, offense

죄수 prisoner, convict

지경 situation, (miserable) condition

지껄이다 to chatter, gabble ▷네가 내 말을 종달새처럼 지껄였나 보구나! It appears
　　　that you chattered to him about me like a skylark. (내 말 words [things]
　　　about me)

집안 family, household, one's relatives

짝 one of a pair, the partner

차려지다 to be set, arranged, prepared. 차리다 to set the table ▷저녁을 차리다 to
　　　set the table for dinner

착하다 to be good, nice, kindhearted

처지 situation, condition, circumstances

처하다 to sentence, deal (with) ▷엄벌에 처하다 to sentence (one) to a heavy
　　　punishment

천지 heaven and earth, universe, world

천하다 to be low, humble (in social status)

청룡 blue dragon

청송 green pine

청하다 to ask, request, invite

촛불 candlelight

춘향 Ch'unhyang, the name of the heroine of the story (*lit.,* spring fragrance).
춘향전 the story of Ch'unhyang

출두 appearance, presence, showing up

충신 loyal subject

치솟다 to rise suddenly and swiftly, shoot up, skyrocket

친정 woman's parents' (old) home, one's maiden home

칭찬하다 to praise, admire, speak highly of

태도 attitude, manner, behavior

파직 dismissal (removal) from office, discharge. 파직하다 to dismiss (a person)
from office

평생 one's whole life, lifetime, throughout one's life

평안하다 to be well, peaceful

풀어 주다 to release, set free

하직 인사 saying good-bye, leave-taking

학정 oppressive government, tyranny, despotism

한 regret; grudge ▷죽어도 한이 없다 to have nothing to regret even if one dies

한없이 endlessly, extremely, greatly ▷한없이 울다 to cry endlessly

함부로 at random, without good reason; rudely

향기 fragrance, scent, sweet odor, aroma

허둥지둥 all flustered (mimetic word)

형리 legal clerk in a local government [obsolete]

형상 shape, appearance, form

형틀 chair in which a criminal is fastened to be interrogated [archaic]

호롱 불 the light of a kerosene lamp

혹하다 to become infatuated, fascinated, charmed

홀로 alone, single-handed

화(를) 내다 to become angry, flare up, give vent to one's anger

화려하다 to be splendid, gorgeous, gay

효녀 filial [dutiful] daughter

후손 descendants, offspring, posterity

흥 mirth, fun, pleasure, excitement. 흥이 나다 to get excited ▷흥에 겨워 in the
excess of mirth, driven by one's enthusiasm ▷흥이 넘치다 to be full of mirth

희뜩희뜩 very dizzy, giddy, shaky (mimetic word)

흰나비 white butterfly

Useful Expressions

1. **~기(가) 짝이 없다** it is extremely ~; there is no match for ~ (*lit.,* 'one of a pair is lacking in ~)

   무식하기(가) 짝이 없구나.

   You are extremely ignorant. (*lit.,* 'your being ignorant is matchless')

   나는 취직하게 되어 기쁘기(가) 짝이 없어요.

   I am extremely happy to get a job.

2. **다른 게 아니라** it is nothing but; for no other reason than; just

   용호가 그렇게 말하는 것은 다른 게 아니라 결국 자기가 옳다는 거야.

   Yongho is saying so just to show that he was right.

   안녕하세요? 다른 게 아니라 (or 다름이 아니라) 좀 부탁할 일이 있어서 왔는데요.

   Hi. I have come for no other reason than to make a request of you.

   선생님: 너 어제 왜 학교에 안 왔니?

   Why were you absent from school yesterday?

   학생: 다른 게 아니라 (다름이 아니라) 어머니가 아프셔서 올 수 없었어요.

   It is only that I couldn't come because my mother was sick.

3. **~(이)란다** you see; you know; it really is

   도령님은 네가 글을 잘 쓴다 하여 청하는 것이란다.

   The young master is inviting you because you are known to be a good writer, you see.

   저 오른 편에 보이는 기는 불란서 대사관의 기란다.

   The flag you can see over on the right is the flag of the French Embassy, you see.

4. **듣자하니** as I have heard; as I understand

   듣자하니 이 학교의 학생들은 모두 아주 열심히 공부 한다더군요.

   As I have heard, all the students at this school study very hard.

5. **The familiar speech style**

   The familiar style endings include ~네 (statement), ~는/은/ㄴ가 (question), ~세 (suggestion), and ~게 (command), as in 나는 가네, 평안한가? 우리 먹세, 허락하여 주게. In contemporary Korean, these endings are not used productively, except perhaps to one's sons-in-law, male's adult younger male cousins or nephews, male's friends' adult children, or male's aged male friends whose friendship started in childhood or adolescence. In old Korea, where a caste system prevailed, however, this style was used much more widely by both males and females, especially to one's social inferiors. Thus, it was usually the case that a younger upper-class person used this style to an older lower-class person, while receiving a deferential or polite ending.

6. **~기나 하다** just do ~

술을 마시기나 합시다.

Let's just drink some wine (forgetting about other things).

노시다가 가시기나 하시지요.

How about just enjoy yourself for a while and leave?

7. **~다고** even though ~; simply because ~

너를 두고 떠난다고 어찌 너를 잊겠느냐?

Even though I am departing leaving you behind, how could I forget you?

가난한 사람이 공부를 잘 한다고 금방 부자가 되겠어요?

Will a poor person become rich at once simply because he or she studies hard?

8. **~(으)ㄴ들/는들** granted that ~; even though ~

너를 잠시인들 잊겠느냐?

How can I forget even if it is a short while?

절벽의 바위가 바람이 분들 무너지며, 청송, 녹죽 푸른색이 눈이 온들 변하겠어요?

Would rocks fall from a cliff by the winds, or would the green pine or green bamboo ever change their color?

9. **~(으)마** I promise ~

너를 꼭 데리러 오마.

I promise to come back to get you by all means.

이 약 이따가 먹으마.

I promise to take this medicine later.

10. **~느니만 못하다** worse than doing ~

사는 것이 죽느니만 못하다.

It is worse for one to remain alive than to die.

일하는 것이 공부하느니만 못한 것 같아요.

It seems that working is worse than studying.

11. **~다니/라니** (as, since) you said that ~ (At the end of a sentence, this often has an added meaning 'I can't believe it' or 'I don't get it'.)

   기생의 딸이라니 빨리 가서 불러오너라.

   As you said she is a daughter of a *kisaeng*, why don't you hurry and call her here!

   이게 웬 말이에요! 서방님이 오시다니.

   What are you saying?! My husband has come! I can't believe it.

   아이고 벌써 봄이라니.

   Oh, it's already spring—I can't believe it.

12. **~자구나** let's ~

   This sentence ending connotes greater intimacy and emotion than the simple ~자, as in 내일 다시 보자 versus 내일 다시 보자구나.

Exercises

1. 관련된 단어들끼리 연결하여 문장을 만들어 보세요.

(1) 시험　•	• 구르다
(2) 글　•	• 급제하다.
(3) 발　•	• 보다
(4) 과거　•	• 짓다
(5) 엄벌　•	• 처하다
(6) 소원　•	• 이루어지다

   _____

   _____

   _____

   _____

   _____

   _____

2. 아래의 설명과 맞는 단어나 표현을 보기에서 찾아 쓰세요.

> 보기: 무식하다, 절경, 효녀, 충신, 동갑

   (1) 효성이 지극한 딸: _____

   (2) 나라와 임금을 위해 충성을 다하는 신하: _____

   (3) 지식이 부족하다: _____

   (4) 뛰어나게 아름다운 경치: _____

   (5) 서로 같은 나이: _____

3. 보기에서 적당한 말을 골라 빈칸을 채우세요.

> 보기: 울렁거렸다, 향하였다, 어두워졌다, 가두었다, 드렸다, 맺었다

   (1) 춘향이 말소리가 귀에 쟁쟁하고 고운 태도가 눈에 삼삼하여 해 지기만 기다렸다. 드디어 날이 _____.

   (2) 도령님이 와 계시다는 말을 듣고 가슴이 _____.

   (3) 방자가 도령님을 모시고 오자 춘향 모친이 뛰어나와 도령님께 문안을 _____.

   (4) 사람들이 춘향이는 기생이 아니고 이몽룡과 백년 가약을 _____고 말했지만 듣지 않았다.

   (5) 이도령은 부모님께 하직 인사를 하고, 걸인처럼 꾸민 후 부하들과 함께 전라도로 _____.

   (6) 변 사또는 반은 죽고 반은 산 춘향이를 감옥에 _____.

4. 밑줄 친 말과 가장 비슷한 단어나 표현을 보기에서 고르세요.

   (1) 춘향이는 갈 마음이 났으나 어머니의 뜻을 몰라 <u>묵묵히</u> 앉아 있었다.
     a. 아무 말도 하지 않고   b. 움직이지 않고
     c. 묵직하게   d. 묵념하고

(2) 춘향이는 이 말을 듣고 가슴이 울렁거려서, <u>허둥지둥</u> 문을 열고 나와
    건넌방에 가서 어머니를 깨웠다.
    a. 몹시 다급하게 서두르며   b. 조심스럽게
    c. 천천히 움직이며   d. 허름하게

(3) 저 건너 꽃 속에서 <u>오락가락</u> 희뜩희뜩 얼른얼른하는 게 뭐냐?
    a. 왔다갔다   b. 오들오들
    c. 하늘하늘   d. 즐겁게

(4) 충신은 두 임금을 <u>섬기지</u> 않습니다.
    a. 무서워하지   b. 이끌지
    c. 알지   d. 모시지

(5) 우리가 처음 만나 하늘에 <u>맹세한</u> 백년 가약은 어떻게 된 거예요?
    a. 바친   b. 소리친
    c. 굳게 약속한   d. 굳게 믿은

5. 주어진 단어나 표현을 이용하여 문장을 만드세요.

(1) ~기(가) 짝이 없다

_____

(2) 다른 게 아니라

_____

(3) ~다니/~라니

_____

(4) ~기나 하세요

_____

(5) ~는들/~은들/~ㄴ들

_____

(6) ~느니만 못하다

_____

6. 춘향전에 나오는 의성어 (sound-imitating words)와 의태어 (manner-imitating
   words)를 찾아서 아래 (1)에 적고 그 외에 여러분이 알고 있는 의성어나 의태어를
   (2)에 적어 보세요.

(1)

_____

_____

_____

(2)

_____

_____

_____

Comprehension Questions

I. Overall comprehension

춘향전은 흔히 한국의 로미오와 줄리엣이라고 합니다. 다음 상자에 춘향전과 로미오와 줄리엣의 공통점과 차이점을 써 보세요.

공통점	
차이점	

II. Finding details

1. 춘향이 아버지와 어머니는 어떤 분이었습니까?

_____

2. 이도령은 왜 춘향이와 백년 가약을 맺은 뒤에 서울로 떠나야 했습니까?

_____

3. 이도령은 언제 과거 시험을 보아 장원 급제를 하였습니까?

_____

4. 변 사또는 춘향이와 이도령이 결혼한 사실을 알고 있었습니까?

_____

5. 춘향이는 어사가 수청을 요구했을 때 뭐라고 했습니까?

_____

6. 이몽룡과 춘향이는 처음 어떻게 해서 만나게 되었습니까?

_____

7. 월매의 꿈과 이몽룡은 무슨 관계가 있습니까?

_____

8. 이 도령이 부모를 따라 서울로 가야 했을 때 왜 춘향이를 데리고 가지
   못했을까요?

_____

9. 춘향이는 뭐라고 하면서 변 사또의 수청 요구를 거절했습니까?

_____

10. 변 사또는 춘향이에게 어떤 벌을 주었습니까?

_____

11. 암행 어사는 어떤 옷차림으로 춘향이 집에 가서 자기 장모에게 뭐라고 했습니까?

_____

12. 옥중의 춘향이는 어사를 보고 뭐라고 했습니까?

_____

13. 어사가 변 사또 생일 잔치에 가서 써 준 글은 어떤 내용이었습니까?

_____

14. 어사가 춘향이에게 수청을 요구했을 때 춘향이의 대답은 무엇이었습니까?

_____

Discussion & Composition

1. 춘향전에는 요즘 잘 쓰지 않는 단어나 표현이 많이 나오는데 찾아서 아래에 적고 그 뜻을 쓰세요. 이 들 단어나 표현이 왜 요즘에는 쓰이지 않는지 그 이유를 생각해 봅시다.

   _____   _____   _____

   _____   _____   _____

   _____   _____   _____

   _____   _____   _____

   _____   _____   _____

   _____   _____   _____

2. 도서관이나 인터넷에서 한국과 중국의 과거 제도(Civil Service Exam)에 대해 조사해 본 후 그 장단점에 관한 글을 아래에 써 보세요.

   _____

   _____

   _____

   _____

   _____

   _____

   _____

   _____

   _____

   _____

   _____

   _____

   _____

---

3. 동양의 유교 문화권에는 여자의 정절과 희생을 미덕으로 알고 권장하는 전통이
   있습니다. 여러분은 이러한 문화적 전통에 대해 어떻게 생각합니까? 여러분의
   의견을 이야기해 보세요.

4. 학생들이 힘을 합하여 춘향전을 연극으로 만들어 보세요. 우선 감독과
   해설자(narrator)를 선출하고 감독의 지시에 따라 배역(the cast)을 정하세요. 각자
   맡은 배역에 따라 대사(one's lines)를 다 외운 다음 모두 모아 여러 차례
   연습하세요. 충분한 연습이 끝나면 클래스에서 공연해 보세요.

    a. 춘향
    b. 이몽룡
    c. 월매
    d. 방자
    e. 변학도
    f. 이한림 (이몽룡의 아버지)
    g. 형리
    h. 엑스트라: 기생들, 나졸들, 양반들

Lesson 20   The story of Ch'unhyang

1. During the reign of Great King Sukchong (1674–1720), in (the town of) Namwŏn in Chŏlla province, lived a *kisaeng* (female entertainer) named Wŏlmae (Moon Plum). When she passed the age of 40, she, with a *yangban* (aristocrat) named Sŏng, gave birth to a daughter as lovely as a jewel. Calling her Ch'unhyang (Spring Fragrance), Wŏlmae cared for her like a precious gem. Ch'unhyang had a remarkably beautiful face, and she was unequalled in her daughterly devotion to her mother. She was wise, honest, courteous, and very good at writing poems. Everyone in Namwŏn praised her.

2. At that time, a *yangban* named Yi Hallim, a descendant of an exemplary loyal subject, received orders from the king and came down to Namwŏn (from the capital) to serve as governor. Governor Yi had a sixteen-year-old son named Yi Mong-nyong. Day and night, Young Master Yi was diligently studying for the state examination. One warm spring day, Young Master Yi called to Pangja (his servant):

Young Master Yi: Is there a scenic spot in this county?

Pangja: You should not look for scenic spots when you are studying, Young Master!

Young Master Yi: How stupid you are! Why, since ancient times viewing nature has been the basis for writing literary pieces!

Pangja named several good spots, and Young Master said they would go to Kwanghan Tower. After securing permission from the governor, Young Master Yi, on a donkey and accompanied by Pangja, arrived at the tower. There, he drank a cup of wine and enjoyed the excellent view. Just then, an oriole cried; and yellow bees and white butterflies flew around the spot in search of a sweet odor.

3. That day happened to be the Tano Festival in the fifth lunar month. Ch'unhyang was swinging on a swing nearby. Holding the ropes of the swing in each hand, she pressed the pedal forward with her sock-clad feet. When she did so, her lovely willow-like body shot up (with the swing) toward the sky.

Young Master Yi: Pangja! What is that glistening thing going dizzily back and forth?

Pangja: What is that! A child named Ch'unhyang, the daughter of

a person named Wŏlmae, a former *kisaeng* in this county.
Her mother is an entertainer, but Ch'unhyang studies a
lot. Why, she's just like a daughter of a *yangban!*

Young Master Yi: Ho ho! A *kisaeng*'s daughter! Go quickly and call her
here!

Pangja went to Ch'unhyang, as he was ordered.

Pangja: Hello there, Ch'unhyang! What a mess I'm in! The
governor's son is at Kwanghan Tower. He saw you
playing on the swing and ordered me to bid you go see
him.

Ch'unhyang: *(angrily)* You're crazy! How can the Young Master call
me when he doesn't even know me? It appears you
chattered to him about me like a skylark!

After saying this, Ch'unhyang went back home.

4. On the Young Master's orders, Pangja then went to Ch'unhyang's house. When
he got there, mother and daughter were seated facing each other, eating their
lunch.

Ch'unhyang: Why are you here again?

Pangja: The Young Master says you are a good writer and has a
favor to ask of you. He wants you to go see him.

Ch'unhyang wanted to go; but she did not know if her mother would mind, so she
just sat quietly.

Ch'unhyang's mother: A blue dragon appeared in my dream last night. I thought
it must be a good omen. It wasn't a chance happening.
I've heard that the governor's son is named Mong,
meaning 'dream', and Ryong, meaning 'dragon'. A
marvelous match with my dream! Anyhow, a *yangban*
has summoned you, and you cannot refuse him. Go and
hurry back!

Only then did Ch'unhyang, feigning reluctance, get up and go to Kwanghan Tower.

Young Master Yi:	What is your family name, and how old are you?
Ch'unhyang:	My surname is Sŏng, and I am sixteen years old.
Young Master Yi:	Ho ho. I'm glad to hear that. Our family name is different and our age is the same. We are fated for each other. How about spending our life (sharing our joys and sorrows) together?
Ch'unhyang:	A loyal subject does not serve two kings, and a virtuous woman does not change husbands. You, Young Master, are a young noble, and I am a girl of low birth. If you abandon me after I entrust my heart to you, I will have to spend my whole life alone and in tears. So do not make such a command.
Young Master Yi:	When we join our fates together, we will do so before Heaven. I will visit your home this evening.

5. After she went home, Ch'unhyang's words rang clearly in the Young Master's ears, and her bearing remained vivid in his eyes. He waited for sundown. As soon as it was dark, he went secretly to Ch'unhyang's house, following the light of the kerosene lamp carried by Pangja.

Pangja:	Hello there, Ch'unhyang! Are you asleep already? The Young Master is here!

When Ch'unhyang heard this, her heart began pounding fast. In a flutter, she opened the door, stepped out, went to her mother's room, and awakened her.

Ch'unhyang:	Pangja has brought the Young Master here!
Ch'unhyang's mother:	*(running outside)* Young Master, please accept my regards.
Young Master Yi:	Are you Ch'unhyang's mother? Are you doing well? I want to make an eternal vow of marriage with Ch'unhyang. How do you feel about it?
Ch'unhyang's mother:	Oh, don't speak of that. Just relax here for a while.
Young Master Yi:	I am a man who has made up his mind. Please give your permission!

Finally, at Young Master Yi's pleas, Chunhyang's mother gave her permission for the two to marry.

6. After the two made their vows to Heaven, they shared from that night the bloom of love and the warmth of each other's affection. One year passed like a dream. But one day, Governor Yi was promoted and went up to Hanyang [now Seoul]. Young Master Yi also had to go and leave Ch'unhyang behind. When Ch'unhyang heard the news, she was dumbstruck:

Ch'unhyang: (*crying sadly*) Young Master! What about our eternal
                     vow before Heaven? Do you leave me purposely because
                     I am of low birth? How I wish to die!
Young Master Yi: Don't cry, Ch'unhyang! I know you are upset because I
                     must leave you. Do you think I will forget you? When I
                     pass the state examination, I will come back for you
                     without fail.

Ch'unhyang sent her dear husband off to Hanyang, and spent her days in sadness and loneliness.

7. Then, a new governor came to Namwŏn: a stubborn, disagreeable *yangban* named Pyŏn Hak-do. Governor Pyŏn heard rumors of Ch'unhyang's loveliness and had her summoned to him. People told him that Ch'unhyang was not a *kisaeng,* and that she had pledged an eternal vow with Yi Mong-ryong. But he did not heed their words. Finally, Ch'unhyang appeared before Governor Pyŏn. Entranced with her beauty, he ordered her to surrender her body to him. Ch'unhyang refused, but the governor was persistent.

Ch'unhyang: A loyal subject does not serve two kings, and a virtuous
                     woman does not serve two husbands. If that is your
                     order, it is better for me to die than to live.
Governor Pyŏn: (*angrily*) Listen, you wench! I will punish you severely
                     for the crime of not obeying a governor's orders!
Ch'unhyang: If raping a married woman isn't a crime, then what is?
Governor Pyŏn: (*shaking in anger*) Guards! Set this wench in the
                     punishment chair, tie her up, and whip her!

Ch'unhyang, though beaten within an inch of her life, would not yield to the governor's command. The governor locked up the half-dead Ch'unhyang in prison. Ch'unhyang spent her days there in desolation, waiting only for her husband's return.

8. Meanwhile, Young Master Yi had gone up to Seoul, where sleep failed him nightly because of his longing for Ch'unhyang. Believing that he would see her again if he passed the state examination, he took great pains to prepare well. After several years passed, Young Master Yi passed the exam with the highest mark. The king summoned Young Master Yi and ordered him to serve as the secret inspector-general of Chŏlla province. His dream of life came true eventually. After taking leave of his parents, he disguised himself as a beggar and headed for Chŏlla province with his subordinates. Near Namwŏn, he heard from some farmers about Governor Pyŏn's cruelty and Ch'unhyang's desperate circumstances.

9. The inspector-general went to Ch'unhyang's home by night.

Inspector:	Is anyone home?
Ch'unhyang's mother:	Who is it?
Inspector:	It's me.
Ch'unhyang's mother:	Who is "me?"
Inspector:	I'm Yi, your son-in law.
Ch'unhyang's mother:	Yi? My son-in-law?
Inspector:	Ho ho! Has my mother-in-law become senile? Don't you know who I am?

Ch'unhyang's mother was exceedingly happy. She took him by the hand ánd led him inside. She set him down in the candelight. She looked at him carefully and saw he was the most wretched of beggars.

Ch'unhyang's mother:	*(startled)* What happened to you?
Inspector:	After I went up to Hanyang, my father's post was terminated. My family was ruined. My father became a teacher at a village schoolhouse, and my mother returned to her parents' home. I came down here to ask Ch'unhyang for some money.
Ch'unhyang's mother:	*(startled)* What in the world will you do about my daughter Ch'unhyang?
Inspector:	At any rate, mother-in-law, I must see her.

10. That evening, he went to see Ch'unhyang at the prison where she was being kept.

Ch'unhyang's mother: Ch'unhyang! Ch'unhyang! Whether he is your spouse or your louse, a beggar has come to see you. Talk to him.

Ch'unhyang: What is happening? You say my husband has come? My love whom I have seen in my dreams is now here in flesh and blood! I can die happily! *(looking carefully at his appearance)* My darling husband, there should be no regrets if I die, but how did you come to such a state as this?

Inspector: *(while Ch'unhyang cries sadly)* Do not be sad, Ch'unhyang. Human life is bound up with Heaven's will. You are not going to die, are you? Even if the heavens crumble, there will be a hole for you to spring up from (i.e., there is a way out of every situation, however bad). I'll see you again tomorrow.

The inspector-general took his leave and came back to Ch'unhyang's house.

11. The following day, a big birthday feast for Governor Pyŏn was held at Kwanghan Tower. Many magistrates and *yangban* from surrounding counties gathered for the occasion. Sumptuous foods were prepared, silk-clad *kisaeng* danced cheerfully, and the entire party was filled with mirth. Just then a beggar entered.

Beggar: Hey! Tell the governor a beggar has come from far off to join in the feast. Tell him I want a drinking table!

The beggar received food and drink. The *yangban,* in their merriment, began to compose poems.

Beggar: I'm sorry to eat and just leave. I would like to write a poem, too.

The beggar wrote the following poem, handed it to them, and left.

The beautiful wine in your golden jars? The blood of ten thousand peasants!
The delicacies on your jade trays? Their fat!
The wax dropped from your candle flames? The tears of the peasantry!
In your loud songs can be heard their grudge against you!

12. In a moment was heard, "The Secret Inspector-General is coming! The Secret Inspector-General is coming! The Secret Inspector-General is coming!"

It was as though the mountains and the rivers were collapsing, and heaven and earth were being overturned. Before long, Governor Pyŏn was on his knees, prostrated before the inspector-general, who immediately ordered him to quit his job. The inspector-general then ordered a legal clerk to bring to him all of the prisoners in the prison. After questioning each one about their crime, he released the poor unfortunates. Then,

Inspector-general:	What is that girl's crime?
Legal clerk:	That is Ch'unhyang. She refused to serve Governor Pyŏn, saying she would remain faithful to her husband. She resisted him in the courtyard of the government office.
Inspector-general:	They say you resisted the governor in the courtyard of the government office. How can you expect to live? Will you refuse to serve me, too?
Ch'unhyang:	Do the rocks crumble when the wind blows on the high cliff? Do the green pines and green bamboo lose their color even under the fallen snow? Please just kill me.
Inspector-general:	Raise your head and look at me!

Ch'unhyang raised her face and looked up at the platform. Was it a dream, or reality? Her husband, who had come to her yesterday as a beggar, was now sitting there as inspector-general! Ch'unhyang was so happy, she embraced him and shed endless tears.

13. After making his inspection of Chŏlla province, Yi Mong-ryong took Ch'unhyang with him to Hanyang. The king approved of Ch'unhyang as Yi Mong-ryong's wife. Yi Mong-ryong received many high government posts. Together with Ch'unhyang, he enjoyed a lifetime (*lit.*, hundred years) of happiness, with three wonderful sons and two wonderful daughters.

Adapted by Ho-min Sohn

Useful Expressions

Item	Meaning	Lesson
A 거나 B	A or B	2.10
A 뒤에는 B이/가 있다	B is behind A	17.4
A ～(이)다기/(이)라기 보다(는) B	B rather than A; not so much A as B	2.3
A(이)라고 하는 B	B which is called A	7.6
A, B 할 것 없이	A and B alike; regardless of A or B	6.10
A, B의 순(으로)	(in) the order of A and B	6.6
A가 B에 넘쳐흐르다	A overflows into B	6.7
A(이)든지 아니면 B	either A or B; if not A then B	8.2
A(으)로 하여금 ～게 하다	make A do ～	18.11
A면서 B게 되다	as A happens, something becomes B	5.11
A에 B을/를 먹이다	soak A with [in]	5.4
A에 달린 것이지 B에 달린 것이 아니다	depend on A, and not on B	14.15
A이/가 B을/를 말한다	A refers to [indicates, shows, proves] B	15.10
A이/가 B의 장래를 어둡게 [밝게] 하다	A makes B's future dark [bright]	14.8
Familiar speech style		20.5
가능한 한	if possible; as ～ as possible	10.14
각각 A와 B를 차지하다	take up A and B, respectively	6.5
각기 다른 길을 걸어오다/걸어가다	each goes through different ways	17.1
갈수록	as time goes by	10.5
거의 ～기 직전에 있는 것처럼 보이다	look as if it is just about to ～	14.7
경우	circumstance; situation; occasion; case; instance	1.5
곧이어	at once; immediately; directly	19.9
그나마	even so; at that	3.17
그만	by mistake; as soon as; no sooner than	9.9
급격히 확산되고 있다	be spreading rapidly	1.4
길(이) 들다	become used to; get accustomed to	3.9
남대문	(trousers) fly (*lit.*, South Gate)	1.8
(남)몰래	secretly; in secret; privately	13.4
납득이 가다	understand; be convinced	15.6
눈에 띄게	remarkably; conspicuously	11.6

눈에 띄다	catch one's eye; be conspicuous [noticeable]	19.6
다른 게 아니라	it is nothing but; for no other reason than; just	20.2
다른 어느 ~ 보다(도)	more [rather] than anything [anybody] else	8.12
다시 말하면	in other words	18.13
다음과 같은	like the following	18.1
단연 주목할 만하다	be definitely worth looking at; be noteworthy	1.3
대대적으로	grandly; immensely; on a large scale	12.4
더구나	besides; moreover; in addition	15.4
더욱이	besides; moreover; in addition (to that); what's more	19.10
도난(을) 당하다	be stolen; be robbed	4.10
동이 나다	run out; run short of; be out; be exhausted; be sold out	19.13
듣자하니	as I have heard, as I understand	20.4
듯이	as if; as though; as	2.8
마찬가지로	as well as; too; likewise	13.2
마치 ~ 처럼	as if; as though; as; just like; as ~ as	15.8
마치 ~는 듯한 느낌을 받다	feel as if ~	6.13
마치 ~듯(이)	(just) as if ~	14.5
만만치 않다	be difficult to deal with; be formidable	10.9
만큼	not so ~ as; as much as	15.3
말도 안 되다	be unreasonable [illogical; absurd]	3.12
말할 나위도 없다	it goes without saying that; it is needless to say that	15.7
모습을 담고 있다	look just as; reflect; keep the features of	2.13
못 버티다	not hold; not maintain; be unable to keep up	16.11
무슨 ~을 하든	no matter what ~ one does	5.8
무엇보다(도)	more than anything else; above all	11.8
뭐니 뭐니 해도	above all; when all is said and done	8.10
별 탈(이) 없다	be without trouble	9.5
별반 다름이 없다	be not particularly different	12.12
삼다	have [take, make] a thing [person] as	9.4
설사 ~라고 해도	even if (something, somebody) were ~	1.10
수없이 많다	be countless [innumerable, incalculable]	19.1
슬슬	slowly; gradually; by degrees	9.1
시원치 않다	be unsatisfying [unsatisfactory, lacking, wanting]	13.8

(기사를) 싣다	publish [carry] (an article)	12.2
아마 ~ 덕분일 것이다	maybe thanks to ~	8.7
아무 때나 ~(으)ㄹ수 있다	be able to ~ whenever (one likes)	8.15
아예	from the beginning; (not) at all	10.13
안달이 나다	grow impatient	9.8
앞서 제시했던 것과 같이	as I showed [presented] earlier	18.12
앞장서다	take the lead [initiative]	8.18
어느새	in no time; quickly; without one's knowledge	8.1
어안이 벙벙하다	be amazed; be struck dumb	18.4
언뜻	in an instant; in a flash	15.5
역사상	from the historical point of view; historically	4.1
역시	as expected; after all	10.10
열변을 토하다	to make an impassioned speech, deliver a fervent speech	16.2
영 + negative (못, 안, 없)	not at all	3.10
예나 지금이나	as always; as it was in bygone days	11.4
예로부터 (= 자고로)	from old times; since time immemorial	11.3
우여곡절을 겪다	have twists and turns; have complications	4.8
우열을 가리다	decide which [who] is better	8.9
위에서 [앞에서] 언급했듯이	as I mentioned above [before]	18.10
유명세를 타다	be well known; gain celebrity	1.1
응어리를 풀다	relieve anxiety [frustration, pent-up feelings]	13.6
이상에서 알 수 있는 것과 같이	as we can learn from the above (discussion)	18.15
이에 반해	on the other hand; by contrast	6.11
이왕이면	as long as one is at it; things being what they are; all in all	11.1
인기를 끌고 있다	be winning popularity	12.10
일단 ~하고 나면	once (one) does ~; if (one) does ~	7.7
일리(가) 있다	there is some reason (truth)	16.4
자고로	from ancient times; traditionally	16.6
자취를 감추다	disappear without a trace; conceal one's whereabouts	2.11
적게는 A에서 많게는 B까지	from (at least) A to (the maximum) B	7.11

적금을 붓다	make deposits into a savings account	16.12
전적으로	wholly; totally; entirely	9.7
전혀 + negative (안, 못, 없)	not at all; not in the least	9.10
조차	even	10.7
좀처럼 + negative (못, 안, 없)	hardly ~; seldom ~	5.10
죄책감에 빠지다	fall into [yield to, be consumed by] a sense of guilt	13.9
주도권을 행사하다 [차지하다]	take the leadership [initiative]	16.9
줄잡아	approximately; roughly	12.7
지갑을 내려 놓다	drop the wallets; stop spending money	14.13
지나치게	too much; over	19.15
쩔쩔매다	become flustered; be at a loss (what to do)	16.10
출신	a native; a graduate; origin; birth; affiliation	8.14
치맛바람을 일으키다	women's influence on (something) grew	16.8
크게 다르지 않다	be no great difference; be much the same	11.5
터무니없다	be unfounded [unreasonable]	16.1
통이 크다 / 통이 큰 사람	a person of character; a magnanimous person	16.14
판이하게 다르다	be completely different	8.3
필두로	the first on the list; as a starting point	16.7
하긴, 하기는	it is true but; indeed	3.8
하나하나	one by one; step-by-step	18.7
한갓 ~에 지나지 않다	be nothing but; only	19.4
~ 가운데/중의 하나이다	one of the ~	12.14
~ 편을 들다	take the side of ~	1.9
~(어/아)도 말이다	you know; although it is the case that ~	14.6
~(으)ㄴ 채	just as it is ~	10.6
~(으)ㄴ/는/(으)ㄹ 것 같다	it seems [appears] ~	3.4
~(으)ㄹ 맛이 나다	feel like doing ~	13.10
~(으)ㄹ 뻔하다	come near ~ing; just barely escape from ~ing	9.2
~(으)ㄹ 생각은 아예 하지도 말다	don't ever think about doing ~	14.2
~(으)ㄹ 수 있다	be able to ~; it is possible that ~	13.1
~(으)ㄹ 위험이 있다	there is a danger of ~	8.13
~(으)ㄹ 지경에 이르다	be on the point [verge] of ~; be about to ~	10.12

~(으)ㄹ 터이다 (=테다)	expect to ~; plan to ~; be going to ~	3.16
~(으)ㄹ 테니까	since ~; as ~	3.13
~(으)ㅁ에도 불구하고	in spite of ~; despite ~	14.3
~(으)로 몰고 가다	drive, chase, or push into ~	17.10
~(으)로 여기다	consider; deem	2.9
~(으)로 이루어지다	consist of ~	5.1
~(으)로 인하다	be due to; be caused by	2.1
~(으)로 인해 [인하여]	owing to ~; caused by ~; due to ~; arising from ~	4.7
~(으)로 인해 발생된 것	a thing caused [occurred] by ~; an event that occurred due to	18.14
~(으)로 추측되다	it is surmised [assumed] that ~	4.11
~(으)로 향하다	be headed to ~	7.8
~(으)로부터	from ~	14.1
~(으)로서	as ~	6.2
~(으)로써	by ~; by means of ~	6.12
~(으)마	I promise ~	20.9
~(으)ㄴ/는 까닭에	because; as; since (= 기 때문에)	2.5
~(으)ㄴ/는 말할 것도 없고	not to mention; say nothing of	11.9
~(으)ㄴ/는 셈이다	be considered [thought] to be	15.12
~(으)ㄴ가/는가 보다	it seems that ~; I guess ~	3.11
~(으)ㄴ지/는지 아닌지 모르다	I don't know whether ~ or not	8.8
~(으)ㄴ지/는지(를) 알아보다	figure out [find out] if (something) is ~	7.3
~(의) 편에 서다	take sides; go over to ~	17.8
~(이)라고 할 수 있다	can be called ~	6.15
~(이)란다	you see, you know, it really is	20.3
~(이)야말로	the very; just; indeed; precisely; exactly	15.13
~거든(요)	surely; certainly; indeed (used to give a polite justification)	3.5
~것은 상상할 수 없다	it is unimaginable that ~	8.4
~게 될까 봐 조심하다	be careful in case ~; be wary of ~	13.11
~게 해주는 효과가 있다	have an effect on ~	5.12
~게/것이 분명하다	it is obvious that ~	9.12
~게/기 마련이다	be natural; be expected; by definition	11.2
~고 말다	end up; finally do	9.6

~곤 하다	used to ~	3.2
~기 위해 [위하여, 위해서]	so as to ~; (in order) to ~	10.3
~기 짝이 없다	be incomparable [matchless]; be extremely ~	9.11
~기(가) 짝이 없다	it is extremely ~ (lit., 'one of a pair is lacking')	20.1
~기나 하다	just do ~	20.6
~기도 하다	be really [quite, indeed] ~	3.14
~기도 하다	do [be] indeed	6.8
~기에 망정이지	be good luck [fortune] that	9.3
~나 싶다	I think ~; I feel ~	3.15
~나 싶다	look ~; seem ~; appear ~	10.2
~느니만 못하다	worse than doing ~	20.10
~느라고	because of ~; owing to ~; while doing ~	10.11
~는 것이 보통이다	(it) is common to do ~, (people) usually do ~	7.9
~는 역할을 하다	function to ~	5.3
~는 측면에서는	from the side [angle, viewpoint] of ~	11.7
~는 한편	while ~; on the other hand	17.7
~(으)ㄴ들/은들	granted that ~; even though ~	20.8
~다/라 해도	even if (one says that) ~	18.17
~다고	even though ~; simply because ~	20.7
~다고/라고 경고하다	warn [caution] that ~	12.6
~다고/라고 해도 지나친 말은 아닐 것이다	it's no exaggeration to say that ~	19.5
~다니/라니	(as, since) you said that ~ (At the end of a sentence, this often has the added meaning 'I can't believe it' or 'I don't get it'.)	20.11
~덕분에	due to ~; thanks to ~; because of ~	5.7
~던데(요)	I found that ~	3.7
~도록 도와 주다	help someone do ~	18.6
~도록 하다	be sure to do; decide to do	14.12
~든(지) ~든(지)	whether ~ or not; either ~ or; 무엇이든(지) whatever	3.3
~듯 싶다	maybe; perhaps	8.6
~란 말이 나왔으니까	having mentioned ~; speaking of ~	15.9
~만 보아도	looking only at ~	18.9
~만을 의미하지 않는다	do not only mean ~; mean more than ~	18.2
~면 그만이다	be the end of it if ~	10.8
~어대다/아대다	do something repeatedly	3.6

~어도/아도 아무렇지도 않다	be unconcerned by ~; think nothing of ~	1.7
~에 귀기울이지 않다	not pay attention to ~	16.15
~에 꼬치꼬치 간섭하다	fuss over ~; interfere in ~	16.13
~에 대한 우려가 크다	there is great worry [concern] about ~	14.11
~에 대한 추억을 느끼다	keep the memory of alive; have recollections of	2.4
~에 도사리고 있다	harbor in; lurk	19.3
~에 뒤지지 않는다	be ahead of others in ~; be second to none in ~	16.5
~에 따라	according to ~; by ~	14.10
~에 따르면	according to ~	4.13
~에 맞서(서)	against ~; in opposition to ~	12.9
~에 못 미치다	do not meet [reach] ~	14.4
~에 못 박히다	be nailed in (one's) heart; be stung to the quick; feel deep rancor [grudge]	19.8
~에 박차를 가하다	spur (someone, something) to ~; accelerate or prompt ~	17.9
~에 비해(서)	considering ~; compared to ~	10.4
~에 뿌리를 두다	originate from ~	4.5
~에 아랑곳하지 않다	be unconcerned about ~; take no notice of ~	19.12
~에 압도되다	be overwhelmed by ~	8.16
~에 어울리다	match; suit	12.13
~에 영향을 주다 [미치다, 끼치다]	influence ~	5.5
~에 의해서	by ~; according to ~	7.1
~에 익숙하다	be accustomed to ~; be used to ~	5.9
~에 자리 잡다	take a position at ~; be located at ~	6.9
~에 초점을 맞추다	focus on	12.8
~에 치중하다	attach weight (importance) to ~; lay stress on ~	17.2
~에 홀딱 빠지다	be fascinated with ~; be obsessed by ~; completely	8.11
~에 흥분하다	to be excited by [at] ~	13.5
~에게 압력을 넣다	put pressure on ~; press ~	12.5
~에도 (불구하고)	despite ~; in spite of ~	6.14
~에서 보는 바와 같이	as you can see in [at] ~	6.4
~에서 비롯되다	start from; originate from	2.7
~에서 오는	coming [originating] from ~	18.3
~에서 한 몫을 톡톡히 하다	play a big role in ~	15.11

~와/과 거의 다를 바 없다	it is hardly different from ~	12.11
~와/과는 달리	unlike; contrary to	2.6
~은/는 그 누구도 부인하지 못 하다	nobody can deny ~	17.5
~은/는 두말할 나위도 없다	it goes without saying that ~; needless to say ~	19.7
~은/는 듯하다	it seems (to me) that ~	2.14
~은/는 물론이고	not to mention; let alone ~	15.2
~은/는 ~의 통제 아래 있다	be under the control of ~	17.6
~을/를 일깨워주다	remind (someone) that ~; make (someone) realize ~	8.17
~을/를 펼쳐 나가다	unfold ~; lay out ~; carry out ~; promote ~	17.3
~을/를 (time) 앞두고	(time) ahead of ~; (time) before ~	4.6
~을/를 거두다	harvest ~; gain ~; achieve ~	4.4
~을/를 기리다	give high praise to ~; pay tribute to ~	4.9
~을/를 기울이다	concentrate on ~; devote oneself to~	4.3
~을/를 둘러싼 논쟁	the controversy [dispute, argument] surrounding ~	12.1
~을/를 뒤흔들다	shake up ~	6.1
~을/를 들먹이지 않더라도	even though you don't refer to [mention] ~	19.2
~을/를 무릅쓰고	risking ~	14.9
~을/를 비롯한	including ~; as well as ~	3.1
~을/를 상징하다	symbolize ~	7.4
~을/를 손에 쥐다	get hold of ~	13.3
~을/를 예로 들다	take as an example [instance]	1.6
~을/를 전후하여	before or after ~; around the time of ~	4.2
~을/를 치르다	hold (an event or party)	7.5
~을/를 타고	taking ~; getting (on) ~; taking advantage of ~	5.2
~을/를 통하여	through ~; by way of ~	7.2
~의 몫	portion of ~	6.3
~의 묵인 하에	under auspices of ~; with ~'s connivance	18.8
~의 입장에서는	from ~'s point of view	7.10
~의 주름살이 펴져야 한다	should get better ~	18.5
~이/가 고작이다	be at most; be at best	10.1
~이/가 대두하다/ 대두되다	~ gain power; ~ rise; ~ be formed	12.3

~이/가 무리는 아니다	it is not unreasonable; it is not unnatural	16.3
~이/가 바람직하다	it is desirable [advisable] that ~	19.14
~이/가 아닌가 여겨지다	it is thought that ~ may	15.12
~이/가 일품이다	be an excellent piece; be superb; be a rarity	12.2
~이다 보니	being ~; as (one) is ~	5.6
~이야말로	indeed; precisely	8.5
~자구나	let's ~	20.12
~자마자	as ~; just as ~; as soon as ~	11.10
~점에서(는)	from the standpoint of ~; in respect of ~	1.2
~중에서 선정하다	choose from ~	4.12
~지 궁금하다	I wonder if [whether, how, when, who, what] ~	15.1
~지 않는 한 ~(으)ㄹ 수밖에 없다	there is no choice but to ~ unless ~	14.14
~지 않도록	so as not to	10.15
~지 않을 수 없다	cannot help (doing) ~; cannot but (do) ~; have to ~	19.11
~지도 ~지도 않다	neither ~ nor ~	2.12
~하는 도리 밖에 없다	there is no choice but to ~	13.7

Korean-English Glossary

-가 street, section of a district
가까스로 barely, just, with difficulty
가끔 sometimes, every now and then
가능성 possibility, potential
가닥 piece, cut(ting), strip, strand, fork (of a road)
가두 시위 street demonstration
가라앉히다 to calm down, pacify, relieve, soothe
가락 key, pitch, tone
가려내다 to separate, single out
가르다 to divide, split, sever
가리다 to distinguish, discriminate (between), tell (one thing) from (another)
가마솥 traditional Korean iron kettle
가소롭다 to be laughable, ridiculous
가약 marriage vow, pledge of eternal love
가열하다 to apply heat, to heat
가옥 house
가입자 member, participant
가입하다 to join, become a member (of), participate (in)
가장 head of a family
가정 형편 family background, family situation
가죽 skin, hide, leather, fur
가축 domestic animal
가치 value, worth, merit
가치관 sense of values
가풍 중시 taking a serious view of family tradition, valuing family tradition
각각 each, every, all, individually
각기 individually, each one
각성 awakening
각종 every kind, every variety
간 liver
간격 gap, discrepancy
간곡히 cordially, sincerely, earnestly
간략히 briefly, concisely

간접적으로 indirectly
간주되다 to be considered
간주하다 to deem, consider
갈등 complication, conflict, discord, trouble
갈래 kind; branch
감격적 impressive, moving, touching
감상하다 to appreciate
감수성 sensibility
감수하다 to be ready to suffer
갑작스럽게 suddenly
강력히 strongly
강렬하다 to be intense, strong
강산 rivers and mountains, landscape, scenery
강요하다 to force, demand
강자 strong person, the strong
갖추다 to equip, furnish, have
갚다 to repay, pay back
개막 raising the curtain, beginning the performance
개막식 opening ceremony
개발 development
개발 도상국 developing country
개발되다 to be developed
개발하다 to develop, cultivate
개방 opening
개방적 frank, candid, open-minded
개봉되다 to be opened, released (of a film at the cinema)
개설하다 to open (up), establish, set up, found
개성 individuality, personality
개입되다 to intervene (in), be involved (in)
개조하다 to remodel, modify
개최 holding (a meeting)
개최국 host country
개최지 site (of an athletic meeting), place where (a meeting) is held
개최하다 to hold (a meeting), open (an exhibition)
개탄 regret, lamentation

개혁	reform, reformation, innovation
객관성	objectivity
객관적인	objective
객관화시키다	to objectify
객차	passenger car; passenger train
거금	huge amount of money
거대하다	to be huge, enormous
거두다	to take in, gain, obtain
거부하다	to reject, refuse
거울	mirror
건강 기록부	record of medical checkups, medical records
건강식	healthy meal, health food
건수	number of items [cases]
걸맞다	to be well matched
걸인	beggar
겁탈하다	to rape, rob, plunder
게시판	bulletin board
겨레	race, nation, people; brethren
격식	formality
격차	gap, difference
겪다	to experience, suffer
견공	dog (honorific term for 개)
견주다	to compare one with another; to compete (with)
견해	view, opinion
결과물	resulting product, outcome
결말	end, conclusion
결성하다	to form, organize
결실	fruit, fruition, result
결정되다	to be decided
결정적으로	definitely
결합	joining together, union, combination, consolidation
결합하다	to unite with, combine, join together
결혼관	outlook on marriage
경고	warning
경고하다	to warn
경공업	light industry
경기장	ground, field
경기 침체	economic stagnation, recession
경력	(career) experience
경로 효친	respecting elderly people and being filial to parents
경시청	police headquarters
경악하다	to be astonished at
경연	contest, match, competitive performance
경쟁국	competing [rival] country
경적	car horn
경제	economy
경제 개발	economic development
경제 교류	economic exchange
경제 대국	major economic power
경제력	economic power
경제 발전	economic development
경제 성장	economic growth
경제 위기	economic crisis
경제적으로	economically
경향	tendency
곁	side, neighborhood, vicinity
곁들이다	to garnish (a dish with vegetables), add (something) as a relish
계기	moment, beginning, opportunity, chance
계정	account
계층	social stratum, class
계피	cinnamon (bark)
고구려	Koguryŏ, the northernmost of the Three Kingdoms on the Korean Peninsula from 37. B.C. to A.D. 668
고급	high-class, high-quality
고루	evenly, equally, uniformly, fairly
고비	climax, crest, peak, crisis, critical moment
고소득	high income
고소하다	to taste like roasted sesame; to be tasty
고스란히	wholly, completely, just as it was, with nothing missing, completely
고안하다	to design, contrive, conceive, devise
고압	high pressure
고약하다	to be wicked, bad
고온	high temperature
고용인	employee
고용자	employer
고위 공무원	high-ranking civil servant
고유의	unique, characteristic, proper

고을	district of a province, county
고작	at (the) most, at (the) best, at the highest
고전적인	classical
고정 관념	prejudice, preconception
고정하다	to fix firmly
고집	stubbornness, obstinacy
고통	pain, agony, anguish, suffering
고통스럽다	to be agonizing
고함	shout, yell, roar
고흐	Vincent Van Gogh
곤란하다	to be difficult, troublesome
골방	back room, small room
골뱅이	top shell; @ symbol
골칫거리	headache, nuisance
공감	sympathy
공격적	offensive, aggressive
공공 기관	public institution
공동	cooperation, union
공식적	official
공약하다	to pledge, make a public commitment
공유하다	to share, have in common
공자	Confucius
공해	pollution
공헌	contribution, service
공헌하다	to contribute (to)
공화국	republic, commonwealth
과거 시험	state examinations in old Korea
과외	extracurricular work, private tutoring
과정	process, step, procedure
과즙	fruit juice
과체중	overweight
관	pipe
관계자	persons [parties] concerned
관광 상품	tourist attractions
관람	inspection, viewing
관람료	admission fee
관람하다	to see, view, inspect
관련되다	to be related
관리	government officials
관명	one's adult name, official title
관세 면제	exemption from tariffs
관철	accomplishment, realization
관철되다	to be accomplished, realized
관철하다	to accomplish
관현악	orchestral music
관현악단	orchestral band
광경	sight, scene, view
광목	wide woof of cotton
광복	restoration of independence
광한루	Kwanghan Tower in Namwŏn, setting of the Ch'unhyang story
교류	interchange
교모	school cap
교문	school gate
교섭	negotiation, bargaining
교섭 단체	bargaining body
교섭하다	to negotiate
교역국	trading partner (as a country)
교외	suburbs
교육 재정	education budget
교육관	views on education
교향악단	symphony orchestra
교훈	lesson, moral
교훈적인	instructive
구닥다리	old-fashioned person or stuff
구별	distinction, discrimination
구별되다	to be classified into, be divided into
구분	division, classification
구분하다	to divide, classify
구사하다	to use freely, make the most of
구석	corner
구성하다	to compose, constitute
구수하다	to be tasty, savory pleasant-tasting (of slightly scorched food and drinks)
구실	excuses
구제하다	to relieve, give relief to
구조[1]	relief, bailout
구조[2]	structure, construction
구조 조정	restructuring
구타하다	to beat (people or animals)
구해 주다	to save, rescue, help, give relief to
구호	slogan, motto, catchword
국가 대표팀	national team

국내	domestic; internal to a country
국내외	domestic and international
국물	soup, broth
국민 총생산	gross national product (GNP)
국악	Korean classical music; Korean folk music
국영화	nationalization
국제 사회	international community
국제 시장	international market
국제 연맹	the League of Nations
국제 통화 기금	International Monetary Fund (IMF)
국토	national territory, national land, country
국회 의원	member of the National Assembly
군림하다	to reign, rule
군비	military expense
군사 독재 정치	military dictatorship
군사 쿠데타	military coup d'état
굴레	bridle, restraint, restriction
굵다	to be thick; to be coarse
굵직하다	to be somewhat thick; to be significant
궁궐	palace
궁극적으로	ultimately, finally
궁극적인	final, ultimate, eventual
궁합	marital harmony as predicted by a fortune-teller
권선징악	promoting good and punishing evil
권하다	to recommend
궤변	sophistry, deceptive talk
귀공자	young noble
귀기울이다	to listen to (what) someone (says) attentively, bend one's ear to someone
귀순자	defector
귀신	ghost
귀하다	to be rare, scarce; to be precious, valuable; to be noble
균형	balance
균형 잡히다	to be well balanced
그간	in the meantime, meanwhile
그대로	as it is

그러나 저러나	at any rate, anyhow, anyway, in any case
그러니까	so; for that [this] reason; therefore
그려내다	to draw out
그릇되다	to become wrong, go amiss, end in failure
극단적이다	to be extreme
극성스럽다	to be frantic, impatient, impetuous
극찬하다	to speak very highly of (a person); to praise (a person) sky-high
극히	extremely, greatly, excessively
근거하다	to be based, founded
근무하다	to do duty, work
근본적	fundamental
글공부	studying (one's books)
글월	letters, literature; letter, epistle; sentence
금기	taboo
금기시되다	to be viewed [regarded] as taboo
금동이	golden jar
금융	circulation of money, finance
금융 관리	management of finance
금융 기관	financial institution
금융 위기	financial crisis
금지	prohibition
급격하게	suddenly, abruptly
급부상하다	to grow rapidly, rise to the surface rapidly
급성장	rapid growth
급성장하다	to grow rapidly
급제하다	to pass (an examination)
기겁하다	to be surprised
기계적으로	mechanically
기고	act of contributing [writing] to a newspaper [magazine]
기고문	contribution [writing] to a newspaper [magazine]
기고하다	to write for, contribute to
기꺼이	gladly, with joy, with pleasure
기다	to crawl, creep
기량	ability, talent, capacity
기록하다	to record, write down

기름	oil, grease
기반	base, basis, foundation, footing
기사	article (in a newspaper, magazine, etc.)
기세	spirit, force
기술자	technician, technical expert
기업체	enterprise, business enterprise
기울어지다	to slant, lean, incline, decline, sink, go down
기울이다	to bend, put (one's mind to); direct (one's attention to); concentrate (one's mind, energy, powers on), devote oneself to
기준	standard
기초적인	fundamental, basic
긴급	urgency, emergency
긴밀하다	to be close; to be rigorous, strict
깊이	depth, deepness, profundity
까닭	reason, cause
까마득하다	to be far off (in space or time), distant, remote
깍쟁이	shrewd person; miser
깔리다	to be covered, scattered
깜짝 놀라다	to be surprised, startled
깨닫다	to realize, perceive, understand; to become aware of
깨우침	awakening, realization
깻잎	sesame leaf
꺼풀	layer
-께	about, around
꼬집다	to pinch; to criticize sarcastically
꼬치꼬치	inquisitively
꼭대기	top, peak
꼼꼼하다	to be a perfectionist, be meticulous
꼼짝없이	helplessly, without any means
꽉꽉	fully
꽹과리	small gong
꾸준히	steadily, constantly, continually
꿰뚫다	to pierce; to see into (a person's heart)

꿰뚫어 보다	to see through
끈끈하게	persistently, tenaciously
끈끈하다	to be sticky
끈적거리다	to be sticky
끌리다	to be attracted
끌어 내리다	to pull down, take down
끔찍하다	to be appalling, terrible
끝마치다	to finish off, complete, terminate
끝없다	to be endless
끼	meal, diet
끼리끼리	group by group
끼여들다	to intrude into, break in on
끼치다	to exert (influence on); to cause, give
나다	to pass; to go or get through (a season)
나동그라지다	to tumble down, topple over
나르시시즘	narcissism
나무라다	to rebuke, scold, blame a person for something
나서다	to come out (forth), appear, present oneself
나선형	spiral, screw
나아지다	to become better, get better
나약하다	to be weak, feeble-minded
나타나다	to appear, present oneself
난국	difficult situation, crisis, deadlock
난도질하다	to chop, mince (meat)
난해하다	to be hard to understand, hard to make out
날로	day by day, daily, from day to day, every day
날카롭다	to be sharp
남녘	south (side)
남미	South America
남사당	male performers in troupe of wandering entertainers
납득	understanding
낭군	one's dear husband
낭만적	romantic
낯선	unfamiliar, strange, unknown
낱말	word
내남없이	irrespective of persons, indiscriminately, without exception

내막	underlying factor
내면	inside
내면적(인)	internal
내밀다	to stretch out; to hand over
내부	inside; interior
내세우다	to set forth, claim, advocate, display (one's learning)
내장	internal organs, intestines, offal
냉정하다	to be calm, cool-headed
너르다	to be wide, spacious, roomy
넋	soul, spirit
널리	widely, broadly, extensively
넘쳐나다	to overflow
넘쳐흐르다	to overflow
넣어주다	to put (in) (for someone)
-네	all of
네티즌	netizen, Internet user
노랑벌	yellow bee
노릇(노릇)하다	to be yellow here and there, yellowish
노자	Lao Tzu (founder of Taoism)
노조 활동	labor union activity
노출	exposure
녹이다	to melt, dissolve
논거	grounds (basis) of an argument; data
논쟁	dispute, argument, controversy
놀랄만하다	to be surprising, amazing
놀림감	object of derision or teasing
농구단	basketball team
농업	agriculture, agricultural industry
농축	concentration
농축되다	to be condensed, concentrated
높이다	to raise, lift
누룽지	crust of overcooked rice, scorched part of boiled rice
누리	the world, this world [archaic]
눈높이	standards, expectations
눈부시다	to be dazzling, brilliant, striking, remarkable
눈치	perceptiveness in social situations, tact, intuition; expression, manner
눈다	to get scorched, be burned
느슨해지다	to become loosened, relaxed
늘어나다	to lengthen, expand
능가하다	to surpass, exceed
능력	ability, capacity, capability, competence
다녀오다	to drop in for a short visit
다름없이	similarly, likewise
다방	teahouse, coffee shop
다수	large number, multitude, majority
다지다	to harden, make hard
다툼	fighting
닥치다	to fall upon, befall, draw near, come round, approach, be near at hand
단골	regular customer, good client
단기 상환	repayment (of a debt) in a short time
단속	keeping under control; control, supervision
단순히	simply, merely
단연	definitely, without hesitation; by far
단오(날)	May festival, the fifth day of the fifth lunar month
단일	singleness, unity
단절	cutting off, separation
단절되다	to be cut off
단절하다	to cut off
단점	weak point, drawback
단정하다	to decide, conclude
달라지다	to become different, change
달래다	to soothe, comfort, calm
달리	differently, in a different way
달리다	to be attached, affixed, appended
담당자	person in charge
답변	reply, answer
당당히	majestically, magnificently, bravely; fairly, justifiably
당면	Chinese noodles
당면한	immediately faced
당사자	person [party] concerned, interested party

당연히	of course, as a matter of fact	도금하다	to plate (with gold or silver)
당하다	to meet with, be confronted with, suffer, receive, sustain	도난	robbery, theft
		도난품	stolen article or goods
대	versus, against; to	도령(님)	young gentleman, unmarried boy (as addressed by servants in old Korea)
대가족 제도	extended family system		
대개	most of, great part of, generally, usually		
		도리	reason, justice, principles, duty, obligation
대걸레	mop		
대공황	Great Depression	도망가다	to escape, run away
대규모	large [grand] scale	도사리다	to harbor (feelings, thoughts); to lurk (in the mind)
대기업	big firms, large companies		
대대적	grand, gigantic, immense, large-scale		
		도살	slaughter, butchery
대략	approximately, roughly	도수	degree, proof
대량	large quantity	도야지	pig (= 돼지)
대류	convection current	도입되다	to be introduced
대륙	continent	도입하다	to introduce, induce, invite, import
대립되다	to be opposed, confront (each other)		
		도장	seal, stamp
대립하다	to oppose, confront	도전적	aggressive
대머리	bald head, bald person	독수공방하다	to live alone, live apart from one's husband
대문자	capital letter		
대범하다	to be big-hearted, magnanimous	독자적인	personal, individual, independent
대비	contrast, contradiction	독특하다	to be unique and special
대사관	embassy	독하다	to be strong, sharp
대수롭다	to be important	독해력	reading comprehension
대우	treatment; pay, salary	돈줄	line of credit
대접	treatment	돌담	stone wall
대출 업무	lending business	돌덩이	piece of stone
대취하다	to get dead drunk	돌잔치	first birthday party
대회	tournament; conference, convention, large meeting	돌파하다	to pass, exceed
		동갑	same age, person of the same age
더러	occasionally, sometimes		
더불어	together with, in addition to	동고 동락하다	to share one's joys and sorrows (with), share the pleasures and pains of life (with)
더욱이	besides, moreover, further, furthermore, what's more		
더위	hot weather	동구 사회주의	socialism of Eastern Europe
덕분에	thanks to	동남아	Southeast Asia
덜다	to lessen, relieve; to subtract, deduct	동독	East Germany
		동명 이인	different person of the same name
덜렁	lonely, alone		
덥히다	to heat	동물 보호 단체	animal protection organization
덩실덩실	(dancing) joyfully, cheerfully		
		동반 자살	joint suicide, suicide pact
덮다	to cover (with a blanket or lid, etc.)	동양적	Oriental, Eastern

동의	consent, assent		question; to distinguish
동조하다	to align oneself with, be in		between right and wrong,
	tune with, be in sympathy		calculate, judge
	with	딱	exactly, just, precisely
동창	schoolmate	딱지	sticker, label, tag
동창생	fellow student; graduate,	땀	sweat
	alumnus	때	dirt, grime
동창회	alumni association	때다	to burn, kindle, make a fire
동행하다	to accompany, go together	때로(는)	sometimes, occasionally, at
동호회	association of like-minded		times
	persons, club	때리다	to beat (a thing, an animal,
되돌아보다	to look back at, look over		or a person)
	one's shoulder	떠받치다	to support, bolster
되살리다	to revive, return to life,	떠오르다	to rise, come to mind
	rekindle	떳떳하게	fairly, honorably
되살아나다	to revive, return to life	똑똑하다	to be smart, bright
되찾다	to take back, regain,	뚜렷하다	to be vivid (clear, distinct)
	recover, retrieve	뚫다	to make a hole, penetrate
되풀이하다	to go over again, repeat	뛰어나다	to be outstanding, superior
두뇌	brain, head	뜸을 들이다	to cook rice completely,
두다	to have (a child); to keep		allowing boiled rice to
두드리다	to strike, beat, hit		settle by its own heat; to
두렵다	to be fearful, afraid of		heat up; to allow warm-up
두루마리	roll of (toilet) paper, scroll		time for a job to be done
둘러싸다	to surround, enclose	뜻밖에(도)	unexpectedly, to one's
뒤꼍	backyard		surprise
뒤집다	to turn over, reverse		
뒤처지다	to fall [lag] behind	레퍼토리	repertoire
뒷받침해 주다	to support	리얼하다	to be real
드리우다	to hang, let (hang) down,		
	suspend	마감하다	to finish, complete
들다	to need, cost, require	마구	recklessly, rashly,
들먹이다	to mention, refer to, specify		excessively, indiscriminately
	by name	마련되다	to be prepared
들이키다	to drink heavily (in large	마련하다	to prepare
	draughts), gulp	마약	drug, narcotic
듬뿍	plenty, much, quite a lot, to	마음가짐	one's mental attitude
	the brim, to the full	마음대로	as one wishes, of one's
등급별	(according to) a rank,		own accord, freely
	grade	마이너스	minus, negative
등록	registration, entry	마주 앉다	to sit face-to-face
등장	appearance, entrance on the	마찬가지	same, same kind
	stage, advent	마찬가지로	in the same manner
등장 인물	characters	마파람	south wind
등장하다	to show up, appear, enter	만듦새	make, workmanship,
	on the stage		craftsmanship
디딤돌	stepping-stone, step	말다	to put (boiled rice) into
디자인	designing, design		soup [water]; to mix (food)
따지다	to call (a matter) into		with soup [water]

말대꾸	retort, response	몹시	very much, exceedingly
말랑말랑	soft; nice and tender	묘사하다	to describe
말리다	to try to stop, prevent, persuade not to do	무더기	pile, heap
맛보다	to taste, sample	무려	as many as, no fewer than
망령	dotage, senility	무릅쓰다	to risk, brave, face (adversity, danger, etc.)
맞선	meeting [interview] with a view to marriage	무엇보다	more than anything else
맞춤	something made to order	무제한의	unlimited, unrestricted
매끄럽다	to be smooth, sleek	무조건	without condition
매달다	to hang	무채색	achromatic color
매달리다	to cling to, hang on	묵묵히	silently, mutely
매도하다	to denounce, condemn	문득	suddenly, by chance, unexpectedly
매를 치다	to whip, cane, flog	문명인	civilized person
맹세하다	to swear, pledge, make an oath, vow	문자	letter, character
맺다	to knot, tie, form, make, contract	문헌	documents, records, written materials, literature
머리 염색	dying hair	문화적	cultural
머리카락	hair	물기	moisture, dampness
머무르다	to stay, remain, stop	물려받다	to inherit (from), take over, obtain by transfer
머물다	to stay, lodge	물론	of course, naturally
멋	taste, elegance, charm, refinement	물리(적)	physical
멜랑콜리하다	to be melancholy	물리력	physical strength
면	aspect, face	물리치다	to defeat, beat; to refuse, reject, spurn
명	order, command	물적	physical, material
명랑하다	to be bright, cheerful	묽다	to be watery, thin
명문대	prestigious university	미군	American forces
명백하다	to be obvious, evident, clear	미덕	virtue
명분	moral duty	미덥다	to be trustworthy, dependable, reliable
명하다	to order, command	미래 지향적	future-oriented
명확하게	clearly, definitely, precisely	미비하다	to be deficient, defective, imperfect, incomplete, weak
몇몇의	several	미성년자	person under age, minor
모녀	mother and daughter	미술 전시회	art exhibition
모뎀	modem	미약하다	to be feeble, weak, faint
모면하다	to escape, avoid, evade	미지근하다	to be lukewarm, tepid
모양	look, appearance	미팅	meeting; blind date
모조리	all, without exception, thoroughly	미화	American dollar
목어	wooden fish (used by Buddhist priests)	민간 교류	civilian exchange
몫	share, proportion	민적	census register, family register
몰고 가다	to chase, drive, push (into)		
몰아내다	drive out, kick out	민족적	national, people's
몰아넣다	to drive or push someone into something	밀려나다	to be driven from
		밍밍하다	to be tasteless, flat
몸무게	weight		
몸살	bodyache	바구니	basket

바깥쪽	outside	배경	background
바라보다	to look at, gaze at	배려하다	to consider, give consideration to
바로	the very, the same, exactly, precisely	배불리 먹다	to eat one's fill, eat heartily
바르다¹	to be straight; to be upright, honest, straightforward	배속	assignment, attachment
		배우자	spouse, mate
		배후	behind the scenes
바르다²	to plaster, rub on, paste	버티다	to endure, tolerate, stand, keep the balance
바보	fool, stupid person		
바이러스	virus	번데기	silkworm, pupa, chrysalis
바짝	closely, tightly; (dried up) completely, scorched	번지다	(of liquid) to spread, run
		벌거숭이	naked body
박박 긁다	to scrape hard	범종	bell of a Buddhist temple, temple bell
박차	spur; acceleration		
박차다	to kick out hard, give a vigorous kick	법고	small stick drum played in front of the statue of Buddha during a Buddhist ritual
반론	objection, refutation		
반복하다	to repeat, reiterate	베테랑	veteran, expert
반주	liquor taken with a meal	벼랑	cliff, precipice
반주자	accompanist	벼슬	government post, official rank in old Korea
반증	counterevidence, evidence to the contrary		
		변모하다	to change, undergo a complete change
받아들이다	to accept, receive, agree with		
		변화 무쌍	endless change
발가락	toe	별 탈 없이	without a hitch
발걸음	step, pace, tread	별미	food with extraordinary taste
발견하다	to discover		
발바닥	sole of the foot	별반	particularly, especially
발생시키다	to make something occur	별수 없이	without any better luck
발신	dispatch of a message	병사	soldier
발을 구르다	to stamp one's feet; to push up (a swing) by pressing the pedal forward with the feet	보관하다	to take custody of, take (a thing) into one's custody, keep
발자취	tracks, traces, footprints	보도하다	to report, inform a person of, notify a person of
발톱	claw, toenail, talon		
밥 한 술	a spoonful of rice	보름달	full moon
방문 교류	visits and exchanges	보선	traditional Korean socks usually made of cotton
방문지	paper of a paper door		
방바닥	floor of a room	보수적인	conservative
방송하다	to broadcast	보신탕	dog-meat soup
방영되다	to be broadcast on TV	보옥	jewel, precious gem
방영하다	to broadcast on TV	보자기	wrapping cloth
방자	servant, footman (in old Korea)	복구	rehabilitation, recovery, restoration
방직 산업	textile industry	복구 사업	restoration task
방황	wandering, roaming	복구하다	to recover, return to a former condition
방황하다	to wander about, roam about		
		복사	radiation; duplication

복잡하다	to be complicated	분석	analysis
복제품	reproduction, replica	분야	area, field
복창하다	to repeat (an order)	분할 통치	rule by partition, divide and rule
본격적인	full-scale, genuine, regular, typical	불가	impropriety; disapproval
본디	originally, by nature, in itself, primarily, from the first	불결하다	to be dirty, unclean, foul
		불교	Buddhism
본받다	to model (oneself) on	불리다	to be called
본보기	example, model	불만	dissatisfaction, discontent, displeasure
본선	main match [contest]	불매 운동	buyers' strike, boycott (movement) against purchasing
본인	I, me, myself, oneself		
봉급	salary, pay, wages		
봉쇄	blockade, closure	불쌍하다	to be poor, pitiable, pitiful
봉쇄되다	to be blocked	불치	incurability
부각시키다	to highlight, bring to the fore	불특정	(being) unspecified
		불평등	inequality, discrimination
부강하다	to be rich and strong	불행하다	to be unhappy
부글부글	boiling briskly	불황	recession, business depression
부끄럽다	to be shy, embarrassed		
부담스럽다	to be burdensome	붐	boom
부두	quay, wharf	붕괴	collapse, fall, breakdown, crumbling
부딪치다	to bump into, strike, hit, knock		
		블랙 푸딩	black pudding
부뚜막	counter area around iron kettles in a traditional Korean kitchen	비극	tragedy
		비극적이다	to be tragic
		비기다	to compare
부문	class, group, department, section, category, branch, line, field	비난	criticism, blame, reproach
		비난하다	to criticise unfavorably, censure, blame, condemn
부사	(old term for) mayor, county chief	비닐 장판	vinyl floor
		비단	silk
부인네	married women	비로소	for the first time (after something happened)
부인하다	to deny, defy		
부작용	side effect	비롯하다	to begin, originate
부정적인	negative	비법	secret method
부쩍	remarkably, greatly	비비다	to rub; to mix (food)
부풀다	to swell up	비율	rate, ratio, percentage, proportion
부하	subordinate, follower		
부합되다	to be matched, agreed upon	비정상적	abnormal
북녘	north, the north side	비중	specific gravity, density; relative importance
분가	branch of a family		
분가하다	to create a new family	비춰 보다	to reflect (in a mirror)
분단	dividing into sections, division, partition	비트	bit
		비판	criticism, comment
분명하다	to be clear, evident, plain, obvious, vivid	비판적	critical
		비판하다	to criticise
분부	order, command, bidding	비하	abasement, humility
분부하다	to bid, order, command	빌미	excuse, curse

빛깔	color, hue	살갑다	to be kind, warmhearted
빠져 나가다	to escape, go out, leak out	살림 도구	household goods
빠져 들다	to fall into	살림하다	to run one's household
빨다	to wash (clothes), launder	살점	piece of flesh
빼놓다	to leave out, miss, skip	삶다	to boil
뻗어 나가다	to extend, stretch out	삼가다	to restrain oneself, abstain from
뻘뻘	(sweat) freely, profusely		
뼈저리게	keenly, severely, acutely	삼각 관계	three-cornered arrangement, triangular relationship or love affair
뽀얗다	to be milk-white, frosty, cream-colored		
뿌리다	to sprinkle, shower, water, scatter, spread	삼계탕	chicken soup with ginseng (and other ingredients)
		삼국사기	*The Record of the Three Kingdoms*
사고[1]	accident, mishap	삼국유사	*Memorabilia of the Three Kingdoms*
사고[2]	thinking, thought		
사나이	a man, a male	삼다	to make, use as
사나흘	three or four days	삽살개	shaggy dog
사당패	troupe of wandering entertainers	–상	on; from the viewpoint, in terms of
사대주의	toadyism	상거래	business transaction, commercial dealings
사또	local magistrate (in old Korea)		
		상걸인	the most wretched of beggars
사라지다	to disappear		
사모 관대	male minister's costume with a silk hat	상공 회의소	chamber of commerce and industry
사물	four musical instruments	상놈	ill-bred fellow, vulgar man, man of low birth, commoner
사상	historically		
사실적	realistic, factual		
사업	project, undertaking, business	상담소	counselor's office
		상당하다	to be considerable, fair, good
사정	circumstances, situation, state of affairs	상대주의	relativism
		상상	imagination, fancy
사정하다	to beg, entreat, implore, solicit (special consideration)	상세하다	to be detailed
		상세히	in detail
		상식하다	to eat normally, live on
사주	the Four Pillars (birth year, month, day, and hour); letter to the house of the fiancé in which the birth year, month, day, and hour of the bride and bridegroom are written	상영되다	to be put on the screen, play
		상인	merchant, shopkeeper
		상좌	high seat of honor
		상주 인구	permanent residents (in an area)
사채 시장	private money market	상징하다	to symbolize
사채 업자	moneylender, loan shark	상태	form, condition, state
사춘기	adolescence, puberty	상표	model, example
사항	matters, facts, articles, items	상호	mutual
		상황	condition, aspect, situation
사회적으로	socially	새끼	fellow, guy, brat
산뜻하다	to be clean, neat	새삼스럽게	anew, afresh; now; again

생년월일(시)	date (and hour) of one's birth	성장률	growth rate
생동적이다	to be active, dynamic, lively	성찬	feast, good table
생리	physiology	성취	achievement, accomplishment, attainment
생산량	output, yield	성취도	achievement rate
생생하게	lively, fresh	성토	censure; debate
생선회	sliced raw fish, sashimi	성향	disposition, tendency
생시	one's lifetime	성 희롱	sexual harassment
생활 방식	lifestyle	세계은행	World Bank
서구	Western Europe, the West	세계인	cosmopolitan
서구 사상	Western ideas	세계화	globalization
서구화	Westernization	세대 차이	generation gap
서당	village schoolhouse in old Korea	세련되다	to be elegant, polished, refined
서독	West Germany	세우다	to set up, build, construct, establish
서두	beginning, inception; prologue	세태	social conditions
서두르다	to hasten, hurry up	셰익스피어	(William) Shakespeare
서론	prologue	소련	Soviet Union
서민	common people, peasantry	소박하다	to be simple, naive
서방	Mr. (familiar title used within the family, especially to one's husband, son-in-law, or younger brother-in-law)	소비자	consumer
		소비하다	to consume, spend, expend
		소유물	possessions, one's property
		소재	material, subject matter
		소주	soju (a type of distilled Korean liquor)
서서히	slowly, gradually	속도	speed, velocity
서양식	Western-style	속독	rapid [fast, quick] reading
석유 화학	petroleum chemistry	손맛	taste from someone's particular cooking skill
석탄	coal		
선	line	손잡이	handle
선정되다	to be chosen, selected	솟구치다	to rise quickly, blaze up
선조	ancestor	솟아오르다	to well up, spring out
선진화되다	to be advanced, modernized	송금	remittance
선호하다	to prefer	송신	transmission of a message
설득하다	to persuade	솥	kettle, pot
설문	questions, questionnaire	쇠	iron, metal
설문 조사	survey by questionnaire	수강하다	to take courses (at a university)
설문지	survey		
설정하다	to establish, create, set up	수단	means, measure, way
설치하다	to install	수령	provincial mandarin, magistrate
섬기다	to serve, be devoted to (one's master)		
		수북이	heaped up, heaping full
성	sex	수시로	as occasion arises
성과	result, fruit, outcome, performance	수신	receipt of a message
		수신자	addressee, recipient
성급하다	to be hasty, rash	수여하다	to give, award
성사	accomplishment, achievement, realization	수입	income, earnings, revenue, proceeds
성욕	sexual desire		

수절하다	to remain chaste, remain faithful to one's deceased husband
수중	in the hands (of)
수차	several times, time and again
수청	serving as a mistress
수출	export
수학	mathematics
순금	solid gold
순환하다	to circulate; to rotate
술상	drinking table
숭늉	water boiled with scorched rice
쉬다	to become hoarse
스미다	to come in (of water), soak in
스스로	by oneself, of one's own accord, for oneself
스태미나	stamina
슬기롭다	to be intelligent, sagacious, wise, bright
슬슬	slowly
승리	victory
승인하다	to approve, admit, acknowledge
시각	point of view, perspective, viewpoint
시사점	suggestions, lessons
시상식	ceremony of awarding prizes
시상하다	to award a prize
시샘	jealousy
시선	one's gaze, one's eye(s)
시야	visual field, field of vision
시위	demonstration
시정되다	to be corrected, be rectified
시청자	TV watchers
시청하다	to watch (TV) (lit., look and listen)
시해	assassination
식성	taste, culinary preference
식습관	eating habits
식용	use as food
식용하다	to use as food, eat
식용화	making something into food
식인종	cannibal
신뢰	trust, confidence
신명나다	to get enthusiastic (about), be enraptured, enter into the spirit (of things)
신방	bridal room, bridal bed
신부	bride
신선하다	to be fresh
신세대	new generation
신통하게	marvelously, admirably
신풀이	Korean exorcism
신호	sign, signal
싣다	to load, carry; to publish
실감	actual feeling
실내	indoor
실리다	to be loaded
실연	failure in love
실정	real situation, actual circumstances, real state of affairs
실증적	positive, empirical
실증하다	to prove, demonstrate
실질적으로	substantially, virtually, practically
실향민	people who had to move from their hometown because of war [disaster], refugees
심각하다	to be serious, grave, acute, poignant
심도 있게	deeply, in depth, in detail
심성	disposition, mentality
심심하다	to taste slightly flat; to be bored
싹트다	to sprout, bud, begin to develop
쏘다	to shoot, discharge
쓰이다	to be used
씁쓸하다	to be rather bitter
아궁이	fuel hole, opening of a firebox
아끼다	to be economical, be sparing
아낙(네)	woman, wife
아녀자	women and children; woman
아랑곳하다	to be concerned with, take an interest in
아랫목	warmest part of an ondol floor
아령	dumbbell
아롱다롱하다	to be variegated, mottled
아명	childhood name

아무튼	anyway, anyhow, at any rate, in any case [event], somehow or other	애완견	pet puppy
아쉬워하다	to be reluctant, loath; to feel the lack of	애원	entreaty, appeal, supplication
아씨	young lady [archaic]	애정	affection, love
아예	from the very first	애지중지하다	to love and prize
아이고	Oh, my God! Oh!	액수	amount of money
악몽	nightmare, bad dream, hideous dream	야단	uproar, clamor
악상	theme, motif, melodic subject	야단나다	to be in a quandary
		야만	savagery, savageness
악수	handshake	야생	wild
악장	movement (of a piece of music), section of a longer musical piece	야생 동물	wild animal
		야외	field, open air
		약혼	engagement
안건	agenda, bill; matter	약혼식	engagement ceremony
안달이다	to be impatient, overanxious	얇다	to be thin
		양가	both families
안목	good eye (for), appreciative eye, discerning eye, sense of discrimination	양국 관계	relationship between two countries
		양론	both arguments, both sides of the argument
안심시키다	to set a person at ease, relieve a person of his [her] anxiety	양변기	toilet bowl
		양보하다	to concede, give in, compromise
알려지다	to become known	양식	mode, fashion, style
암기	learning by heart, memorization	양지	sunny spot, bright place
		어김없이	surely, without fail, certainly
암행 어사	secret inspector-general, undercover emissary of the king	어느새	before one is aware, in no time at all
		어른거리다	to flicker, glimmer, shimmer
압도되다	to be overwhelmed, overpowered	어리석다	to be foolish, stupid, silly
압도하다	to overwhelm, overpower, surpass	어색하다	to feel awkward, be embarrassed
압력	pressure	어안이 벙벙하다	to be dumbfounded, amazed, struck dumb
앞당기다	to do something ahead of its due date	어우러지다	to be well matched with, be joined together
앞두고	with a period or a distance ahead	어울리다	to mix with, mingle with, join
앞장서다	to lead, be at the head, be the first (to do), take the lead [initiative]	어원	etymology
		어지간하다	to be fair, tolerable, considerable
앞치마	apron	어질다	to be wise, gentle, considerate
애사당	children in a troupe of wandering entertainers	어쨌거나	however, anyway
		어쨌든	anyhow, anyway
애쓰다	to take pains [trouble], make an effort, endeavor, strive	어쩌다(가)	how, by doing what, by chance

어찌하여	why, for what reason
억양	intonation
억울하다	to suffer unfairness, feel victimized, be mistreated
억제하다	to suppress, repress, restrain, constrain
억척스럽다	to be unyielding, steadfast
언뜻	in an instant, in a flash
언론	media, press
얻다	to get, obtain
얼떨결에	in a moment of bewilderment
얼른얼른하다	to glisten (mimetic word)
얼큰하다	to be rather hot, somewhat peppery
얼키설키	all mingled up; in a disorderly way, confusedly, complicatedly
얽매다	to tie [bind] up tight
엄벌	severe [heavy] punishment
엄연히	solemnly, gravely
엄청나게	terribly, absurdly, massively
업무	business, duty
업체	company, firm
엉기다	to coagulate, congeal, clot
엉키다	to be entangled
에스콰이어	esquire
에티켓	etiquette
여기다	to think of, regard (as), consider
여력	remaining power, strength; financial ability
여론	public opinion
여봐라	hey! [archaic]
여사당	female performers in a troupe of wandering entertainers
여신	goddess
여염집	ordinary household
여유로움	surplus, richness
여전하다	to be as usual, be as before, as ever
여주인공	female protagonist
여쭙다	to tell, say, inform, ask, inquire
여필종부	wives should be submissive to their husbands
역대	many generations, generation after generation, successive generations
역사상	historically
역삼각형	inverted triangle shape
역설	paradox
역설적으로	paradoxically
역학 관계	dynamic relationship
역할	role, function
역행하다	to be contrary (to), retrogress
엮다	to plait, weave
연계되다	to be connected, linked (with)
연기	smoke
연도	year, period, term
연료	fuel
연맹	association, union, confederation, alliance
연분	preordained tie, bond, fate, relation
연예	entertainment
연예인	entertainer
연주	(musical) performance
연탄	briquette of coal
연 평균	annual average
연하다	to be light, mild, soft, tender
연합군	Allied Forces
연휴	consecutive holidays
열	heat, fever
열강	great powers, superpowers
열광하다	to be wildly excited, go wild with excitement
열녀	heroine, woman of chaste reputation, exceptionally virtuous woman
열등하다	to be inferior
열띠다	to get excited, become heated
열리다	to be held, take place
열망	desire
열변	passionate eloquence, fervent speech
열병	febrile disease, fever
열정적이다	to be passionate, ardent, fervent
열풍	heat, hot wind, fervor
염두	mind, thought
염세주의자	pessimist
영구적	lasting, permanent
영구히	permanently

영국 왕실	British royal household	외눈박이	one-eyed person
영상 자료	visual aids, visual materials	외래어	loanwords, words of foreign origin
영역	territory, domain		
영원히	eternally, perpetually	외면하다	to ignore, turn one's face
영혼	spirit, soul	외부	outside, exterior
영화광	film fan	외부인	outside, exterior
예법	etiquette, manners, courtesy	외세	foreign power(s)
예복	ritual or formal costumes	외채	foreign debt
예술	art	외환	foreign exchange (currency)
예술단	performing art group, performance group	요구하다	to ask, request, demand
		요소	essential element, factor, constituent
예식장	wedding hall		
예의상	by courtesy	요인	cause, reason, primary factor
예전에는	in the old days		
예측하다	to predict, estimate	욕정	feelings of passion, sexual desire
오도독	with a crunching sound (onomatopoeic word)		
		욕하다	to curse, swear, abuse, insult
오라이	Japanese-style pronunciation of 'all right'	용도	use, service
오락	entertainment	용돈	pocket money
오락가락	coming and going, milling (mimetic word)	용어	terminology, term
		우람하다	to be grand, magnificent, impressive, imposing
오만	arrogance, insolence		
오순도순	people gathering in a small group (mimetic word)	우려	worry, concern, fear
		우수한	excellent
오슬오슬	person shivering with cold (mimetic word)	우승	championship, win
		우승팀	winning team
오일 쇼크	the oil shock	우승하다	to win the victory [championship]
오직	only, merely, solely		
오징어	squid	우여곡절	twists and turns, meandering, complications
옥소반	jade tray, small jade dining table		
		우열	superiority or inferiority
옥중	inside of a jail	우주	universe, cosmos
옥황상제	King of Heaven (in Taoism)	운명	destiny
온몸	whole body	울렁거리다	to palpitate, throb, pound, beat
온수	hot water		
올려 놓다	to raise, lift	원동력	motive power, driving force
올리다	to offer, give, present (humble form); to put on record, enter (a name)	원만한	harmonious, peaceful
		원망	resentment, reproach, grievance, grudge
올바르다	to be straight, upright, correct, straightforward, honest	원삼	woman's royal costume, worn by the bride in the traditional wedding ceremony
옹호하다	to protect, safeguard		
왕래	comings and goings, interaction	원초적	basic, original, first
		원형	original form, prototype
왕실	royal household	월드컵	World Cup
외교적(인)	diplomatic	웬일	what matter, what cause, what reason
외국인	foreigner, alien		

위계 질서	hierarchical order
위기	crisis, emergency, critical moment, critical situation
위배되다	to be violated
위배하다	to breach, violate
위상	status of (a country or an organization in a bigger community)
위생	hygiene, sanitation
위생 시설	sanitary facilities
위험	danger, peril
위험선	danger line, danger signal
유교	Confucianism
유랑	wandering, roaming
유랑자	nomadic people, nomads
유랑하다	to wander [roam] about
유래	history, origin
유래하다	to originate in, result from
유별나다	to be distinctive
유부녀	married woman
유사성	similarity, resemblance
유유히	at ease, in comfort
유인물	printed matter
유일하다	to be single, unique
유전자	gene
유출	effluence, outflow, spillage
유출하다	to flow out
유치	lure, enticement
유통	distribution
유통하다	to distribute, circulate
유학	studying abroad, studying overseas
육성	promotion, upbringing
육신	body, flesh
융자금	loan
융통성	adaptability, flexibility
으레	habitually, commonly, usually, naturally
은근히	secretly, privately, inwardly, not overtly
은은하다	to be dim, vague, indistinct, misty
은행잎	ginkgo leaf
음료	drink, beverage
음미	tasting, sampling, appreciation, savoring
음색	(musical) tone color
음양	yin and yang (negative and positive forces [elements])

음울하다	to be gloomy, melancholy
음지	shady spot, dark place
응어리	unpleasant feeling, anxiety
의견	opinion, view
의미	meaning, sense
의미 있다	to be meaningful, important
의식	ceremony
의식하다	to be conscious of, be aware of
의아해 하다	to be dubious, suspicious
이끌다	to lead, head, command, take along, guide
이데올로기	ideology
이듬해	the following year
이루다	to form, make, constitute
이루어지다	to be formed of, composed of, made up of; to get accomplished
이르다	to arrive, reach; to result in
이른바	what is called, what we call, so-called
이마	forehead
이미지	image
이방인	stranger, alien, foreigner
이산 가족	separated families
이상	ideal
이상적(인)	ideal
이상형	ideal type
이어지다	to be connected, continued
이용자	user
이윽고	after a while, before long
이전	before, in former times
이질감	sense [feeling] of difference [disparateness]
인격	character, personality
인근	nearby
인내심	patience, endurance, perseverance
인내하다	to tolerate, endure
인도적	humane, humanitarian
인식	cognition, recognition, perception, knowledge, impression
인식되다	to be recognized, understood, appreciated
인연	karma, fate, tie, bond, relation
인정	recognition, acknowledgment

인정받다	to receive recognition	자동문	automatic door
인정하다	to admit, recognize, acknowledge, authorize	자동 판매기	vending machine
인지상정	human nature, humaneness	자랑스럽게	boastfully, proudly
일간	daily publication	자랑스럽다	to be boastful, proud
일간지	daily newspaper	자리잡다	to take one's seat or position, occupy, locate
일과	daily work, daily task	자립적인	to be independent
일깨워 주다	to awake, arouse, enlighten, open (a person's) eyes	자본주의	capitalism
일다	to rise, go up, become active	자살하다	to commit suicide
일대	whole area [district]; neighborhood (of)	자손	offspring
일반	all; general	자유주의적	liberal
일반인	general people, the public	자주성	independence, sovereignty
일방적이다	one-sided, unilateral	자체	oneself, itself; one's own body
일상 생활	everyday life, daily life	자취	trace
일상적인	daily, usual	자판기	vending machine
일시	once, one time	작용하다	to operate on, affect, function (as)
일어나다	to happen, occur, arise	작위	(noble) title, peerage
일원	a member (of society)	잔뜩	extremely, to the fullest, to the utmost
일으키다	to cause, raise, give rise to	잔인하다	to be cruel, heartless
일자리	job, position, employment	잔치	party, feast
일정액	certain amount of money, fixed sum	잠자리	sleeping place, bed
일제	Japanese imperialism	잡종견	mongrel (dog)
일종의	a kind of, a sort of	잣대	measuring stick; standard
일치하다	to match, agree, fit	장고	hourglass-shaped drum
일품	article of top quality, excellent piece	장관	minister, director, governor
임	lover, sweetheart	장기 투자	long-term investment
임금(님)	king, monarch	장난	game, mischief, prank, practical joke, fun, amusement, pastime
임하다	to deal with, face, meet; to be confronted (by)	장난 삼아	for fun
입가심	taking away the aftertaste from one's mouth	장단	rhythm
입금	receipt of money	장래	future, time to come
입시	entrance exam	장려	promotion, encouragement
입시철	entrance exam period	장모	man's mother-in-law
자	name or style taken at the age of twenty, one's "courtesy name"	장문	lengthy writing
자개	mother-of-pearl	장악하다	to hold, seize, grasp
자개장	furniture decorated with mother-of-pearl	장원	highest mark in the state examination in old Korea
자금 융자	capital loan	장유유서	there is an order between the young and the old
자동	automatism, automatic movement; automatic	장차	in the future, some day
		장치	equipment, facility
		장판지	oiled paper (for traditional *ondol* floor)
		잦다	to be frequent, often
		재계	financial world

재벌 기업	chaebol, (financial) conglomerates
재빨리	quickly, agilely, rapidly
재산세	property tax
재정	budget, finances
재즈 그룹	jazz group
쟁쟁하다[1]	to be clear, sonorous, resonant
쟁쟁하다[2]	to be famous
저명하다	to be famous
저물다	(the day or year) closes, it grows dark
적극적(인)	positive, active, constructive
적극적이다	to be positive, active, constructive
적응	adaptation
적응하다	to adapt oneself (to), adjust oneself (to)
적장	enemy general, commander of the enemy force
적절하게	appropriately, properly
적지 않은	many, not a little
전세계	the whole world
전개되다	to be unfolded; to develop
전개하다	to unfold, develop, spread out, unroll
전권	total control
전달하다	to deliver
전담하다	to bear total responsibility, be fully responsible (for)
전도	conduction
전략	strategy, tactics
전면	front [side, part], frontage
전문가	specialist, expert
전문 대학	technical college
전문직	professional occupation
전반적	general, overall
전반적으로	generally
전산	computer computation
전산망	information system
전송	electrical transmission
전송하다	to transmit, convey, deliver
전시하다	to show, exhibit
전신	predecessor
전자 우편	electronic mail, e-mail
전적으로	totally, overall, wholly, entirely
전전하다	to wander from place to place, roam about

전통적으로	traditionally
전투적	combating, military
전파하다	to circulate, transmit
전학하다	to change school
전후	postwar days
절	bow (on one's knees), deep bow
절경	magnificent view, fine scenery
절묘하다	to be miraculous, exquisite
절반	half
절벽	(sheer) cliff, inaccessible precipice
절실하게	desperately, urgently
절실하다	to be earnest, urgent
절차	procedures, steps
절하다	to make a bow
젊은이	youth, young person
점유하다	to occupy
점잖게	gently, in a gentle manner
점쟁이	fortune-teller
점차	gradually, more and more
접속하다	to connect (with)
정	compassion, sentiment
정겹다	to be friendly, affectionate, tender
정경 유착	tie between politicians and businessmen
정계	political world
정교하다	to be elaborate, exquisite
정국	political situation
정권	political power, regime
정규(의)	regular, formal, proper
정기적으로	regularly
정독	careful reading
정독하다	to read carefully, peruse
정리하다	to arrange, put in order
정보화 시대	information age
정부	government
정부 기관	government agency
정상[1]	normal, normality
정상[2]	top, summit, peak
정상 회담	summit meeting
정서	emotion, feeling, sentiment
정식	proper [regular] form
정유	oil refinery
정작	actually, really, practically
정착시키다	to make (something) settle down

정책	policy
정치력	political power, political influence
정치인	politician, statesman
정치적으로	politically
정화	purification, purgation
정확하다	to be correct, accurate
정확히	accurately, exactly, precisely
제2차 대전	Second World War
제고	improvement, heightening
제공하다	to provide, give, offer, present
제대로	formally, regularly, in a formal way, in style
제도	system, institution, organization, regime
제사	memorial service, ancestor-worship ceremony
제수	things needed in the ancestor-memorial service
제시하다	to present, show
제약	restriction, condition
제작	production, manufacture
제작하다	to produce
제전	big event, festival
제품	product, article
조각품	(piece of) sculpture
조급하게	hastily
조선	shipbuilding
조선 시대	Chosŏn dynasty (1392 – 1910)
조언하다	to advise, counsel
조연	supporting player, supporting actor
조의금	condolence money
조차(도)	even; besides, in addition
조화	harmony, accord, agreement
족두리	headpiece (like a crown), which goes with a woman's traditional ceremonial costume
족보	genealogy, family register
존재	existence, being, presence
종달새	lark, skylark
종목	item
종식	cessation, end
종식하다	to cease, come to an end
좌우하다	to dominate, influence, affect
좌절	breakdown, frustration, setback
죄수	prisoner, convict
죄 의식	feeling of guilt [sin]
죄책감	feeling of liability for a crime
주간지	weekly magazine
주걱	spatula, scoop
주관하다	to convene, organize, be in charge of (an event)
주기	period, cycle
주도	leading
주도권	leadership, initiative
주도면밀하다	to be meticulous, careful, cautious, scrupulous, circumspect
주도적	leading
주도하다	to lead, take the lead in
주되다	to be chief, principal, main
주류	main current, maintream
주름살	wrinkles (on skin)
주목	attention
주목하다	to pay attention to
주민	residents, inhabitants, dwellers
주변	surroundings, periphery
주석	notes, commentary
주식	staple food
주역	leading player, leader
주요 도시	major cities
주요한	principal, chief, main, major
주의 깊게	attentively, cautiously
주입식	cramming method (in teaching)
주전부리	habitual snacking
주차	parking
주체성	independence, autonomy
주춤거리다	to hesitate, waver, hold back, shy away
주한	Korea-based, resident in Korea
죽	completely; roughly
준	semi-, quasi-
준결승	semi-final
줄곧	all the time, at all hours, constantly
줏대	strength of character, moral fiber, conviction
중공업	heavy industry

중단	interruption, stopping, breaking off
중단하다	to cease, discontinue, stop
중매 결혼	marriage arranged by a go-between
중매쟁이	matchmaker
중미	Central America
중시하다	to attach great importance to, take a serious view of a matter
중화학 공업	heavy-chemical industry
쥐다	to grasp, clasp, grip, clutch
즉	in other words
즉각	instantly, at once, immediately
즐거움	joy, delight, pleasure, happiness
즐겨	willingly
증가하다	to increase, multiply
증기	steam
증액	increasing the amount
지경	situation, (miserable) condition
지국장	head manager of a branch
지껄이다	to chatter, gabble
지나치다	to go beyond, go too far, go to excess
지니다	to carry, wear, have something along, hold
지다	to carry (something on one's back)
지도자	leader
지도층	the ruling class
지방 정부	local government
지배하다	to govern, dominate
지상 과제	someone's purpose, mission
지속적이다	to be continual, continuous
지식층	intellectual class
지역	area
지원	support, backup, aid
지위	position, status
지적하다	to point out, indicate
지점	place, point
지지	support, upholding, backing
지천	abundance
지천으로	in great abundance
지출 경쟁	competition in spending
지탄	criticism, blame
지향	intention, aim, inclination
지향하다	to intend to do
직무 유기	neglectful of one's duty
직전(에)	just before
진수	essence, spirit, soul, gist
진원지	original source, real origin
진정으로	heartily, from the bottom of one's heart
진정한	true, sincere, earnest
진출	advance, march
진출하다	to advance, gain ground
진하게	deeply, strongly, thickly
진하다	to be thick, rich, strong; to be dark
진학	entrance into a school of higher grade
진행하다	to proceed, progress
질기다	to be tough, strong
질러대다	to shout [yell, holler] a lot, shout repeatedly
질리다	to become disgusted with, get sick of, become fed up with
질박하다	to be simple, plain
질투	jealousy
짐승	beast, animal
짐작하다	to guess, conjecture, estimate
집게발	claws, nippers
집단	group
집단 강도	organized burglars
집단 토론	group discussion
집단으로	in a group
집단적으로	as a group, collectively
집중	concentration, convergence
집착	attachment, adherence, persistence
집착하다	to get hung up
짓거리	act, deed, behavior
짓다	to make (rice), build (a house), compose (a poem)
징	large gong
짚어내다	to point out, describe
쪼개다	to split, cleave, divide, cut
쪽지	slip of paper, memo
쫀득거리다	to be sticky, glutinous, adhesive, elastic, rubbery
찌개	pot stew
찌르다	to pierce, prick, stab
찍다	to imprint, stamp; to dip (into)

차관[1]	national loan, debt (from overseas)
차관[2]	vice minister
차등화	differentiation, gradation
차량 행렬	procession of cars
차려지다	to be set, arranged, prepared
차례	order, sequence
차례로	by turns
차리다	to set the table
차별	discrimination
차분히	calmly, quietly, composedly
차원	(mathematical) dimension
차지하다	to occupy, hold, take up, have a share [portion], make (a thing) one's own
착각하다	to mistake, misunderstand, get the wrong end of the stick
착하다	to be good, nice, kindhearted
찬미하다	to praise, admire
찬사	praise, eulogy, laudatory remarks
찬찬히	staidly, deliberately, quietly
참가하다	to participate in
참게	king crab
참고 문헌	literature cited
참고 자료	reference materials
참신하다	to be fresh, new
참여	participation
참여하다	to participate in, take part in
참조	reference
참조하다	to refer to, consult
참혹하다	to be cruel, brutal
찹쌀	sticky rice
찻집	teahouse
창안자	inventor, originator
창작	creation, production
채우다	to fill, pack, cram, charge
책임	responsibility, liability, accountability
책임감	sense of responsibility
처리하다	to handle, manage, treat, deal with
처신	behavior, actions, conduct
처지	situation, condition, circumstances
처하다	to sentence, deal (with)
천	fabric, cloth
천국	heaven
천차만별	infinite variety
철분	iron (content)
철자	spelling
철저하다	to be perfect, thorough, complete, exhaustive, all-embracing
첨단 기술	high technology
첨부	attachment
첨부 파일	attached file
첨부하다	to attach
첫날밤	first night
첫머리	head, opening, beginning
청년	young people, youth
청룡	blue dragon
청실	blue thread
청홍	blue and red
체결	conclusion (of an agreement or treaty)
체류	stay, visit
체질	(physical) constitution
체험	experience
초반	early stage
초점	focus, focal point
촉구하다	to press, urge, demand, call upon
촉촉하다	to be wet, damp, moist
촌극	short dramatic performance; happening
총각	bachelor, unmarried man
총기	firearms
최고 경영자	CEO (chief executive officer)
최대	(being) the largest; the maximum
최장	longest
최저가	lowest price
최초	very first
추상 명사	abstract noun
추세	tendency
추억	recollection, reminiscence, remembrance, reflection
추임새	sound of encouragement made by accompanist or audience during performance of traditional Korean music

추정하다   to presume, assume, infer, estimate

추진하다   to promote, pursue

추하다   to be ugly, bad-looking, plain; to be indecent, disgraceful, shameful, dishonorable, mean

축의금   wedding gift in cash

축제   festival

춘향전   *The Story of Ch'unhyang*

출두   appearance, presence, showing up

출세   rising in the world, making one's way, success

출신지   one's hometown, birthplace

출전   participating in a contest; going into a war

출전하다   to participate in a contest; to go into a war

충격   shock, impact

충고   advice, warning, caution

충분히   enough, sufficiently, fairly, fully

충신   loyal subject

취급하다   to treat (in a certain way), handle, deal with

취업   going to work, employment, commencement of work,

취향   taste, liking, inclination

측면   side, aspect, flank

-층   class, stratum, level, layer

치다   to take, undergo (an exam)

치르다   to carry out, go through; to pay, settle one's account; to experience, go through

치마 저고리   skirts and upper garments (of traditional Korean women's costume)

치맛바람   female influence, female power

치밀하다   to be elaborate, fine, nice, delicate

치중하다   to put weight (on), emphasize

친정   woman's parent's (old) home, one's maiden home

침략군   invading army

침체하다   to stagnate, become sluggish, be dull

카아   phew (onomatopoeic word describing sound made after drinking *soju*)

캐럿   carat, karat

컵   trophy, cup

쾌재를 부르다   to cry out 'bravo', shout with exultation

쾌활하다   to be cheerful, gay, cheery, lively

크기   size, volume

큰절   bow on ceremonial occasions

키우다   to grow, bring up

타악기   percussion instrument

탄생   birth, nativity

탄생시키다   to make (something) be born

탄생하다   to be born

탄압하다   to suppress, oppress, repress, crush

탐색   search, hunt

탐색하다   to search

탕   soup; broth

태반   mostly, generally, the majority (of)

택일   selection of a day (to hold a ceremony or an event)

터무니없다   to be unfounded, unreasonable, outrageous

터져 나오다   to get broken, be torn; to explode, burst

털   hair

토론회   forum, debate

통   counter for letters and documents

통과하다   to pass through

통로   passage

통일   unification

통제   control, regulation, regimentation

통째   all, whole, altogether

통틀어   taking all things together, altogether

통하여   through

통화   currency, medium of circulation

투우   bullfighting, bullfight

투자	investment
투자자	investor
튀기다	to fry
튀김	fried food
특권	privilege
특별하다	to be special, peculiar
특색	characteristics
특유의	characteristic, peculiar
특정	specification, specifics
특집	special edition
특징	(special, distinctive) feature
특징적인	characteristic
특혜	privilege, special favor
틀	convention, formality, frame, framework
틀어쥐다	to take control
파격적	exceptional, unprecedented, extraordinary, special; abnormal, irregular
파견	dispatch
파고 들어가다	to dig into, make a thorough investigation of
파산	bankruptcy, insolvency
파일	file
파직	dismissal [removal] from office, discharge
파직하다	to dismiss (a person) from office
판단	judgment, decision
판명	becoming clear
판명되다	to become clear
판이하다	to be completely different
팔각형	octagon
팔씨름	arm wrestling
패	party, company, group
패다	to beat (a thing or a person)
패싸움	group fight, gang fight
편	piece (counter for a movie)
편성하다	to draw up, compose, organize
편안하다	to be comfortable
편입	transfer (from one school [university] to another)
편지체	epistolary style
펼치다	to spread, extend, expand, carry out, unfold
평등	equality, impartiality
평등하다	to be equal

평범하다	to be common, ordinary
평상시	normal times
평소(에)	ordinary times
평화	peace
폐백	ceremony in which the bride greets the groom's family
폐쇄	closing, closure
폐쇄되다	to be closed.
폐해	evil, abuse, vice, evil practices
포식	predation
포장마차	street food stall, (lit., covered wagon)
폭력물	violent matters (like movies)
폭로하다	to expose, reveal, disclose
폭발적인	explosive
표면적으로	superficially, outwardly, externally
표시	indication, expression, sign
표지판	signboard
표현되다	to be expressed
표현하다	to express, give expression to
푸근하다	to be comfortably warm
푸념하다	to complain of, grumble at
푸다	to scoop up, dip up
푹푹	thoroughly, well
풀어 주다	to release, set free
풀이되다	to be interpreted
풍경	scenery, scene
풍미하다	to dominate, predominate
풍속	customs
풍자	satire, sarcasm, innuendo, irony
피로감	fatigue
피붙이	family member
필독	must-read
필두	first on a list, role model
필연적이다	to be necessary, inevitable
필연적인	necessary, inevitable
필요 충분한	necessary and sufficient
핑계	excuse, pretext, pretense
하나하나	one by one
하룻밤	one night
학대	cruelty, mistreatment, maltreatment

학대하다	to be cruel to, mistreat
학업 성취도	academic achievement rate
학위	university degree
학위 논문	thesis for a degree
학정	oppressive government, tyranny, despotism
학창	school, campus
한가하다	to be leisurely
한갓	only, alone
한겨레	one people
한결같다	to be constant, consistent
한결같이	consistently, invariably
한국은행	Bank of Korea
한기	cold air or cold feeling
한때	once
한류	Korean Wave
한바탕	a scene, a round
한소끔 끓이다	to boil briskly
한심하다	to be a pity, be lamentable, pitiful, pitiable
한편	on the other hand, besides
함	present [gift] box for the bride
함진아비	person who is carrying a box of presents from the groom to the bride's family
합동	joint, united, combined
합리적(인)	rational, reasonable
합법화	legalization
합숙	staying together in a camp for training
합의	agreement, consent
합의하다	to consent, agree
합작 투자	joint investment
항렬자	generation name, Chinese character used in the names of family members of a particular generation
항목	item, head, heading
항아리	pot, jar
항의하다	to protest
해결책	solution
해물탕	Korean seafood soup
해방	emancipation, discharge, release, liberation
해삼	trepang, sea cucumber
해외	foreign countries, overseas
해외 여행	overseas travel
핵심	core, nucleus

행세	pose as, assume the air of
행위	act, action, behavior, conduct
행정 기관	administrative machinery
허가	permission, approval, license
허락하다	to consent to, assent to, permit
허용하다	to allow, permit
헤매다	to wander about
헤프게	wastefully, lavishly
혁명	revolution
혁신적(인)	innovative
현실적	realistic, practical
현지	actual spot, locale
혈통	bloodline, descent
협상	negotiation
협주곡	concerto
협회	society, association
형리	legal clerk in a local government [obsolete]
형벌	punishment
형상	shape, appearance, form
형틀	chair in which a criminal is fastened to be interrogated [archaic]
혜택	favor, kind indulgence, benevolence
호	pen name, title
호롱불	light of a kerosene lamp
호소력	power of appealing
호적	census registration, family register
혹하다	to become infatuated, fascinated, charmed
혼란	confusion, disorder, derangement
혼란하다	to be confused, disordered, messy, chaotic
혼례	marriage ceremony
홀딱	completely (mimetic word)
홍보	public information, publicity
홍실	red thread
화기애애하다	to be peaceful, be harmonious
화려하다	to be splendid, gorgeous, magnificent
화목	harmony, happiness
화장	makeup, beauty care

화학 작용	chemical action	후진국	undeveloped country
화합	harmony, concord	후진성	underdevelopment, backwardness
화합하다	to harmonize		
확고히	firmly, determinedly	후하다	to be rich, hospitable
확산	spread, dissemination	후회	regret, repentance, remorse
확산되다	to be diffused, dispersed, expanded	훌륭하다	to be excellent, splendid, praiseworthy
확산시키다	to spread (something)	훔쳐보기	peeking
확산하다	to expand	훔쳐보다	to steal a glance at, look furtively at
확실하다	to be certain, sure, reliable		
환갑 잔치	sixtieth birthday party	훼손되다	to be damaged or ruined
환상	fantasy	훼손하다	to damage, ruin
황당하다	to be baffled, puzzled; to be absurd, preposterous	휘영청	brightly
		흉계	evil plot
회복	recovery, restoration, retrieval, rehabilitation, recuperation	흐르다	to flow
		흔하다	to be common, plentiful
		흙	earth, soil, clay
회복하다	to recover, regain, restore, rehabilitate, retrieve	흠잡다	to find fault with
		흡인력	suction, attractive power
회비	membership fee	흥미롭게	interestingly
회상하다	to recollect, recall	흥미롭다	to be interesting
회원	member, membership	흥분하다	to be excited
획수	number of strokes	희귀 동물	rare animal
획일적	uniform	희뜩희뜩	very dizzy, giddy, shaky (mimetic word)
후반	second half		
후반전	second half of the game	희한하다	to be rare, curious, scarce, uncommon
후손	descendants, offspring, posterity		
		흰색	white color
후원	support		

English-Korean Glossary

@ symbol	골뱅이
abasement	비하
ability	기량, 능력
abnormal	비정상적, 파격적
about (time)	~께, 무렵
abruptly	급격하게
abstain from	삼가다
abstract noun	추상 명사
absurd	불합리한, 황당한
absurdly	불합리하게, 엄청나게
abundance	풍부, 지천
in great ~	대량으로, 지천으로
abuse	욕하다; 폐해
acceleration	가속, 박차
accept	받아들이다
accident	사고
accidental	우연한
(be) accompanied	데리다
accompanist	반주자
accompany	동행하다, 모시다
accomplish	관철하다, 이루다
accomplishment	관철, 성사, 성취
accord	조화, 일치; 일치하다
of one's own ~	마음대로, 스스로
account	계정
accountability	책임
accumulate	쌓다, 모으다; 쌓이다
accurate	정확한
accurately	정확히
accustom	익숙케 하다
(be) accustomed to	익숙해지다
achievement	성공, 성사, 성취
~ rate	성취도
achromatic color	무채색
acknowledge	승인하다, 인정하다
acknowledgment	인정
act	짓거리, 행위
action	행위, 활동, 행동
actions	처신, 행실
active	생동적(인), 적극적(인)
activity	활동
actual	실제의
~ feeling	실감
actually	정작, 실제로
acute	심각한, 날카로운

acutely	뼈저리게; 날카롭게
adapt	적응하다
adaptability	융통성
adaptation	적응
(in) addition	게다가, 그 위에
addressee	수신자
adherence	집착, 부착
adhesive	쫀득거리는, 접착성의; 접착제
adjust	적응하다
administrative machinery	행정 기관
admirably	신통하게
admire	찬미하다, 칭찬하다
admission fee	관람료, 입장료
admit	승인하다, 인정하다
adolescence	사춘기
adult name	관명
advance	진출; 진출하다; 앞당기다
advanced	발달한, 선진화된; 첨단(의)
advantage	장점
advantageous	유리한
advent	등장
advertisement	광고
advice	충고, 조언
advise	조언하다
advocate	내세우다, 주장하다; 주장자
affect	작용하다, 좌우하다; ~에게 영향을 주다
affection	애정
affectionate	정겨운
affix	붙이다, 첨부하다, 달다
(be) afraid of	두렵다
afresh	새삼스럽게, 새로이, 다시
after a while	이윽고
after all	결국
again	새삼스럽게, 다시
against	대; ~에 대비하여
age	시대, 나이
agenda	안건
aggressive	공격적, 도전적

agilely	재빨리	(power of) appealing	호소력
agonizing	고통스러운	appearance	등장, 출두; 모습, 모양,
agony	고민, 고통		형상
in ~	고민하여	append	달다, 붙이다
agree	일치하다, 합의하다	appetite	식욕, 입맛
~ with	받아들이다, ~에	appreciate	감상하다, 평가하다,
	동의하다		인식하다
agreement	조화, 합의	appreciation	음미, 감사, 평가
agricultural industry	농업	appreciative eye	안목
aid	지원	approach	다가오다, 닥치다
aim	지향, 목적; 겨누다	appropriately	적절하게
(be) alarmed	놀라다	approval	허가, 승인
alien	외국인, 이방인	approve	승인하다, 허가하다
align oneself	동조하다	approximately	대략, 대강
alliance	연맹	apron	앞치마
Allied Forces	연합군	ardent	열정적인
allover	두루	area	분야, 지역
allow	허용하다	argument	논쟁
alone	덜렁; 한갓; 홀로	both ~s	양론
although	그렇지만; 비록	grounds of an	
	~일지라도	~	논거
altogether	다, 통째, 통틀어	arise	일어나다, 벌어지다
alumni reunion	동창회	aristocrat	양반
alumnus	동창생	arm wrestling	팔씨름
(be) amazed	기(가) 막히다, 어안이	aroma	향기
	벙벙하다	around (of time)	~께, 무렵
amazing	놀랄만한	arouse	깨우다, 일깨워 주다
ambience	분위기	arrange	정리하다, 마련하다
American dollar	미화	~d marriage	중매 결혼
American forces	미군	arrogance	오만
amount of money	액수	art exhibition	미술 전시회
amusement	장난, 오락; 즐거움	article	기사, 제품, 사항
analysis	분석	superior ~	일품
ancestor	선조, 조상	as a matter of fact	당연히, 사실상
ancestor worship	제사	as ever	여전히
anew	새삼스럽게, 새로이	as it is	그냥, 그대로
(get) angry	화(를) 내다	as usual	여전히
anguish	고민, 고통	as you know	아시다시피
animal	짐승	ask	부탁하다, 요구하다,
~ protection			청하다, 여쭙다
organization	동물 보호 단체	~ after a person	~의 안부를 묻다,
answer	답변, 대답		문안드리다
anticipation	기대	aspect	면, 측면; 모습, 상황
anxiety	응어리, 걱정, 근심	assassination	시해, 암살
anyhow	그러나 저러나, 아무튼,	assault	공격하다
	어쨌든, 어쨌거나	assent	동의; 동의하다,
apart	따로		허락하다
appalling	끔찍한	assignment	배속, 할당, 담당, 숙제
appeal	애원, 호소, 간청	assist	돕다, 보충하다

association	연맹, 협회, 동호회	(be) baffled	황당하다; 실패하다
assume	추정하다, 떠맡다	bailout	긴급 구조, 구제
(be) astonished at	경악하다, 놀라다	balance	균형
at all	도대체, 전혀	keep the ~	버티다, 균형을
at all hours	줄곧, 언제든지		유지하다
at any rate	그러나 저러나, 아무튼	lack of ~	불균형
at last	그제야, 마침내	(well) balanced	균형 잡힌
atmosphere	분위기	baldheaded	대머리
at once	당장, 즉각, 한꺼번에	ban	금지하다
attach	첨부하다, 붙이다	bankruptcy	파산
attachment	배속; 집착; 첨부	barely	가까스로, 겨우
attack	공격하다	bargaining	교섭, 거래
attainment	성취, 달성	~ body	교섭 단체
attend	모시다, ~에 출석하다	barter	교환하다
(be) attended by	데리고 가다 [오다]	base	기반, 기초
attendance	청중; 출석, 참석	(be) based (on)	근거하다
attention	주목	basic	기초적인, 원초적
pay ~ to	주목하다	basis	근본, 기반
attentively	주의 깊게	basket	바구니
attitude	태도	basketball team	농구단
(be) attracted	끌리다	bead	구슬
attractive power	흡인력	bear	견디다; 떠맡다
audience	관객, 청중	beast	짐승
auditorium	공연장, 강당	beat	때리다, 패다, 구타하다,
auditor	청중; 청강생		두드리다; 물리치다;
authorize	인정하다, 승인하다		울렁거리다
automatic	자동	beauty care	화장
~ door	자동문	befall	닥치다
~ movement	자동	before long	이윽고
automatism	자동	beg	사정하다, 얻어먹다,
autonomy	주체성, 자치		빌다
average	평균	beggar	걸인
annual ~	연평균	begin	비롯하다, 시작하다
avoid	모면하다, 피하다	beginning	계기, 서두, 첫머리
awake	깨우다; 깨다	behavior	태도, 행위, 처신,
awakening	각성, 깨우침		짓거리
award	수여하다, 시상하다	behind-the-scenes	배후
(be) aware of	의식하다, 깨닫다	being	존재
awkward	어색한, 서투른	come into ~	생기다
		belittlement	비하
bachelor	총각	bend	기울이다, 구부리다
background	배경	benevolence	혜택
backing	지지	besides	한편; 더욱, ~ 조차(도)
back room	골방	(at) best	고작
backup	지원	(become) better	나아지다
backwardness	후진성	beverage	음료
backyard	뒤곁, 뒤뜰	beyond	~을 넘어서
bad	고약한, 나쁜	go ~	지나치다
~ dream	악몽	bidding	명령
~-looking	추한	~ of a superior	분부

big-hearted	대범한	brief	간단한, 잠깐의
bill	안건	briefly	간략히, 간단히
birth	탄생	bright	똑똑하다, 슬기롭다;
(sixtieth) birthday	환갑		명랑하다, 밝다
birthplace	출신지, 출생지	~ place	양지
bit	비트	brilliant	눈부신
bitter	씁쓸한, 쓴	(to the) brim	듬뿍
blame	비난, 지탄; 비난하다,	brim over	넘치다
	나무라다	bring	불러 오다
blaze up	솟구치다	~ about	빚다, 야기하다
blind date	미팅, 선	~ into	끌어들이다
blockade	봉쇄	~ to the fore	부각시키다
(be) blocked	봉쇄되다, 막히다	~ up	키우다
bloodline	혈통	briquette of coal	연탄
blue and red	청홍	(Great) Britain	영국
blue dragon	청룡	British royal	
blue thread	청실	household	영국 왕실
boastful	자랑스러운	broad	넓은
boastfully	자랑스럽게	broad-minded	대범한, 마음이 넓은
body	육신, 몸	broadcast	방송; 방송하다,
bodyache	몸살		방영하다
boil	삶다, 끓이다	broadly	널리
~ briskly	한소끔 끓이다	broth	국물, 탕
bolster	떠받치다, 지지하다	brother	형제, 형, (남)동생
bond	연분, 인연	brutal	참혹한
boom	붐	bud	싹트다; 싹
(be) bored	심심하다	Buddhism	불교
(be) born	탄생하다, 태어나다	Buddhist temple	절
(be) bound up with	~에 매이다	budget	재정, 예산
bow	절	build	짓다, 세우다
deep ~	큰절	bulletin board	게시판
make a ~	절하다	bullfight(ing)	투우
boycott	불매 운동	bump into	부딪치다
box	함, 상자	burden	부담, 짐
brain	두뇌	burdensome	부담스러운
branch	갈래, 부문	burn	때다; 태우다
~ of a family	분가	get ~ed	눈다
brat	새끼, 자식	burst	터지다
brave	무릅쓰다; 용감한	business	사업; 업무; 근무
bravely	당당히	~ enterprise	기업체
breach	위배하다; 절교	~ suit	양복
break (down)	끊어지다	~ transaction	상거래
break in on	끼어들다	butchery	도살
breakdown	붕괴, 좌절	buyers' strike	불매 운동
breaking off	중단	by far	단연, 뛰어나게
brew (alcohol)	빚다		
bridal room	신방	calculate	따지다, 계산하다
bride	신부	call at	다녀가다, 방문하다
bridegroom	신랑	call out	외치다

call upon	촉구하다; 방문하다
(be) called	불리다
calm down	가라앉히다
calmly	차분히, 냉정히
campus	학창, 대학
candid	개방적, 솔직한
candlelight	촛불
cane	매를 치다; 지팡이
cannibal	식인종
capability	능력, 실력
capacity	능력, 기량
capital letter	대문자
capital loan	자금 융자
capitalism	자본주의
car horn	경적
carat	캐럿
career experience	경력
careful	주도 면밀한, 신중한
~ reading	정독
carrot	당근
carry	지다, 싣다, 지니다
~ out	치르다, 수행하다
catchword	구호
category	부문
cause	까닭, 요인, 원인; 빚다, 끼치다, 일으키다
caution	충고, 주의
cautious	주도 면밀한
cautiously	주의 깊게
cease	종식하다, 중단하다
censure	비난하다; 성토
census register	민적, 호적
Central America	중미
CEO	최고 경영자
ceremony	의식
~ of awarding prizes	시상식
certain	확실한
certainly	반드시, 어김없이
cessation	종식
challenge	도전
chamber of commerce and industry	상공 회의소
championship	우승, 선수권
chance	계기, 기회
by ~	문득, 어쩌다(가)
change	변하다, 변모하다, 달라지다; 변화
endless ~	변화 무쌍
~ school	전학하다

chaotic	혼란한
character	모습; 성격, 인격; 문자
characteristic	고유의, 특유의, 특징적인
characteristics	특색
characters	등장 인물
charge	채우다, 담당하다
in ~ of	주관한, 담당한
person in ~	담당자
charm	멋, 매력
charmed	매혹된
chase	몰고 가다, 쫓다
(remain) chaste	수절하다
chatter	지껄이다
cheerful	명랑한, 쾌활한
cheery	쾌활한
chemical action	화학 작용
chicken soup with ginseng	삼계탕
chief	주된, 주요한
childhood name	아명
children	자녀, 자제
~ and women	아녀자
children's story	동화
Chinese character	한자
Chinese date	대추
Chinese noodles	당면
chivalrous man	대장부
Chŏlla Province	전라도
chop	난도질하다, 자르다
Chosŏn dynasty	조선
chrysalis	번데기
cinnamon	계피
circulate	순환하다, 전파하다, 유통하다, 돌리다
circulation of money	금융
circumstances	사정, 처지
actual ~	실정
civilian	민간
civilized person	문명인
claim	내세우다; 요구하다
clamor	야단
clasp	쥐다
class	~층, 계층, 부문
classical	고전적인
Korean ~ music	국악
classification	구분
classify	구분하다
claw	발톱
clay	흙, 진흙

clean	산뜻한, 깨끗한	common	평범한, 흔한
clear	명백한, 분명한, 쟁쟁한	~ people	백성, 서민, 상놈
make ~	밝히다	commonly	으레, 보통
become ~	판명되다	commonwealth	공화국
clearly	명확하게	company	회사, 업체; 패
cleave	쪼개다	compare	비기다, 견주다
clever	현명한, 영리한	(have no)	
click one's tongue	혀를 차다	comparison	비길 데 없다
cliff	벼랑, 절벽	compassion	정
climax	고비	compete	견주다, 경쟁하다
cling to	매달리다	competence	능력
close	긴밀한; 닫다	competing country	경쟁국
closely	바짝, 가깝게	competition	경쟁
closure	폐쇄	~ rate	경쟁률
clot	엉기다	competitive	
cloth	천	performance	경연
club	동호회, 동아리	complacency	여유로움
clutch	쥐다	complain of	푸념하다
coagulate	엉기다	complete	끝마치다, 마감하다;
coal	석탄		철저한, 완전한
coarse	굵은, 거친	completely	바짝; 홀딱, 고스란히,
coffee shop	다방		죽, 완전히
cognition	인식	complex	복잡한
cold air	한기	complicated	복잡한
cold buckwheat		complicatedly	얼키설키, 복잡하게
noodles	냉면	complication	갈등, 복잡, 우여곡절
collapse	무너지다; 붕괴	compliment	찬사, 칭찬
color	빛깔, 색	compose	짓다, 구성하다,
combating	전투적		편성하다
combination	결합	(be) composed of	이루어지다
combine	결합하다	composedly	차분히
combined	합동(의)	comprise	포함하다
come near	다가오다	compromise	양보하다
come out (forth)	나서다	computation	계산
come round	닥치다, 닥쳐오다	computer ~	전산
comfort	달래다, 위안하다	concede	양보하다
in ~	유유히	conceive	고안하다, 상상하다
comfortable	편안한	concentrate	기울이다, 집중하다
comfortably warm	푸근한	concentration	농축, 집중
coming and going	오락가락; 왕래	conception	관념
command	명, 명령, 분부; 명하다,	concern	관심, 우려
	분부하다, 이끌다	concerned party	당사자
commander of the		concerto	협주곡
enemy force	적장	concisely	간략히
comment	비판, 평	conclude	단정하다; 끝내다
commentary	주석	conclusion	결말; 체결; 결론
commercial dealings	상거래	concord	화합, 일치
commit suicide	자살하다	condemn	매도하다; 비난하다
commit oneself	공약하다, 약속하다	condensed	농축된

condition	모습, 상태, 상황, 처지,	continual	지속적인, 계속적인
	지경; 조건, 제약	continually	계속해서, 꾸준히
without ~	무조건	(be) continued	이어지다
condolence money	조의금	continuous	지속적인
conduct	처신, 행위	continuously	계속해서
conduction	전도	contract	맺다; 계약
confederation	연맹	contradiction	대비, 모순
conference	대회	contrary (to)	역행하는, 반대의
confidence	신뢰	on the ~	오히려, 반대로
conflict	갈등	contrast	대비, 대조
confront	대립하다	contribute (to)	공헌하다, 기고하다
Confucian	유교적인	contribution	공헌
Confucianism	유교	contrive	고안하다
Confucius	공자	control	단속, 통제
confuse	혼란시키다	controversy	논쟁
confusedly	얼키설키	convection current	대류
confusion	혼란	convene	주관하다; 소집하다
congeal	엉기다	convention	대회; 관습
conglomerate	재벌 기업	conventional	전통적
conjecture	짐작하다; 짐작, 추측	convergence	집중
connect (with)	접속하다, 잇다	convey	전송하다, 전하다
(be) connected	연계되다, 이어지다	convict	죄수
connection	연결, 관계	conviction	줏대, 신념
conscious of	의식한	cook (rice)	짓다
consent	동의, 합의; 합의하다	cool-headed	냉정한
~ to	허락하다, 동의하다	cooperation	공동, 협력, 협동
conservative	보수적인	cordially	간곡히
consider	간주하다, 여기다;	core	핵심
	배려하다	corner	구석
considerable	상당한, 어지간한	correct	올바른, 정확한;
considerate	어진, 생각이 깊은		시정하다, 정정하다
consideration	고려, 배려	cosmopolitan	세계주의적인; 세계인,
give ~ to	배려하다		세계주의자
consistent	한결같은	cosmos	우주
consistently	한결같이	cost	비용; 들다
consolidation	결합	counsel	상담; 조언하다,
constant	한결같은, 일정한		상의하다
constantly	꾸준히, 줄곧	counselor's office	상담소
constituent	요소	count	세다, 꼽다
constitute	구성하다, 이루다	counterevidence	반증
constrain	억제하다	country	나라, 국가; 지방, 시골
construct	세우다, 짜 맞추다	court	마당
construction	구조, 건설, 건축	courtesy	예법, 예의
constructive	적극적(인)	by ~	예의상
consult	참조하다, 의논하다	cover	덮다, 싸다, 깔다
consume	소비하다	crack	벌어지다; 틈
consumer	소비자	craftsmanship	만듦새
contest	경연, 경기	cram	채우다
continent	대륙	crawl	기다

cream-colored	뽀얀	data	논거, 자료
create	설정하다, 창조하다	date of birth	생년월일
creation	창작, 창조	day by day	날로
creep	기다	(in those) days	당시
crest	고비, 꼭대기	dazzling	눈부신
crime	죄, 범죄	deadlock	난국
crisis	고비, 난국, 위기	deal (with)	처하다, 처리하다,
critical	비판적		취급하다, 임하다
~ moment	고비, 위기	dear	그리운, 다정한
~ situation	위기	debate	성토; 토론
criticism	비난, 비판, 지탄	debt	차관, 빚
criticize	비판하다, 비난하다,	deceptive talk	궤변
	꼬집다	decide	결정하다, 단정하다,
cruel	잔인한, 참혹한		판단하다
cruelty	학대, 잔인성	decision	판단, 결정
crumbling	붕괴	decline	기울어지다; 거절하다
crush	탄압하다	decorate	꾸미다, 장식하다
crust of overcooked		decrease	줄이다, 줄다
rice	누룽지	deduct	덜다, 감하다
cry out	외치다	deed	짓거리, 행위
~ 'bravo'	쾌재를 부르다	deem	간주하다
culinary preference	식성	deep	진한, 깊은
cultivate	개발하다	deep bow	큰절
cultural	문화적	deeply	심도 있게, 진하게
curiosity	호기심	defeat	물리치다
curious	희한한, 호기심 있는	defective	미비한, 불완전한
currency	통화	defector	귀순자
curse	욕하다; 저주	deficient	미비한, 모자란
custom	습관, 풍속	definitely	결정적으로, 단연,
cut	쪼개다, 단절하다;		명확하게
	끊어지다	defy	부인하다, 무시하다
cycle	주기	degree	도수, 도
		deliberately	찬찬히; 일부러
daily	날로; 일상적인	delicacy	별미
~ life	일상 생활	delicate	치밀한
~ newspaper	일간지	delight	즐거움
~ publication	일간	deliver	전달하다, 전송하다
~ task	일과	demand	강요하다, 요구하다,
~ work	일과		촉구하다
damage	훼손하다; 손해	demonstrate	실증하다, 설명하다
damp	촉촉한	demonstration	시위, 실증
dampness	물기	denounce	매도하다, 비난하다
dance cheerfully	덩실덩실 춤추다	density	비중, 밀도, 농도
danger	위험	deny	부인하다
~ line	위험선	department	부문, 학과
dangerous	위험한	dependable	미더운
dark	진한, 어두운	deploring	개탄
~ place	음지	depression	불황
get ~	저물다, 어두워지다	Great ~	대공황

depth	깊이	discord	갈등; 불화하다
in ~	심도 있게, 깊게	discover	발견하다
descendant	후손	discrepancy	간격, 불일치, 모순
descent	혈통	discriminate	가리다, 차별하다
describe	묘사하다, 짚어내다	discrimination	구별, 불평등, 차별
design	디자인; 고안하다	sense of ~	안목
desire	바람, 열망, 소원	disgraceful	추한, 수치스러운
desperately	절실하게	disguise oneself	꾸미다, 가장하다
despotism	학정, 독재	dishonorable	추한, 불명예스러운
destiny	운명	dismiss	파직하다, 해고하다
(in) detail	상세히, 심도 있게, 자세히	dismissal	파직, 해고
		disobey	반항하다, 불복종하다
determine	결정하다	disorder	혼란
determinedly	확고히	disordered	혼란한
develop	개발하다, 전개하다	disparagement	비하
developing country	개발 도상국	dispatch	파견
development	개발, 발달	~ of a message	발신
deviate (from)	벗어나다	disperse	확산하다
devise	고안하다	display	내세우다, 전시하다
devote oneself to	~에 전념하다	displeasure	불만
die out	망하다	disposition	성향, 심성, 논쟁
diet	끼, 끼니	dispute	논쟁
difference	격차, 차이	dissatisfaction	불만
sense of ~	이질감	dissemination	확산
(completely) different	판이하다	dissolve	녹이다
differentiation	차등화, 구별	distance	사이, 거리
differently	달리	distant	까마득한, 먼
difficult	곤란한, 어려운	distinction	구별; 명예
~ situation	난국	distinctive	유별난, 특징적인
(with) difficulty	가까스로, 어렵게	distinguish	가리다, 구별하다
diffuse	확산하다	distribute	유통하다, 분배하다
dig into	파고 들어가다	distribution	유통, 분배
dim	은은한, 희미한	district	고을, 지방
dimension	차원	diverse	다양한
diminish	줄이다; 줄다	divide	가르다, 쪼개다, 구분하다, 나누다
dip (into)	찍다; 담그다		
dip up	푸다	~ and rule	분할 통치
diplomatic	외교적(인)	division	구분, 분단
direct	기울이다; 지도하다; 똑바른	document	기록, 문헌, 서류
		dog of mixed breeds	잡종견
director	소장	dog-meat soup	보신탕
dirt	때	domain	영역
dirty	불결한, 더러운	domestic	국내
disappear	사라지다	~ and international	국내외
disapproval	불가, 부결		
discerning eye	안목	~ animal	가축
discharge	쏘다; 파직; 해방	~ chores	살림
disclose	폭로하다	dominate	좌우하다, 풍미하다, 지배하다
discontent	불만		
discontinue	그만두다, 중단하다	donkey	나귀

dotage	망령
drawback	단점
draw into	끌어들이다
draw out	그려내다
draw up	편성하다
drink	음료
~ heavily	들이키다
drinking table	술상
dripping	뻘뻘
drive	몰고 가다
~ into	몰아넣다
~ out	몰아내다
driving force	원동력
drop in	다녀가다, 다녀오다
drug	약, 마약
drum	북
drunk	취한
get dead ~	대취하다
dubious	의아해 하는, 어안이 병벙한
dumbbell	아령
dumbfounded	기(가) 막힌, 어안이 병벙한
duty	근무, 업무; 도리
do ~	근무하다
dweller	주민
dying hair	머리 염색
dynamic	생동적인
~ relationship	역학 관계
each	각각, 각기
(bend someone's) ear	귀기울이다
early days	초기
early stage	초반
earnest	절실한, 진정한
earnestly	간곡히
earnings	수입, 소득
earth	흙, 땅
(at) ease	유유히, 마음 편히
Eastern	동양적
Eastern Europe	동구
East Germany	동독
eat	먹다, 식용하다
~ heartily	배불리 먹다
~ one's fill	배불리 먹다
~ usually	상식하다
eating habit	식습관
economic	경제적
~ crisis	경제 위기
~ development	경제 개발, 경제 발전

~ exchange	경제 교류
~ growth	경제 성장
~ power	경제력
~ stagnation	경기 침체
economical	아끼는, 경제적인
economically	경제적으로
economy	경제
education budget	교육 재정
effect	영향, 효과
effectiveness	효과
effluence	유출, 발산, 방출
elaborate	정교한, 치밀한
elastic	쫀득거리는, 탄력 있는
electrical transmission	전송
electronic mail	이메일, 전자 우편
elegance	멋, 우아, 고상
elegant (passionate)	세련된, 우아한
eloquence	열변
e-mail	전자 우편
emancipation	해방
embarrass	난처하게 하다
embarrassing	부끄러운, 난처한
embassy	대사관
embrace tightly	끌어안다
emergency	긴급, 위기
emotion	정서, 감정
emphasize	강조하다, 치중하다
empirical	실증적
employee	고용인
employer	고용자
employment	일자리, 취업
enclose	둘러싸다
encouragement	장려, 격려
end	결말, 종식, 끝
come to an ~	종식하다
~ in failure	실패하다, 그릇되다
in the ~	마침내
endeavor	애쓰다, 노력하다
endless	끝없는, 끊임없는
endlessly	한없이
endurance	인내심
endure	견디다, 인내하다, 버티다, 참다
enemy general	적장
energetic	힘찬
engagement	약혼
~ ceremony	약혼식
England	영국

enjoy	즐기다	evident	명백한, 분명한
enlighten	일깨워 주다	evil	나쁜; 악, 폐해
enormous	거대한	~ plot	흉계
enough	충분히; 충분한	~ practices	폐해
entangled	엉킨	exactly	딱, 바로, 정확히
enterprise	기업체	examine	살펴보다, 조사하다
entertainer	연예인	example	본보기, 예
entertainment	연예, 오락	exceed	능가하다, 돌파하다
~ hall	공연장	exceedingly	몹시, 무척
(get) enthusiastic	신명나다, 열광적이다	excellent	우수한, 훌륭한
enticement	유치	~ piece	일품
entirely	전적으로	(without) exception	모조리, 예외 없이
entrance exam	입시, 입학 시험	exceptional	파격적, 예외적
~ period	입시철	excessively	극히, 마구
entreat	사정하다	exchange	교환하다
entreaty	애원	excited	흥분한
entry	등록; 입장	get ~	열띠다, 흥분하다
epistle	글월	excitement	흥, 흥분
epistolary style	편지체	exclaim	외치다
equal	평등한, 동등한	excuse	빌미, 핑계, 구실
equality	평등	exemption	면제
equally	고루, 평등하게	exhaustive	철저한
equip	갖추다	exhibit	전시하다
equipment	장치, 장비	existence	존재
era	시대	exorbitant	엄청난, 터무니 없는
escape	도망가다, 모면하다,	(Korean) exorcism	신풀이
	빠져나가다, 벗어나다	expand	늘어나다; 펼치다,
escort	모시다, 동행하다		확산하다
especial	특별한	expectation	기대, 눈높이
especially	별반, 특별히	expend	소비하다
essence	진수, 본질	expenditure	비용, 지출, 소비
essential element	요소	expense	비용, 경비
establish	개설하다, 세우다,	experience	겪다, 치르다; 경험,
	설정하다		체험
estimate	예측하다, 짐작하다,	expert	전문가, 베테랑
	추정하다	explode	터지다, 폭발하다
eternally	영원히	explosive	폭발적인
etiquette	에티켓, 예법	export	수출; 수출하다
etymology	어원	expose	폭로하다
eulogy	찬사	exposure	노출
evade	모면하다, 피하다	(be) expressed	표현되다
evenly	고루	expression	눈치, 표시; 표현
event	사건, 행사	give ~ to	표현하다
eventual	궁극적인	exquisite	절묘한, 정교한
every	각각의, 모든	extend	뻗어나가다, 펼치다
~ day	날로	extended family	
~ kind of	온갖, 각종	system	대가족 제도
~ now and then	가끔	extensively	두루, 널리
~ variety	각종	exterior	외부, 외부의
everyday life	일상 생활	externally	표면적으로

extracurricular work	과외	feast	성찬, 잔치
extraordinary	파격적, 비상한	feature	특징, 모습
extreme	극단적인	febrile disease	열병
extremely	극히, 무척, 잔뜩, 극단적으로	fed up with	질린
		feeble	미약한
		feeble-minded	나약한
		feeling	정서, 느낌
fabric	천; 구조	fellow student	동창생
face	맞다, 임하다; 면, 얼굴	female	여자
facility	장치, 시설	~ influence	치맛바람
factor	요소, 원인	~ power	치맛바람
facts	사항	~ protagonist	여주인공
factual	사실적	fervent	열정적인
fail	실패하다	~ speech	열변
without ~	반드시, 어김없이	festival	제전, 축제
failure in love	실연	festive day	명절
faint	미약한	fever	열
fair	상당한, 어지간한	fiction	소설
fairly	당당히, 떳떳하게; 충분히, 고루	field	부문, 분야; 경기장; 야외
fairy tale	동화	~ of vision	시야
fall	붕괴; 떨어지다	fighting	다툼, 싸움
~ behind	뒤쳐지다	figure	모습
~ down	무너지다	file	파일
~ into	빠져들다, 빠지다	attached ~	첨부 파일
~ upon	닥치다	filial daughter	효녀
family	집안, 가정, 가족	fill	채우다
both ~s	양가	film	영화
~ background	가정 형편	~ fan	영화광
~ member	피붙이, 가족	final	궁극적인
~ name	성	finally	궁극적으로, 마침내
~ register	민적, 족보, 호적	finance	금융, 재정
~ situation	가정 형편	financial crisis	금융 위기
famous	저명한, 쟁쟁한	financial institution	금융 기관
fancy	상상	financial world	재계
fantasy	환상	financing	금융
far and wide	두루	find fault with	흠잡다
far off	까마득한	finish	마감하다, 끝마치다
farmer	농부	fire	불
farmers' music	농악	make a ~	불을 때다, 피우다
(be) fascinated	혹하다, 빠지다	firearms	총기
fashion	양식, 유행	firm	업체
fate	연분, 인연, 운명	big ~	대기업
fatigue	피로	firmly	확고히
feeling of ~	피로감	first	원초적, 처음의
favor	혜택	be the ~ (to do)	앞장서다
favorable	유리한	~ birthday party	돌잔치
fear	우려, 두려움	~ night	첫날밤
fearful	두려운	~ on a list	필두

from the ~	아예, 본디	foundation	근본, 기반
fit	일치하다, 알맞다	fragrance	향기
fix	확정하다; 고정시키다	frame	틀
flank	측면	framework	틀, 구조
flare up	화(를) 내다	frank	개방적, 솔직한
flash	번쩍임; 번쩍거리다	frantic	극성스러운
flat	밍밍한, 평평한	freely	마음대로, 자유로
flesh	육신	frequent	잦은
flexibility	융통성	fresh	신선한, 참신한
flicker	어른거리다	freshly	생생하게
flog	매를 치다	fried food	튀김
floor	방바닥, 마룻바닥	friendly	정겨운, 친한
flow	흐르다	front	전면, 앞
~ out	유출하다	frosty	뽀얀 서리가 내리는
(all) flustered	허둥지둥	fruit	결실, 성과; 과일
focal point	초점	~ juice	과즙
focus	초점	fruition	결실, 성과
(Korean) folk music	국악	frustration	좌절
follow	따르다	fry	(기름으로) 튀기다
follower	부하	fuel	연료
following year	이듬해	~ hole	아궁이
(use as) food	식용; 식용하다	full	가득한
foolish	어리석은	~ moon	보름달
footing	기반	~ of strength	힘찬
footprint	발자취	in ~	자세히
forbid	금지하다	to the ~	듬뿍
force	강요하다; 기세, 힘	full-scale	본격적인
forefather	조상	fully	꽉꽉, 충분히
forehead	이마	fun	장난, 흥
foreign	외국의	for ~	장난 삼아
~ countries	해외	function	역할; 행사; 작용하다
~ debt	외채	fundamental	근본적, 기초적인
~ exchange	외환	fur	가죽
~ power(s)	외세	furnish	갖추다
foreigner	외국인, 이방인	furniture	가구
form	결성하다, 이루다, 맺다,	further	더욱이
	생기다; 모습, 상태	furthermore	더욱이
formal	정규(의), 형식적인	furtively	몰래
in a ~ way	제대로, 정식으로	future	장래
formality	격식, 틀	in the ~	장차
formally	제대로, 정식으로	future-oriented	미래 지향적
former	전의, 앞의		
~ days	예전	gabble	지껄이다
in ~ times	이전에	gain	늘다; 거두다
fortunately	다행히	~ ground	진출하다
fortune-teller	점쟁이	game	장난
forum	토론회	main ~	본선
foul	불결한	gang fight	패싸움
found	개설하다, 설립하다	gap	간격, 격차, 차이, 틈

garden	뜰	~ post	벼슬, 관직
garlic	마늘	governor	지사
garnish	곁들이다	gradation	차등화
gaze	시선; 바라보다	grade	등급; 학년
gem	보석, 구슬	gradually	서서히, 점차
gene	유전자	graduate	동창생, 졸업생;
genealogy	족보		졸업하다
general	일반, 전반적	grand	대대적, 우람한
in ~	대개, 대체로	grasp	장악하다, 쥐다
~ people	일반인	grave	심각한
generally	대개, 대체로,	gravely	엄연히
	전반적으로, 태반	grease	기름
generation	세대	greatly	극히, 부쩍, 한없이
~ after ~	역대	green bamboo	녹죽
~ gap	세대 차이	green pine	청송
gentle	어진, 점잖은	grievance	원망
in a ~ manner	점잖게	grime	때, 먼지
gently	점잖게	grip	쥐다
genuine	본격적인; 진짜의	ground	경기장; 뜰, 마당
get better	나아지다	group	집단, 동아리, 패
get out of	벗어나다	as a ~	집단적으로
get used to	익숙해지다	~ discussion	집단 토론
ghost	귀신	in a ~	집단으로
gibber	지껄이다	group fight	패싸움
giddy	희뜩희뜩, 어지러운	grow rapidly	급부상하다, 급성장하다
gigantic	대대적; 거대한	growth rate	성장률
ginkgo leaf	은행잎	grudge	원망, 한
gist	진수, 요점	grumble at	푸념하다, 불평하다
give in	양보하다	guess	짐작하다
give rise to	빚다, 일으키다	guide	이끌다, 안내하다
gladly	기꺼이	guilt	죄
glimmer	어른거리다	feeling of ~	죄의식
glisten	얼른얼른하다	gulp	들이키다
globalization	세계화		
gloomy	음울한	habit	습관, 버릇
glory	명예	habitual snacking	주전부리
glutinous	쫀득거리는	habitually	으레, 습관적으로
GNP	국민 총생산	hair	털, 머리카락
goddess	여신	half	절반
golden jar	금동이	handle	손잡이; 취급하다,
(large) gong	징		처리하다
(small) gong	꽹과리	handshake	악수
(saying) good-bye	하직 인사	hang	드리우다, 매달다;
gorgeous	화려한		매달리다
govern	지배하다	~ down	드리우다
government	정부	happen	벌어지다, 생기다,
~ agency	정부 기관		일어나다
~ office	관청	happiness	즐거움, 화목, 행복
~ officials	관리	harden	다지다

harmonious	원만한, 화기 애애한	high-ranking official	고위 공무원
harmoniously	오순도순, 화목하게	historically	역사상, 사상
harmonize	화합하다	history	유래, 역사
harmony	조화, 화목, 화합	hit	두드리다, (부딪)치다
hasten	서두르다	hoarse	목쉰
hastily	조급하게	hold	개최하다; 끌어안다;
hasty	성급한		지니다, 차지하다
have	차지하다, 갖다, 갖추다;	~ back	주춤거리다
	두다; 맞다	holding	개최
~ a share	차지하다	(consecutive)	
~ in common	공유하다	holidays	연휴
head	머리, 두뇌; 이끌다;	homely	질박한, 가정적인
	항목	hometown	출신지, 고향
~ of a family	가장	honest	바른, 올바른, 정직한
take the ~	앞장서다	honeymoon trip	신혼 여행
headache	골칫거리, 두통	honor	명예
heading	항목	honorably	떳떳하게, 명예롭게
health food	건강식	hope	기대, 희망
heap	무더기	horrible	두려운
hearers	청중	hospitable	후한
hearsay	소문	host country	개최국
heart	가슴, 심장	hot weather	더위, 더운 날씨
heartily	배불리, 진정으로	household	집안
heartless	잔인한	~ goods	살림 도구
heat	열, 열풍; 가열하다,	housework	살림, 집안일, 가사
	덥히다, 달구다	hover around	헤매다
apply ~	가열하다	however	어쨌거나, 그러나
~ up	뜸을 들이다	hue	빛깔
heated	열띤	hug	끌어안다
heating	난방	huge	거대한
heaven	천국	~ amount of	
~ and earth	천지	money	거금
heavy industry	중공업	human	인적, 인간의; 인간
heavy-chemical		~ nature	인간성, 인정
industry	중화학 공업	humane	인도적
(be) held	열리다	humaneness	인지상정
help	구해 주다, 돕다	humanitarian	인도적
helplessly	꼼짝없이	humble	천한, 겸손한
hero	대장부, 영웅	humbleness	비하, 겸손
heroine	열녀, 여장부, 여주인공	hunger	굶주림, 배고픔
hesitate	주춤거리다, 주저하다	hunt	탐색, 사냥; 사냥하다
(without) hesitation	단연코, 주저 없이	hurry up	서두르다
hide	가죽	husband	낭군, 남편
hierarchy	위계 질서	hygiene	위생
high	높은		
at the ~est	고작	idea	관념, 생각
~ income	고소득	ideal	이상; 이상적(인)
~ pressure	고압	~ type	이상형
~ quality	고급	identical	마찬가지인, 동일한
highlight	부각시키다	ideology	이데올로기

ignorant	무식한, 무지한	individually	각각, 각기
ignore	외면하다, 무시하다	indoor	실내
ill-bred fellow	상놈	induce	도입하다, 권유하다
illiterate	무식한, 문맹의	induction	유치, 유도
image	이미지	indulge in	빠지다
imagination	상상	inequality	불평등
power of ~	상상력	inevitable	필연적인, 불가피한
imagine	상상하다	(become) infatuated	혹하다, 반하다
imbalance	불균형	infer	추정하다
imbed	박다, 끼워 넣다	inferior	열등한
immediately	당장, 즉각	influence	감동, 영향; 좌우하다
~ faced	당면한	inform	알리다, 보도하다
immense	대대적, 거대한	information	정보
impact	충격	~ age	정보화 시대
impartiality	평등	~ system	전산망
impatient	극성스러운, 안달이 난	inhabitant	주민
imperfect	미비한, 불완전한	inherit (from)	물려받다
impetuous	극성스러운	initiative	주도권
implore	사정하다	innovation	개혁
imply	의미하다	innovative	혁신적(인)
import	도입하다, 수입하다	innuendo	풍자; 빈정거리다
importance	중요성	in other words	즉
attach ~ to	중시하다	inquire	묻다, 여쭙다
important	소중한, 중요한	inquisitively	꼬치꼬치
impression	감동, 인식, 인상	(become) insane	미치다
impressive	감격적, 인상적	inside	내부, 안쪽
imprint	찍다	insist	주장하다
impropriety	불가, 부적당, 잘못	insolence	오만
improvement	제고, 개량, 개선	insolvency	파산, 지불 불능
in any case	아무튼, 그러나 저러나	inspect	관람하다, 시찰하다
inception	서두, 발단	inspection	관람, 시찰, 조사
incidental	우연한	install	설치하다
inclination	지향, 취향, 경향	instant	순간, 즉시
incline	기울다; 경향	in an ~	언뜻, 순간적으로
include	포함하다	instantly	즉각
income	수입	instead	오히려, 대신
incomplete	미비한, 불완전한	institution	제도; 공공 시설
increase	늘다, 증가하다; 증액	instructive	교훈적인
incurability	불치	insult	욕하다; 모욕(하다)
indecent	추한, 버릇없는	intellectual class	지식층
independence	자주성, 주체성, 독립	intelligence	정보
independent	독자적인, 자립적인	intelligent	슬기로운, 현명한
indicate	지적하다	intend to do	지향하다, 의도하다
indication	지적, 표시	intense	강렬한
indirectly	간접적으로	intent	뜻
indiscriminately	마구, 무차별로	intention	뜻, 지향
indistinct	은은한, 희미한	interaction	왕래, 상호 작용
individual	독자적인, 개인적	interchange	교류
individuality	개성	intercourse	왕래, 교제

interest	관심, 흥미	jealousy	시샘, 질투
interested party	당사자	jewel	보석
interesting	흥미로운	job	일자리, 일, 직장
interestingly	흥미롭게	join	가입하다, 어울리다
interior	내부	~ together	결합하다
internal	내적, 내면적(인)	joining together	결합
~ organs	내장	joint	합동
international	국제적(인)	~ investment	합작 투자
~ community	국제 사회	~ suicide	동반 자살
~ market	국제 시장	journey	왕래, 여행
International		joy	즐거움
Monetary Fund	국제 통화 기금	with ~	기꺼이
Internet user	네티즌	joyfully	덩실덩실, 즐겁게
interpret	풀이하다, 해석하다	judge	판단하다, 따지다
interruption	중단	judgment	판단
interval	사이, 틈	jujube	대추
intervene	개입하다	just	가까스로, 그냥, 딱
intestine	내장	justice	도리, 정의
intonation	억양	justifiably	당당히
introduce	도입하다, 소개하다		
intrude in	끼어들다, 침입하다	karat	캐럿
intuition	눈치	karma	인연
invading army	침략군	keenly	뼈저리게, 예민하게
invariably	한결같이	keep	갖다, 두다, 보관하다,
inventor	창안자, 발명자		유지하다
inverted triangle	역삼각형	kettle	솥
investigate	조사하다	iron ~	가마솥
investment	투자	key	가락, 열쇠, 키
long-term ~	장기 투자	kick out	몰아내다; 박차다
investor	투자자	kind	갈래, 종류
invite	도입하다, 청하다	~ of	일종의
(be) involved (in)	개입되다, 열중하다	kindhearted	착한, 친절한
inwardly	은근히, 몰래	kindle	때다, 태우다
iron	쇠; 철분	king	임금(님), 왕
irony	풍자	king crab	참게
irregular	파격적, 불규칙적	knock	부딪치다, 치다
irrespective of	~에 관계 없이	knot	맺다; 매듭
item	종목, 항목, 사항	knowledge	인식, 지식
iterate	반복하다	(become) known	알려지다
itself	자체		
in ~	본디	label	딱지, 꼬리표
		labor union	노조
jade	옥	(feel the) lack of	아쉬워하다
~ tray	옥소반, 옥쟁반	lag	뒤쳐지다
jail	옥, 감옥	lamentable	한심스러운
inside of a ~	옥중	lamentation	개탄
Japanese imperialism	일제	landscape	강산, 풍경
jar	항아리	Lao Tzu	노자
jazz group	재즈 그룹	large number	다수

large quantity	대량	liking	취향
large scale	대규모	line	부문; 선
large-scale	대대적	(be) linked (with)	연계되다
largest	최대	liquor taken with a	
lark	종달새	meal	반주
last night	간밤	listen	귀기울이다
lasting	영구적	literature	문학, 문헌, 글
lately	최근	literature cited	참고 문헌
laudatory remarks	찬사	live alone	독수공방하다
laughable	가소로운	lively	생동적인, 생생한,
laughingstock	놀림감		쾌활한
launder	빨다	liver	간
lavishly	헤프게	living style	생활 방식
lay	깔다	load	싣다; 부담
layer	층, 꺼풀	loan	융자금, 빚
lead	앞장서다, 이끌다,	~ shark	사채 업자
	주도하다	loanword	외래어
leader	주역, 지도자	loath	아쉬워하다
leadership	주도권	(the) locale	현지
leading	주도, 주도적	local government	지방 정부
~ player	주역	locate	자리잡다
leak out	빠져나가다	lodge	머물다
lean	기울어지다, 기대다	lonely	덩렁; 고독한, 쓸쓸한
learning by heart	암기	longest	최장
leather	가죽	long for	그리워하다, 열망하다
(take) leave	작별하다	look	모양, 모습; 보다
leave out	빼놓다	~ all around	살펴보다
leave-taking	하직 인사	~ at	바라보다
legalization	합법화	~ back at	되돌아보다
leisurely	한가한; 느긋하게	~ furtively	훔쳐보다
lending	대출	~ into	살펴보다
lengthen	늘어나다; 늘이다	~ over	되돌아보다, 훑어보다
lengthy writing	장문	loosened	느슨해진
lessen	덜다, 줄이다	love	애정, 사랑
lesson	교훈, 시사점; 과	love and prize	애지중지하다
letter	문자, 글(월), 편지	lovely	고운, 사랑스러운
level	층, 정도	lover	임, 애인
liability	책임	low	천한, 낮은
liberal	자유주의적, 관대한	lowest	최저
liberation	해방	~ price	최저가
license	허가, 면허증	lowly	천한
lie	엎드리다, 눕다	loyal subject	충신
life	목숨, 생명	luckily	다행히
~style	생활 방식	lukewarm	미지근한
~time	생시, 평생	lure	유치; 유치하다,
lift	높이다, 올려 놓다		유혹하다
light	밝은; 가벼운	lurk	도사리다, 숨다
~ industry	경공업		
likewise	다름없이, 마찬가지로	(be) made up of	이루어지다

magistrate	수령, 사또	maximum	최대
magnificent	화려한, 우람한	May Festival	단오(날)
~ view	절경	mayor	시장, 부사
magnificently	당당히, 장엄하게	meal	끼, 식사
maiden	처녀	mean[1]	의미하다
~ home	친정	mean[2]	추한, 천한
main	주된, 주요한	meaningful	의미 있는
~ current	주류	means	수단
~ly	주로	by any ~	설마; 어떻게 해서든지
~ stream	주류	(in the) meantime	그간
maintain	유지하다, 주장하다	meanwhile	그간
majestically	당당히	measure	수단, 한도; 측정하다
major	주요한	measuring stick	잣대
~ cities	주요 도시	mechanically	기계적으로
~ economic power	경제 대국	media	언론
majority	다수, 태반	medical records	건강 기록부
makeup	화장	meeting	회의, 모임
making one's way	출세	general ~	대회
male	사나이, 남자	marriage ~	맞선
~ chauvinism	남존 여비	melancholy	멜랑콜리하다, 음울하다
maltreatment	학대	melodic subject	악상
man	남자, 사람	melt	녹이다, 녹다
~ of low birth	상놈	member	가입자, 회원, 일원
~'s mother-in-law	장모	become a ~	가입하다
manage	처리하다, 관리하다	membership	회원
management	관리	~ fee	회비
manly man	대장부	memo	쪽지
manner	눈치, 모습, 습관, 태도	memorial service	제사
(well) mannered	예절바른	memorization	암기
manners	예법, 예절	mental attitude	마음가짐, 정신적 태도
have good ~	예절 바르다	mentality	심성, 정신 상태
~ and customs	풍습	mention	들먹이다, 언급하다
manufacture	제작, 제조	merchant	상인
march	진출, 행진; 진출하다	merely	단순히, 오직
marital harmony	궁합	merit	가치, 장점, 공적
marriage ceremony	혼례, 결혼식	message	메시지, 전갈
marriage vow	가약	messy	혼란한, 지저분한
married woman	유부녀, 부인네	metal	쇠, 금속
marvelously	신통하게, 놀랍게	meticulous	꼼꼼한, 주도 면밀한
massively	엄청나게	mild	연한, 부드러운
match	경연; 일치하다	military	전투적
(be) ~ed	부합되다	~ coup d'état	군사 쿠데타
(get) ~ed with	어우러지다	~ dictatorship	군사 독재 정치
well ~ed	걸맞는	~ expense	군비
matchmaker	중매쟁이	milk-white	뽀얀
matchmaking	중매	mince	잘게 썰다, 난도질하다
mate	배우자, 짝	mind	마음, 정신; 염두, 뜻
material	물적, 소재, 재료	come to ~	떠오르다
mathematics	수학	mingle with	어울리다
matter	사항, 안건; 물질	minister	장관

minus	마이너스	multitude	다수
minutely	자세히	musical instrument	악기
miraculous	절묘한, 기적적인	mutely	묵묵히
mirror	거울	mutual	상호(적)
mirth	흥, 환희, 즐거움		
mischief	장난	naive	소박한, 자기 나라의
miser	깍쟁이, 구두쇠	naked body	벌거숭이
mishap	사고	narcissism	나르시시즘, 자기 도취
miss	빼놓다, 놓치다	narcotic	마약
mission	지상 과제, 사명	national	민족적, 국가적
mistake	실수하다; 잘못	~ holiday	명절
mistreat	학대하다	~ loan	차관
mistreated	억울한, 학대받은	~ team	국가 대표팀
mistreatment	학대	~ territory	국토
misty	은은한, 안개가 짙은	nationalization	국영화
misunderstand	착각하다, 오해하다	National Assembly	국회
mix (food)	비비다, 섞다	member of the ~	국회 의원
mix (food) with		naturally	물론, 원래, 으레
soup [water]	말다	(by) nature	본디, 원래
mix with	~과 어울리다; 섞다	nearby	인근
mode	양식, 유행	neat	산뜻한
model	본보기, 상표	necessary	필연적인, 필요한
modem	모뎀	~ and sufficient	필요 충분한
modernization	현대화, 선진화	need	들다, 필요하다
(be) modernized	선진화되다	negative	마이너스, 부정적인
modify	개조하다, 수정하다	neglectful of one's	
moist	촉촉한, 젖은	duty	직무 유기
moisture	물기, 습기	negotiate	교섭하다
moment	계기, 순간	negotiation	교섭, 협상
(for) a ~	잠깐	netizen	네티즌
monarch	임금(님), 군주	never	아예, 결코 ~ 않다
mongrel (dog)	잡종견	new	참신한, 새로운
mop	대걸레, 자루걸레	~ generation	신세대
moral	교훈; 도덕상의	news	소문, 뉴스
~ duty	명분	nice	좋은, 착한; 치밀한
~ fiber	줏대	~ and tender	말랑말랑
moreover	더욱이	nice-looking	고운, 예쁜
mostly	태반, 거의	(Korean) nightingale	꾀꼬리
most of	대개	nightmare	악몽
mother and daughter	모녀	nippers	집게발, 집게
mother-of-pearl	자개	no less than	무려, 적어도
motion	활동, 운동	nobility	양반, 귀족
motive	이유, 동기	noble	귀한
~ power	원동력	nobleman	양반
mottled	아롱다롱한	nomadic people	유랑자, 유목 민족
motto	구호	normal	정상(적)
move	움직이다, 이동하다	~ times	평상시
movement	악장; 운동, 이동	normality	정상
multiply	증가하다	north side	북녘, 북쪽

not a little	적지 않은	on	위(에)
not at all	전혀	~ earth	도대체
not different (from)	다름(이) 없다	~ no account	설마
notes	주석	~ the other hand	한편
notify	보도하다, 알리다	~ the spur of the	
notion	관념	moment	얼떨결에
not overtly	은근히	one	일, 하나
not till	비로소, 그제야	~ by one	하나하나, 하나씩
novel	소설	~ night	하룻밤, 어느날 밤
nowadays	요새, 요즘	~ of a pair	짝
nucleus	핵심	~ time	일시, 한때
nuisance	골칫거리	one-eyed person	외눈박이
number of items	건수	oneself	자신
		by [for] ~	스스로
(take an) oath	맹세하다	one-sided	일방적인
object	대상	only	오직, 한갓
objectify	객관화시키다	~ then	그제야
objection	반론, 반대	open	개방하다; 열다
objective	객관적인	~ air	야외
objectivity	객관성	~ an exhibition	개최하다
obligation	도리, 의무	~ one's eyes	일깨워 주다
observe	살펴보다, 관찰하다	~ up	개설하다
obstinacy	고집	opening	개방; 첫머리
obtain	거두다, 얻다, 차지하다	~ ceremony	개막식
~ by transfer	물려받다	~ of a firebox	아궁이
obvious	명백한, 분명한	open-minded	개방적
occasion	마당, 경우	operate on	작용하다
as ~ arises	수시로	opinion	견해, 의견
occasionally	더러, 때로(는), 때때로	opportunity	계기, 기회
occupy	자리잡다, 점유하다,	oppose	대립하다, 반항하다
	차지하다	opposite room	건넌방
occur	벌어지다, 생기다,	oppress	탄압하다
	일어나다; 발생하다	oppressive	
octagon	팔각형	government	학정
offal	내장 (짐승의); 부스러기	orchestral band	관현악단
offense	죄, 위반; 공격	orchestral music	관현악
offensive	공격적	order	명, 명령, 분부; 명하다,
offer	올리다, 제공하다		분부하다; 차례
official	공식적	put in ~	정리하다
~ rank	벼슬, 관직	ordinary	평범한, 보통의
~ title	관명	~ household	여염집
offspring	자손, 후손	~ times	평소(에)
Oh, my God!	아이고	organization	기관, 제도
oil	기름	organize	결성하다, 주관하다,
~ed floor paper	장판지		편성하다
~ refinery	정유	~d burglars	집단 강도
~ shock	오일 쇼크	Oriental	동양적, 동양의
old-fashioned person		origin	원인, 유래
or stuff	구닥다리	original	원초적, 본래의

~ form	원형	pass	나다, 돌파하다,
~ source	진원지, 근원		통과하다; 급제하다
originally	본디, 원래	passage	통로
originate	비롯하다, 시작하다	passenger train	객차
originator	창안자	passionate	열정적인
oriole	꾀꼬리	paste	바르다
other side of	건너	pastime	장난, 오락, 놀이
outcome	성과, 결과	patience	인내심
outcomes	결과물	pay	대우, 봉급; 치르다
outflow	유출	~ back	갚다
outlook on marriage	결혼관	peace	평화
output	생산량, 생산; 출격	peaceful	원만한, 평안한, 화기
outrageous	터무니없는		애애한
outside	바깥쪽, 외부, 외부인	peak	고비, 꼭대기, 정상
outstanding	뛰어난	peasant	농부, 서민
outstandingly	뛰어나게	peasantry	농부, 농민
outwardly	표면적으로	peculiar	특별한, 특유의
overall	전반적, 전적으로	peeking	훔쳐보기
overanxious	안달인, 안달하는	peerage	작위
overflow	넘치다, 넘쳐나다,	penetrate	뚫다, 통과하다
	넘쳐흐르다	pen name	호
overpower	압도하다	people	겨레, 백성, 국민, 민족
overseas	해외	peppery	얼큰한
~ travel	해외 여행	perceive	깨닫다
overweight	과체중	percentage	비율
overwhelm	압도하다	perception	인식
own	갖다, 소유하다	percussion	
		instrument	타악기
pace	발걸음	perfect	철저한, 완전한
pacify	가라앉히다	perfectionist	완벽주의자
pack	채우다	perform	연주하다; 실행하다
pain	고통	performance	공연; 성과; 실행
take ~s	애쓰다	musical ~	연주
palace	궁궐	~ group	예술단
palpitate	울렁거리다	peril	위험
paradox	역설	period	기간, 시대, 연도, 주기
paradoxically	역설적으로	periphery	주변
parch	마르다; 볶다, 말리다	perish	망하다
parking	주차	permanent	영구적
part	작별하다, 이별하다	~ residents	상주 인구, 영주권자
participant	가입자, 참가자	permanently	영구히
participate	가입하다; 참가하다,	permission	허가
	참여하다, 출전하다	permit	허락하다, 허용하다
participation	참가, 참여, 출전	perpetually	영원히
particularly	별로, 별반, 특별히	perseverance	인내심
partition	분단	persistence	집착, 고집
rule by ~	분할 통치	persistently	끈끈하게, 완고히
partner	짝, 파트너	personal	독자적인, 사적인
party	잔치; 패	personality	개성, 성격, 인격

person concerned	당사자	policy	정책
person of the same age	동갑	polished	세련된
person under age	미성년자	political	정치적
perspective	시각, 관점	~ influence	정치력
persuade	설득하다	~ power	정권, 정치력
~ not to do	말리다	~ situation	정국
peruse	정독하다	~ world	정계
pessimist	염세주의자	politically	정치적으로
pet puppy	애완견	politician	정치인, 정치가
petroleum chemistry	석유 화학	pollution	공해
physical	물리(적), 물적	poor	불쌍한, 가난한
~ constitution	체질	popularity	인기
~ strength	물리력	position	위치, 일자리, 지위
physiology	생리	take a ~	자리잡다
piece	가닥, 조각	positive	실증적, 적극적(인)
~ of flesh	살점	possess	갖다, 소유하다
~ (of movie)	편	possessions	소유물
~ (of poem)	수	possibility	가능성
~ of stone	돌덩이	possible	가능한
pierce	꿰뚫다, 찌르다	posterity	후손
pig	도야지, 돼지	postwar days	전후
pile	무더기, 더미; 쌓다	pot	솥, 항아리
pinch	꼬집다	~ stew	찌개
pipe	관	potential	가능성, 잠재력; 가능한
pith and marrow	진수, 골수	pound	울렁거리다; 빻다
pitiable	불쌍한, 한심스런	(great) powers	열강
pitiful	불쌍한, 비참한	practicable	가능한
plain	분명한, 질박한, 추한	practical	현실적, 실제의
plait	엮다	~ joke	장난
plaster	바르다	practically	정작, 실질적으로
plate	도금하다	practice	풍습; 실행, 연습
play	장난; 연주하다	praise	찬미하다, 칭찬하다,
pleasant-tasting	구수한		찬사
pleasure	즐거움, 흥	~ highly	극찬하다
get ~	즐기다	praiseworthy	훌륭한, 감탄할
pledge	맹세하다	prank	장난
~ of eternal love	가약	pray	기원하다, 빌다
plentiful	흔한, 풍부한	precious	귀한, 소중한
plenty	듬뿍, 풍부	precipice	벼랑
plunder	겁탈하다, 약탈하다	precisely	딱, 명확하게, 바로,
pocket money	용돈		정확히
poem	시	preconception	고정 관념
poignant	심각한, 매서운,	predation	포식
	날카로운	predecessor	전신, 전임자; 조상
point	점	predict	예측하다
~ of view	시각, 관점	predominate	풍미하다, 우세하다
~ out	지적하다, 짚어내다	preeminently	뛰어나게
police headquarters	경시청, 경찰청	preestimate	예측하다
		prefer	선호하다

prejudice	고정 관념, 편견	prohibition	금지
preordained tie	연분	project	사업
prepare	마련하다, 준비하다	prologue	서두, 서론
preposterous	엄청난, 황당한	promote	추진하다
presence	존재, 출두	(get) promoted	승진하다
present	제공하다; 제시하다	promotion	육성, 장려, 승진
~ oneself	나서다, 나타나다	proof	도수; 증거
press	언론; 촉구하다	proper	고유의, 정규(의)
pressure	압력	~ form	정식
prestige	명예, 위신, 명성	properly	적절하게
prestigious university	명문대	property	소유물, 재산
presume	추정하다	~ tax	재산세
pretense	핑계, 구실	proportion	몫, 비율
pretext	핑계, 구실	propriety	예절
prevailing style	유행	prostrate	엎드리다
prevent	말리다, 예방하다	protect	옹호하다, 보호하다
prick	찌르다	prototype	원형
primarily	본디, 주로	proud	자랑스런
primary factor	요인	proudly	자랑스럽게
principal	주된, 주요한	prove	실증하다, 증명하다
principally	주로	provide	제공하다
principle	도리, 원칙	provinces	지방
printed matter	유인물	puberty	사춘기
prison	옥, 감옥	public	일반의, 공적인
prisoner	죄수	~ information	홍보
private academy	학원	~ institution	공공 기관
privately	은근히, 사적으로	~ opinion	여론
private money market	사채 시장	publicity	홍보
private moneylender	사채업자	publish	싣다, 출판하다
private tutoring	과외	pull down	끌어내리다
privilege	특권, 특혜	pull into	끌어들이다
procedure	과정, 절차	punishment	형벌, 벌
proceed	진행하다, 나아가다	pupa	번데기
proceeds	수입, 수익	purification	정화
process	과정	pursue	추진하다
procession of cars	차량 행렬	push into	몰아넣다, 밀어넣다
produce	제작하다, 연출하다,	(be) puzzled	황당하다
	생산하다		
product	제품, 생산품	(in a) quandary	야단나다
production	제작, 창작, 생산	quasi-	준-
professional		quay	부두
occupation	전문직	(call into) question	따지다; 의심하다
profitable	유리한	questionnaire	설문
profundity	깊이, 심오	quickly	재빨리
profusely	뻘뻘; 풍부하게	quietly	조용히, 차분히, 찬찬히
progenitor	조상, 선조	quite a lot	듬뿍, 톡톡히; 많은
progress	진행하다		
prohibit	금지하다	race	겨레, 종족

radiation	복사, 방사
raise	기르다; 높이다, 올려놓다, 일으키다
raising the curtain	개막
(at) random	함부로
rank	등급
rape	겁탈하다, 강간하다
rapid growth	급성장
rapidly	재빨리, 급속히
rare	귀한, 드문, 희한한
~ animal	희귀 동물
rash	성급한
rashly	마구, 함부로
rate	비율
rather	오히려
ratio	비율
rational	합리적(인)
(sliced) raw fish	생선회
reach	도착하다, 이르다
read carefully	정독하다
(rapid) reading	속독
reading comprehension	독해
real	리얼한, 실재적
~ ability	실력
~ origin	진원지
~ situation	실정
~ state of affairs	실정
realistic	사실적, 현실적
realization	관철, 깨우침, 성사
realize	깨닫다; 실현하다
really	정작, 실제로, 참으로
rear	기르다
reason	까닭, 원인, 이유
for that ~	그러니까, 그 때문에
for what ~	어찌하여
reasonable	합리적(인)
rebel against	반항하다, 반역하다
rebuke	나무라다, 꾸짖다
recall	회상하다
receipt	수신; 입금, 영수증
receive	당하다, 받아들이다
recently	요새, 최근
recession	경기 침체, 불황
recipient	수신자
recklessly	마구, 함부로
recognition	인식, 인정
recognize	인정하다, 인식하다
recollect	회상하다
recollection	추억
recommend	권하다, 추천하다
record	기록; 기록하다
put on ~	올리다, 기록하다
recover	되찾다; 복구하다, 회복하다
recovery	복구, 회복
rectify	시정하다
recuperation	회복
red thread	홍실
reduce	줄이다
refer to	들먹이다, 참조하다
reference	참조
~ materials	참고 자료
refined	세련된
refinement	멋, 세련
reflect	비춰 보다; 반사하다
reflection	추억; 반사
reform	개혁;개혁하다
reformation	개혁
refreshing	시원한
refugee	실향민, 피난민
refuse	거부하다, 거절하다, 물리치다
refutation	반론, 반박
regain	되찾다, 회복하다
regard (as)	여기다, ~라고 간주하다
regime	정권, 제도
regimentation	통제, 규격화
registration	등록
regret	개탄, 한, 후회; 후회하다
regular	본격적인, 정규(의)
~ customer	단골
regularly	정기적으로, 제대로
regulation	통제
rehabilitate	회복하다
rehabilitation	복구, 회복
reign	군림하다
reject	거부하다, 거절하다
rekindle	되살리다
related	관련된
relation	관계, 연분, 인연
relationship	관계
relatives	집안, 친척
relativism	상대주의
relax	느슨하다; 늦추다
release	풀어 주다, 개봉하다; 해방

reliable	미더운, 확실한	restoration task	복구 사업
relief	구조	restore	회복하다
give ~ to	구제하다	restrain	억제하다, 삼가다
relieve	가라앉히다, 덜다,	restraint	굴레, 억제, 구속
	안심시키다; 구제하다;	restriction	제한, 제약, 굴레
	소생하다	restructuring	구조 조정
reluctant	싫어하는	result	결실, 성과, 결과
remain	머무르다	~ from	유래하다
remaining power	여력	~ in	이르다, 귀착하다
remarkable	눈부신, 현저한	resulting product	결과물
remarkably	부쩍, 몹시, 뚜렷하게	retrieval	회복
remembrance	추억, 기억	retrieve	되찾다, 회복하다
reminiscence	추억, 회상	retrogress	역행하다
remittance	송금	reveal	폭로하다
remodel	개조하다	revenue	수입
remorse	후회, 죄책감	reverse	뒤집다; 역전, 거꾸로의
remote	까마득한	revive	되살리다, 되살아나다
repay	갚다	revolution	혁명
repeat	되풀이하다, 반복하다	rhythm	장단, 리듬
repent of	후회하다	rich	진한, 후한, 풍부한
repentance	후회	~ and strong	부강한
repertoire	레퍼토리	richness	여유로움, 부
replica	복제품	ridiculous	가소로운
reply	답변, 말대꾸; 답하다	rigorous	긴밀한, 엄격한
report	보도하다; 보도	rise	떠오르다, 일다,
represent	대표하다		일어나다
repress	억제하다, 탄압하다	~ quickly	솟구치다
reproach	비난, 원망	~ swiftly	치솟다
reproduction	복제품, 복사, 재생	~ to the surface	
republic	공화국	rapidly	급부상하다
reputation	명예, 명성	rising in the world	출세
request	부탁하다, 요구하다,	risk	무릅쓰다
	청하다	ritual costumes	예복
require	들다; 요구하다	rivalry	경쟁
rescue	구하다	rivers and	
resemblance	유사성	mountains	강산
resentment	원망, 분노	roam	방황하다, 전전하다
resident	주민	roamer	유랑자
resist	반항하다, 저항하다	roaming	방황, 유랑
resonant	쟁쟁한, 울리는	roar	고함; 고함치다
respect	관점; 존경	rob	겁탈하다, 강탈하다
response	말대꾸, 응답	robber	도둑, 강도
responsibility	책임	robbery	도난, 약탈, 강탈
bear total ~	전담하다	role	역할
sense of ~	책임감	roll of (toilet) paper	두루마리
rest	대, 받침대; 휴식; 쉬다	romantic	낭만적
restitution	복구, 회복	roomy	넓은, 널찍한
restoration of		root	근본, 뿌리
independence	광복	rotate	순환하다, 돌다

roughly	대략, 죽	scorched rice	누룽지
royal household	왕실	scrape hard	박박 긁다
rub	비비다, 바르다	scream	외치다, 소리치다
rubbery	쫀득거리는, 탄력 있는	screw	나사, 나선형
rudely	함부로, 무례하게	scroll	두루마리
ruin	훼손하다, 망치다	scrupulous	주도 면밀한, 꼼꼼한
rule	규칙, 법칙; 지배하다	(piece of) sculpture	조각품
ruling class	지도층	(Korean) seafood	
rumor	소문	soup	해물탕
run	달리다, 번지다;	seal	도장
	경영하다	search	탐색; 탐색하다
~ away	도망가다	sea slug	해삼
~ one's household	살림하다	second half	후반, 후반전
		secretly	은근히, 몰래, 비밀히
safeguard	옹호하다, 보호하다	secret method	비법
sagacious	슬기로운	section	부문, 구분; 절
salary	대우, 봉급	see through	꿰뚫어보다
saliva	침	seize	장악하다
same age	동갑	select	선정하다, 고르다
sample	맛보다; 견본	selection of a day	택일
sampling	음미, 시식, 시음	semi-	준
sanitary facilities	위생 시설	semi-final	준결승
sanitation	위생	send (one) off	떠나 보내다
sarcasm	풍자	senility	망령
sashimi	생선회	sense	의미; 감각; 느끼다
satire	풍자	sensibility	감수성
savage	야만적인; 야만인	sentence	문장, 글월; 처하다
savagery	야만 상태; 잔인	sentiment	정, 정서
save	구하다	separate	가려내다
savory	구수한, 맛좋은	separated families	이산 가족
scarce	귀한, 희한한	separately	따로
scatter	뿌리다, 깔다	separation	단절
scene	광경, 장면, 풍경;	sequence	차례
	한바탕	serious	심각한, 진지한
scenery	경치, 풍경, 강산	servant	방자, 하인
fine ~	절경	serve	모시다, 섬기다
scenic beauty	경치	service	공헌, 근무, 서비스
scent	향기	sesame leaf	깻잎
school	학교, 학창	set	놓다, 두다
~ cap	교모	~ forth	내세우다
~ gate	교문	~ free	풀어 주다
~ record	성적	~ (one) at ease	안심시키다
(village) schoolhouse		~ the table	차리다
(in old Korea)	서당	~ up	개설하다, 설정하다,
schoolmate	동창		세우다
scold	나무라다, 꾸짖다	setback	좌절, 퇴보
scoop	주걱	settle down	정착하다
~ up	푸다	sever	가르다
(get) scorched	눋다	several	몇몇의

~ times	수차	similar	다름(이) 없는, 비슷한
severe punishment	엄벌	similarity	유사성
severely	뼈저리게, 엄하게	similarly	다름없이
sex	성	simple	간단한, 소박한, 질박한
sexual desire	성욕, 욕정	simply	단순히
sexual harassment	성희롱	sin	죄; 죄를 짓다
shady spot	음지	sincere	진정한, 성실한
shaggy dog	삽살개	sincerely	간곡히
shameful	부끄러운, 추한	single	유일한; 독신
shape	모습, 형상; 만들다	single out	가려 내다, 골라 내다
~ dough	빚다	single-handed	홀로, 혼자
share	공유하다, 나누다; 몫	singleness	단일, 단독
~ one's joys and		sink	기울어지다, 가라앉다
sorrows (with)	~과 동고동락하다	Sino-Korean word	한자어
sharp	날카로운, 독한	sit face-to-face	마주 앉다
shed (light) on	비추다	situation	사정, 상황, 지경, 처지
shimmer	어른거리다	size	크기
shipbuilding	조선	skin	가죽, 피부
shirk	피하다, 회피하다	skip	빼놓다, 뛰어 넘다
shiveringly	오슬오슬	~ a meal	굶다, 식사를 거르다
shock	충격	skirts and upper	
shoot	쏘다	garments	치마 저고리
~ up	치솟다	skylark	종달새
shopkeeper	상인, 가게 주인	skyrocket	치솟다
short	간단한, 짧은	slant	기울다; 기울어진
shout	고함; 고함치다	slaughter	도살
~ out	외치다	sleek	매끄러운
~ repeatedly	질러대다	sleeping place	잠자리
~ with exultation	쾌재를 부르다	slim	날씬한
show	전시하다, 제시하다	slip of paper	쪽지
~ up	등장하다, 나타나다	slogan	구호
shower	뿌리다; 샤워; 소나기	slow	느린
showing up	출두	slowly	서서히, 슬슬
shun	피하다	sluggish	느린
shy	부끄럼 타는, 수줍은	become ~	침체하다
side	곁, 측면, 편	smart	똑똑한, 영리한
~ dish taken		smoke	연기
with drink	안주	smooth	매끄러운, 매끈매끈한
~ effect	부작용	soak in	스미다
sight	광경	so-called	이른바
sign	신호, 표시	soccer	축구
signal	신호	social conditions	세태
signboard	표지판, 간판	socialism	사회주의
significant	중요한, 굵직한	socially	사회적으로
signify	의미하다	social stratum	사회 계층
silently	묵묵히, 조용히	society	협회; 사회
silk	비단	(Korean) socks	버선
silkworm	번데기	soil	흙, 땅
silly	어리석은	soldier	병사, 군인

solely	오직; 혼자서	split	가르다, 쪼개다
solemnly	엄연히, 진지하게	spoonful	술, 숟가락 하나 가득
sole (of a foot)	발바닥	(on the) spot	당장
solicit	사정하다, 간청하다	spouse	배우자
solid gold	순금	spread	번지다, 펼치다, 뿌리다;
solution	해결책, 해결		확산; 펴다, 확산시키다
somehow or other	아무튼, 어떻게	~ out	깔다, 전개하다
	해서든지	sprinkle	뿌리다
sonorous	쟁쟁한, 울리는	sprout	싹트다
soothe	가라앉히다, 달래다	spur	박차
sophistry	궤변	spurn	물리치다
(a) sort of	일종의	squid	오징어
(all) sorts of	온갖	stab	찌르다
soul	넋, 영혼, 정신	stagnate	침체하다
soup	탕, 국물	staidly	찬찬히, 침착하게
sour	신	stamina	스태미나
source	근본, 원인, 출처	stamp	도장; 찍다
~ of money	돈줄, 돈의 출처	~ (a seal)	(도장을) 찍다
South America	남미	~ one's feet	발을 구르다
Southeast Asia	동남아	stand[1]	대
south side	남녘, 남방, 남쪽	stand[2]	버티다
south wind	마파람, 남풍	standard	기준, 눈높이, 잣대,
sovereignty	자주성, 주권		정도; 표준의
Soviet Union	소련	standardize	표준화하다
soybean-paste stew	된장찌개	standpoint	관점, 견해
spacious	넓은	staple food	주식
sparing	아끼는, 절약하는	(be) startled	깜짝 놀라다
spatula	주걱	starve	굶다
speak highly of	칭찬하다, 극찬하다	state	모습, 상태
special	독특한, 특별한	statesman	정치인
~ edition	특집	status	지위, 위상
~ favor	특혜	stay	머무르다, 머물다; 체류
specialist	전문가	steadfast	억척스러운, 확고한
specially	별(로), 특별히	steadily	꾸준히, 착실하게
specialty	전문	steal a glance at	훔쳐보다
specific	특정	stealthily	몰래
~ gravity	비중	steam	증기
specification	특정; 설명서, 명세	step	과정, 절차; 발걸음;
specify	상술하다		디딤돌
spectator	관객, 구경꾼	~ in	들어서다
speed	속도, 속력	stepping-stone	디딤돌
spelling	철자	sticker	딱지
spend	소비하다, 쓰다	sticky	끈끈한, 끈적거리는,
spending	지출, 소비		쫀득거리는
spillage	유출	~ rice	찹쌀
spiral	나선형(의)	stolen goods	도난품
spirit	넋, 영혼, 정신, 진수,	stone wall	돌담
	기세	stop	그만두다, 머무르다,
spit	침; 토하다, 뱉다		중단하다
splendid	화려한, 훌륭한	~ at (a place)	다녀가다, 머물다

English	Korean
stopping	중단
story	소설, 이야기
straight	(올)바른, 곧은, 똑바른
strand	가닥
strange	낯선
stranger	이방인, 낯선 사람
strategy	전략
stratum	층
street	거리
~ demonstration	가두 시위
~ food stall	포장 마차
stretch out	내밀다, 뻗어나가다
strict	긴밀한, 엄격한
strike	두드리다, 부딪치다
striking	눈부신, 뚜렷한
strip	가닥, 조각; 벗기다
strive	애쓰다, 노력하다
stroke	획; 타격
strong	강렬한, 진한, 질긴, 독한
~ person	강자
~ point	장점
strongly	강력(히), 진하게
struck dumb	어안이 벙벙한
structure	구조
stubbornness	고집
(get) stuck	박히다
studying	공부, 연구
~ abroad	유학
stunned	기(가) 막힌
stupid	어리석은
~ person	바보
style	양식, 스타일
subject	대상, 주제, 주어
~ matter	소재
subordinate	부하
substantially	실질적으로
subtract	덜다, 빼다, 감하다
suburb	교외, 도시 주변
success	성공
~ in life	출세
successive generations	역대
suction	흡인력, 빨기
suddenly	갑작스럽게, 급격하게, 문득
suffer	겪다, 당하다
~ unfairness	억울하다
suffering	고통

English	Korean
sufficiently	충분히
suggestion	시사점, 암시; 제안
summit	정상, 꼭대기
~ meeting	정상 회담
summon	불러 오다, 소환하다
sunny spot	양지
superficially	표면적으로
superior to	뛰어나다
superiority or inferiority	우열
superpower	열강, 초강대국
supervision	단속, 감독
supplement	보충하다
supplication	애원, 간청
support	뒷받침하다, 지지하다; 지원, 지지, 후원
supporting actor	조연
suppress	억제하다, 탄압하다
sure	확실한
surely	어김없이, 확실히
surname	성
surpass	능가하다, 압도하다
surplus	여유로움, 나머지
(be) surprised	기겁하다, (깜짝) 놀라다
surprising	놀랄만한
surprisingly	뜻밖에(도), 놀랍게도
surround	둘러싸다
surrounding	주변
survey	조사; 살펴보다
suspend	드리우다
suspicious	의아해 하는, 의심스러운
sustain	당하다, 견디다
swap	바꾸다, 교환하다
swear	맹세하다; 욕하다
sweat	땀
sweetheart	임, 애인
swell up	부풀다
swing	그네
symbolize	상징하다
sympathy	공감, 동정
in ~ with	동조하여
symphony orchestra	교향악단
system	제도
taboo	금기, 터부
viewed as ~	금기시된
tact	눈치

tactics	전략	thin	날씬한, 얇은; 묽은
tag	딱지	thinking	사고
take	잡다, 가지다; 타다	way of ~	사고 방식
~ along	데리다, 이끌다	think out	고안하다
~ a serious view	중시하다	thoroughly	푹푹; 모조리, 철저히
~ courses	수강하다	though	그렇지만
~ custody	보관하다	thought	관념, 사고, 염두
~ down	끌어내리다	thoughtlessly	함부로, 생각 없이
~ over	물려받다	three-cornered	
~ part in	참여하다	arrangement	삼각 관계
~ place	열리다	Three	
~ up	차지하다	Kingdoms	삼국
talent	기량, 재능	throb	울렁거리다, 떨리다
talon	발톱	through	통하여
tariff	관세	throughout	두루; 완전히
taste	맛보다; 입맛, 식성,	throw away	던지다
	취향; 멋	throw up	토하다
~ flat	심심하다	tie	맺다; 인연
tasteless	밍밍한	~ up tight	얽매다, 단단히 묶다
tasting	음미	tightly	바짝, 단단히
tasty	고소한, 구수한	time	시간, 시기; 틈
teahouse	찻집, 다방	all the ~	줄곧
technical college	전문 대학	at a ~	한꺼번에
technician	기술자	at that ~	당시
(high) technology	첨단 기술	at ~s	때로(는)
(high) temperature	고온	~ and again	수차
temple bell	범종	~ and tide	세월
tenaciously	끈끈하게, 끈기 있게	~ of year	시기
tendency	경향, 성향, 추세	~ to come	장래
tender	연한, 정겨운	title	호, 표제, 타이틀
tepid	미지근한	toadyism	사대주의
term	기간, 연도; 용어	toe	발가락
(in) terms of	~상	toenail	발톱
terminate	끝마치다, 끝내다	together with	~와/과 더불어
terminology	용어	(go) together	동행하다
terrible	끔찍한, 무서운	toilet bowl	양변기
terribly	엄청나게, 지독하게	tolerable	어지간한, 참을 수 있는
territory	영역, 영토	tolerate	버티다, 인내하다
test	시도하다, 시험하다	tone	가락
textile industry	방직 산업	top	꼭대기, 정상
thanks to	덕분에	topple over	넘어지다
theft	도난, 절도	top shell	골뱅이
then and there	당장	totally	전적으로
therefore	그러니까, 그러므로	touching	감격적
these days	요즘	tough	질진, 단단한, 곤란하
thesis for a degree	학위 논문	tourist attraction	관광 상품
thick	굵은, 굵직한; 진한	tournament	대회, 토너먼트
thickly	진하게, 두텁게	trace	자취, 발자취
thief	도둑	trading partner	교역국

tradition	전통
traditional	전통적
traditionally	전통적으로
traffic	왕래, 교통
tragedy	비극
tragic	비극적인
transfer	편입, 이전; 옮기다
transform	변하다, 변형하다
transformation	변화, 변형
transmission	
of a message	송신
transmit	전송하다, 전파하다
tread	발걸음
treasure	보물
treat	취급하다, 처리하다
treatment	대우, 대접
trepang	해삼
triangular	
relationship	삼각 관계
trophy	우승컵, 트로피
trouble-free	별 탈 없는
troublesome	곤란한
true	진정한, 참된
truly	진정으로
trust	신뢰, 신임
trustworthy	미더운
try out	시도하다
tumble down	나동그라지다
(in) tune with	동조하여
turn down	거절하다
(be) turned inside	
out	뒤집히다
turn one's face	외면하다
turn over	뒤집다
(in) turns	차례로
tut	혀를 차다
TV watcher	시청자
twisting	우여 곡절, 꼬임
typical	본격적인, 대표적인
tyranny	학정, 전제 정치
ugly	추한, 못생긴
ultimate	궁극적인
ultimately	궁극적으로
unbalance	불균형
unclean	불결한
uncommon	드문, 희한한
underdevelopment	후진성
undergo (an exam)	(시험을) 치다

underlying factor	내막
understand	깨닫다, 이해하다
understanding	납득, 이해
undertaking	사업
undeveloped country	후진국
unexpectedly	뜻밖에(도), 문득
unfamiliar	낯선
unfold	전개하다, 펼치다
unfounded	터무니없는
unhappiness	불행
unhappy	불행한
unification	통일
uniform	획일적
uniformly	고루, 한결같이
unilateral	일방적인
union	결합, 공동; 연맹
unique	고유의, 유일한, 독특한
united	합동(의)
United Kingdom	영국
unite with	~와/과 결합하다
unity	단일, 통일, 조화
universe	우주, 천지
university degree	학위
unknown	낯선
unlimited	무제한의
unmarried man	총각
unmarried woman	처녀
unparalleled	비길 데 없는
unpleasant feeling	응어리, 싫은 감정
unprecedented	파격적, 전에 없던
unreasonable	터무니없는, 불합리한
unrelenting	억척스러운
unrestricted	무제한의
unroll	전개하다
unusual	드문, 별난
unyielding	억척스러운
upbringing	육성, 양육
upholding	지지
upright	바른, 똑바로 선
uproar	야단, 소란
urge	촉구하다, 재촉하다
urgency	긴급
urgent	절실한, 긴급한
use	용도, 사용; 쓰다
of no ~	소용없는
~ freely	구사하다
user	이용자, 사용자
usual	일상적인, 보통의
as ~	여전히

usually	대개, 으레, 주로	wandering	방황, 유랑
(to the) utmost	잔뜩; 최대한으로	war	전쟁, 전쟁하다
		go into a ~	출전하다
vagabond	유랑자	going into a ~	출전
vague	은은한, 애매한	warmhearted	살가운, 인정 있는
valuable	귀한, 소중한	warn	경고하다
value	가치	warning	경고, 충고
sense of ~	가치관	wash (clothes)	빨다
valuing family		wastefully	헤프게
tradition	가풍 중시	watch (TV)	시청하다
variegated	아롱다롱한	water	물을 뿌리다
variety	변화; 천차만별	hot ~	온수
various	다양한	watery	묽은
become ~	다양해지다	waver	주춤거리다, 흔들리다
velocity	속도, 속력	way	수단, 방법; 길
vending machine	자동 판매기, 자판기	weak	나약한, 미비한, 미약한
versus	대	~ point	단점
veteran	베테랑	wear	지니다; 입다
vice	폐해, 악덕, 결함	weariness	피로
vice minister	차관	weave	엮다, 짜다
vicinity	곁, 근처, 부근	wedding gift in cash	축의금
(feel) victimized	억울하다	wedding hall	예식장
victory	승리	weekly magazine	주간지
view	견해, 경치, 광경, 의견;	weight	몸무게, 무게
	관람하다	well	평안한, 잘
~ of education	교육관	well up	솟아오르다
viewing	관람	(the) West	서구
viewpoint	시각, 관점	Western ideas	서구 사상
vinyl floor	비닐 장판	Westernization	서구화
violate	위배하다, 위반하다	West Germany	서독
violence	폭력	Western style	서양식
virgin	처녀	wet	촉촉한, 젖은
virtue	미덕, 덕, 장점	wharf	부두
virtuous woman	열녀	what is called	이른바, 소위
virus	바이러스	what's more	더욱이
visit	체류, 방문	whip	매를 치다
visual aids	영상 자료	whole	통째, 전체의, 온
visual field	시야	~ area	일대
visual materials	영상 자료	~ body	온몸
vivid	분명한, 생생한	~ life	평생
very ~	뚜렷한	on the ~	대체로
vocabulary	낱말, 어휘	wholly	고스란히, 다, 전적으로
volume	크기	wicked	고약한
vow	맹세하다	wide	너른, 넓은
vulgar man	상놈	~ woof of cotton	광목
		widely	널리, 두루
wages	봉급, 급료, 임금	widen	벌어지다
wander	유랑하다, 방황하다,	wild	야생의, 거친
	헤매다, 전전하다	~ animal	야생 동물

willingly	즐겨, 기꺼이	worry	우려, 걱정
willow	버들	worth	가치
win the victory	우승하다	wrap	싸다
winning	우승	wrapping cloth	보자기
～ team	우승팀	wrinkles (on skin)	주름살
wise	슬기로운, 어진, 현명한	write a composition	글 짓다
wish	기원하다, 빌다; 뜻,	write down	기록하다
	소원, 바람	written materials	문헌
as one ～s	마음대로, 소원대로	(be) wrong	그릇되다
dearest ～	바람		
woman's parent's		yard	뜰, 마당
(old) home	친정	year	해, 연도, 년
work	일, 근무; 근무하다	yell	고함
workmanship	만듦새	yellowish	노릇(노릇)한
(the) world	누리, 천지, 세계	yield	생산량
Second ～ War	제2차 대전	yin and yang	음양
whole ～	전 세계	young people	청소년, 젊은이
～ Cup	월드컵	youth	젊은이, 청년, 청소년